Maternal Sensitivity

Mary Ainsworth's work on the importance of maternal sensitivity for the development of infant attachment security is widely recognized as one of the most revolutionary and influential contributions to developmental psychology in the twentieth-century. Her longitudinal studies of naturalistic mother–infant interactions in Uganda and Baltimore played a pivotal role in the formulation and acceptance of attachment theory as a new paradigm with implications for developmental, personality, social, and clinical psychology. The chapters in this volume collectively reveal not only the origins and depth of her conceptualizations and the originality of her assessment methods, but also the many different ways in which her ideas about maternal sensitivity continue to inspire innovative research and clinical applications in Western and non-Western cultures. The contributors are leading attachment researchers, including some of Mary Ainsworth's most influential students and colleagues, who have taken time to step back from their day to day research and reflect on the significance of the work she initiated and the challenges inherent in assessing parental sensitivity during naturalistic interactions in infancy and beyond. This volume makes Ainsworth's pioneering conceptual and methodological breakthroughs and their continuing research and clinical impact accessible to theorists, researchers and mental health specialists.

This book was originally published as a special issue of *Attachment & Human Development.*

Klaus E. Grossmann, PhD, is Professor Emeritus in the Department of Psychology at the University of Regensburg, Germany.

Inge Bretherton, PhD, is Professor Emerita in the Department of Human Development and Family Studies at the University of Wisconsin–Madison, USA.

Everett Waters, PhD, is Professor in the Department of Psychology at the State University of New York at Stony Brook, USA.

Karin Grossmann, PhD, is a Senior Research Scientist (retired) in the Department of Psychology at the University of Regensburg, Germany.

Maternal Sensitivity

Mary Ainsworth's Enduring Influence on Attachment Theory, Research, and Clinical Applications

Edited by

Klaus E. Grossmann, Inge Bretherton, Everett Waters and Karin Grossmann

Routledge
Taylor & Francis Group
LONDON AND NEW YORK

First published 2015 by Routledge

2 Park Square, Milton Park, Abingdon, Oxon, OX14 4RN
605 Third Avenue, New York, NY 10017

Routledge is an imprint of the Taylor & Francis Group, an informa business

First issued in paperback 2020

British Library Cataloguing in Publication Data
A catalogue record for this book is available from the British Library

ISBN 13: 978-1-138-81071-6 (hbk)
ISBN 13: 978-0-367-73926-3 (pbk)

Typeset in Times New Roman
by RefineCatch Limited, Bungay, Suffolk

Publisher's Note
The publisher accepts responsibility for any inconsistencies that may have arisen during the conversion of this book from journal articles to book chapters, namely the possible inclusion of journal terminology.

Contents

Citation Information

The chapters in this book were originally published in the *Attachment & Human Development*, volume 15, nos. 5–6 (September–November 2013). When citing this material, please use the original page numbering for each article, as follows:

Chapter 1
Introduction to the Special Issue: Maternal sensitivity: observational studies honoring Mary Ainsworth's 100th year
Klaus E. Grossmann, Inge Bretherton, Everett Waters and Karin Grossmann
Attachment & Human Development, volume 15, nos. 5–6 (September–November 2013) pp. 443–447

Chapter 2
Mary D. Salter Ainsworth: an autobiographical sketch
Mary D. Salter Ainsworth
Attachment & Human Development, volume 15, nos. 5–6 (September–November 2013) pp. 448–459

Chapter 3
Revisiting Mary Ainsworth's conceptualization and assessments of maternal sensitivity-insensitivity
Inge Bretherton
Attachment & Human Development, volume 15, nos. 5–6 (September–November 2013) pp. 460–484

Chapter 4
Mary Ainsworth's legacy: a systematic review of observational instruments measuring parental sensitivity
Judi Mesman and Rosanneke A.G. Emmen
Attachment & Human Development, volume 15, nos. 5–6 (September–November 2013) pp. 485–506

Chapter 5
Parental synchrony and nurturance as targets in an attachment based intervention: building upon Mary Ainsworth's insights about mother–infant interaction
Kristin Bernard, EB Meade and Mary Dozier
Attachment & Human Development, volume 15, nos. 5–6 (September–November 2013) pp. 507–523

Chapter 6

Sensitive attunement to infants' internal states: operationalizing the construct of mind-mindedness
Elizabeth Meins
Attachment & Human Development, volume 15, nos. 5–6 (September–November 2013) pp. 524–544

Chapter 7

The insightfulness assessment: measuring the internal processes underlying maternal sensitivity
David Oppenheim and Nina Koren-Karie
Attachment & Human Development, volume 15, nos. 5–6 (September–November 2013) pp. 545–561

Chapter 8

Parsing the construct of maternal insensitivity: distinct longitudinal pathways associated with early maternal withdrawal
Karlen Lyons-Ruth, Jean-Francois Bureau, M. Ann Easterbrooks, Ingrid Obsuth, Kate Hennighausen and Lauriane Vulliez-Coady
Attachment & Human Development, volume 15, nos. 5–6 (September–November 2013) pp. 562–582

Chapter 9

How does microanalysis of mother–infant communication inform maternal sensitivity and infant attachment?
Beatrice Beebe and Miriam Steele
Attachment & Human Development, volume 15, nos. 5–6 (September–November 2013) pp. 583–602

Chapter 10

One doll fits all: validation of the Leiden Infant Simulator Sensitivity Assessment (LISSA)
Alexandra Voorthuis, Dorothée Out, Rixt van der Veen, Ritu Bhandari, Marinus H. van IJzendoorn and Marian J. Bakermans-Kranenburg
Attachment & Human Development, volume 15, nos. 5–6 (September–November 2013) pp. 603–617

Chapter 11

Maternal anxiety, maternal sensitivity, and attachment
Joan Stevenson-Hinde, Rebecca Chicot, Anne Shouldice and Camilla A. Hinde
Attachment & Human Development, volume 15, nos. 5–6 (September–November 2013) pp. 618–636

Chapter 12

Piecing together the sensitivity construct: ethology and cross-cultural research
Germán Posada
Attachment & Human Development, volume 15, nos. 5–6 (September–November 2013) pp. 637–656

Chapter 13
Individual dispositions as precursors of differences in attachment quality: why maternal sensitivity is nevertheless important
Gottfried Spangler
Attachment & Human Development, volume 15, nos. 5–6 (September–November 2013) pp. 657–672

Chapter 14
Epilogue: reflections on a Special Issue of Attachment & Human Development *in Mary Ainsworth's 100*th *year*
Everett Waters, Dean Petters and Christopher Facompre
Attachment & Human Development, volume 15, nos. 5–6 (September–November 2013) pp. 673–681

Please direct any queries you may have about the citations to clsuk.permissions@cengage.com

INTRODUCTION

Maternal sensitivity: observational studies honoring Mary Ainsworth's 100th year

Klaus E. Grossmann[a], Inge Bretherton[b], Everett Waters[c] and Karin Grossmann[a]

[a]*Department of Psychology, University of Regensburg, Regensburg, Germany;* [b]*Department of Human Development and Family Studies, University of Wisconsin-Madison, Madison, WI, USA;* [c]*Department of Psychology, State University of New York, Stony Brook, NY, USA*

This special double issue of *Attachment & Human Development* celebrates and honors Mary D. Salter Ainsworth and her lifetime achievements on the 100th anniversary of her birth. The papers we have invited focus on maternal sensitivity, broadly construed, and its links to the development of secure and insecure attachment. Mary Ainsworth's contributions to this important topic have been central and enduring.

Mary Ainsworth spent the years 1949–1953 working with John Bowlby and James Robertson at the Tavistock Institute in London, where one of her tasks was to analyze Robertsons' field notes in which he had recorded his observations of children who were separated from their families for shorter or longer periods. She described his notes as "the most sensitive and perceptive direct observations I had ever encountered," but Robertson did not allow her (as a psychologist) to "transgress into direct observations" because she had not been trained (Myers, 1969).

Thus, when Mary Ainsworth moved to Uganda with her husband Leonard, in 1954, she eagerly seized the opportunity to conduct her own home observations of mother–infant interactions in a non-Western culture. She emulated Robertson's skilful observational methods, but, on the theory side, she was influenced by ethological studies of social bond-formation in animals that John Bowlby had begun to incorporate into this emerging Darwinian approach to infant–mother attachment (Bowlby, 1953). Bowlby's views persuaded her, once she began observing, to drop the "theory of cupboard love" (that babies love their mother because mothers feeds them).

The Uganda study (Ainsworth, 1967) yielded a number of important insights and findings regarding the development of attachment and the use of the mother as a secure base. She built upon and extended this work in her Baltimore longitudinal study, where she and her research team implemented a much more detailed system for observing mother–infant interactions in real life situations. Observer notes taken during lengthy 3-weekly visits throughout the infant's first year were translated into audio-recorded narratives and then transcribed. The resulting narrative records allowed Mary Ainsworth to identify four key dimensions of maternal care: sensitivity-insensitivity, cooperation-interference, acceptance rejection and accessibility-ignoring/neglecting and to develop corresponding rating scales (Ainsworth, 1969). Overall ratings of the 9–12 months narrative records turned out to be strong predictors of infant–mother attachment security in the Strange Situation at 1 year of age (Ainsworth, Bell, & Stayton, 1971; Ainsworth, Blehar, Waters, & Wall, 1978).

It often goes unrecognized that Mary Ainsworth's evaluation of maternal care as adapted to an individual infant's characteristics was revolutionary. The phylogenetic programme is sufficiently open to allow all babies to become attached to caregivers, even if the quality of care they receive is insensitive or even abusive. Infants' attachment to the caregiver under these circumstances, however, is likely to be insecure. Sensitivity, hence, is a key to understanding the development of individual differences in attachment relationships. As Mary Ainsworth later said, observational research on maternal sensitivity, broadly construed in ethological terms, was an entirely different paradigm from then current behaviorist notions that sensitive responding amounts to spoiling a baby (Ainsworth & Bell, 1977).

In the late 1960s Klaus Grossmann began to read about John Bowlby's ethological orientation and the observational studies of preverbal infants by Mary Ainsworth and her research team. In 1973, having acquired a doctorate in ethology, he expressed an interest in learning the new methods, and Mary Ainsworth invited him to her Baltimore lab where she and her research team shared insights and transcripts and demonstrated the Strange Situation. Inspired by Klaus' reports of his Baltimore visit, Karin Grossmann initiated a 1-year observational pilot study of six mothers and babies in their homes in Bielefeld, Germany. In 1975, with Mary Ainsworth's encouragement, the Grossmanns began a larger longitudinal study whose methods during the first-year phase were closely modeled on those used in Baltimore. The Bielefeld study confirmed that many detailed findings obtained in Baltimore (Ainsworth et al., 1978) held also in North Germany (K. Grossmann, K. E. Grossmann, Spangler, Suess, & Unzner, 1985). Longitudinal studies in Regensburg followed (K. Grossmann & K. E. Grossmann, 2012; K. Grossmann, K. E. Grossmann, & Kindler, 2005). Throughout this work the Grossmanns were generously helped by Mary Ainsworth and her former graduate students, particularly Mary Main, who classified Strange Situations, and Inge Bretherton, who acted as reliability rater of maternal sensitivity for Bielefeld home visit narratives. In the mid-1970s a number of other influential longitudinal attachment studies were initiated in Minnesota, Berkeley and Israel, demonstrating that Ainsworth's insights and methods travelled well (see summaries in K. Grossmann, K. E. Grossmann, and Waters, 2005).

The Grossmanns' longitudinal research, and that by others too numerous to cite here, showed that parental sensitivity can be observed well beyond infancy. They found that sensitive parents not only respond with prompt and appropriate behavior, but interpret and give words to their children's feelings and experiences. They serve as translators between child and environment, and between the child and her peers or other adults, and for this reason caregiver sensitivity has become pivotal to attachment-based clinical interventions with troubled families.

Over and above responding to an infant's or child's needs for protection and affection, sensitivity, as conceptualized in Mary Ainsworth's scales, also involves respect for the child as a valuable person with autonomous feelings, needs, wishes, goals and a mind of her own. To the child, a caregiver's sensitivity means that her or his communications are understood, worthy of attention, and appropriately and promptly responded to. In addition, a caregiver's sensitive responses foster the child's competence.

Given the complexity of the sensitivity construct, however, the scientific assessment of caregiver sensitivity remains a challenge. One problem has been the availability of the four scales. Only the text of the Sensitivity-Insensitivity scale has been published in full (Ainsworth, Bell, & Stayton, 1974). Although the complete instructions for the full set of

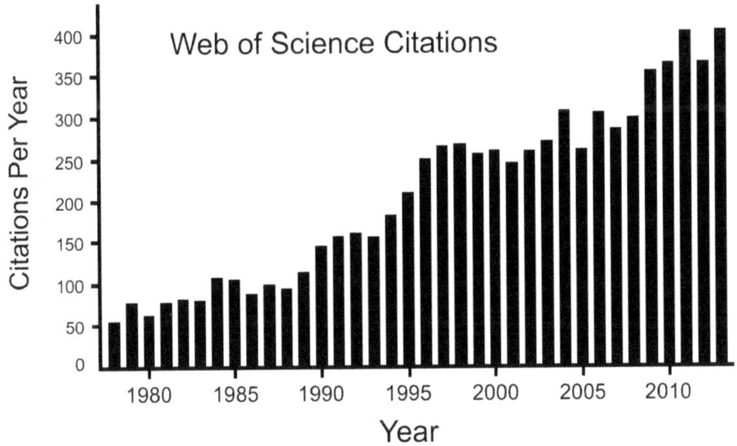

Figure 1. Number of citations per year of Mary Ainsworth's publications. (Web of Science 1978–2013).

four scales have long been available in mimeographed form and online (Ainsworth, 1969), the whole set will appear in print for the first time in a new edition of Ainsworth et al.'s classic volume, *Patterns of Attachment,* scheduled for 2014. In the 100th year after Mary Ainsworth's birth, and almost exactly 60 years after the beginning of the Baltimore Study in 1964, it is clear that her work on maternal sensitivity and infant attachment is more relevant than ever. Her observations and insights have generated an entire new field of study and, as noted by Howard Steele, "this journal would not exist without her" (personal communication, July 2013). Moreover, as Figure 1 documents, interest in Mary Ainsworth's work over the years has only increased.

Mary Ainsworth's productive influence is also evident in the contributions to this Special Issue by eminent researchers who have creatively extended and elaborated the construct of caregiver sensitivity-insensitivity and its relation to secure and various insecure forms of attachment.

We open this special double issue of *Attachment & Human Development* with Mary Ainsworth's own account of her life, work and career. Although her 1983 autobiographical essay is not widely known, it conveys both her commitment to her work and her concern for children and mothers. It is followed by two reviews. In the first review, Inge Bretherton provides a thoroughgoing summary and analysis of the complete corpus of work by Ainsworth and her Baltimore research team that relates to the sensitivity construct, the scales and the link between maternal sensitivity and infant security. In the second review, Judi Mesman and Rosanneke Emmen describe and analyze eight of the most commonly used global assessments of caregiver sensitivity. The remaining contributions illustrate various new applications of the sensitivity construct. Kristin Bernard, E. B. Meade and Mary Dozier show how assessment of sensitivity in distress and non-distress situations can be used *in vivo* during clinical interventions with troubled families. Elizabeth Meins documents how sensitivity manifests itself in a mother's ability to empathize with her infant's feelings and internal states, revealed by appropriate versus inappropriate mind-minded verbalizations during interactions with a preverbal infant. David Oppenheim and Nina Koren-Karie demonstrate how facets of sensitivity are revealed in mothers' talk about the relationship with their child as they respond to questions about a video-taped interaction with their child. Karlen Lyons-Ruth and her colleagues report that, in high risk groups, maternal withdrawal – a neglected facet of insensitivity – predicts D-secure patterns of attachment in infancy, controlling-caregiving attachment in middle childhood and adolescent psychopathology as well as maternal role confusion at age 20. Beatrice Beebe and Miriam Steele show that derailed dyadic communication processes, observed micro-analytically during brief mother–infant face-to-face interactions at 4 months, already foreshadow the infant's disorganized attachment classification at 1 year. Along very different lines, Alexandra Voorthuis and colleagues assessed sensitivity in female college students who were asked to provide care to a standard "difficult baby" (simulated by a programmable robotic doll). Sensitivity scores were stable across settings and related to positive affect while caring for the doll. Joan Stevenson-Hinde, Rebecca Chico, Anne Shouldice and Camilla Hinde showed that multiple assessments of sensitivity in different contexts provide stronger predictions of attachment security than single assessments and mediate the link between maternal anxiety and security in a study of preschoolers. German Posada assessed maternal sensitivity in several contexts (home, hospital, and playground) in infants and preschoolers. Sensitivity ratings in different situations were correlated with each other and children's secure base behavior. He demonstrates the validity of the sensitivity construct in Latin America, even when assessed ethnographically. Finally, Gottfried Spangler presents evidence that some potentially deleterious gene polymorphisms associated with emotion regulation have an adverse developmental effect primarily under conditions of maternal insensitivity. Also notable, several authors were able to go beyond the secure/insecure dichotomy and document that specific aspects of insensitivity predicted insecure-avoidant, -resistant, and -disorganized attachment patterns. The epilogue for the Special Issue by Everett Waters and co-authors indicates that there is a great deal of work ahead and ample opportunities to make significant contributions built upon Mary Ainsworth's work.

We wish to express our deepest thanks to all contributors who participated in the arduous and exciting effort to produce this Special Issue. In addition, we gratefully acknowledge the unstinting and responsive support by the editor of *Attachment & Human Development*, Howard Steele. We also thank Taylor & Francis who contributed in many ways to making this Special Issue possible.

References

Ainsworth, M. D. S. (1967). *Infancy in Uganda: Infant care and the growth of love*. Baltimore, MD: Johns Hopkins University Press.

Ainsworth, M. D. S. (1969). *Scales for home visits*. Retrievable as "Sensitivity scales" from http://www.psychology.sunysb.edu/attachment/measures/content/ainsworth_scales.html. Also available from the Harvard Dataverse Network (Baltimore Longitudinal Study of Attachment 1963–1967).

Ainsworth, M. D. S., & Bell, S. M. (1977). Infant crying and maternal responsiveness: A rejoinder to Gewirtz and Boyd. *Child Development, 48*, 1208–1216.

Ainsworth, M. D. S., Bell, S. M., & Stayton, D. J. (1971). Individual differences in Strange Situation behaviour of one-year-olds. In H. R. Schaffer (Ed.), *The origins of human social relations* (pp. 17–57). London: Academic Press.

Ainsworth, M. D. S., Bell, S. M., & Stayton, D. J. (1974). Infant–mother attachment and social development: "Socialization" as a product of reciprocal responsiveness to signals. In P. M. Richards (Ed.), *The integration of a child into a social world* (pp. 99–135). Cambridge: Cambridge University Press.

Ainsworth, M. D. S., Blehar, M. C., Waters, E., & Wall, S. (1978). *Patterns of attachment: A psychological study of the Strange Situation*. Mahwah, NJ: Erlbaum.

Bowlby, J. (1953). The contributions of studies of animal behavior. In J. M. Tanner (Ed.), *Prospects in psychiatric research* (pp. 80–108). Oxford: Blackwell Scientific Publications.

Grossmann, K., & Grossmann, K. E. (2012). *Bindungen – Das Gefüge psychischer Sicherheit* [Attachments – The framework of psychological security] (5th ed.). Stuttgart: Klett-Cotta.

Grossmann, K., Grossmann, K. E., & Kindler, H. (2005). Early care and the roots of attachment and partnership representation in the Bielefeld and Regensburg Longitudinal studies. In K. E. Grossmann, K. Grossmann, & E. Waters (Eds.), *Attachment from infancy to adulthood: The major longitudinal studies* (pp. 98–136). New York, NY: Guilford Press.

Grossmann, K., Grossmann, K. E., Spangler, G., Suess, G., & Unzner, L. (1985). Maternal sensitivity and newborns' orientation responses as related to quality of attachment in northern Germany. In I. Bretherton & E. Waters (Eds.), Growing points in attachment theory and research. *Monographs of the Society for Research in Child Development, 50* (1–2, Serial No. 209), 233–256.

Grossmann, K. E., Grossmann, K., & Waters, E. (Eds.). (2005). *Attachment from infancy to adulthood: The major longitudinal studies*. New York, NY: Guilford.

Myers, R. (1969). *Interview of Mary Ainsworth*. Oral history of psychology in Canada. Retrieved from www.feministvoices.com/mary-ainsworth/

Mary D. Salter Ainsworth: an autobiographical sketch

Reprinted from: O'Connell, A. N., & Russo, N. F. (Eds.). (1983) *Models of achievement: Reflections of eminent women in psychology* (pp. 200–219). New York: Columbia University Press.

If this were a clinical history rather than a brief sketch of a career, it would begin with my family, and continue to discuss in detail my relationships with my parents and two younger sisters as they changed in the course of my development. Except for stating that we were a close-knit family with a not unusual mixture of warmth and tensions and deficiencies, I shall confine myself to a few bare facts.

My parents were Pennsylvanians, both graduates of Dickinson College, where my father earned a Master's degree in history before he went to work for a large manufacturing firm in its Cincinnati office. My mother groped for a vocation after her graduation, tried teaching, began nursing training, then was called home because of her mother's illness. Five years after her graduation she married my father, and henceforward had no thought of a career other than homemaking. I was born late in 1913, and my sisters two and seven years later, respectively. In 1918 the family moved to Toronto, my father having been transferred to a Canadian branch of his company. Later the foreign branches split from the parent company, and in due course he became president of his branch. Realizing that he was committed to a career in Canada, he became a naturalized citizen, as did I as a minor.

From the beginning it was assumed that we girls would go to college, for both of our parents placed high value on a good liberal arts education. My parents' expectations of outstanding academic achievement were reinforced by my eagerness to learn to read when I was three years old. It was my mother who located appropriate materials and got me off to a good start. With this early beginning, both grade school and high school were easy. I thoroughly enjoyed learning, which posed no problems until high school when I pretended to be indifferent to learning in order to ingratiate myself with peers.

A regular event in our family life was the weekly trip to the library. We returned home with the maximum number of books that our five cards would allow. When I was fifteen and in my final year in high school, one of the books brought home was William McDougall's *Character and the Conduct of Life* (1927), which I read with great excitement. It had not previously occurred to me that one might look within oneself for some explanation of how one felt and behaved, rather than feeling entirely at the mercy of external forces. What a vista that opened up! I decided thereupon to become a psychologist.

This decision was half forgotten when I first enrolled at the University of Toronto in the fall of 1929. Because I was underage I had to enroll in the first year of the "Pass Course," and could not take psychology until my second year, but after an introductory course then my enthusiasm was renewed, and I transferred to the honor psychology course for my final three years. The honor course had a very intensive, comprehensive, structured curriculum, which I was privileged to explore with only four classmates.

I gobbled everything up with great enjoyment and shared in the messianic spirit that permeated the department – a belief that the science of psychology was the touchstone for great improvements in the quality of life. Although now this belief seems naive, we all firmly held it then, even in the midst of the Great Depression – and it has never entirely deserted me. Nothing that I studied seemed irrelevant, and no one who taught me failed to engage my interest in his or her field of expertise.

Before I graduated in 1935, I had already decided that I wanted to continue in graduate work in psychology, and it did not occur to me to apply elsewhere than Toronto. My parents went along with my wishes, although my father had previously thought that it would be nice for me to be a stenographer for a while before marrying. Although my undergraduate record had been excellent, I did not assume that I would be accepted, and was delighted when I was not only accepted but also offered a stipend of $200 for the year as a teaching assistant to the head of the department, Professor Edward A. Bott, in his introductory course for medical students. If the stipend was low, so were other costs in the thirties. Moreover, I lived at home and my parents refused to let me pay board, which I could have done because from my second year of graduate work on I had quite adequate financial support through scholarships, teaching evening courses, and higher teaching assistant stipends.

I cannot recall how many graduate students there were in the department of psychology. My retrospective impression is that the sexes were evenly balanced, although more of the women than men were headed toward a terminal master's degree. Let me mention a few with whom I overlapped: Mary Northway, who studied for her doctorate at Cambridge with Bartlett, and returned to a position in the university's Institute of Child Study; Donald Snygg who was enthusiastic about phenomenology and subsequently became well-known in American psychology; Louis McQuitty, who went to Illinois after his Ph.D., and subsequently Michigan State, then Miami; Carl Williams, who after faculty appointments at the Universities of Manitoba and Toronto, became president of the University of Western Ontario; Gordon Turner, who had been a classmate in the undergraduate honor course, later went to the University of Western Ontario where he was chairman of psychology for some time; Mary Wright, who also wound up at the University of Western Ontario and also served as chairman there; Herbert Pottle, who eventually became Minister of Education for Newfoundland; and Nora Weckler, who is a member of the faculty of California State University at Northridge.

To me it seemed to be a tightly integrated group of graduate students. We had tea together in the late afternoon in the graduate lounge, and planned numerous social events, including an annual picnic with faculty that featured a softball game, and an annual Christmas party with skits and songs prepared for the occasion. I remember our morale as being high.

During the seven years of undergraduate and graduate studies in the department of psychology, three professors emerged as major influences: Sperrin N. F. Chant, William E. Blatz, and Edward A. Bott. Chant spent a year with our fourth-year undergraduate class in an experimental project involving the galvanic skin response. I owe to him chiefly the discovery that research can be fun. When I decided to enter graduate work, he immediately offered to supervise my master's research, and we proceeded to investigate the relationship between attitudes and emotional response, using the GSR as the measure of emotion (with Chant, 1937). Whatever skills I now have in supervising the theses and dissertations of graduate students owe much to the supervision he offered.

Blatz's influence also began while I was an undergraduate. I was impressed by his courses in genetic (developmental) and abnormal psychology, in which he talked of his own theory of development–security theory. This was a programmatic theory that owed much to Freud – although Blatz was careful not to acknowledge this because of the very strong anti-psychoanalytic bias in Toronto at that time. It was a theory of personality development, and that was what I had been waiting for! I was honored when, having completed my master's thesis, Blatz proposed that I undertake my dissertation research within the framework of his security theory.

In briefest summary, his position was that in infancy and early childhood the individual needed to develop a secure dependence on parents in order to gain the courage necessary to brave the insecurity implicit in exploring the unfamiliar world and learning to cope with it. A child needs to feel confidence in the secure base provided by parents to learn the skills and to develop the knowledge that will gradually enable him or her to depend confidently on self and eventually to gain a secure emancipation from parents. However, since it is impossible in this social world to be totally independent of others, the immature dependent security of the relationship with parents should be gradually supplanted by a mature secure dependence on peers from the individual's own age group and eventually on a heterosexual partner, implying a relationship in which each partner finds security in the skills, knowledge, and emotional support contributed by the other. Of course, some persons are characterized by more insecurity than security from all three sources combined, and some rely on defensive maneuvers (which Blatz termed "deputy agents") to hold their insecure feelings at bay.

Blatz's proposition was to develop instruments to assess the balance between security (from all three sources) and insecurity/defensive maneuvers in all major aspects of a person's life. My dissertation research was to be devoted to the construction of two self-report pencil-paper scales to assess young adults regarding their relations with parents and with age peers (Salter, 1940). There was at that time no approved quantitative technique for selection and weighing of items on such scales, but with Chant I settled on a roughly satisfactory method. Validation of the scales also presented a problem. This was handled by using the same college student subjects who had written autobiographies for a course of Professor J. Davidson Ketchum's. I found no way of quantifying the autobiographical material, but it "blew my mind" to find out how similar this material was for persons yielding the same pattern of scores on the two scales. I emphasize patterns. I have been searching for – and finding – patterns in my research ever since.

The third person who exerted a profound influence on my career development was Professor Bott, the head of the department. I continued for four years as his teaching assistant, not just in his introductory course, but soon in two experimental/statistical courses that he taught. As a graduate student, I attended his seminar in systematic psychology, which he conducted in a Socratic manner. Like many other Toronto Ph.D. students, I failed to appreciate at the time the significance of Bott's thinking, for his manner was dry. But in later years I came to realize what an important influence he had been in the way I viewed the scientific approach. I believe that science is a "state of mind" – not that he ever said just that. Science is implicit in the way one thinks about problems and approaches data, rather than being irretrievably vested in the hypothetico-deductive method, experiment, or specific quantitative techniques.

Since I later became a clinical psychologist I should mention that I did indeed think of becoming one during my first year as a graduate student. Through the help of one of the faculty, C. Roger Myers, I was appointed as a psychological intern at the Ontario Hospital in Orillia in the summer of 1936. Discouraged by the seeming impossibility of helping effectively the mental patients served by this hospital, I abandoned thoughts of a clinical career in favor of research relevant to personality development.

In the spring of 1939, Professor Bott did what he could to find jobs for all of the new Ph.D.'s, arranging job interviews with potential employers. I did not want to leave Toronto. I was in the full flush of excitement about my Ph.D. research based on Blatz's theory of security. Blatz himself wanted me to stay to become co-director of an expanded program of security research. In blissful ignorance of the academic facts of life, including such matters as vacancies, and tenure-line slots, I told Professor Bott that I wanted a faculty appointment in his department and did not want to go elsewhere.

Nevertheless he arranged an interview for me with Professor George Humphrey, then head of the psychology department at Queens University in Kingston, Ontario, who was searching for a young experimental psychologist to establish a new laboratory. Because I did not want the position I downplayed my skills and abilities and was honest in my admissions of weakness. Perhaps because of this openness, Humphrey decided that I was precisely the person he wanted for the job. Two weeks later he visited again to tell me sorrowfully that the Senate of Queens University refused to appoint a woman. This is the only instance of discrimination in regard to employment that I encountered in my career.

As for Humphrey and Queens, everything turned out well, for they hired Donald Hebb. Even then I believed that they made the better bargain. As for me, my naive faith was rewarded by an appointment as lecturer at the University of Toronto, beginning in the fall of 1939.

Great Britain (and Canada) declared war on Germany in September 1939, and everyone's career plans were changed. Professor Bott immediately threw himself into plans for maximum contribution by Canadian psychologists to the war effort, and turned over all of his undergraduate classes to me with scarcely two weeks' warning. Within a year Professors Bott and Myers had left to become advisors to the RAF in regard to pilot selection, Line to head personnel selection in the Canadian Army, Chant to do likewise in the RCAF, and Blatz to set up model wartime day nurseries in Great Britain. Male graduate students and recent Ph.D.s joined the armed services in personnel selection, and several members of the staff of the Institute of Child Study joined Blatz in England. Several recent female Ph.D.s, including Magda Arnold (who subsequently became well-known for her work in the field of emotion), were appointed to help carry on the work of the department. I remained for three years, and then no longer content to be away from where the action was – and belatedly wanting to get away from home – joined the Canadian Women's Army Corps in July 1942.

I spent that summer in basic and officer's training and then was tapped by Bill Line – then Colonel William Line, Director of Personnel Selection – to become an Army Examiner, as the personnel selection officers were called. In this capacity I was posted to the Canadian Women's Army Corps Training Center at Kitchener, Ontario. The work had a distinctly clinical flavor, including administering tests, interviewing, history-taking, and counseling, as well as recommending placement. I was impressed with how much could be learned from such an approach and entertained the idea of becoming a clinical psychologist at war's end in order to pursue more effectively my interest in personality development. A few months later, however, I was posted to headquarters in Ottawa, as the CWAC advisor to the director of Personnel Selection. There I encountered the reverse of sex discrimination, despite the fact that CWAC pay was four-fifths of men's pay. After arriving at Headquarters as a second lieutenant, I was promoted to major within a year.

The directorate of Personnel Selection was under the director general of Medical Services – a psychiatrist, General Brock Chisholm, who subsequently became director of the World Health Organization. He and Line shared the idealistic perspective that personnel selection should be a thoroughgoing clinical service to army personnel with the Army Examiners working closely with company officers on the one hand and with the various professionals of the Medical Corps on the other – physicians, psychiatrists, and social workers. So acute was the manpower shortage, however, that the need for infantrymen frustrated the male Army Examiners in their efforts to place men in the work to which they were best suited. But Line's goal was feasible for the women in the service, and it was my job to work with CWAC Army Examiners all over Canada to see that the goal was approximated. My work was entirely administrative, entailing much traveling back and forth across Canada. In the winter of 1943–44 I was assigned to a four-month tour in England, where I especially enjoyed visiting the Personnel Selection service of the British Army. My opposite number there, Senior Commander Edith Mercer, not only made me welcome at that time, but also later played an important role in my career.

After V-E Day, I was invited to retire from the Army to become the superintendent of Women's Rehabilitation in the Department of Veterans' Affairs. The director general of Rehabilitation Services was my previous mentor, Sperrin Chant, although he was about to leave to become head of psychology at the University of British Columbia. Doubtless he thought that I was set up for a continuing administrative career in government service. The work was significant and demanding, but much like what I had done in the Army. Within a year I felt that I had done all that I could to set up the women's rehabilitation program and was tired of administrative work. When Professor Bott, back at the University of Toronto, invited me to return as an assistant professor, I accepted with pleasure and anticipation. Nonetheless I valued highly my four years in army and government service. I came to value a clinical perspective. I learned a great deal about administration. I learned to value and to work within a multidisciplinary perspective.

Upon returning to Toronto, I taught introductory psychology to medical students and experimental psychology as before – a twelve-hour teaching load, made light because of it being my first year. The problem was what to teach, especially to graduate students, the following year. The courses I especially wanted to teach were being dealt with very competently by Magda Arnold, whom I admired. Knowing that it was uncertain whether her war-time appointment was to continue, I wanted to propose nothing to Professor Bott that might encroach on her territory. I asked her how we might share teaching in the personality area. Since she was teaching the theoretical courses, she suggested that I teach personality assessment. I protested that I knew nothing about this specialty, but she replied "You can learn, can't you!" Therefore, at her suggestion, I attended a summer workshop in the Rorschach technique directed by Bruno Klopfer, and contacted William Henry of the University of Chicago for references to his work on the Thematic Apperception Test. I read all that I could lay my hands on relevant to both projective and paper-pencil tests, practiced administering these various appraisal techniques to volunteers. I offered my volunteer services to a Department of Veterans' Affairs hospital, where at least I received neuropsychiatric supervision from the clinical director. And that is how I began as a clinical psychologist.

Next autumn, 1947, I offered a graduate course in personality appraisal, and it captured the interest of my students as well as engrossing me. The following summer I attended another Klopfer workshop, this time at the advanced level. I prepared a mimeographed booklet for the use of my students – to fill in the gaps that I observed in The Rorschach Technique by Klopfer and Kelly (1942), which was distributed by the university bookstore.

Magda Arnold departed for an appointment at Loyola University in Chicago, and I fell heir to the courses of hers that I had coveted – emotion and motivation and theories of personality. And throughout the years 1946–50 I was co-director, with Bill Blatz, of a research team focused on developing scales to assess security in various aspects of life – a clear sequel to my dissertation research.

I became engaged to marry one of that team – a veteran student, Leonard Ainsworth, who was just completing his master's degree. The prospect of his continuing for a Ph.D. in the same department in which I had a faculty appointment seemed uncomfortable, so when he was accepted by University College, London, as a doctoral student it was there that we went after our marriage in the summer of 1950. Len had DVA educational benefits and expected to be able to pick up the same kind of teaching and research assistantships there had been available to him in Toronto, although that proved not to be the case. My efforts to line up a position for myself in advance proved to be unavailing. But I thought that I might write a book. Since my mimeographed manual on the Rorschach technique had unexpectedly sold hundreds of copies, a book-length version of it seemed worth considering. I wrote to Bruno Klopfer seeking his approval, since it was his version of the technique that I proposed to write about. He replied with an invitation to be a co-author in a book he was planning. So we set off for London in September 1950, with high hopes but inadequate financial resources. As it turned out, I did collaborate with Bruno and Walter Klopfer and Robert Holt in Developments in the Rorschach Technique, volume 1, conducting all our exchanges by correspondence. The book was not finally published until 1954, so it did not help at all with our immediate financial needs, but royalties have been steady ever since.

Upon arrival in London, I immediately cast about for a job. I also looked up relatives and friends, including Edith Mercer from my army days. One day she drew my attention to an advertisement in the London Times Educational Supplement for a job that seemed precisely suited to my qualifications. It was for a research position at the Tavistock Clinic in an investigation, directed by Dr. John Bowlby, into the effect on personality development of separation from the mother in early childhood. I applied, was interviewed, was enthusiastic about the project, and was hired. So Edith Mercer and a newspaper advertisement reset the whole direction of my research career.

Psychologists do not ordinarily expect crucial research to stem from a psychoanalytic setting, so it may seem paradoxical that it was at the Tavistock Clinic that I finally realized what kind of research strategy would best serve me in exploring the problems of personality development in which I had been interested from the beginning. First, the clinical perspective tends to emphasize patterns of personality or behavior (syndromes) as they relate to patterns of antecedents, rather than searching for a one-to-one cause effect relationship between a single antecedent and a single outcome variable. Second, James Robertson, one of my new colleagues, had been observing at first hand the responses of young children to separation from and reunion with their families in the course of visits to the home before and after the separation and to the separation environment to observe the child's responses. Although he himself was very modest about his data – transcriptions of his observational notes – I was deeply impressed with their value. I was entranced with the prospect of a future study of my own in which I would employ simple, direct, naturalistic observation, and use simple descriptive statistics to deal with its findings.

Third, both the problems in which John Bowlby was interested and his non-doctrinaire approach to theory were very congenial to me. To be sure, Blatz had been theory-oriented, but my experience with Bowlby was my first with a theory in the making. John became increasingly interested in the implications of evolutionary theory and the ethological approach in accounting for the findings of separation research – findings that could not be accounted for adequately by either psychoanalytic theory or psychological learning theory. Although I was intrigued with Lorenz's imprinting studies, I myself was so brainwashed by psychological theories of the day that I felt uneasy. To me at that time it seemed self-evident that a baby becomes attached to his mother because she fulfills his basic needs or drives. Indeed, after I left London, John and I had an exchange of correspondence in which I urged him to reconsider his new theoretical position. He may have reconsidered, but fortunately he was not deterred by my reaction.

My husband, who was completing his Ph.D. in the autumn of 1953, had been talking about how much he would like to go to Africa. Again it was our friend Edith Mercer who drew his attention to an advertisement in the London Times for a research psychologist in the East African Institute of Social Research in Kampala, Uganda. I was not enthusiastic about this prospect, fearing that it would be even more difficult to break into the academic stream in Canada or the United States after such a venture than before it. Nevertheless, Len's application and interview resulted in an appointment. We had scarcely arrived home in Canada when the news of the appointment reached us, and on New Year's Day, 1954, we sailed from Halifax, bound for London, and then Mombasa and Kampala.

Although I had it in mind to undertake a short-term longitudinal and naturalistic study of mother-infant interaction at the first opportunity – and now the opportunity was in Uganda – I was unsuccessful in obtaining funding from such a distance and at such short notice. I was happy that Dr. Audrey Richards, director of the institute, scraped together enough salary for me and for an interpreter to make such a study feasible. The study of Ganda mother-infant dyads turned out to be every bit as rewarding as I had hoped a short-term longitudinal, naturalistic study could be. I welcomed Dr. Richards' directive that there be an anthropological component to the study, for this ensured that I would view current mother-infant interaction and maternal care practices in their cultural context, and I valued the opportunities presented by the institute again to interact with a multidisciplinary team.

It is a pity that one cannot require field work in another society of every aspiring investigator of child development. Despite all the language and other difficulties, I am convinced that it is easier to be objective when viewing another society, and then, as I discovered later, it is easier to take a fresh, unbiased view when later undertaking research in one's own society. Despite many cultural differences, it was a profoundly moving experience for me to perceive the basic common core of parental concern for their children's welfare. Furthermore, I had not spent many weeks in observation before I was convinced that the previous "self-evident view" of the basis of an infant's attachment to its parents squared not at all with what my eyes saw, and that Bowlby's new ethological approach did indeed provide a much more useful framework. I am sorry that I did not immediately inform him of my *volte face*.

For complex reasons, the analysis and publication of the Ganda data was substantially delayed (1963, 1967), but perhaps a few reflections are pertinent here. The hypothetico-deductive method that has guided so much psychological research is inapplicable to the kind of exploratory, naturalistic study that I undertook in Uganda. To be sure, one needs to have some notion of what one is looking for, and hence some selectivity of observations – and indeed I did have some such notions. But I left myself open to observe and descriptively record as much as possible beyond these initial notions, rather than boxing myself in with check lists conceived a priori. I learned so much new that was not covered by my initial notions (hypotheses) that ever since I have tried to avoid deciding in advance what the relevant variables must be and how I am going to analyze my data. I let the raw observational data suggest to me what the relevant variables are. In exploratory studies post hoc variables may well be the most valuable. Whereas I acknowledge that later replicatory studies of a more rigid kind are needed, for hypothesis-discovering studies, too rigid an adherence to the hypothetico-deductive approach is clearly counterproductive.

At the end of our two-year tour in Uganda, it was not easy to find jobs in Canada or the United States from our Kampala base. Acting on the assumption that it would be more difficult for Len, with his relatively new Ph.D., to get placed than for me to do so, we put the emphasis on the position for him. With the initial aid of the APA Employment Bulletin, he found a position as a forensic psychologist in Baltimore. It was not until late 1955 that our visa arrangements were completed and we were settled. I then began my explorations for a job by visiting the chairman of the department of psychology at Johns Hopkins University, Wendell Garner. Extrapolating from Professor Bott's intimate knowledge of opportunities in Ontario, I expected Garner to be knowledgeable about opportunities in the Baltimore area. He did offer me an evening course (which I snapped up), and made several suggestions about possibilities for full-time jobs in the area. I began to follow up his suggestions, but within two weeks Dean Wilson Shaffer of Johns Hopkins called me in to offer me a position. It emerged that he and Garner had been hoping to find someone to offer some clinical-type instruction in an otherwise highly experimental department, and to provide supervised clinical experience to a few students who wished it. There was no ready-made slot for such a person, but they patched up a position for me, supported in part by the department, in part by the evening college, and in part by Sheppard and Enoch Pratt Hospital, where I was to work two days a week providing psychological service with the aid of one graduate student assistant. I jumped at the opportunity to join the Hopkins faculty, even though I was disappointed to be appointed as a mere lecturer.

Paradoxically, it was this academic appointment that gave me my first extended opportunity to gain clinical experience. The work at Sheppard Pratt was essentially diagnostic evaluation, and I had no difficulty with this. I have never been able to understand why American clinical psychologists have so chafed at the diagnostic role, feeling that this limited them to being mere psychometricians, subordinate to all medical personnel. On the contrary, I found that diagnostic skills gave me very substantial status and respect. In addition to a quite heavy hospital load, I gradually set up a part time private practice, on referral from psychiatrists, psychoanalysts, social agencies, and schools in the Baltimore area, being mostly concerned with children. In the beginning, my research experience at the Tavistock Clinic was especially useful. At that time there was almost no literature pertaining to diagnostic evaluation of children. It was necessary to extrapolate principles from adult evaluation to work with children, and of course research experience with disturbed children was very helpful.

Our marriage came to an end in the summer of 1960. Although I do not wish to write about this personal disaster, I can say that I do not believe career conflicts to have been a factor. A depressive reaction to divorce led me to seek professional help, which culminated in an eight-year psychoanalytic experience. Sometimes I believe that this was the most important positive influence on my career, despite the fact that I had already been very fortunate in both mentors and turns of fortune. Certainly analysis helped me to become very much more at peace with myself and very much more productive.

I felt a great urge to immerse myself in the psychoanalytic literature, especially Freud. I emerged with a profound respect for psychoanalytic therapy, and with a firsthand understanding of the psychoanalytic process – unconscious processes, repression, transference, resistance, and the like – experience that has made me a better psychologist, even though there remains much in classical psychoanalytic theory that I believe to be obsolete, especially instinct theory and metapsychology. All of this both enriched my teaching of courses focusing on personality and various approaches to assessment and my understanding of research data.

The Sheppard-Pratt responsibility left very little opportunity for research. All that I could do was to work on the data analysis and publication of research from previous years and settings. I proposed to Garner, my chairman and good friend, that I withdraw from the hospital commitment, shift my teaching to developmental psychology, and begin the naturalistic, longitudinal research into mother-infant interaction that I had been longing to do ever since leaving Uganda. He readily agreed, and indeed both then and since could not have been more encouragingly supportive of what I wanted to accomplish. So in 1961 the shift was implemented.

Let me interrupt this narrative to mention the degree to which I experienced discrimination. It must be clear that I had experienced none in regard to appointments since 1939, and that for a position that I did not want. It was otherwise in regard to salary at Johns Hopkins. My low initial salary was understandable because the appointment was not to a "tenure-track" slot; I had to wait only two years before being appointed associate professor, but it took a very long time to overcome the initial salary handicap. Three chairmen in a row recommended me for annual increments designed to bring my salary to the level appropriate to my age, experience, and contribution; year after year these were cut back, and it was clear that the difficulty was sex-linked. It was not until Hopkins faced the pressures of affirmative action that the situation was rectified, and then only after I wrote a strong letter to the Dean.

It rankled also that at noon the Johns Hopkins Club relegated women to a separate dining room for lunch, so that female faculty could not meet members of other departments in the normal way. The House Committee felt that it would be offensive to the sensitivities of the gentler sex to encounter male faculty in informal garb at lunchtime, not seeming to recognize that they encountered their male colleagues in the same garb in their departmental interactions. It was not until late in 1968 that this ridiculous restriction was lifted.

Soon reverse discrimination set in! Suddenly the few women faculty members were in great demand. Every university committee had to include a woman. We were very overworked, and this situation still continues in many universities. At Hopkins I was eventually elected by the faculty to the Academic Council – the body responsible for advising the administration on matters of academic policy, appointment, promotion, and tenure. I could detect no signs of discrimination against women in these matters in this council, nor could I do so later when I moved to the University of Virginia, neither in the department of psychology nor during the year when I was a member of the dean's Promotion and Tenure Committee.

I find it difficult to write about my major project – the short-term longitudinal research into the development of infant-mother attachment that I launched at Johns Hopkins in 1962. There is too much to be said, and much of it has already been said in piecemeal publications. This research has turned out to be everything that I had hoped it would be, and it has drawn together all the threads of my professional career. I opted for direct observation in the natural environment of the home supported by a specifically designed laboratory situation – the strange situation. The combination of the two highlighted the importance of observing in various contexts if we are to understand infant behavior and development – a lesson that was also implicit in the cross-cultural comparisons I made with the findings of the Ganda study. Indeed there are many other areas of science in which the mutual feedback between observations in the natural environment and observations in the laboratory yield more understanding than observations in either context alone.

At the Tavistock Clinic I heard the dictum "no research without therapy." In no position to give therapy and not wishing to deliberately intervene, I adapted this dictum in both Ganda and Baltimore studies to a principle of not attempting to take data away from participants without giving something appropriate in return, and I took some pains to find what would be most appropriate in each instance.

Visits were made to the home at three-week intervals from three to fifty-four weeks after the baby's birth, each visit lasting about four hours, which resulted in about seventy-two hours of observation for each infant. These long, frequent visits had several clear advantages. The mother could be more easily induced to behave as usual and to follow her normal routine. We attempted to span all aspects of a baby's day, although we could not cover nighttime hours. Frequent visits made up for the inevitable variability of behavior from day to day, so that measures could be used that combined the findings from four visits together, thus making for more stable measures without unduly sacrificing the picture of developmental changes. Seventy-two hours provided a broad data base. Finally, we got to know our families very well, which helped enormously in the identification of possible variables that might be involved in individual differences, and that could then be put to a systematic test.

The evolutionary-ethological orientation provided by even the earliest formulations of Bowlby's theory of attachment (e.g., Bowlby 1958) proved indeed to be helpful. It, as well as my experience in Uganda, suggested behaviors and possible "activating and terminating" situations that we wanted to be especially alert to when they occurred. On the other hand, I tried to keep our observations as open and comprehensive as possible to maximize the chances of finding new hypotheses about how behaviors become organized together and linked to situations. Thus, although benefiting from theory-based expectations, we felt free to undertake post hoc analyses of data. From the beginning emphasis was on understanding the variables involved in individual differences as well as on learning about the normative course of development – as might be expected of a clinician. Finally, although I had for a long time deliberately put my Blatzian orientation and research aside in the interests of making a fresh start with a new approach, I was eventually delighted to realize that there was a striking congruence between the old and the new, and especially in the phenomenon of an infant using his attachment figures as a secure base from which to explore the world. Furthermore, the pattern approach that I had found so useful in my Ph.D. dissertation emerged as the obvious way in which our new data could be ordered to describe qualitative differences in infant-mother attachment.

Soon after I shifted my academic field from clinical to developmental psychology increased numbers of graduate students began to seek me for a supervisor. The ongoing longitudinal research project provided a convenient focus for an aspect of their research training. I have been very fortunate in the associates and students who collaborated with me, and indeed the success of the project owes very much to their time, efforts, and ideas. Of those who remain primarily in academic teaching and research, I want to thank: Mary Main, who is now a professor at the University of California, Berkeley; Everett Waters, who is now at the State University of New York at Stony Brook; Mark Greenberg, now at the University of Washington; Inge Bretherton, at University of Wisconsin; Rob Woodson, at the University of Texas at Austin; Sally Wall, who teaches at Towson State University in Maryland; and Michael Lamb, who was with me at Hopkins for only one year. It is perhaps not surprising that even more of my ex-students and ex-associates have moved from research into clinical applications, although they are still known chiefly for their research publications: Silvia Bell, Donelda Stayton, Robert Marvin, George Allyn, Alicia Lieberman, Russel Tracy, and others. Mary Blehar, with whom I have co-authored several publications, has been at NIMH for some years. Barbara Wittig, whose sensitive observations were crucial to my Baltimore project, was a clinical psychologist before working in the project, but has moved into other fields of endeavor. Including also the undergraduates in my project who contributed through laborious coding and the undergraduates in my courses who have gone on to careers in psychology, psychiatry, or pediatrics, I although childless find myself to have a large academic family – dear to me and very gratifying.

As a developmental psychologist at Johns Hopkins, and a relative newcomer to the American scene of development research, I suffered the disadvantages of isolation, as the only one of my kind in the department. Nevertheless, "support systems" soon became available. The friendship and encouragement of my colleagues Wendell Garner and James Deese were significantly helpful; although in the experimental tradition they valued the kind of research I was doing. The Society for Research in Child Development was important to me, both because of its meetings and because of the between-meeting contacts with friends I made through the society. My long-distance interaction with John Bowlby had never lapsed, but from 1960 on it picked up impetus when we realized that our thinking had developed along extraordinarily similar lines. Ever since, we have functioned as partners in attachment research and theory. The renewal of contact with John led to my inclusion in the Tavistock Mother-Infant Interaction Study Group which established a basis of communication with leading developmental scientists of various nationalities and disciplines. For a long time this combination of resources functioned very well for me.

But Garner left Hopkins for Yale, and later Deese left for the University of Virginia. With their departure I felt that I had lost effective intra-departmental encouragement for my approach, and began to feel restive. In due course I accepted a position at the University of Virginia, beginning in the fall of 1975. The Virginia department included a number of other developmental psychologists; communication with them has been a significant feature in my enjoyment of this new and congenial milieu.

Finally, I would like to consider the relation of my research contribution to the women's movement. By some it has been viewed as a stroke against women's liberation, since it has highlighted the importance of sensitive responsiveness to infant behavioral cues on the part of the mother figure and the desirability of continuity of the infant's relationship with that figure, unbroken by separations that are unduly long or frequent. It has been assumed that I believe in full-time mothering during the child's earliest years, and indeed this does seem to be the most usual way of ensuring adequate responsiveness and continuity. I acknowledge that satisfactory supplementary mothering arrangements can and have been made by a not inconsiderable few. Had I myself had the children for whom I vainly longed, I like to believe that I could have arrived at some satisfactory combination of mothering and a career, but I do not believe that there is any universal, easy, ready-made solution to the problem.

I have sometimes been accused of being out of touch with current changes in life-styles, but I believe that the problem is that infants are perhaps a million or so years out of touch with them. Their inbuilt evolutionary adaptations tend not to match new life-styles, much as we would like to believe infants to be infinitely adaptable. In a sense the traditional role of women is also tied to evolutionary considerations. The child-bearing and -rearing role is so essential to the survival of the species – and has for so long absorbed women's energies – that it is small wonder that women have been constrained to that role over many millennia.

Now, however, it is clear that the human species has been too successful in that the world is overpopulated; at least some women have been relieved of their age-old responsibilities for at least some period of their lives. There seems little reason to doubt that the intelligence and dedication that women have devoted to their traditional role can now, when not required by that role, be channeled elsewhere without undue hindrance.

References

Ainsworth, M., & Chant, S. N. F. (1937). The measurement of attitude toward war and the galvanic skin response. *Journal of Educational Psychology*, *28*, 281–289.

Bowlby, J. (1958). The nature of a child's tie to his mother. *International Journal of Psychoanalysis*, *39*, 350–373.

Klopfer, B., & Kelly, D. M. (1948). *The Rorschach technique*. Yonkers-on-Hudson, NY: World Book.

McDougall, W. (1927). *Character and the conduct of life*. London: Methuen.

Salter, M. D. (1940). An evaluation of adjustment based upon the concept of security. *University of Toronto Studies, Child Development Series*, no. 9. Toronto: University of Toronto Press.

Revisiting Mary Ainsworth's conceptualization and assessments of maternal sensitivity-insensitivity

Inge Bretherton

University of Wisconsin-Madison, Madison, WI, USA

This paper describes the evolution of Ainsworth's construct of maternal sensitivity-insensitivity to infant signals from its beginnings in her research in Uganda to its explicit emergence in the findings from the Baltimore study. It provides an analysis of her bipolar Maternal Care Scales (Sensivity-Insensitivity, Cooperation-Interference, Acceptance-Rejection, and Accessibility-Ignoring and Neglecting) and associated findings from the Baltimore study, including studies of specific maternal and infant interactive behaviors also rooted in the sensitivity construct. In addition, the four Maternal Care ratings of observed maternal behavior in the home environment are considered in relation to Strange Situation subgroups and Ainsworth's home classifications of infant attachment and exploratory behavior. A brief comparison of Ainworth's with Bowlby's contributions follows. The paper ends with a discussion of Ainsworth's approach to science.

With the passage of time, constructs once regarded as groundbreaking and for that reason contentious tend to be taken for granted or considerably simplified as they gain general acceptance. Illustrating this effect, the last edition of the *Handbook of Attachment* (Cassidy & Shaver, 2008) references a fair number of studies linking various measures of maternal sensitivity to infant–mother attachment security but does not also include a comprehensive treatment of Mary Ainsworth's construct of maternal sensitivity-insensitivity despite its central role in attachment theory. The centenary of her birth thus provides a fitting occasion to revisit her conception of maternal sensitivity-insensitivity in its full complexity.

In this paper, I will begin by charting the origins of the sensitivity construct as it began to evolve from Ainsworth's observational research in Uganda and became explicit in her subsequent Baltimore study. In addition to published findings, I will pay particular attention to her four Maternal Care Scales (Sensitivity-Insensitivity, Cooperation-Interference, Acceptance-Rejection, Accessibility-Ignoring), three of which have never been published in their entirety, as well as to several of her 22 also never-published scales that she devised for rating aspects of maternal care during infants' first 3 months of life. These scales illuminate the construct of sensitivity beyond the reported summaries in published work. Next, I will review findings from the Baltimore study that link maternal and infant behaviors to maternal sensitivity ratings and the Strange Situation Procedure (SSP). I will also consider Ainsworth's less well known five home classifications as related to the Maternal

Care Scales and the SSP subgroups. I will then compare her contributions and methods to Bowlby's and end by discussing her approach to science and research.

Beginnings in Uganda

Ainsworth conducted her first observational study of infant–mother interaction during a 2-year (1954–1955) stay at the East African Institute for Social Research in Kampala, Uganda, after an almost 4-year collaboration with John Bowlby and his colleague James Robertson in London. As a member of Bowlby's research team at the Tavistock Institute, Ainsworth had become cognizant of his attempts to introduce ideas from ethology and evolutionary science into his initial formulations of attachment theory. She had also come to admire the work of her team-mate James Robertson who was observing children undergoing long- and short-term separations from their mothers and whose methods she had decided to emulate should she ever have an opportunity to conduct an observational study of her own. This opportunity presented itself when she arrived in Kampala where her husband had obtained a postdoctoral position.

With the help of local chiefs, Ainsworth recruited 26 families with young infants (two with twins) who lived in villages near Kampala. Over a period of 9 months and as regularly as possible she observed mothers, infants, and any family members in their homes during bi-monthly 2-hour visits. She was accompanied by an English-speaking Ganda social worker who served as interpreter and collaborator, but she had also learned a few expressions in the local language, Baganda. Data collection consisted of detailed note-taking, expanded after each visit into a typed report that her interpreter-colleague checked for factual accuracy. The notes included observations of infants' interactions with their mothers and with others present. They also summarized what mothers said in response to Ainsworth's questions about many aspects of infant care in Uganda (Ainsworth, 1963, 1967).

Although Ainsworth initially concentrated on the emergence of infant attachment behavior (e.g., crying, vocalizing, smiling, and postural adjustment) as it became differentially directed to the mother and a few other family members, she soon became particularly intrigued by individual differences in infant–mother relationships. At the end of her 9-month study, she was able to discern three patterns in Ganda infants' use of the mother as a secure base for exploration at home. Attached (vs. non-attached) infants showed age-appropriate discriminating attachment behavior toward the mother. However, secure-attached infants cried little and engaged in exploration when their mother was present while insecure-attached infants were frequently fussy even with mother in the same room. Although Ainsworth was also struck by individual differences in *maternal* behavior and had written detailed and vivid case summaries about each family (see pp. 125–316 in *Infancy in Uganda*), these summaries were not sufficiently detailed for identifying specific maternal behaviors that might be linked to the infant attachment classifications. She tried several simple group comparisons (i.e., sole maternal vs. multiple caregivers, degree of acculturation, demand versus schedule feeding, or maternal warmth) but these failed to distinguish mothers of secure- from those of insecure-attached babies. Only three yielded significant differences: (a) the amount of care provided by the *mother* (not the amount of care an infant received from the totality of caregivers); (b) the mother's excellence as informant; and (c) the mother's enjoyment of breastfeeding. Ainsworth (1967, p. 400) regarded these variables "as mere rough approximations of underlying maternal care variables which are more crucial in determining infant attachment quality," but for which she had not yet developed a name.

The emergence of the sensitivity construct

Ainsworth first mentioned the term maternal "sensitivity to infant signals" in the final chapter of her book on *Infancy in Uganda* (1967). A footnote, citing the work of French clinicians Miriam David and Genevieve Appel, hints at the origin of this somewhat unusual but very fitting label. Based on an exploratory study of routine and individualized care of institutionalized infants, David and Appell (1961, p. 132) had suggested that observing the quality of nurse–infant relationships required that one ask several questions at each moment of interaction. The primary questions were: "Is the nurse *sensitive and responsive to signals* coming from the child or the child's state? Does the infant take any notice of the caregiver? Does he react to her and how?" The term, "sensitivity and responsiveness to infant signals" may have appealed to Ainsworth because it accorded with the dyadic conception of maternal care for which she was searching.

Next step: the Baltimore study

Although Ainsworth introduced her ideas about maternal sensitivity in the volume *Infancy in Uganda* (1967), she did so in reference to preliminary findings from her, by then completed, second observational study in Baltimore. For that study she had trained three observers (Barbara Wittig, Robert Marvin, and George Allyn) to record maternal and infant behavior in much richer detail than had been possible in Uganda (Ainsworth & Bell, 1969). The observers took running notes, scored by time markers every 5 minutes. The notes included not only detailed behavioral descriptions of infant–mother interactions, but also captured what the mother said to the observer, both casually and during short interviews that were often conducted in the beginning of a visit or when the baby slept. This type of information is usually not available when home observations are brief and not repeated.

Considered less threatening, the observers were instructed not to assume a pure spectator role but to be responsive to overtures by mother and baby, but they assiduously avoided interfering, giving advice, or implying criticism (Ainsworth, 1977a, p. 2). They occasionally initiated interactions with the infants to assess their "cuddliness" when very young (all proved cuddly) and to test their responses to a relatively unfamiliar person. They also performed regular cognitive tests. Ainsworth herself was the regular visitor of five of the families and served as occasional reliability observer for each member of her research team.

The 26 white middle-class mothers who took part in the Baltimore study were recruited via pediatricians, mostly before the baby's birth, and none dropped out after observations began (Ainsworth, Blehar, Waters, & Wall, 1978). For the first 15 families, 4-hour home visits started at 3 weeks and continued at 3-week intervals until 54 months. For a second group of 11, there were weekly visits during the first month, lasting 2 hours each, but beginning at 6 weeks the schedule of the two sub-samples was identical. Immediately after each visit, the observers translated their notes into audio-recorded narratives.

Ainsworth (1977a, p. 145) had rejected the idea of using checklists to record observations. She felt that checklists cannot fully capture the larger context in which interactions occur and do not allow for the discovery of unanticipated behaviors. However, as she later commented:

> [this had] at least one disadvantage. It took years to get the accounts of the home visits transcribed from the tapes that had been dictated after the visits. And it took even longer to

> complete the coding of infant and maternal behavior at home. In comparison, it was relatively easy to get the dictated accounts of the strange-situation behavior transcribed. (Ainsworth, 1988, p. 11)

At the end of the infants' first year of life the Strange Situation Procedure (SSP), a 20-minute observational procedure including infant, mother, and a stranger, was conducted in a laboratory playroom. Participants' behavior was recorded by two or more observers who dictated continuous narratives from behind a one-way mirror. The initial goal had been to investigate infants' exploration and responses to a stranger in an unfamiliar environment in the presence and the absence of the mother. However, individual differences in infants' responses to maternal separations and reunions turned out to be so striking that Ainsworth and Wittig (1969) create a provisional SSP classification system. This system preceded the systematic coding of home observations, and was first presented in 1965 at a research meeting organized by Bowlby in London. The definitive SSP classification system included data from a second sample observed by Bell (1970), was completed between 1967–1968, and published in Ainsworth, Bell, and Stayton (1971).

As typed home narratives became available, Ainsworth examined 4th quarter (9–12 months) transcripts in relation to each SSP group and made notes, a procedure she called "back-and-forthing." She stressed that "this type of back-and-forthing between antecedent and outcome can be very productive in pioneer studies" (Ainsworth, 1988, pp. 10–11). From this exploratory exercise emerged the first explicit conceptualization of maternal sensitivity:

> (1) Sensitivity in response to signals implies that signals are *perceived* and *correctly interpreted*, and that the response to signals is *prompt and appropriate*. The signals may be of *need and distress* or they may be *social* signals.
> (2) Sensitivity to signals tends to ensure that the care the mother gives the baby, including her *playful* interaction with him, is *attuned* to the baby's state and mood – at the baby's own *timing*, not the mother's timing.
> (3) Routine care may be undertaken with little interaction. It is *interaction* that seems to be most important, not mere care, and particularly conspicuous in mother–child pairs who have achieved good interaction is *the quality of mutual delight* which characterizes their exchanges. (Ainsworth, 1967, p. 397, italics added)

A major but often unrecognized innovation of Ainsworth's Sensitivity-Insensitivity construct is its dyadic or relational emphasis:

> [It] does not consider maternal behavior in any absolute terms. The most important aspect of it, I repeat, was the mother's ability to gear her interactions to infant behavioral cues, so that despite inevitable constitutional differences among infants who later became securely attached, all had had experiences of a good "mesh." (1977b, p. 6)

Instead of interpreting maternal behavior and infant behavior in terms of unidirectional relations between cause (mother) and effect (infant), Ainsworth and Bell contended that:

> Whatever role may be played by the baby's constitutional characteristics, it seems quite clear that the mother's contribution to the interaction and the baby's contributions are caught up in an *interacting spiral*. It is because of these spiral effects – some vicious and some virtuous – that the variables are so confounded that it is not possible to distinguish independent from dependent variables. (Ainsworth & Bell, 1969, p. 160, italics added)

Other advances were to interpret all infant and maternal interactive behaviors as having a communicative function (whether so intended or merely expressive) and to propose that the dyadic patterning of these "behavioral conversations" formed the basis for infants' developing personality structure. Also new was the emphasis on maternal co-regulation or co-determination, achieved through sensitive attunement, pacing, and timing, aspects of mother–infant interaction that became important in subsequent work on mother–child play by Stern (1974) and others during the 1970s.

Whereas Bowlby (1969/1982) had proposed that the predictable outcome of infant signaling is proximity to the mother (implying her responsiveness), Ainsworth pointed out that infant signaling can achieve this outcome only if it activates appropriate caregiving responses in the adult (Ainsworth, Bell, & Stayton, 1974, p. 119). When experiencing sensitive feedback in a fairly consistent way a baby can:

> build up a set of expectancies about what his mother will do in each of a variety of sets of commonly occurring circumstances. He gradually builds up a working model of his mother, in representational terms, as someone in whom he can have confidence as being accessible and responsive when he wants or needs her. Therein lies his feeling of security in his relations with her. (Ainsworth, 1977b, p. 6)

Finally, it is often overlooked that Ainsworth applied the notion of maternal sensitivity to infants' *positive* social overtures as well as to secure base and safe haven behavior.

The four Maternal Care Scales

When infants' SSP classifications were compared to their mothers' 4th quarter Sensitivity-Insensitivity ratings, strong differences emerged between mothers of infants classified as secure versus those classified as insecure (avoidant or ambivalent). To differentiate mothers of insecure-avoidant from those of insecure-ambivalent infants, Ainsworth developed three additional scales (Cooperation-Interference, Acceptance-Rejection, and Accessibility-Ignoring). All four scales are summarized in Ainsworth et al. (1971) and are available online (see Ainsworth 1969a), but only the full text of the Sensitivity scale was ever published in Ainsworth et al. (1974).

As Ainsworth stressed, these were not ordinary scales, "drawn up in sketchy fashion in advance of data collection" (Ainsworth et al., 1978, p. 138), but scales based on a careful examination of behaviors described in the narrative records. Each 9-point scale begins with a long preamble (between 2 and 3 single-spaced typed pages) defining the bipolar construct, followed by text drawn from the narrative records that anchors the uneven numbered rating points (9, 7, 5, 3, and 1).

The four scales were applied to the 4th quarter home narratives by five independent judges, three of whom had no other knowledge of project data. Rating schedules were drawn up to avoid halo effects across variables and visits. All interrater correlations were above 0.85. The overall rating for each scale across five visits was agreed upon by conference, and usually turned out to be the median (Ainsworth et al., 1978, p. 143).

Correlations among Sensitivity, Acceptance, and Cooperation scores were above 0.85, but those with Accessibility were a little lower (r = 0.82, 0.58, and 0.72, respectively). Inspection of scatter diagrams (unpublished) showed that mothers with high Sensitivity ratings also scored highly on Cooperation, Acceptance, and Accessibility, whereas scores of mothers with lower ratings varied by scale. The summaries in Table 1 describe, at the high end: (1) sensitive maternal behavior that is flexibly adapted to a specific infant's

Table 1. Summary of the four Maternal Care Scales.

Sensitivity-insensitivity to infant signals	Cooperation-interference with infant's ongoing activities	Acceptance-rejection	Accessibility-ignoring
M's prompt and appropriate responsiveness to B's accurately perceived signals and communications	M's attitude to B as an autonomous person. The extent to which M's interventions or initiations of interaction break into, interrupt, or cut cross B's ongoing activity	Balance of M's positive and negative feelings about her particular B. The extent to which M has been able to integrate these conflicting feelings or to resolve the conflict	Degree of M's physical and psychological accessibility to B (acknowledgement of and responsiveness to B)
Sensitive. Able to see things and feel things from B's point of view. Sensitive to idiosyncratic ways of B's signals, behavior, and preferences by responding promptly and appropriately	**Cooperative:** M gears her behavior to the B's state, goals, and current interests. If she invites play, but B does not respond, she either desists or shifts her approach. Uses mood-setting techniques	**Accepting:** M cheerfully accepts the responsibility of caring for B. She may occasionally be irritated, but does not make an opponent of B even though B places temporary limitations on her other activities	**Accessible:** nearly always tuned in to B's signals and communications even when B is in another room. Can attend to B's communications despite distractions by other demands and interests
Insensitive. M gears interventions and initiations almost exclusively to her own wishes, moods, and activities. Interprets B's communications in line with her own wishes or defences, or does not respond to them at all	**Interfering:** M does not respect B as an autonomous person whose wishes have a validity of their own. Interventions break into or interrupt B's ongoing activity (includes frequency and extent of physical interference or being "at the baby" most of the time, training, eliciting, controlling)	**Rejecting.** Frequent angry, resentful feelings overwhelm M's positive feelings toward B. M may openly voice rejection, constantly oppose B's wishes or maintain an atmosphere of irritation and scolding	**Inaccessible** M ignores and thus neglects B. M is so preoccupied with her own concerns that she cannot perceive B's signals. Or she is aware but ignores B deliberately, noticing B only when doing something for B. Cannot sufficiently *feel* things from B's point of view

signals and communications, (2) cooperation with the baby's ongoing behavior (3) acceptance or a positive balance of feelings regarding the baby and being a mother, and (4) accessibility or attention to the baby's signals. The low scale-points describe mothers who appear preoccupied with themselves and engage in more or less arbitrary behavior. Scale mid-points (ratings of 5) capture maternal inconsistencies (inconsistently sensitive, mildly interfering, ambivalently accepting, and inconsistently accessible).

Aside from the Table 1 definitions, several additional features of the scales bear emphasizing:

Emotion. The scales place considerable stress on affect and emotions (the mother's own and the infant's). High ratings on the Sensitivity scale are given to mothers who have insight into their own mood and its effect on their infant. Over and above mere intellectual awareness of infant signals, Ainsworth (1970) proposed that a mother must empathize with her baby's feelings or "*feel things from his point of view*" before she can respond appropriately. In turn, mothers learn about the appropriateness their responses from infant feedback via emotional signals such as pleasure, relief, or negative responses indicating when to desist. Mothers given low Sensitivity ratings seem predominantly governed by their own needs, feelings, and fantasies, particularly hindering accurate perception of infant signals during the early months when the meaning of signals is often ambiguous.

Ainsworth also considered maternal delight in the baby (including the capacity to express it verbally) to be an important aspect of sensitivity. This delight can be tender and gentle, and is not necessarily intense. It emerges during situations and behavior specific to the baby, and should not to be confused with pride. Delight may be present in some mothers from beginning but may develop in others only gradually.

Opposing positive and negative feelings are addressed in the Acceptance-Rejection scale. At the positive pole, mothers accept that the baby has a will of his or her own and even find the baby's anger worthy of respect. At the rejecting pole, mothers experience the baby as a burden whose needs are seen as unwelcome demands. However, because it is the norm that mothers love their babies, Ainsworth cautions that maternal anger at or about the baby is often likely to be repressed or suppressed, leading some mothers to put on a show of affection or hide their genuine feelings. She also cautions that not too much weight is to be given to momentary outbursts of irritation if embedded in an otherwise positive, warm relationship, but pseudo-accepting mothers who respond to infant signals in a long-suffering manner should receive lower ratings.

In her Ganda study, Ainsworth (1967, p. 394) had noted that emotional warmth (which can be shown without sensitivity) did not distinguish mothers of secure-attached from those of insecure-attached infants. In connection with the Baltimore study, however, she repeatedly highlighted the dyadic affective quality of *harmony*:

> Insofar as there is a single, quantifiable dimension of mother–infant interaction implicit in our hypotheses, it is a crude one of harmony-disharmony, with the implication that towards the disharmonious pole qualitative differences are so great that it is difficult to order them magnitudinally, let alone quantify them. (Ainsworth et al., 1971, pp. 49–50)

Relatedly, Stayton, Hogan and Ainsworth (1971, p. 1060) state that the purpose of the Sensitivity, Acceptance, and Cooperation scales was to assess the harmony in the mother–infant relationship.

Cooperation and control. Ainsworth defined sensitive mothers as those who usually give their young babies what they seem to want but respond tactfully when they cannot go along with their baby's wishes (e.g., offering an acceptable alternative). Sensitive mothers also rely on mood-setting (e.g., slowing down the pace at bedtime) and plan to avoid situations that would require interfering interventions (e.g., by baby-proofing the house to allow safe exploration). Impersonal restraints, such as strapping the baby in a high-chair or placing him or her in a play-pen, are only interfering if the baby does not accept them willingly. In short, Ainsworth regarded maternal cooperation as incompatible with coercion but as compatible with foresightful "nudging." Finally, she commented that, at the end of first year, there may come a point when parents can show a baby that they are not an instrument of the baby's will. Sensitivity at that point consists of warmly encouraging infant behaviors that *invite* maternal cooperation.

Defensive operations. As noted, the Baltimore observers – in addition to recording interactive behavior – also noted what the mother said to and about her baby in the course of home visits. This allowed comparisons between what mothers said and did, something not possible during "pure" observations. If discrepancies were noticed, Ainsworth advised coders to give greatest credence to what had been observed.

Consistent with a background in clinical diagnostics and her appreciation of Freud's ideas about the unconscious, Ainsworth (1969a) attributed mismatches between what mothers said and the observers noticed (e.g. apparent misinterpretations or ignoring of unmistakable signals) to defensive operations such as projection and denial. If the baby's signals did break through the mother's defensive barrier, a second line of defense was to somehow remove "from the stimuli emanating from the baby their signal quality." Ainsworth also referred to the defense mechanism of intellectualization, noting that some mothers can accurately perceive infant signals only if they submerge their own feelings, but in that case their perceptions appear detached.

Relevant in this connection is Ainsworth's emphasis on mothers' excellence as informant for which she had already developed a special scale during her Ganda study (1967, p. 45). Mothers with high ratings stick to the topic, volunteer information with much spontaneous detail, and never seem impatient. In the preamble of a scale by the same name (in a collection of 22 unpublished scales on 1st quarter maternal care) Ainsworth clarifies that Excellence as Informant does not mean reporting precise schedules, hours, and dates, but details "about idiosyncracies and sensitive little things that testify to a mother's interested perception." Such (nondefensive) mothers make observers feel they had been there. Unless mothers evade requests for information, however, they should not be given lower scores merely because they want occasionally to talk about themselves.

Maternal and infant learning. Ainsworth observed that optimal synchronization may require learning or mutual adaptation by both mother and baby and may therefore take time. However, given that mothers have more control over their behavior than infants, Ainsworth et al. (1978, p. 142) categorized synchronization as a maternal variable. Mother-supported synchrony assists the baby in learning to stabilize his or her rhythms, whereas these natural rhythms may become disorganized if synchronization is not achieved. Synchronization implies that the baby should not be allowed to build up to a state of distressing tension whereas slight delays may nudge the baby towards regularization.

After completing the rating of the five 4th quarter home observation narratives and demonstrating their highly significant associations with the SSP classifications (Ainsworth et al., 1971), Ainsworth and her team initiated a series of meticulous analyses of the narrative records that focused on specific domains of maternal and infant interactive behavior. These, too, were inspired by the sensitivity construct and will be discussed next. As Ainsworth and colleagues (1971, p. 36) commented; "Broader significance can be attributed to strange-situation behavior … only if it emerges as consistently related to characteristic behavior in everyday life."

Home behavior as linked to the Maternal Care Scales and Strange Situation classifications

A subset of publications on mother–infant interactive behavior at home focused entirely on normative age trends and intercorrelations among variables within and across domains (see Bell and Ainsworth, 1972, on infant crying and nonverbal communication; Stayton, Ainsworth, and Main, 1973, on infant and maternal behaviors during brief everyday separations; Ainsworth, Bell, and Stayton, 1972, on close bodily contact; and Main and Stadtman, 1981, on maternal contact aversion and infant anger). Although I will include findings from some of these articles and chapters (which deserve a detailed analysis of their own), my emphasis here is on the corpus of writings linking maternal and infant interactive behaviors to 4th quarter maternal sensitivity ratings as well as to secure (B), avoidant (A), and resistant or ambivalent (C) infant–mother classifications in the Strange Situation. Table 2 provides excerpts from narrative records to demonstrate the detailed

Table 2. Brief Illustrative Excerpts from Baltimore Home Visit Narrative Records.

Boy 1, Visit 14, 33 weeks

M comes back into the room now and B is very excited. M is about 8 feet away from him and she's coaxing B to come over to her. B is even more excited now as he works his way over to her. Finally he gets close enough for M to pick him up and she does so. B is still excited as she picks him up.

B is obviously getting tired. He turns around to M now, and M puts him in a face-to-face position, and B opens his mouth and puts it on M's cheek, giving her a great big slobbery kiss. Now M begins to snuggle B. B rears back and starts exploring M's face with his hands. He lets out a huge yawn and M decides that it is time to put B to bed.

Boy 2, Visit 19, 48 weeks

Suddenly B loses his balance and topples over and bangs his head on the wheel of the stroller. Then there is a fuss. M pats him without picking him up and asks "where's your spoon?" [with which B had been playing].

He kneels holding on to this table and reaches for something on the table. It's a stack of orange coasters. M says no-no repeatedly and B pays no attention to her so M moves them away, not quite before he's managed to knock the coasters on the floor.

B is still crying. M picks him up and says with a very scornful voice "Oh brother, you're pitiful." She carries B out to the kitchen.

Girl, Visit 13, 31 weeks

B gets a little fussy now and she makes a cryish sound, so M picks B up and B quiets. M says she might be wet. M holds B so she can get into the diaper, checks B, and carries B into the bedroom and puts her down on her back on the bed. B rolls over, and M says: "Before too long we'll have a nap." M says this in response to my question as to napping. M rolls B on to her back, and B rubs her eyes and sucks on her thumb. She kind of squints her eyes and makes a growling sound. B touches M's face and I ask M about this. M says "she'll push and pull on you." Now M brings her face down close to B's face and she reaches up and touches M's face.

M gets out the highchair and B watches. Then she makes a little neutral call, and I would interpret this call as follows: "Hurry up." I'm really translating from baby talk to adult talk. B is silent right now. Now she makes another call, which I feel signifies to M to hurry up, There's no cry. B appears very confident that she will get her food. Now she makes a little protest. M goes over and picks B up and B makes a grunt; it's kind of guttural.

behavior captured in a variety of situations. The behavioral coding was undertaken by trained undergraduates with no knowledge of infants' maternal Sensitivity ratings and SSP classifications.

The voluminous findings from this set of studies are summarized in Tables 3 and 4, together with their sources (chapters, articles, manuscripts, and the book *Patterns of Attachment*). For each domain, maternal behaviors are listed before corresponding infant behaviors, highlighting their complementarity. Correlations with 4th quarter sensitivity are reported when available, and means are listed for the three major SSP classifications.

Table 3 presents 1st quarter (1–3 months) maternal and infant behaviors, showing mean differences between B (secure) and A/C groups combined (avoidant- and ambivalent-insecure) assessed with *t*-tests. Differences between A- and C-dyads were not tested owing to the small group sizes, but will nevertheless be discussed here because they suggested "different forms of mother–infant interaction that tie into different dynamic processes affecting infant development" (Ainsworth et al., 1978, p. 240).

The feeding classifications listed at the top of Table 3 were first reported at a meeting in London in 1967. They appeared in a chapter by Ainsworth and Bell (1969) that illustrates Ainsworth's methods especially well but has, unfortunately, almost "dropped out" of the attachment literature. It focused on feeding practices and their correlates, because feeding takes up much of infants 1st quarter waking time.

As in Uganda, Ainsworth found simplistic categories (schedule vs. demand feeding) useless for evaluating feeding practices and, as in *Infancy in Uganda*, the chapter lists summary descriptions and raw data for each mother so that readers can draw their own conclusions and perform their own computations. Ainsworth and Bell list details of nine maternal patterns, extracted from 1st quarter narrative records and rank-ordered to form a scale. The top-ranked patterns refer to feeding practices that allow a baby to be an active participant and thus provide him or her with a feeling of efficacy. These patterns were characteristic of mothers who synchronized their behavior with the baby's rhythms and pace (neither too fast nor slow) and handled solid food preferences tactfully. Mothers in the middle ranks staved off feedings for prolonged periods, overfed by coaxing, or were impatient and ended feeding too soon. The lowest ranked patterns describe highly arbitrary feedings with unpredictable timing and long delays, force-feeding, and disregard for infant rhythms (i.e., speeding up feeding by enlarging the hole in the nipple of the feeding bottle causing choking). In these groups, feedings were often a battle. Ainsworth and Bell commented that mothers who tried to use forcible methods to influence their baby's feeding behavior usually ended up with the opposite results. The authors' basic assumption was that a good feeding is a happy feeding.

Also reported were ratings based on six of Ainsworth's 22 unpublished 1st quarter Maternal Care Scales that were not concerned with feeding. Ainsworth credited Barbara Wittig for help with scale development and Robert Marvin and George Allyn for independent rating of the 1st quarter narrative records (interrater correlations of 0.86–0.93). Four of these scales pertained to mothers' general attitude (perception of, delight in, and acceptance of the baby as well as mother's excellence as informant). The 5th and 6th scales pertained to variations in specific maternal behaviors (effectiveness in calming a crying infant and amount of physical contact). Maternal scores on these six 9-point scales were highly intercorrelated (0.81–0.94). Table 3 therefore lists the averaged ratings for the six scales.

Clear-cut differences emerged between feeding practices of mothers whose babies were later classified as secure (B) and insecure (A and C combined) with their mothers in

Table 3. Maternal and baby behavior in the 1st quarter: correlations with 4th quarter maternal sensitivity ratings and means for Strange Situation groups at 12 months (Baltimore study data reported in various sources).

	M sensitivity (4th quarter)		Strange Situation groups (12 months)			
Home behaviour 1st quarter	in[a]	*r*	in[a]	B	A	C
Feeding						
M feeding practices (9 ranked groups)			1	3.1***	7.2	7.7
M feeding synchronized w/B's rhythms (rating)			2	6.4***	2.7	2.4
M lets B determine end of feeding (rating)			2	6.5***	3.2	2.8
M tactful re food preferences (rating)			2	6.7**	3.9	3.8
M synchronizes feeding with B's pace (rating)			2	6.8**	3.4	3.3
Mean of the 4 (above) feeding scales	3	.77***				
1st Quarter Maternal Care Scales						
Mean of 6 scales (see text)			1	6.8***	2.5	2.9
Crying						
Crying episodes ignored by M			2	1.6	3.1	1.6
M unresponsive to crying (mins/hour)			2	3.6**	6.8	9.3
B crying episodes/hour	4	−.61**	2	3.4*	5.4	3.8
B crying minutes/hour	4	−.72**	2	6.9**	13.0	11.8
Holding						
Mean contact episode (minutes)			2	8.7[+]	5.2	7.8
M behavior affectionate %			2	16.9*	6.5	8.7
M holding tender careful %			2	55.0***	22.0	2.2
M inept holding %			2	5.0***	28.0	41.0
M appears averse to close bodily contact (rating)			2	2.3**	7.3	1.7
B positive to hold			2	24.8*	6.7	1.8
B negative to hold			2	19.5	16.3	32.5
B positive to put-down			2	11.4	5.3	6.5
B negative to put-down			2	36.0*	46.7	61.2
Face-to-face interaction[b]						
M contingent pacing			2	52.9**	20.7	10.9
M silent, unsmiling initiation			2	12.2	28.7	11.3
M routine manner			2	11.0**	29.7	25.5
M unresponsive to B initiation[c]			5	4.6* B3	15.3 (*A* + C)	
M abrupt			5	.6*** B3	12.0 (*A* + C)	

(*continued*)

Table 3. *(Continued)*.

	M sensitivity (4th quarter)		Strange Situation groups (12 months)			
Home behaviour 1st quarter	in[a]	*r*	in[a]	B	A	C
M encourages further interaction			5	25.2*** B3	3.4 (*A* + C)	
M playfulness			5	18.6^{+} B3	8.5 (*A* + C)	
Liveliness of M stimulation			5	4.9^{+} B3	3.7 (*A* + C)	
Episodes brief			5	35.6** B3	62.5 (*A* + C)	
B bounce			5	21.3** B3	5.4 (*A* + C)	
B smile			2	45.3	39.3	26.3
B vocalize			2	23.9	26.7	6.9
B no response to M initiation			2	4.9*	17.7	16.6
B terminates interaction			2	11.4*	26.1	14.7
Affection and Expressiveness						
M kisses B (median frequency)[d]			6	.30	.58	.21
M hugs/cuddles B (median frequency)[d]			6	.17	$.03^{+}$	.30*
M lack of facial expressiveness (rating)[e]			2	2.7*	6.2	3.5

Note: [a] Indicates source of information: 1 = Ainsworth and Bell (1969); 2 = Ainsworth et al. (1978, chapter 7 for B variables, chapter 8 for M variables); 3 = Ainsworth and Tracy (1973); 4 = Stayton and Ainsworth (1973); 5 = Blehar, Lieberman, and Ainsworth (1977); 6 = Tracy & Ainsworth, 1981; [b] includes 6–15 week visits; [c] for this and the following 7 variables only the B3 vs. A + C comparison is available; [d] first and second quarter; [e] whole year.
$^{+}p < .10$; $^{*}p < .05$; $^{**}p < .01$; $^{***}p < .001$ (two-tailed); if asterisk is on B, B is different from A/C combined, if asterisk is on A or C, that mean is different from B.

the SSP at 12 months, but the mean scores of group A- and C-mothers were indistinguishable (Ainsworth & Bell, 1969). This held, also, for the four 9-point feeding scales (from the collection of 22 1st quarter Maternal Care Scales listed in Ainsworth et al., 1978), and the average of the six 1st quarter scales (maternal attitudes, response to crying, and amount of physical contact), computed from Ainsworth and Bell (1969).

The remainder of Table 3 lists maternal and infant behaviors related to infant crying, close bodily contact, face-to-face play, and affection. For almost all of these variable sets, group-B mothers and infants (those later categorized as secure in the SSP) received significantly more favorable scores than A- and C-dyads, but the untested differences between A- and C-dyads also deserve attention (to conserve space, group A, B, and C mothers will henceforth be called A-, B-, and C-mothers).

C-mothers ignored crying most often and delayed their responses longest, but A-infants cried both most frequently and longer per hour. B-mothers held their babies longest, most tenderly, and affectionately, and their babies responded most positively to being held and being put-down (presumably because the mother sensed when they were satisfied). C-mothers most often held their babies ineptly and least often tenderly, and their infants received the lowest scores for positive responses and the highest scores for negative responses to being held. A-mothers, on the other hand, had the lowest percentage of affectionate holding episodes and A-infants responded least positively to being put down. It is necessary to interject here that many holding episodes were coded as neutral, thus there was no a priori necessity for negative correlations between positive and negative infant and maternal responses.

Face-to-face interactions were examined by Blehar et al. (1977) who compared mothers and infants in the B3 subgroup (optimally secure in the SSP) with A- and C-infants combined (the less optimal B1/B2 group was consistently intermediate on all variables, a point to which I return in the next section). However, for some face-to-face behaviors the A/B/C means were reported in *Patterns of Attachment* (Ainsworth et al., 1978), and are listed this way in the table. Maternal pacing that was attuned to infants' level of arousal characterized B-mothers who were also most playful, and engaged in the longest face-to-face bouts. Reciprocally, B-infants displayed more active pleasure (e.g., bouncing) and smiled most during face-to-face interactions. In contrast, A-mothers most often initiated silent, unsmiling face-to-face episodes, and their babies terminated face-to-face episodes sooner than B- and C-babies. Overall, however, A-babies smiled almost as often and vocalized more often during face-to-face episodes than B-infants. Finally, A-mothers kissed their babies (without engaging in close bodily contact) more frequently than B-mothers during the first half-year, but both C- and B-mothers cuddled their babies considerably more than A-mothers. In fact, at this age C-mothers cuddled their babies most often, but this code did not include the quality of physical contact (Tracy & Ainsworth, 1981).

Table 4 pertains to the 4th quarter home narratives. For most variables, *t*-test showed that B-infants and their mothers differed significantly both from A- and from C-dyads. With respect to feeding, Ainsworth and Tracy (1973) discovered that the four 1st quarter feeding scales were no longer useful in the 4th quarter because many babies had begun to feed themselves (finger foods, holding own bottle). However, happy 4th quarter feedings were strongly associated with concurrent maternal Sensitivity.

Infant crying declined over the first year for the sample as a whole (Bell & Ainsworth, 1972). Nevertheless, maternal Sensitivity ratings were strongly (inversely) correlated with 4th quarter crying variables (Stayton & Ainsworth, 1973). In addition, crying differed by SSP-classification. A-babies still cried slightly more frequently than C-infants during the 4th quarter, but not as long as C-infants overall. B-babies cried least, but used non-crying modes of communication (gestural, vocal, facial) more than the other two groups (rated 1 to 3; see Bell & Ainsworth, 1972).

Total maternal holding time also declined in the course of the first year, mostly because many mothers no longer held their babies during feedings (Ainsworth et al., 1972). B-mothers were still most affectionate and tender-careful while holding their babies, whereas C-mothers had the lowest means for these categories, and the highest percentage of inept holding and routine holding episodes. A-mothers were more abrupt or interfering (20% of the time) while picking their baby up than either B- or C-mothers. B-infants responded most positively and A-infants least positively to being held. A-infants also engaged least in active contact behavior (molding their body to the adult), and "sinking" in. Overall, they responded negatively to being held as much as C-babies. As in the first half year, B-mothers cuddled their infants most during the 3rd and 4th quarters, C-mothers did so half as often, and A-mothers hardly at all, although A-mothers again kissed their babies (absent cuddling) more often than B- and C-mothers (Tracy & Ainsworth, 1981).

As infants became mobile, Stayton and Ainsworth (1973) found that A- and B-infants followed the mother about equally often when she left the room while C-infants did so only half as much. B-infants cried least and C-infants most when the mother left the room, but

Table 4. Maternal and baby behavior in the 4th quarter: correlations with 4th quarter maternal sensitivity ratings and means for Strange Situation groups at 12 months (Baltimore study data reported in various sources).

	M sensitivity (4th quarter)		Strange Situation groups (12 months)			
Home behavior 4th quarter	in[a]	r	in[a]	B	A	C
Feeding						
Feedings rated as happy	3	.83***				
Crying (general)						
M unresponsive to cry min/hour	7	−.58**	2	1.3	3.3***	4.4**
M ignores crying episodes/hour	7	−.41*	2	1.5	2.1	2.3
B frequency crying/hour	9	−.63**	2	3.7	4.7	4.2
B duration crying minutes/hour			2	3.0	5.6**	8.1**
B non-crying communication rating			2	2.6	1.8	1.2*
Holding						
M affectionate episodes %			2	24.0	8.8*	4.0***
M tender careful holding episodes %			2	21.6	8.7	3.0+
M abrupt/interfering pick-up episodes %			2	9.1	20.3**	14.2
M holding time engaged in routines %			2	17.4	21.3	46.2*
M inept holding episodes %			2	3.8	9.8^{+}	15.0*
B initiates pick-up %			2	22.1	16.2	9.5*
B positive to hold %	9	.71***	2	40.0	14.3**	20.7*
B active contact behavior			2	.40	.02*	.12
B sinks in %			2	.25	.02**	.20
B positive to put-down %	9	.43*	2	68.7	59.8	50.2**
B negative to hold %	9	−.53**	2	6.1	21.2**	23.0
B initiates put-down %	9	−.36	2	2.5	3.5	6.7
Affection and Expressiveness						
M kisses B (median frequency/hr)[b]			6	.47	.66	.19^{+}
M hugs/cuddles B (median frequency/hr)[b]			6	.66	.02**	.31*
B mood dominated by anger (rating)			2	3.0	7.8***	5.7**
Brief separations/reunions						
M acknowledges B on return (%)	7	.60**	2	34.5	17.8*	23.0^{+}
M Frequency of leaving room	7	−.29				
B cries when M leaves room (%)	7	−.40*	2	14.1	20.3**	29.0**
B follows when M leaves room (%)	7	.40*	2	55.6	56.3	21.5**
B greets M on return (%)	7	.46*	2	39.0	28.2*	23.0*

(continued)

Table 4. (*Continued*).

	M sensitivity (4th quarter)		Strange Situation groups (12 months)			
Home behavior 4th quarter	in[a]	*r*	in[a]	B	A	C
B greets M crying/mixed response (%)	7	−.28	2	9.5	12.3	17.2**
Obedience						
M verbal commands frequency	8	−.14	2	2.6	2.4	2.0
M physical interventions frequency	8	−.44*	2	.6	1.3⁺	1.3
B complies with M command (%)	8	.63**	2	81.1	54.0**	44.0**
B internalized control	8	.40*				
4th Quarter Maternal Care Scales						
Sensitive-Insensitive	7	1.00	2	6.5	2.4***	2.4***
Acceptance-Rejection	7	.89**	2	7.6	3.7***	5.4**
Cooperation-Interference	7	.86**	2	7.3	3.6***	4.2***
Accessibility-Ignoring	7	.82**	2	6.6	3.8**	3.5**
C Attachment-Exploration Balance						
Ranked groups I – V (I = optimal)			2	1.5	3.3***	4.7***
Other						
Griffiths Scale IQ	8	.46*	2	119	110	107
M grants B floor freedom	8	.07				

Notes: [a]Indicates source of information for maternal sensitivity correlations and Strange Situation groups (sources numbered 1, 4, and 5 are only used in Table 3): 2 = Ainsworth et al. (1978); 3 = Ainsworth and Tracy (1973); 6 = Tracy and Ainsworth (1981); 7 = Stayton and Ainsworth (1973); 8 = Stayton et al. (1971); 9 = unpublished computations by I. Bretherton for Stayton and Ainsworth (1973). [b]3rd and 4th quarter.
⁺ $p < .10$; *$p < .05$; **$p < .01$; ***$p < .001$ (two-tailed); if asterisk is on A or C mean, that mean is different from B.

overall A-infants cried significantly more than B-infants. B-mothers acknowledged their babies most often when re-entering the room whereas A-mothers did so least (here again many responses were neutral). B-infants greeted their mothers most positively (40% of enter-room episodes), A-infants did so less (about 30%), and C-infants least (just over 20%). C-infants most often greeted the mothers with a mixed response that included a fuss.

During the 4th quarter, mothers intervened in their babies' undesirable ongoing behavior either physically by removing them from the source of concern or through verbal requests and commands (Stayton et al., 1971). B-infants cooperated with maternal verbal requests/commands about 80% of the time, but even A-infants complied just over half and C-infants just under half of the time. A few (usually B-infants) manifested the beginnings of internalized control or self-prohibition. As the authors comment: "There is little evidence that obedience is achieved through training or specific schedules of reward or punishment. Rather, the affectional tie itself seems to foster a willingness to comply with parental signals" (Stayton et al., 1971, p. 1067).

In addition to domains of behavioral interaction, Table 4 presents correlations of maternal Sensitivity with the other three 4th quarter Maternal Care Scales (all *r*s exceeded 0.80) and infant Strange Situation patterns. B-mothers received the highest means, but there were differences in the rank order of A- and C-means that I discuss in the next section.

It is less well known that Ainsworth also constructed a classification system of infant secure base and exploratory behavior at home (see Ainsworth et al., 1971). She identified five groups, labeled with Roman numerals I to V (I being optimal). Table 4 shows that B-infants were placed in optimal home groups significantly more often than A- and C-infants, but a detailed discussion of A/C differences related to this measure is also postponed to the next section.

Finally, 11-month IQ scores obtained with the Griffiths scale were significantly correlated with maternal Sensitivity, but separate comparisons of A- and C-infants' scores with those of B-infants were not significant (Ainsworth et al., 1978, p. 131). Ainsworth and Bell (1974, p. 108) ventured that maternal sensitivity may have a facilitating effect on the infant's exploration of the environment, but permitting more floor freedom was not related to maternal Sensitivity ratings.

In summary, the 1st quarter studies presented in Table 3 reveal that future A-dyads scored less favorably than C-dyads on a few behavioral categories. A-mothers were least expressive of positive emotions (lowest percentage of affectionate holding episodes, silent, unsmiling face-to-face initiations, and routine interactions) while A-infants responded least positively to being put-down and terminated face-to-face interactions more often than C-infants. A larger number of differences emerged during the 4th quarter (see Table 4). Mothers of A-infants were somewhat more often abrupt when picking the baby up, had the highest percentage of brief holding episodes, acknowledged their infants least when re-entering the room, and – as in the 1st quarter – showed affection through kissing rather than cuddling (Tracy & Ainsworth, 1981). A-infants reciprocated by responding least positively to being held, failing to sink in and mold their body to the mother's, but were also least satisfied when put down. C-infants cried longest per hour and cried most often when their mother departed from the room, but A-infants cried somewhat more frequently per hour than C-infants, and cried proportionately more often at home than B-infants when mothers left the room. Possible meanings of differences between the A1/A2 and C1/C2 subgroups will be discussed in the next section.

Strange Situation subgroups in relation to the Maternal Care ratings and infant home classifications

In addition to documenting the mean Maternal Care ratings and infant–mother home classifications as related to the three major SSP classifications, Ainsworth examined these ratings by SSP subgroups (B3, B1/B2, A1, A2, C1, and C2). She reasoned that "a more refined identification of outcome patterns offers more aid to the identification of relevant antecedent variables than does a cruder kind of identification" (Ainsworth et al., 1978, pp. 234–235). Following a method she often used in classification procedures, she had identified the SSP subgroups before creating the three major ABC classifications and predicted that subgroup distinctions would, in time, prove even more useful than placement into the three major groups (Ainsworth et al., 1978, p. 251).

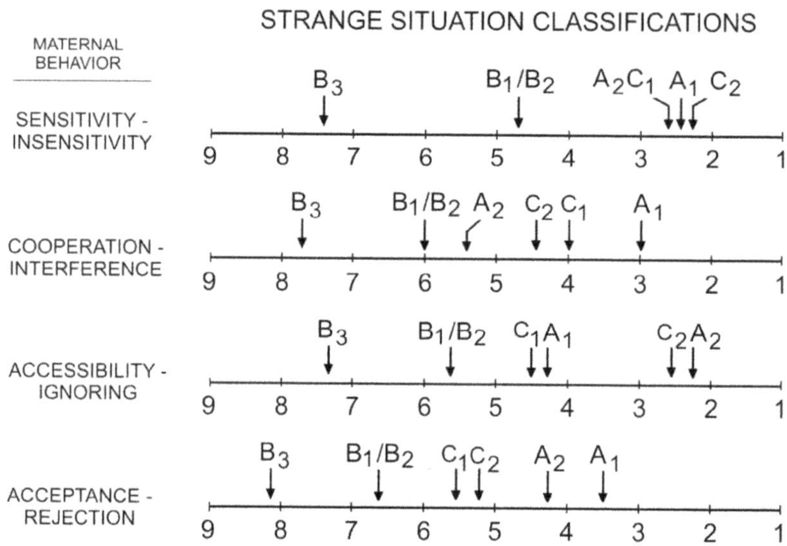

Figure 1. Mean Maternal Care ratings by Strange Situation sub-groups. This graph is adapted from Ainsworth, Bell, and Stayton (1971, p. 43).

Maternal Care ratings and SSP subgroups. Figure 1 (from Ainsworth et al., 1971, p. 43) graphically displays maternal Sensitivity, Acceptance, Cooperation, and Accessibility ratings by SSP subgroup. Consistently, mothers with the highest ratings on the four scales had infants who were classified as B3 (optimally secure) in the SSP but as consistently, the means of B1/B2-mothers on these scales were 1–3 points lower. On Sensitivity B1/B2-mothers actually scored slightly below 5 (inconsistently sensitive). However, on the Acceptance-Rejection scale, the gap with the B3 group shrank, with clearly positive ratings just short of 7 (accepting). On Cooperation, means for B1/B2 mothers were also quite positive (between cooperative and slightly interfering), yet on Accessibility-Ignoring, their means were only just above 5 (inconsistently accessible).

Mothers of infants in the four *insecure* SSP sub-groups had lower means than mothers of the B1/B2 group on every scale. On Sensitivity, all mothers with insecure infants were closely bunched below 3 (insensitive), but on the other three scales their scores diverged. On Acceptance-Rejection C1- and C2-mothers were rated slightly above 5 (i.e., on the positive side of ambivalent) whereas A2- and A1-mothers received the lowest ratings (between ambivalent and rejecting). The negative pole of the Acceptance ratings implies that “anger, resentment, hurt, or irritation conflict conspicuously with and limit positive feelings and result in more or less overt rejection of the baby.” Scale-point 3 (rejecting) reads: “Putting him away from her if he doesn’t do what she wants – or by deliberate ignoring as retaliation”; “long-suffering pseudo-patient compliance with his demands (which are perfunctory compliances and hence not satisfying)”; or constantly dwelling on the baby’s defects, shortcomings, and problems. Even the scale mid-point (ambivalent) describes mothers who react to infant anger or assertion of will as if it revealed the infant’s deep-seated hostility, opposition, or rejection toward the mother, albeit with the proviso that these negative feelings are not dominant.

On the Cooperation-Interference scale, in contrast, the A2-mothers’ means were slightly above the midpoint (mildly interfering) and only one half point below that of B1/B2-mothers. The means for C1- and C2-mothers were one scale-point lower (just below 5), but it was A1-mothers who received by far the lowest ratings (3 = interfering), described in the manual as "frequent displays of physical interference or restraint, or very frequent mild interference – instructing, eliciting, prohibiting, and commanding," with the proviso that these maternal behaviors have some rationale (training, scheduling) rather than being completely arbitrary which would deserve a rating of 1.

On Accessibility, A1- and C1-mothers had similar mean scores just below 5 (inconsistently accessible) whereas the also similar means of the A2- and C2-mothers were about two-scale points lower (below 3 = often inaccessible, neglecting, and ignoring). In the manual a score of 3 is described as: "Occasionally seems responsive to B's behavior and to the signals implicit in it, but … She may be too preoccupied with her own thoughts or activities to notice him, or she may notice and correctly interpret his signals without being moved to acknowledge them … Although she frequently ignores him, she is not entirely oblivious. If the baby signals strongly enough or persistently enough, M may respond to him – and in this she differs from mothers with even lower ratings."

Home classifications, Maternal Care ratings and SSP subgroups. The findings graphed in Figure 1 raise the question whether similar patterns would emerge if Ainsworth's less well known five home classifications of infant attachment and exploratory behavior were plotted against means of the Maternal Care Scales. Although this information is not directly available, it can be estimated. In what follows I therefore describe each of the five home-classifications in relation to the Maternal Care Scales and the SSP subgroups. I reflect on the phenotypic differences between infant behavior in the home and lab settings, and consider the appropriateness of SSP-labels for patterns of infant attachment and exploratory behavior at home in the context of the four Maternal Care ratings.

Ainsworth found the task of identifying 4th quarter patterns of infant–mother behavior in Baltimore homes considerably more daunting than the home classification of Ganda infants. This is perhaps not surprising, because the Ganda observations were conducted during the traditional afternoon visiting hour (Ainsworth, 1967) and did not include, as in Baltimore, all aspects of infant care.

Although Ainsworth named her home classification manual "Criteria for Classification of One-Year-Olds in Terms of the Balance between Exploratory and Attachment Behavior at Home" (Ainsworth, 1970, summarized in Ainsworth et al., 1971), the classification system focuses not so much on the *balance* of infant attachment and exploratory behavior of each group as on qualitative differences in their *integration* and quality. Classifications are labeled with Roman numerals rather than descriptive names, because Ainsworth was considering a revision that would not be geared primarily to the concept of the attachment-exploration balance (Ainsworth et al., 1978, p. 241). The original plan, to have research assistants independently classify each 4th quarter visit proved unworkable, because infants sometimes behaved quite differently from one visit to the next. Importantly, the variability of infant behavior was therefore incorporated into the classification system, and all classifications, conducted by Ainsworth herself, were based on joint consideration of the complete set of 4th quarter narrative records.

Just as the four Maternal Care Scales require that infant behavior be taken into account in rating maternal behavior, some of the infant home classifications required that aspects of *maternal* responses be considered to classify infants. Infants in Home Group I moved freely away from the mother to engage in locomotor and constructive object exploration while keeping track of the mother's whereabouts and gravitating back to her from time to time for brief, but satisfying, physical contact. Minor separations at home tended not to distress infants in Group I. All eight were classified as B3 in the SSP (hence had mothers with the highest maternal Sensitivity, Acceptance, Cooperation, and Accessibility scores; see Figure 1). The label "secure" fit these infants' home interaction patterns particularly well and was consonant with their ability to use the mother as secure base and safe haven during the initial SSP episode during which they eagerly approached and investigated the attractive set of toys. However, when left with a stranger in an unfamiliar room they responded with distress, and approached and sought contact with the mother on her return. Although they were relatively quickly soothed, their exploratory behavior did not return to its initial level (Ainsworth et al., 1971, p. 31). An observer should expect little distress from these babies at home, however.

Home Group II infants differed from Group I in that they used the mother as a secure base *intermittently*, that is, at times when she was *intermittently* accessible and non-interfering. If Group II mothers picked their babies up in an interfering way, they resisted and even ignored or avoided her. Conversely, when infants approached the mother while she was in an ignoring or rebuffing mood, infants responded with insistent attachment behavior. Three of the four Group II infants were B2/B1 and one was B3 in the SSP. In the SSP, B1/B2 infants did not cry when the mother left, but became distressed when the stranger left and they were completely alone. In contrast to Group I/B3 infants, they interacted with the returning mother more over a distance, and some showed moderate avoidance. Because of the variability of infant and maternal behavior, and the uneven pattern of Maternal Care ratings, the unqualified label "secure" fit the home behavior of Group II less clearly than that of Group I.

Infants placed in home Group III absorbed themselves in independent exploration around the house, often moving out of the mother's sight. Their mothers, conversely, ignored them for long periods. Although these babies approached the mother rather infrequently, if they did and she failed to respond, they were easily discouraged (in contrast to the more feisty Group II infants who became peremptory under these conditions). The quality of Group III infants' exploration was (it appears) constructive, but Ainsworth (1970, p. 4) describes them as having a "take-it-or-leave-it attitude" to maternal presence and absence at home. If picked up, Group III infants did not mold to mother's body, and tended not to protest when put down. In the SSP two of these infants were A2 and one was B2. The A2-infants' home behavior resembled their SSP exploratory behavior in the mother's absence. However, in the SSP they did cry when left completely alone, and responded with incomplete or aborted attachment behavior when the mother returned, mildly avoidant behavior that was less evident in the B2 infant. The SSP designation "avoidant" fit the home behavior of Group III reasonably well, although Ainsworth and colleagues, at times, referred to them as "independent" (Ainsworth et al., 1971, p. 38).

Group IV infants behaved very differently at home than Group III. They made active attempts to remain in the vicinity of the mother, and became distressed when losing track of her or she left the room and they could not follow. Yet, they seemed conflicted about close bodily contact, both wanting and resisting it (Ainsworth, 1970). If the mother picked them up when they sought contact they often squirmed to get down again right away, but then protested when released. Ainsworth et al., 1978 (p. 242) labeled them as the "conflicted" group. At home, they explored more briefly and with less focused attention than groups I, II, and III. In the SSP, three Group IV infants were classified as A1, and one as C1. Whereas the C1-infant showed conflicted attachment behavior in both settings, A1-infants anxious home behavior was in stark contrast to their lack of separation distress and proximity- and interaction-seeking during the SSP, even though they searched for the absent mother as much as the other groups (Ainsworth et al., 1978, p. 370). The label "avoidant" that fit the A1-classified SSP behavior of Group III infants was quite inconsistent with their conflicted home behavior.

Ainsworth initially attributed A1 infants' avoidant SSP reunion behavior to a severe approach-avoidance conflict engendered by maternal rejection and interference, but suppressed by defensive processes available to these infants under conditions of high stress (Ainsworth et al., 1971). Later she shifted to an ethology-based explanation proposed by Main wherein avoidance is a displacement behavior that allows the infant to remain in the mother's proximity without showing attachment behavior that the mother might rebuff (cited in Ainsworth et al., 1978, pp. 316–321). In my view, neither these nor subsequent explanations, often couched in terms of minimizing the output of the attachment behavioral system (Main, 1990) or deactivating attachment (Kobak, Cole, Ferenc-Gillies, Fleming, & Gamble, 1993), are entirely satisfactory. Even though their overt behavior obscures it, studies by Sroufe and Waters (1977) and by Spangler and Grossmann (1993) reveal that avoidant infants are as physiologically aroused during separation and reunions as secure infants.

Whatever the explanation for the divergence of A1-infants' home and SSP behavior, their approach-avoidance conflict at home is hard to overlook, especially with respect to interactions involving close bodily contact. At home, their mood during 4th quarter visits was rated as considerably angrier than that of B- and C-infants, and they showed more instances of aggression toward the mother (for definitions of these behaviors, see Main & Stadtman, 1981). Ainsworth attributed A1-infants' anger at home to unassuaged attachment behavior, but an additional reason could be that A1-mothers' pick-ups frequently occurred in the context of interfering with infant exploration (Ainsworth et al., 1972, p. 47). Although facially inexpressive, A1-mothers' considerable dislike of close bodily contact was evident in the abrupt manner in which they initiated physical contact and the frequency with which they rebuffed bids for contact, behaviors in line with their low scores on the Acceptance-Rejection scale. In short, A1-infants' conflicted attachment behavior at home was matched by A1-mothers'conflicted and controlling (interfering) behavior. Hence, the SSP-designation "avoidant" should not be taken to mean that A1 infants rarely cry or fuss at home and fail to show proximity-seeking or separation distress in that context.

Group V infants behaved passively at home, in terms of both attachment and exploratory behaviors. Some were chronically passive and others intermittently so. They seemed anxious about the mother's whereabouts without signaling this clearly, and while they did not actively seek contact, they were described as accepting it passively when offered. They explored little, except visually, or required their mothers to initiate active behavior. Although of some these infants occasionally undertook independent locomotor explorations (often of forbidden areas), when they were ignored or confined, Group V infants tended to engage in repetitive, stereotyped behavior (e.g., rocking, chewing on objects, hair-pulling). Ainsworth et al., 1971 (p. 44) describe group V mothers as invested in motherhood, but emotionally fragile rather than angry. To hold themselves together, they often tuned the baby out and let it cry for long periods during the early months. The combination of maternal ignoring and interference may have encouraged these infants' passivity at home. In the SSP, one Group V infant was classified as C1, two as C2, and one as A1. The SSP label "resistant" was chosen to describe both types of C-infants because they signaled for contact during reunions, but then reacted angrily after the mother picked them up and offered toys as a distraction. "Resistant" does not, however, fit their intermittently or consistently passive behavior at home.

In sum, the appellations Ainsworth coined to highlight characteristic aspects of infant behavior in the SSP should *not* be expected to apply in literal fashion to infants' behavior with their mothers at home (the disorganized classification had not yet been identified, and will not be discussed). Despite the very impressive convergence of SSP subgroups with the five home classifications, the home patterns may, in some instances, offer greater insight into the reciprocal fit between maternal sensitivity in relation to infant behavior. Ainsworth expected that additional insecure patterns and associated maternal patterns of care remained to be discovered, citing in that connection Tolstoy's remark "Happy families are all alike; every unhappy family is unhappy in its own way" (cited in Ainsworth, 1977a, p. 19).

Finally, whereas Ainsworth believed that mothers have the most profound initial influence on infants, she did not discount infants' effect on their mothers, and also encouraged closer consideration of attachment figures other than the mother, including fathers, siblings, and daycare providers (Ainsworth et al., 1978, pp. 307–308).

Ainsworth: contrast and relation to Bowlby

Until now I have almost completely refrained from linking Ainsworth's name with Bowlby's. My goal was to clearly highlight her innovative contributions rather than, as is more usual, to evaluate it terms of its roots in and impact on Bowlby's formulation of attachment theory.

It is, of course, undeniable that Ainsworth was much influenced by Bowlby's reliance on ethology and his evolutionary perspective on attachment. It is also undeniable that ethological studies, particular of nonhuman primates, influenced the interactive behaviors Ainsworth chose to study (e.g., greetings) and how she chose to study them. From time to time, too, she adopted Bowlby's control systems language whereby attachment behaviors are switched on and off (activated and terminated) when an infant has gained sufficient proximity to and contact with the attachment figure (Ainsworth et al., 1978, p. 22). Indeed, in many of her theoretical writings she devoted considerably more space to explaining Bowlby's ethologically-oriented attachment theory than to the conceptual and methodological innovations of her own work. No single publication contains a complete description of all aspects of the constructs and methodology derived from the Baltimore home observations. Conversely, Bowlby acknowledged and incorporated Ainsworth's empirical work in Uganda (Bowlby, 1969/1982) and in Baltimore (Bowlby, 1973) into attachment theory, but I believe he underestimated her conceptual influence on attachment theory, especially with respect to individual differences.

I submit that Ainsworth differed from Bowlby in several ways. First, she showed more boldness in the topics she selected for study. Bowlby encouraged his research team to focus on parent–child separation because the effects of relationship disruption were clear-cut, undeniable, and hence easier to document than more subtle variations in parent–child and familial interactions (see Bretherton, 1992). Ainsworth, in contrast, set her mind on what she wanted to study and proceeded to collect relevant naturalistic data. Drawing on techniques of pattern recognition that she had already found fruitful when analyzing her dissertation data (Salter, 1939) she trusted that she would discover an effective way of analyzing her observational records.

Second, whereas Bowlby charted the broader principles of attachment theory and emphasized the infant's side of the relationship, Ainsworth focused on mother–infant relationships and linked attachment to love. Through close perusal of narrative records describing maternal and infant interactive behavior she identified the construct of sensitivity. She noted how some mothers empathically adapted their behavior to the behavior of their individual infant and, by responding to infant signals appropriately and promptly, engendered a more harmonious relationship. Most likely inspired by ethology, she viewed all maternal and infant interactive behaviors (including postural adjustments) as communicative. Ainsworth and colleagues also demonstrated that maternal attempts to cure an infant of making demands or "show the child who is boss" led to much less satisfying attachment relationships and to less infant cooperation with the mother than when the mother went "with the grain." Finally, Ainsworth discovered that maternal interference in infants' ongoing activities affected the quality, not just the amount, of infant exploratory behavior although that aspect of her work is less elaborated. In making these complex judgments about the quality of relationships she never took a mechanical approach.

Third, in addition to being enormously influenced by ethology, Ainsworth's work was imbued with clinical and diagnostic insights. Like Bowlby she rejected Freudian drive theory and the theory of "cupboard love," but she appreciated some aspects of Freud's thinking more than Bowlby did. Although she toned down references to Freud and defense mechanisms in *Patterns of Attachment* (Ainsworth et al., 1978), this was not a change of heart, as demonstrated in her subsequent interview with psychoanalyst Rudnytsky (1997, p. 399) and her autobiographical note (Ainsworth, 1983, p. 212; reprinted in this Special Issue). In the latter, she described her 8-year psychoanalytic experience (undertaken because of a depressive reaction to divorce) as the most important positive influence on her career, that also led her to immerse herself in the psychoanalytic literature, especially Freud. Freud's views on the unconscious particularly appealed to her, as well as the psychoanalytic focus on inner structure and processes (Ainsworth, 1969b, p. 1016). She thus emphasized that the attachment behavioral system is not to be solely characterized by its outward manifestations, but by an inner organization that is presumably rooted in neurophysiological processes, is subject to developmental change, and requires further study.

Her view on the communicative and relational role of close bodily contact may also have been inspired by psychoanalytic writings. Thus, she cited Freud's statement that the mother in stroking, kissing, and rocking the baby is fulfilling her task "in teaching him how to love" (Ainsworth, 1969b, p. 972) and referred to Winnicott "who considered physical holding as so 'basic a form of loving' that he extended it to cover the total environmental provision" (Ainsworth, 1969b, p. 978). Relatedly, drawing on her Ganda study, she tentatively proposed that, under certain conditions, sucking and rooting are precursor attachment behaviors that may become tied into the attachment relationship when mothers engage in thoroughgoing demand feeding and allow the baby to seek the breast for comfort. If deferred well beyond the first year, Ganda babies responded to the final stage of weaning (withdrawing night-time access) with relatively little disturbance, but for four secure-attached infants final weaning began at the end of the first year and resulted in traumatic relationship disruptions that lasted for weeks (Ainsworth & Tracy, 1973).

Concluding remarks: validity and trustworthiness

A number of developmental psychologists immediately recognized the originality and importance of Ainsworth's pioneering constructs and her pioneering methodology. Major longitudinal studies replicating and extending her research (e.g., the Grossmanns' Bielefeld study and the Sroufe-Egeland Minnesota study; summarized in Grossmann,

Grossman, and Waters, 2005) were initiated even before the publication of the definitive book, *Patterns of Attachment* (Ainsworth et al., 1978). However, criticisms of Ainsworth's methods and findings also erupted because she did not hesitate to use her Ganda and Baltimore findings to suggest that parental responsiveness to crying and provision of close bodily contact do not spoil young infants (e.g., Ainsworth, 1967, p. 464). These recommendations went counter to the then prevalent behaviorist Zeitgeist, but have influenced what are now accepted infant caregiving practices. Others questioned her qualitative methods, evaluative variable labels, and post hoc derivation of constructs.

Some critiques of Ainsworth's work, including her reliance on post hoc analyses, are in my view based on misunderstandings of her research philosophy. "Science," she maintained, "is implicit in the way one thinks about problems and approaches to data, rather than being irretrievably vested in the hypothetico-deductive method, experiment, or specific quantitative techniques" (Ainsworth, 1983, p. 204; reprinted in this issue). Although she had had strong training in experimental methods, when exploring new territory from an ethological perspective, she opted for Lewin's (1951) principle of "levels of successive approximation." According to this principle, it is necessary to understand how the behavior in question relates to an animal's total behavioral repertoire in its everyday environment before engaging in hypothesis-guided experimentation (Ainsworth, 1969b, p. 1019).

I would call Ainsworth's approach *spiral theory-building*. In her Ganda study, persuaded by Bowlby ethological notions about social bonds, she became fascinated with qualitative variations in observed mother–infant interactions. Her notes on infant behavior helped her classify patterns of secure base behavior, but were insufficient for detailed assessments of the quality of maternal care. For the study of Baltimore families she therefore devised a context-preserving method of data collection that allowed her and her team to record aspects of individual differences in mother–infant interactions not included in the Ganda findings while also permitting new connections and constructs (including the sensitivity construct) to emerge. Over and beyond what any checklist could provide, the narrative records enabled her not only to discover and define the maternal sensitivity construct but to devise the Maternal Care Scales with descriptive behavioral anchor points. Her identification of interaction patterns and behavioral ratings from post hoc analyses of the narrative records resembles the approach Darwin used when he derived notions about evolution and natural section from variations in the beaks of finches from various Galapagos Islands – one of the best known examples of his inductive theory-building. In still relatively unexplored research domains precocious armchair theorizing often gives rise to simplistic hypotheses and a priori measures that can preclude the discovery of innovative or theory-changing constructs. What is, of course, required to establish trustworthiness of inductively derived findings are replications. Unfortunately Ainsworth's own proposal to replicate the methods used in the Baltimore study with a new sample was rejected by the NICHD as worthless (Stevenson, 1998).

Ainsworth passed the principle of "levels of successive approximation" on to many of her graduate students. As one of these former students, I frequently find, on completing a project, that I have used a way of analyzing naturalistic or qualitative data that emulates aspects of methods she had invented and successfully used. Her legacy lies not only in the constructs she developed and the findings she reported, but in her way of conducting developmental science.

Acknowledgements

I dedicate this paper to Mary Ainsworth, my challenging and supportive doctoral advisor. I would like to thank Klaus Grossmann and Everett Waters for helpful suggestions and my husband for his sensitive patience while I was writing this article.

References

Ainsworth, M. D. S. (1963). The development of infant-mother interaction among the Ganda. In B. M. Foss (Ed.), *Determinants of infant behavior* (pp. 67–103). New York, NY: Wiley.

Ainsworth, M. D. S. (1967). *Infancy in Uganda: Infant care and the growth of love*. Baltimore, MD: Johns Hopkins University Press.

Ainsworth, M. D. S. (1969a). *Maternal care scales*. Unpublished manuscript. Retrievable as Maternal Sensitivity Scales from http://www.psychology.sunysb.edu/attachment/measures/content/ainsworth_scales.html

Ainsworth, M. D. S. (1969b). Object relations, dependency and attachment: A theoretical review of the infant-mother relationship. *Child Development, 40*, 969–1025.

Ainsworth, M. D. S. (1970). *Criteria for classification of one-year-olds in terms of the balance between exploratory and attachment behavior at home*. Unpublished manuscript. Retrievable as Ainsworth Secure Base Behavior Scales from http://www.psychology.sunysb.edu/attachment/measures/content/home_secure_base_patterns.pdf

Ainsworth, M. D. S. (1977a). Social development in the first year of life: Maternal influences on infant-mother attachment. In J. M. Tanner (Ed.), *Developments in psychiatric research: Essays based on the Sir Geoffrey Vickers Lectures of the Mental Health Foundation* (pp. 1–20). London: Hodder & Stoughton.

Ainsworth, M. D. S. (1977b). *Affective aspects of the attachment of infant to mother: Individual differences and their correlates to maternal behavior*. Paper presented at the symposium on emotional development in infants at the meeting of the American Association for the Advancement of Science, Washington, DC.

Ainsworth, M. D. S. (1983). *Mary D. Salter Ainsworth*. In A. N. O'Connell & N. F. Russo (Eds.), *Models of achievement: Reflections of eminent women in psychology* (pp. 200–219). New York, NY: Columbia University Press.

Ainsworth, M. D. S. (1988). *Security*. Unpublished discussion paper prepared for the Foundations of AttachmentTheory Workshop. Convened for the New York Attachment Consortium by G. Cox-Steiner & E. Waters. Port Jefferson, NY.

Ainsworth, M. D. S., & Bell, S. M. (1969). Some contemporary patterns in the feeding situation. In A. Ambrose (Ed.), *Stimulation in early infancy* (pp. 133–170). London: Academic Press.

Ainsworth, M. D. S., & Bell, S. M. (1974). Mother-infant interaction and the development of competence. In K. J. Connolly & J. Bruner (Eds.), *The growth of competence* (pp. 97–118). New York, NY: Academic Press.

Ainsworth, M. D. S., Bell, S. M., & Stayton, D. (1974). Infant–mother attachment and social development: "Socialization" as a product of reciprocal responsiveness to signals. In P. M. Richards (Ed.), *The integration of a child into a social world* (pp. 99–135). Cambridge: Cambridge University Press.

Ainsworth, M. D. S., Bell, S. M., & Stayton, D. J. (1971). Individual differences in Strange Situation behaviour of one-year-olds. In H. R. Schaffer (Ed.), *The origins of human social relations* (pp. 17–57). London: Academic Press.

Ainsworth, M. D. S., Bell, S. M., & Stayton, D. J. (1972). Individual differences in the development of some attachment behaviors. *Merrill-Palmer Quarterly, 18*, 123–143.

Ainsworth, M. D. S., Blehar, M. C., Waters, E., & Wall, S. (1978). *Patterns of attachment: A psychological study of the strange situation*. Hillsdale, NJ: Erlbaum Associates.

Ainsworth, M. D. S., & Tracy, R. L. (1973). *Infant feeding and attachment*. Paper presented at a symposium on infant feeding at the annual meetings of the American Psychological Society, Montreal, QC.

Ainsworth, M. D. S., & Wittig, B. A. (1969). Attachment and the exploratory behaviour of one-year-olds in a strange situation. In B. M. Foss (Ed.), *Determinants of infant behaviour* (Vol. 4, pp. 113–136). London: Methuen.

Bell, S. M. (1970). The development of the concept of the object as related to infant-mother attachment. *Child Development, 41*, 291–311.

Bell, S. M., & Ainsworth, M. D. S. (1972). Infant crying and maternal responsiveness. *Child Development, 43*, 1171–1190.

Blehar, M. C., Lieberman, A. E., & Ainsworth, M. D. S. (1977). Early face-to-face interaction and its relation to later infant-mother attachment. *Child Development, 48*, 182–194.

Bowlby, J. (1969/1982). *Attachment and loss: Vol. 1. Attachment.* New York, NY: Basic Books.

Bowlby, J. (1973). *Attachment and loss: Vol. 2. Separation: Anxiety and anger.* New York, NY: Basic Books.

Bretherton, I. (1992). The origins of attachment theory: John Bowlby and Mary Ainsworth. *Developmental Psychology, 28*, 759–775.

Cassidy, J., & Shaver, P. R. (2008). *Handbook of attachment: Theory, research and clinical application* (2nd ed.). New York, NY: Guilford.

David, M., & Appel, G. (1961). A study of nursing care and nurse-infant interaction. In B. Foss (Ed.), *Determinants of infant behavior* (pp. 121–141). London: Methuen.

Grossmann, K. E., Grossmann, K., & Waters, E. (2005). *Attachment from infancy to adulthood: The major longitudinal studies.* New York, NY: Guilford Press.

Kobak, R. R., Cole, H. E., Ferenc-Gillies, R., Fleming, W. S., & Gamble, W. (1993). Attachment and emotion regulation during mother-teen problem-solving: A control theory analysis. *Child Development, 64*, 231–235.

Lewin, K. (1951). *Field theory in psychological science: Selected theoretical papers.* In D. Cartwright (Ed.), New York, NY: Harper.

Main, M. (1990). Cross-cultural studies of attachment organization: Recent studies, changing metholologies, and the concept of conditional strategies. *Human Development, 33*, 48–61.

Main, M., & Stadtman, J. (1981). Infant response to rejection of physical contact by the mother: Aggression, avoidance and conflict. *American Academy of Child Psychiatry, 20*, 292–307.

Rudnytsky, P. L. (1997). The personal origins of attachment theory: An interview with Mary Salter Ainsworth. *Psychoanalytic Study of the Child, 51*, 386–405.

Salter, M. D. (1939). *An evaluation of adjustment based on the concept of security.* Toronto, ON: University of Toronto Press.

Spangler, G., & Grossmann, K. E. (1993). Biobehavioral organization in securely and insecurely attached infants. *Child Development, 64*, 1439–1450.

Sroufe, L. A., & Waters, E. (1977). Heartrate as a convergent measure in clinical and developmental research. *Merrill-Palmer Quarterly, 23*, 3–27.

Stayton, D., & Ainsworth, M. D. S. (1973). Individual differences in infant responses to brief separations in the first year of life: Protest, following, and greeting. *Developmental Psychology, 9*, 226–235.

Stayton, D., Ainsworth, M. D. S., & Main, M. B. (1973). The development of separation behavior in the first year of life: Protest, following and greeting. *Developmental Psychology, 9*, 213–225.

Stayton, D., Hogan, R., & Ainsworth, M. D. S. (1971). Infant obedience and maternal behavior: The origins of socialization reconsidered. *Child Development, 42*, 1057–1069.

Stern, D. N. (1974). Mother and infant at play; the dyadic interaction involving facial, vocal. and gaze behaviors. In M. Lewis & L. A. Rosenblum (Eds.), *The effect of the infant on its caregiver.* New York, NY: Wiley.

Stevenson, H. (1998) Oral history interview of Mary Ainsworth. Retrieved from http://srcd.org/about-us/oral-history-project

Tracy, R. L., & Ainsworth, M. D. S. (1981). Maternal affectionate behavior and infant mother-attachment patterns. *Child Development, 52*, 1341–1343.

Mary Ainsworth's legacy: a systematic review of observational instruments measuring parental sensitivity

Judi Mesman and Rosanneke A.G. Emmen

Centre for Child and Family Studies, Leiden University, Leiden, The Netherlands

Since Mary Ainsworth's formulation of the Sensitivity-Insensitivity to Infant Signals and Communications observational scale, new instruments have been developed to observe parental sensitivity. In this paper, we provide an overview of eight commonly used observational instruments to measure parental sensitivity. Their similarities and differences in comparison to the original Ainsworth sensitivity construct and its applications will be discussed. Consistent with the search criteria, each of the instruments clearly includes the key elements of Ainsworth's definition of sensitivity. Notable deviations from the original scale are the use of composite scales rather than a single global scale and the related inclusion of new elements, and specifically the inclusion of positive affect as an indicator of sensitivity. Further, most of the instruments have a wider scope than Ainsworth's sensitivity scale in terms of target age groups and the assessment of sensitivity in fathers. We discuss the interpretation of the sensitivity construct depending on variations in how the construct is defined in different observational instruments, and advances in the application of the construct.

The introduction of the maternal sensitivity construct has proven to be one of Mary Ainsworth's most valuable contributions to the field of parenting and child development. The Sensitivity-Insensitivity to Infant Signals and Communications scale is part of the Maternal Care scales. These scales are clearly grounded in attachment theory and were designed to assess the quality of maternal behavior tailored to a specific infant and to explain individual differences in attachment quality (Ainsworth, Bell, & Stayton, 1971; Ainsworth, Blehar, Waters, & Wall, 1978). To this day the original Ainsworth sensitivity observation scale (Ainsworth, Bell, & Stayton, 1974), is still used in empirical studies (e.g., Fearon et al., 2006; Gonzalez, Jenkins, Steiner, & Fleming, 2012; Spangler, Johann, Ronai, & Zimmerman, 2009).

In addition, a number of new observation instruments have been designed to measure parental sensitivity. These newer instruments vary in their formulation of the sensitivity construct (Seifer, Schiller, Sameroff, Resnick, & Riordan, 1996), with some being very similar to the original construct, and others including new elements or leaving out certain aspects. They also vary in their focus in terms of target age group and observational setting. The choice for one instrument over another when designing an observational study of sensitivity may be based on several theoretical and practical considerations. However, to date there is a lack of systematic comparisons between measures that may inform researchers about each instrument's qualities, and their representation of the sensitivity construct. In this systematic review, we provide an overview of observational instruments that are used to measure parental sensitivity, and analyze them in terms of their relation to the original Ainsworth sensitivity construct and practical aspects of their application. We focus on the sensitivity scale rather than the total set of Ainsworth's Maternal Care scales, as Ainsworth herself identified the sensitivity construct as pivotal to secure attachment development (Ainsworth et al., 1978). The other scales were developed primarily to differentiate between mothers of babies classified as avoidant and ambivalent in the Strange Situation (Ainsworth et al., 1971). In addition, the sensitivity construct and its label have been far more dominant in the empirical attachment literature than the auxiliary scales.

Mary Ainsworth's definition of sensitivity is a parent's ability to (1) notice child signals, (2) interpret these signals correctly, and (3) respond to these signals promptly and appropriately (Ainsworth et al., 1974). These components of parental behavior refer to universally relevant aspects of caregiving, including proximity to the child (necessary for protection and meeting basic needs), contingent responding (promoting social development), and appropriateness of parental interventions based on the child's responses rather than on a fixed list of specific parenting behaviors (Mesman, Oster, & Camras, 2012; Mesman, Van IJzendoorn, & Bakermans-Kranenburg, 2012). To provide a clear representation of Ainsworth's Sensitivity-Insensitivity to Infant Signals and Communications scale, the descriptions of the two extreme scores (9 = highly sensitive, and 1 = highly insensitive) are shown below (Ainsworth et al., 1974, pp. 131–133):

> ***9. Highly sensitive.*** *This mother is exquisitely attuned to B's signals; and responds to them promptly and appropriately. She is able to see things from B's point of view; her perceptions of his signals and communications are not distorted by her own needs and defenses. She "reads" B's signals and communications skillfully, and knows what the meaning is of even his subtle, minimal, and understated cues. She nearly always gives B what he indicates that he wants, although perhaps not invariably so. When she feels that it is best not to comply with his demands – for example, when he is too excited, over-imperious, or wants something he should not have – she is tactful in acknowledging his communication and in offering an acceptable alternative. She has "well-rounded" interactions with B, so that the transaction is smoothly completed and both she and B feel satisfied. Finally, she makes her responses temporally contingent upon B's signals and communications.*

> ***1. Highly insensitive.*** *The extremely insensitive mother seems geared almost exclusively to her own wishes, moods, and activity. That is M's interventions and initiations of interaction are prompted or shaped largely by signals within herself; if they mesh with B's signals, this is often no more than coincidence. This is not to say that M never responds to B's signals; for sometimes she does if the signals are intense enough, prolonged enough, or often enough repeated. The delay in response is in itself insensitive. Furthermore, since there is usually a disparity between one's own wishes and activity and B's signals, M who is geared largely to her own signals routinely ignores or distorts the meaning of behavior. Thus, when M responds to B's signals, her response is inappropriate in kind or fragmented and incomplete.*

These descriptions of highly sensitive and highly insensitive parents illustrate the key role of appropriate responding, and the child-centered definition of appropriateness (i.e., does it make the child content?) in Ainsworth's conceptualization of sensitivity. It is also interesting to note the absence of any references to parental positive affect or warmth in the descriptions of the scores (although warmth is mentioned briefly in the introduction to the scale descriptions), whereas several more recent approaches to parent–child interactions explicitly emphasize the importance of positive affect and warmth in conceptualizations of sensitivity in the score descriptions (e.g., Biringen & Easterbrooks, 2012). In Ainsworth's Maternal Care scales, positive affect and warmth are represented most clearly in a different scale: the Acceptance versus Rejection scale, which she introduces as follows: "This scale deals with the balance between the mother's positive and negative feelings about her baby". Thus, the constructs of sensitivity and positive affect are part of the Maternal Care scales, but are rated as separate constructs.

Regarding theoretical background, Ainsworth's sensitivity scale was developed within the attachment framework and aimed at explaining individual differences in Strange Situation attachment classification (Ainsworth et al., 1971, 1978). Ainsworth's Baltimore study showed that maternal sensitivity was indeed related to attachment security (Ainsworth et al., 1978), a finding that has been replicated in a meta-analysis based on 66 studies (De Wolff & Van IJzendoorn, 1997), and confirmed by a meta-analysis showing that improvements in parental sensitivity induced by parenting interventions improves child attachment quality (Bakermans-Kranenburg, Van IJzendoorn, & Juffer, 2003). More recent work on the sensitivity construct has moved beyond the attachment framework and examines relations with a large variety of parental and child characteristics such as maternal depression (e.g., Campbell, Matestic, Stauffenberg, Mohan, & Kirchner, 2007) and child cognitive outcomes (e.g., Bernier, Carlson, & Whipple, 2010).

Regarding the observational setting, Ainsworth based her coding of maternal sensitivity in the Baltimore study on narrative accounts of naturalistic interactions during multiple home visits with five home visits lasting 4 hours each in the last quarter of the first year for each dyad (Ainsworth et al., 1978), and in subsequent studies it has generally been used to assess parent–infant interactions across the first year of life. In current-day research such intensive and naturalistic observations are rare and sensitivity is usually observed in time frames between 10 and 30 minutes (with some exceptions using longer observation periods, e.g., Grossman, Grossman, Spangler, Suess, & Unzner, 1985; Kochanska, Kim, Barry, & Philibert, 2011). As was common at the time, Ainsworth focused on mothers only, although her sensitivity scale has since been used with fathers (e.g., Grossman et al., 2002; Schoppe-Sullivan et al., 2006). In addition, adaptations of the sensitivity construct to father-specific interaction patterns have been designed (e.g., the Sensitive and Challenging Interactive Play Scale by Grossman et al., 2002). Ainsworth's sensitivity construct seems to have been inspired in part by her observations in Uganda, and her scale has been used in non-Western countries since then (e.g., True, Pisani, & Oumar, 2001; Yovsi, Kärtner, Keller, & Lohaus, 2009). However, observational research on parental sensitivity in non-Western countries is still very rare.

The growing research interest in sensitivity beyond the original use of the Ainsworth scale in terms of theoretical orientation, child age, caregiver identity, and observational settings is likely to have been a driving factor in the development of new observation instruments to measure sensitivity in the past decades. In the present paper we aim to provide an account of the legacy of Ainsworth's sensitivity scale by reviewing currently-used global observational instruments assessing parental sensitivity (or sensitive responsiveness). To find these instruments, we conducted a systematic literature search. Given the fact that the original Ainsworth sensitivity scale is a global rating scale, and the conceptual differences between such scales and other approaches such as behavior counts, event-based coding, or micro-level coding (Mesman, 2010), we decided to focus only on global rating scales. We examine these instruments in light of the original Ainsworth sensitivity scale, its behavioral descriptors, and its applications in terms of target population and setting.

Method

We conducted a systematic literature search for papers reporting on studies using observational instruments of parental sensitivity in Web of Science. The following keywords were used: Topic=((“maternal sensitiv*” OR ”maternal responsive*” OR “paternal sensitiv*” OR ”paternal responsive*” OR “mother* sensitiv*” OR ”mother* responsive*” OR “father* sensitiv*” OR ”father* responsive*” OR “parent* sensitiv*” OR ”parent* responsive*” OR “sensitive parenting”) AND (child* OR infan* OR adolescen* OR toddler OR preschooler OR baby OR babies)). The use of “Topic” as the search field means that the titles, abstracts, author keywords, and Web of Science keywords (KeyWords Plus) were searched.

In addition, we filtered on categories by excluding those that are obviously unrelated to our field (e.g., agriculture). We further selected only papers published in the English language. This search yielded 1014 publications (7 December 2012). Each of these publications was screened to find out whether they indeed included global observational instruments of parental sensitivity or sensitive responsiveness (and not just responsiveness in terms of frequency of responses) and a literature reference or specific name for the scale. This led to a set of 50 observation instruments. For the purpose of selecting instruments to discuss in the current review, we selected the eight instruments that were used in the highest number of publications (all in more than 10) within our search results. These eight instruments were coded regarding several characteristics, based on the coding manuals, the method sections of papers in our search results, their reference lists, but also other sources of information such as the authors of the scales. To correctly indentify instrument characteristics, we also conducted additional literature searches to uncover studies using the instruments for specific purposes and in specific populations relevant to our review. We coded: (1) availability of the instrument; (2) age range for which the instrument is applicable; (3) the observational settings in which the instrument is used; (4) whether the scale has been used to code father sensitivity; (5) whether the scale has been used in non-Western countries; (6) the inclusion of a single sensitivity scale versus a composite sensitivity scale; (7) the inclusion of positive affect or warmth in the definition of sensitivity; and (8) the link with attachment quality.

On a cautionary note we would like to emphasize that the aim of the current review is to provide an account of observational measures that researchers have used to assess sensitivity. The guiding principle is the use of the term sensitivity (or responsiveness including sensitivity elements and not just response frequency) in empirical papers reporting on the instrument. This also means that instruments that do include a sensitivity(-like) or responsiveness(-like) construct but are not described as such by the researchers reporting on the instrument are not included in this review.

Results

Table 1 shows the characteristics of the eight selected instruments for observing parental sensitivity and sensitive responsiveness developed after Ainsworth’s original scale. The characteristics of these instruments can be summarized as follows: five are freely available without cost or mandatory training, the target age ranges vary substantially, free play is the most-often used observational setting, all eight have been used for coding maternal as well as paternal sensitivity, six have been applied in non-Western cultures, three include a single sensitivity scale (rather than a composite of separate subscales), seven included positive affect as a criterion or indicator for sensitivity, and seven have been found to

Table 1. The Ainsworth sensitivity scale and eight commonly used newer observation instruments measuring parental sensitivity and their characteristics.

Instrument name	Freely available[1]	Age range[2]	Observation setting[3]	Fathers[4]	Non-Western cultures[5]	Single global rating[6]	Positive affect[7]	Link with attachment[8]
Ainsworth sensitivity scale (Ainsworth et al., 1974)	Yes	Infancy	N; P; F; T; D	Yes	Yes	Yes	–	Yes
CARE-Index (Crittenden, 2001)	No	Infancy – Preschool	P; FF	Yes	Yes	No	++	Yes
Coding Interactive Behavior (CIB; Feldman, 1998)	No	Infancy – Adolescence	P; F	Yes	Yes	No	++	No
Emotional Availability Scales (EA Scales; Biringen, 2008; Biringen et al., 1998)	No	Infancy – Adolescence	P; T; D	Yes	Yes	Yes/No*	++	Yes
Erickson scales (Erickson et al., 1985)	Yes	Toddler – Preschool	T	Yes	Yes	No	+	Yes
Global Ratings of Mother–Infant Interaction (Murray et al., 1996)	Yes	Infancy	P; FF	Yes	Yes	Yes	+	Yes
Maternal Behavior Q-Sort (MBQS; Pederson & Moran, 1995)	Yes	Infancy – Preschool	Mix**	Yes	Yes	No	+	Yes
NICHD-SECCYD sensitivity scales (Owen, 1992).	Yes	Infancy***	P	Yes	No	Yes	–	Yes
Parent–Child Early Relational Assessment (PCERA; Clark, 1985)	Yes	Infancy – Toddler	F; P; T	Yes	No	No	++	Yes

Notes: We have done our best to uncover all relevant information about the instruments in the table.
[1]No if the instrument is only made available when attending an official training.
[2]Age range as reported in the manual (if mentioned) combined with the ages found in the papers in our search results.
[3]Observational setting as found in the papers within our search results: N = Naturalistic; F = Feeding; P = Play (with or without toys); FF = Face-to-face interaction (with or without toys); T = Teaching task (e.g., puzzle, problem-solving); D = Demanding task (e.g., clean-up, no-touch, competing demands).
[4]Has the instrument's sensitivity scale been used with fathers?
[5]Has the instrument's sensitivity scale been used in a non-Western cultures?
[6]Does the instrument include a single global sensitivity rating? (No if a composite of several scales or items is used to derive a sensitivity or responsiveness scale.)
[7]Is positive affect included in the definition of sensitivity? ++ = prominently included; + = minimally included; – not included.
[8]Is there evidence for a link between the instrument's sensitivity scale and child attachment security?
*In the 3rd edition a single global sensitivity rating is used, but in the 4th edition the sensitivity scale consists of seven subscales.
**The MBQS is coded during extensive home visits based on observations of parental behavior throughout the visit, often in the context of an interview, including naturalistic interactions, and sometimes specific play or teaching settings are added.
***For older ages the Erickson scales are used in the NICHD-SECCYD.

relate to child attachment quality. We will now discuss each of the instruments in some more detail, in alphabetical order. The provided information is based on the instruments' coding manuals, supplementary information materials, and the method sections of papers reporting on the instruments. We describe the characteristics summarized in Table 1 for each instrument (in alphabetical order). We also discuss the theoretical background of the instrument, specifically whether it is grounded in attachment theory as Ainsworth's scale was, and we summarize empirical studies using the instrument in relation to attachment constructs.

The Child–Adult Relationship Experimental Index (CARE-Index)

The CARE-Index was first developed for scoring adult interactions with infants and was later adapted to fit interactions with toddlers up to age 36 months (Crittenden, 2001), and can even be used up to 70 months (Künster, Fegert, & Ziegenhain, 2010). The instrument is described as a screening tool and seems to be mostly used to code sensitivity in free play settings, although there does not seem to be any reason not to use it in other settings. As is common in this field, the CARE-Index has been mostly used with mothers, but there are studies that have employed the instrument to rate father–child interactions (e.g., Kelley, Smith, Green, Berndt, & Rogers, 1998). The CARE-Index is only made available to those who follow the training. The instrument does not have a single sensitivity scale. Instead, seven aspects of maternal interactive behavior are evaluated, including facial expression, vocal expression, position and body contact, expressions of affection, pacing of turns, control, and choice of activity. Scores on each of these aspects are then evaluated in terms of sensitivity, control, and unresponsiveness (on 0–2 scales), and for each of these three parenting constructs the seven items are summed (yielding scores 0–14). The CARE-Index information materials do not describe a specific theoretical framework, although they do briefly mention attachment and, on the scale authors' website, it is mentioned that the CARE-Index was developed under Mary Ainsworth's guidance, and in consultation with John Bowlby.

The CARE-Index scale descriptions clearly include salient aspects of Ainsworth's definitions of sensitivity relating to availability to meet the child's needs, contingent responsiveness, and appropriate timing and content of activities. Although not found explicitly in Ainsworth's descriptions, affection and warmth are coded as important aspects of sensitivity. The CARE-Index sensitivity scores have been found to predict attachment security in the USA as measured in the Strange Situation (e.g., Fuertes, Lopes-dos-Santos, Beeghly, & Tronick, 2009), and using a representational attachment measure (Goodman, Aber, Berlin, & Brooks-Gunn, 1998). It has also been found to predict attachment security in a study in Chile (Valenzuela, 1997). In addition, the sensitivity scale differentiated between mothers with different attachment states of mind (Ward & Carlson, 1995), Finally, the scale can detect improvements in sensitivity following parenting intervention (e.g., Barlow et al., 2007).

Coding Interactive Behavior (CIB)

The observation instrument Coding Interactive Behavior (CIB; Feldman, 1998) consists of 22 scales measuring different aspects of adult–child interactions (rated on a scale from 1 = a little to 5 = a lot). There are versions of the CIB for newborns, infants, toddlers, preschoolers, and adolescents, but we did not uncover the specific age-related changes made for each version. The instrument appears to have been used only in (face-to-face) free-play settings, except for parental sensitivity with 13-year-olds which was assessed during a conversation aimed at planning an enjoyable activity (Feldman, 2010). There is also a modified version specifically tailored to assessing sensitivity in feeding situations (Feldman, Keren, Gross-Rozval, & Tyano, 2004). In addition to being used for coding mother–child interactions, the CIB has also been used to code father–child interactions (e.g., Feldman & Eidelman, 2007) and caregiver–child interactions (e.g., Klein & Feldman, 2007). The CIB is only made available in the context of training. The instrument does not have a single sensitivity scale. A parental sensitivity construct is derived by combining scores on a selection of the 22 adult scales, generally including scales such as acknowledgement of child signals, positive affect, gaze, appropriate vocal quality, consistency of style, resourcefulness, and supportive presence. Several scales clearly refer to the most salient behaviors from Ainsworth's definition as they focus on noticing child signals and appropriate responding across different modalities of interaction. Warmth and positive affect are also explicitly part of the sensitivity construct, which is not the case in Ainsworth's sensitivity scale.

The CIB information materials mention attachment and the work of Mary Ainsworth, and some studies using the CIB sensitivity scale refer to salient aspects of attachment theory (e.g., Kim et al., 2011). The CIB sensitivity scale appears to be used mostly in relation to parental or child social-emotional risk (e.g., Feldman et al., 2009; Feldman & Klein, 2003; Keren, Feldman, & Tyano, 2001). Finally, the scale is able to detect improvements in maternal sensitivity following intervention (e.g., Feldman, Weller, Sirota, & Eidelman, 2003), and has also been used in a non-Western context in Palestinian families in Ramallah and the West Bank, revealing interesting culture-specific patterns of sensitivity and child outcomes (Feldman & Masalha, 2010).

Emotional Availability Scales (EA Scales)

The 3rd edition of the Emotional Availability scales (EA scales; Biringen, Robinson, & Emde, 1998) has been widely used in studies on sensitivity. It has been applied to mothers as well as fathers (e.g., Atzaba-Poria et al., 2010; Lovas, 2005), generally in free-play settings. The 4th edition of the EA scales (Biringen, 2008) is still relatively new and studies using this edition are only just starting to be published (e.g., Flykt et al., 2012). According to the manual, the newest edition can be applied to any adult caregiver interacting with children aged 0–14 years (with an infancy/early childhood version and a middle childhood/youth version), although the two versions are nearly identical. It is suggested that the version for older children may be extended to older ages.

The EA sensitivity scale in the 3rd edition consists of a single 9-point rating scale, and a highly sensitive parent is described as follows: "Emotional communication between parent and infant is for the most part positive, appropriate, and creative. The highly sensitive parent displays much genuine, authentic and congruent interest, pleasure, and amusement with the infant" (Biringen et al., 1998, p. 257). It is clear from this description that the EA sensitivity scale is much broader than the original sensitivity scale and includes strong references to parental affect. This is consistent with the theoretical background of the EA scales (Biringen & Easterbrooks, 2012), which includes clear references to attachment theory, but also explicitly acknowledges the influence of frameworks emphasizing affective attunement (e.g., Emde & Easterbrooks, 1985).

In contrast to the 3rd edition, the 4th edition of the EA scales is not freely available, as it is only released to those who follow the EA training. The 4th edition does not have a single sensitivity scale, but instead includes seven subscales for coding sensitivity, of which the first two are the most salient (scored on a 1–7 scale) and the last five contributing less to the overall score (1–3 scale). The two main subscales are labeled "Affect and Clarity of Perceptions" and "Appropriate Responsiveness". As in the 3rd edition, affect plays a far more important role than in Ainsworth's original sensitivity scale as evidenced by the following sentence from the manual: "The key characteristic of the sensitivity construct, in our view, is affect" (Biringen, 2008, p. 17, underlining by Biringen).

The 3rd edition of the EA sensitivity scale shows meaningful relations with child attachment security in risk samples in Western countries (Oppenheim, Koren-Karie, Dolev, & Yirmiya, 2012; Van IJzendoorn et al., 2007) and in a non-Western country (John, Morris, & Halliburton, 2012, in India). The sensitivity scale also relates to parental attachment state of mind (Aviezer, Sagi, Joels, & Ziv, 1999; Coppola, Cassibba, & Costantini, 2007; Edelstein et al., 2004), and has been shown the ability to detect changes in maternal sensitivity following intervention (e.g., Salomonsson & Sandell, 2011).

Erickson scales

The Erickson scales (Egeland, Erickson, Clemenhagen-Moon, Hiester, & Korfmacher, 1990; Erickson, Sroufe, & Egeland, 1985) are generally used to code interactions in teaching situations (e.g., making a puzzle that is too difficult for the child to solve on his/ her own) with toddlers and preschoolers. The Erickson scales have also been used with fathers in the context of the NICHD-SECCYD study (see below; NICHD Early Childcare Research Network, 2000). Although the manual does not provide a theoretical framework, the first study to use these scales (Erickson et al., 1985) was clearly grounded in attachment theory. The scales include supportive presence, lack of respect for autonomy (later labeled as intrusiveness), hostility, clarity of instruction, sensitivity and timing of instruction, and confidence. These scales are coded using scores 1 to 7, each with specific behavioral descriptions and without shorthand labels. The instrument does not actually include a scale with the label "sensitivity", but several research groups have used composites of (a selection of) these scales to measure the construct of sensitivity (e.g., Alink et al., 2009; Bell & Belsky, 2008). Interestingly, the Erickson scales are also part of the observational battery in the NICHD study where they are also used to derive an overall sensitivity construct (see also the description of the NICHD sensitivity scales below). Various elements of the Erickson scales are indeed relevant to the sensitivity construct, such as the parent's ability to provide support when the child needs it, and tailoring support to the needs of the child in terms of timing and content. Positive regard is mentioned as an aspect of supportive presence, but is not prominent in the descriptions.

The sensitivity construct based on the Erickson scales has been found to be related to child attachment security in a USA sample (McElwain, Cox, Burchinal, & MacFie, 2003) and in a Japanese sample (Vereijken, Riksen-Walraven, & Kondo-Ikemura, 1997), and can detect improvements in maternal sensitivity as a result of intervention (e.g., Stams, Juffer, Van IJzendoorn, & Hoksbergen, 2001; Stolk et al., 2008).

Global Ratings of Mother–Infant Interaction

As the name suggest, the Global Ratings of Mother–Infant Interaction (Murray, Fiori-Cowley, Hooper, & Cooper, 1996) was specifically designed to assess maternal interactions with infants. The manual states that it is intended to measure interactions with 2- to 5-month-old infants in a face-to-face setting. It has been applied to interactions during the Still-Face Paradigm (e.g., Grant, McMahon, Reilly, & Austin, 2010), but also to free play settings (e.g., Stein et al., 2012) and with older infants up to age 12 months in our search results (e.g., Hobson, Patrick, Crandell, García-Pérez, & Lee, 2005). Despite its name it has also been used to code father–infant interactions (Ramchandani et al., 2013). The manual does not provide a theoretical background, but the first study using the scales (Murray et al., 1996) also included the Strange Situation and found no relations between the scales and attachment security. The instrument includes a single specific sensitivity scale (scored 1 to 5) that can be seen as a summary of scales regarding warmth, acceptance, responsiveness, and non-demandingness that are scored first, but it is coded separately. The sensitivity scale description clearly reflects Ainsworth's original definition as it includes references to signal perception, empathy, and appropriate responsiveness. The developers of the scale also specifically mention taking the child's perspective as a guiding principle. Positive affect as reflected in the scale assessing warmth is also part of the sensitivity construct in this instrument. However, the manual explicitly mentions that high maternal warmth without appropriate responsiveness can not lead to a very high sensitivity score.

The sensitivity construct derived from the Global Ratings of Mother–Infant Interaction is related meaningfully to infant attachment security in a South African sample (Tomlinson, Cooper, & Murray, 2005), and has been found to detect improvement in sensitivity through intervention in mothers of very-low-birth-weight infants (Feeley, Zelkowitz, & Shrier, 2012).

Maternal Behavior Q-Sort (MBQS)

The MBQS (Pederson et al., 1990; Pederson & Moran, 1995; Pederson, Moran, & Bento, 1999) is a Q-set consisting of 90 cards with statements about maternal behaviors. The MBQS is not a regular global rating scale, but it was included here because it yields a global sensitivity score. The cards are sorted into nine piles of 10 items each ranging from highly uncharacteristic to highly characteristic. A single sensitivity score is derived by correlating the scores for each mother's Q-sort with a criterion sort provided by experts describing the prototypically sensitive mother. The MBQS was originally designed for home observations of maternal interactions with infants, but has also been used with fathers (Colonnesi et al., 2013). The MBQS has also been used beyond infancy (e.g., Selcuk et al., 2010), and a preschool version of the instrument has been developed (Maternal Behavior for Preschoolers Q-Set; Posada, Kaloustian, Richmond, & Moreno, 2007).

The developers of the MBQS explicitly mention the work of Mary Ainsworth as a major source for the item descriptions (Pederson et al., 1990). The 90 items indeed include clear references to Mary Ainsworth's definition of sensitivity, with descriptions of signal perception (e.g., "notices when baby smiles, vocalizes"), and prompt and child-centered appropriate responding (e.g., "responds accurately to signals of distress") with the aim of satisfying the child (e.g., "interventions satisfy baby"). There are also some references to positive affect (e.g., "displays affection by touching, caressing"), but only sporadically within the total set of 90 items, and thus unlikely to make the difference between ratings reflecting highly sensitive interactions versus ratings reflecting insensitive interactions.

The MBQS sensitivity score is highly correlated with the Ainsworth sensitivity scale (Behrens, Hart, & Parker, 2012), and shows associations with infant attachment quality in Western samples (Bailey, Moran, Pederson, & Bento, 2007; Behrens, Parker, & Haltigan, 2011; Kim & Kim, 2009; Pederson et al., 1990) and in a Colombian sample (Posada et al., 1999). It has also been found to relate meaningfully to maternal attachment state of mind (Bailey, Moran, Pederson, & Bento, 2007; Lindhiem, Bernard, & Dozier, 2011; Whipple,

Bernier, & Mageau, 2011). Finally, the MBQS sensitivity scale has been found to be sensitive to improvements in parenting quality following intervention (Moss et al., 2011).

NICHD-SECCYD sensitivity scales

In the National Institute of Child Health and Human Development study of Early Child Care and Youth Development (NICHD-SECCYD), several single scales are used to assess sensitivity. From infancy up to 24 months, two sensitivity scales are used: one for sensitivity to nondistress and one for sensitivity to distress, scored on a scale from 1 (not at all characteristic) to 4 or 5 (highly characteristic), and generally used in semi-structured free play settings (Owen, 1992). For older ages, slightly adapted versions of the Erickson scales are used to code parental behavior in free play and teaching tasks (also focusing more on teaching-related interactions), and a sensitivity construct is derived by combining the scales for supportive presence, respect for autonomy, and hostility (see discussion of Erickson scales above).

In this section we focus on the infancy scales that were specifically designed for the NICHD-SECCYD. In one of the scale documents, it is stated that the sensitivity to distress scale was adapted from Ainsworth et al. (1978), whereas the sensitivity to nondistress is based on work by Margaret Fish, who in turn acknowledges Ainsworth's work when introducing her measure (Fish, Belsky, & Stifter, 1991). Thus it appears that the attachment framework was used as a guiding principle for both infant sensitivity scales. Given the context of a large longitudinal study, these sensitivity scales have been widely used in research publications, and have been applied to both mothers and fathers (e.g., Barnett, Deng, Mills-Koonce, Willoughby, & Cox, 2008). In both of the sensitivity scales that are used up to age 24 months, the focus is on appropriate responsiveness judged on the basis of the effectiveness of parental responses. In the case of distress this means the child is soothed and in the case of nondistress that the child is engaged and content. These descriptions clearly reflect the main elements of Ainsworth's sensitivity scale. The scales do not include specific mention of parental positive affect as a main element of sensitivity. However, in some studies a composite sensitivity score is used that does include a specific rating of positive regard (e.g., Bradley & Corwyn, 2008; Hirsch-Pasek & Burchinal, 2006).

The NICHD sensitivity scales used for infants up to age 24 months have been found to relate to infant attachment quality (e.g., Bakermans-Kranenburg, Van IJzendoorn, & Kroonenberg, 2004; McElwain & Booth-LaForce, 2006; NICHD Early Child Care Research Network, 2006) and child separation anxiety (Dallaire & Weinraub, 2005). Finally, the scale has been found to reveal improvements in maternal sensitivity towards preterm infants following a parenting intervention (Ravn et al., 2011).

Parent–Child Early Relational Assessment (PCERA)

The Parent–Child Early Relational Assessment (PCERA; Clark, 1985) is an observational rating scale with 65 items (scored 1–5) designed to comprehensively assess the frequency, duration, and intensity of adaptive behavior in terms of social-emotional and task-related qualities. In the manual four coding situations are mentioned, including feeding, structured task, free play, and separation/reunion. Regarding target population, the scale title suggests applicability to both parents, and potentially a range of child ages. We were unable to find out the intended age range of the scales, but found almost exclusively papers reporting on mothers and infants up to 12 months and only one on toddlers with fathers (Eiden, Edwards, & Leonard, 2006). One of the items is labeled "parent reads child's cues and responds sensitively and appropriately". The item title captures the scale's content well, in that the focus is clearly on signal perception and appropriate responsiveness. Similar to Ainsworth's scale descriptions, empathic awareness is specifically mentioned. In addition, some other items also refer to contingent responsiveness to specific child behaviors, thus also reflecting sensitivity. Positive affect is not a part of the sensitivity construct described in the sensitivity item. However, the studies that use the PCERA do not report on a single sensitivity scale, but all report on composite sensitive responsiveness scales that include other PCERA items that do clearly refer to positive affect (e.g., Brown, 2007; Bystrova et al., 2009; Scher, 2001). Thus, it seems that the sensitivity item is not used as a separate scale.

The manual does not provide a theoretical background, although in one paper Ainsworth's work is mentioned in the introduction of the section on the PCERA (Kivijarvi et al., 2001). The PCERA maternal sensitivity construct has been found to predict attachment security in infants born prematurely (Shah, Clements, & Poehlmann, 2011). The PCERA has been used to evaluate intervention effectiveness (e.g., Clark, Tluczek, & Brown, 2008), but we did not find any studies reporting on significant intervention effects on PCERA constructs labeled sensitivity. Finally, the PCERA sensitivity scale does not seem to have been used in non-Western countries.

Discussion

For this review we unearthed no less than 50 different observational instruments used to measure parental sensitivity in early childhood, showing the viability of Mary Ainsworth's formulation of this construct. The selected eight instruments that were used most often to measure sensitivity within our search results do show marked differences in the conceptualization of the construct and in their applications. Nonetheless, consistent with the original aim of the sensitivity construct, for most instruments we found studies reporting on meaningful associations with child attachment security.

Interestingly, only three of the eight most-used instruments include a single global rating scale for sensitivity (EA scales 3rd ed., Global Ratings of Mother–Infant Interaction, and NICHD-SECCYD sensitivity scales), whereas the others require the summing of several scales. This is in contrast to the original Ainsworth sensitivity scale that requires the observer to make one global assessment of sensitivity, rather than separately evaluate specific maternal behaviors that contribute to the sensitivity construct. In addition, the multi-aspect composites used in some instruments extend beyond Ainsworth's core elements. Some of these specific additions seem to reflect the extension to older ages in which other types of interactions are observed than in infancy and need to be rated on sensitivity as well (e.g., teaching behavior in the Erickson scales). In other cases, elements are split up into more specific pieces. For instance, in the CARE-Index each modality of interaction (e.g., facial, vocal, body) is rated separately regarding sensitivity. From a cross-cultural perspective this is an interesting approach, as there is evidence that the use of specific modalities in maternal interactions with infants may vary across cultures (e.g., Kärtner, Keller, & Yovsi, 2010). Specifying separate subscales per modality could thus provide interesting information about culture-specific patterns of sensitive responding.

Some have suggested that the use of a multi-aspect composite is actually a better approach because sensitivity is a complex construct (Seifer et al., 1996). However, studies on the components of sensitivity are surprisingly rare. In a study by Lohaus, Keller, Ball, Elben, and Voelker (2001), independent ratings were obtained for overall sensitivity and each of the main elements of the sensitivity construct. The results showed high correlations between the overall rating of sensitivity and its elements: signal perception ($r = 0.56$), correct interpretation ($r = 0.77$), prompt reaction ($r = 0.75$), and appropriate reaction ($r = 0.72$). These findings could be taken to suggest that when it comes to the main components of sensitivity, coding separate scales is not really necessary, as they are also captured largely by one overall rating. However, high correlations do not mean that the elements can not contribute uniquely to specific aspects of child development. Assessing particular aspects of sensitive parent–child interactions separately may bring to light specific patterns and associations with child outcomes. In most cases however, the subscales are not used separately and are instead used as a part of the final total sensitivity score, including not only the original elements of sensitivity, but also other added elements. To enhance our understanding of the sensitivity construct it may be worthwhile to explore the independent contributions of each of its core and added elements, and to compare this to the contribution of composite constructs. This would require independent coding and sufficient intercoder reliability for each subscale. Independent coding may be quite a challenge given the larger number of coders needed, and regarding reliability it is our experience that the reliability on the final aggregate score can be high even when reliabilities on separate subscales are insufficient. But if separate subscales are thought to reflect significantly different aspects of sensitivity, it may be worthwhile investing in solving these issues.

Another notable deviation from the original Ainsworth sensitivity scale is the inclusion of positive affect or warmth as a criterion or indicator for sensitivity in seven out of eight instruments reviewed. In some instruments this aspect is particularly salient (e.g., the EA scales, the CARE-index), whereas in others it is a rather minor part of the scale descriptions (e.g., the MBQS, the Erickson scales). The terms positive affect and warmth usually refer to maternal smiling and positive tone of voice, and often also to physical affection like caressing. There is something to be said for including positive affect in the definition of sensitivity, as significant correlations between the two constructs have been observed. However, when rated independently these correlations are generally only moderate in size (e.g., 0.12 to 0.45 in Lohaus, Keller, Ball, Voelker, & Elben, 2004, 0.37 in Oppenheimer, Hankin, Jenness, Young, & Smolen, 2013, and 0.49 in Spinrad, Eisenberg, & Silva, 2012), especially compared to the correlations with the basic elements of sensitivity as described above. In addition, there is evidence that warmth and sensitive responsiveness show differential predictive associations with child outcomes. For instance, observed sensitivity was found to predict child regulation of negative affect and empathy towards distressed others, whereas warmth (a multi-method composite including observations) predicted child regulation of positive affect (Davidov & Grusec, 2006). In another study, maternal sensitivity to distress predicted security of attachment whereas maternal affect (defined as social/affective interactions) did not (Del Carmen, Pedersen, Huffman, & Bryan, 1993), and both maternal sensitivity and positive regard (defined as demonstrations of affirmation, warmth, and affection toward the child) have been found to be independent predictors of child ADHD symptoms (Keown, 2012). In a related vein, it has been suggested that warmth and sensitive responsiveness belong to different motivational systems, with different evolutionary functions (MacDonald, 1992). However, to complicate matters, there is also evidence that attachment security is predicted by positive affect and several other aspects of parenting to the same extent as by sensitivity (De Wolff & Van IJzendoorn, 1997).

Supporting the idea that positive affect and prompt appropriate responding to infant signals to facilitate infant secure-base behavior are distinct, Ainsworth reported warmth and affection in all but two mothers in her Uganda study, which by her own interpretation ruled out warmth as a predictor of secure attachment patterns (Ainsworth, 1967). In a related vein, our own extensive experiences with coding parent–child interactions in a variety of samples and observational settings reveal that in a subgroup of parents, high levels of positive affect are accompanied by extreme intrusiveness and lack of signal perception. These parents play with their children vigorously, with a lot of tickling, poking, and fun-making, while not noticing that their child is not enjoying the interaction. The parent's positive affect is genuine, in that she really does enjoy this type of play with her child, but it is not accompanied by sensitivity at all. This interaction pattern appears to have also been noted by Mary Ainsworth as shown in her description of a mother of an infant in the resistant attachment group (C_1): "She continually interrupted her daughter to train her, to show off her accomplishments, or merely because she herself felt like playing with the baby or showing her affection" (Ainsworth et al., 1978, p. 238). Of course in the observational instruments which include positive affect this type of parent could never receive a top score on sensitivity because of the lack of appropriate responsiveness, but her sensitivity score is likely to be at least inflated because of the presence of high levels of positive affect. This particular interaction pattern would yield a relatively high sensitivity score if positive affect is included in the definition of sensitivity, thus obscuring the fact that the mother actually did not show appropriate responsiveness. Thus, Ainsworth certainly acknowledged the importance of positive affect and since it also relates to attachment security, it may be helpful to rate sensitivity and positive affect separately, consistent with the structure of the original Maternal Care scales. It then also becomes possible to examine both the unique and additive or even interactive effects of each of these components on child outcomes.

Regarding the target age range of the children, the focus of the reviewed instruments is predominantly on early childhood, although there are some exceptions (EA scales and CIB). Those studies that do assess sensitivity towards adolescents are generally conducted by researchers who also study early childhood parenting, often longitudinally (e.g., Feldman, 2010). The idea that the attachment framework is also relevant to adolescent as a developmental period in its own right was pointed out by Allen (2008) who suggests that the balance between exploration and attachment behaviors in infancy can be translated to the balance between autonomy and attachment processes in adolescence. In addition, indirect assessments of maternal sensitivity (i.e., concordance between maternal and adolescent reports on the adolescent's characteristics) have shown meaningful relations with adolescent attachment states of mind (Allen et al., 2003; Berger, Jodl, Allen, McElhaney, & Kuperminc, 2005).

There are very few studies reporting on directly observed sensitivity in adolescence in relation to adolescent development, but there is some evidence that such relations exist. For instance, observed maternal sensitivity in adolescence has been found to predict adolescent social development (e.g., Jaffari-Bimmel, Juffer, Van IJzendoorn, Bakermans-Kranenburg, & Mooijaart, 2006), and higher levels of observed maternal support during a discussion task has been found to predict adolescent autonomy problems, and a greater susceptibility to the influence of peers regarding substance use (Allen, Chango, Szwedo, Schad, & Marston, 2011). One study also showed that a variety of risk factors increased adolescent allostatic load, but only for adolescents with mothers observed to show low levels of sensitive responsiveness (e.g., Evans, Kim, Ting, Tesher, & Shannis, 2007). Overall it seems that extending research on sensitivity to older ages and adapting observational instruments accordingly is a worthwhile endeavor.

The extension of the observation of sensitivity to fathers is a notable advance in the field of attachment research (Bretherton, 2010). All instruments reviewed in this paper have also been used with fathers and have shown meaningful associations between paternal sensitivity and a variety of other variables (e.g., Kelley et al., 1998; Lewis & Lamb, 2003; Lucassen et al., 2011; Shannon, Tamis-LeMonda, & Cabrera, 2006; Shannon, Tamis-LeMonda, London, & Cabrera, 2002). However, it has been suggested that other aspects of father–child interactions may be more salient for child development, such as challenging and stimulating play (Grossmann, Grossmann, Kindler, & Zimmermann, 2008). In a recent meta-analysis this idea was not confirmed, as paternal sensitivity including stimulating play was not more strongly predictive of attachment security than paternal sensitivity alone (Lucassen et al., 2011). Nevertheless, studies with observations of father–child interactions are still scarce, and more research is needed to understand the role of paternal sensitivity and related behaviors in predicting child outcomes.

Another important issue regarding the observation targets is the fact that the vast majority of studies assessing parental sensitivity is conducted in Western ethnic majority samples, although a recent review has shown that sensitivity is relevant for child development in ethnic minority families as well (Mesman et al., 2012). As described in our review of the eight observation instruments, some have indeed been used in non-Western samples and have contributed to the notion that parental sensitivity is a universal phenomenon that can be successfully assessed using existing observational instruments. However, we still know relatively little about the nature of predictive relations between sensitivity and child outcomes outside the USA and Europe, and this area of research deserves our full attention in the future.

Going back to the staggering 50 new sensitivity observational instruments that we found, we wondered whether the field needs that many different instruments, each with their own minor and/or major variations on the original conceptualization of the sensitivity construct. At the very least our review results suggest that there is no need for the development of additional instruments to measure sensitivity, because there are already so many of them to choose from. Taking this point a bit further, it may be beneficial to the field if the set of instruments was more restricted and above all include only those with clearly-defined behavioral descriptions of its elements so that readers may know exactly what was measured. Conceptual clarity is of key importance for the interpretation of research results based on different observational instruments. In a related vein, it was surprising to find that most manuals do not provide a clear theoretical framework. The EA scales and the MBQS are notable exceptions as their manuals include explicit theoretical backgrounds. This of course does not mean that the other scales are not grounded in theory. Most do seem to relate to attachment theory, given that seven out of eight have been found to predict attachment security, but it would be helpful to researchers trying to choose an observation instrument if the theoretical background of each instrument was explicitly described.

To promote conceptual clarity, the term sensitivity should not be used too lightly to retain a clear distinction between the original clearly defined and delineated construct and other more elaborate constructs. The instrument that comes closest to Ainsworth's sensitivity scale is the NICHD-SECCYD sensitivity scale as used up to age 24 months, since it consists of a single global rating scale that does not call for evaluating maternal warmth, positive affect, or other added elements. The MBQS is also very close to Ainsworth's sensitivity construct, as the formulation of the items was explicitly guided by her work (Pederson et al., 1990). Instruments using broader conceptualizations can certainly be an asset to the field, but only when its elements are clearly defined. When there are many added elements, it may be advisable to not use the term sensitivity to describe the construct being measured.

There are some limitations to the current review. First, our literature search to find observational instruments measuring parental sensitivity did not uncover all relevant papers, as was shown by additional searches conducted to find more information about specific instruments or topics. Unfortunately it was not possible to perform a cited-reference search for most of the selected instruments, because the instrument manuals were generally unpublished manuscripts. We therefore had to rely on a search with keywords. Our extra searches revealed that some relevant papers only include terms such as "parenting quality" or "parent–child interactions" and were not captured by our search if the terms sensitivity or responsiveness were not explicitly mentioned in the abstract or keywords of the papers, even though they were measured. Expanding our keywords to capture such papers would have led to a much larger number of hits far too great to process within a reasonable time. However, our goal was not to find all existing papers on parental sensitivity, but to find observational measures assessing parental sensitivity. Although it may be that the total set of 50 instruments that we found represents an underestimation of the actual number, it is very unlikely that an expanded search would have led to a change in the set of eight most commonly used instruments that we discussed in detail. Second, although we have done our best to adequately describe the eight selected instruments, it was sometimes surprisingly difficult to obtain information. Some coding manuals were hard to find and in some cases the instrument was used in many different ways, making it more difficult to provide a description that captures all its applications. We did attempt to contact the authors of each of the scales, but were not always successful. Nevertheless, anyone interested in a particular instrument is encouraged to contact the authors of the instrument to make sure that they receive all relevant information, independent of this review.

Although there are some limitations, this is the first systematic review of observational instruments assessing parental sensitivity, and the first attempt to analyze these instruments in relation to the original Ainsworth sensitivity construct. The number of observational instruments to measure sensitivity is very impressive and reflects the value of the construct. However, the interpretation of research results would be served by a more limited and clearly defined set of instruments. The eight observational instruments reviewed in detail all include the main elements from Ainsworth's sensitivity scale. Salient and common deviations from the original scale include the use of composite scales rather than a single global scale and the related inclusion of new elements, and specifically the inclusion of positive affect as an indicator of sensitivity. The variety of parental behaviors that constitute the sensitivity construct across instruments highlights the importance of conceptual clarity. The potential danger of adding elements to scales labeled as assessing sensitivity is that the measures will reflect overall good/positive parenting rather than sensitive responsiveness specifically. Indeed, there is evidence that separating the core sensitivity construct from additions such as warmth and positive affect is worthwhile, and even that distinguishing between the core elements of sensitivity might be helpful. Regarding the targets of observation, the extension of the assessment of sensitivity to older age groups, fathers, and non-parental caregivers has clearly been very valuable to the field and is likely to foster new studies in the future. Most instruments appear to be applicable to both Western and non-Western samples, which is encouraging for the field of cross-cultural studies on parenting and child development. In sum, the legacy of Mary Ainsworth's sensitivity construct and observational scale is truly impressive and her work will continue to inspire researchers across the globe for many decades to come.

Acknowledgements

The authors acknowledge the support of a grant from the New Opportunities for Research Funding Agency Co-operation in Europe (NORFACE, awarded to JM as co-PI) and a European Research Council Starting Grant (awarded to JM).

References

Ainsworth, M. D. S. (1967). *Infancy in Uganda: Infant care and the growth of love.* Baltimore, MD: Johns Hopkins Press.

Ainsworth, M. D. S., Bell, S. M., & Stayton, D. (1974). Infant-mother attachment and social development. In M. P. Richards (Ed.), *The introduction of the child into a social world* (pp. 99–135). London: Cambridge University Press.

Ainsworth, M. D. S., Bell, S. M., & Stayton, D. J. (1971). Individual differences in strange-situation behavior of one-year-olds. In H. R. Schaffer (Ed.), *The origins of human social relations* (pp. 17–58). London: Academic Press.

Ainsworth, M. D. S., Blehar, M. C., Waters, E., & Wall, S. (1978). *Patterns of attachment: A psychological study of the strange situation.* Hillsdale, NJ: Lawrence Erlbaum Associates.

Alink, L. R. A., Mesman, J., Van Zeijl, J., Stolk, M. N., Juffer, F., Bakermans-Kranenburg, M. J., Koot, H. M. (2009). Maternal sensitivity moderates the relation between negative discipline and aggression in early childhood. *Social Development, 18,* 99–120. doi:10.1111/j.1467-9507.2008.00478.x

Allen, J. P. (2008). The attachment system in adolescence. In J. Cassidy & P. R. Shaver (Eds.), *Handbook of attachment: Theory, research, and clinical applications* (pp. 419–435). New York, NY: Guilford.

Allen, J. P., Chango, J., Szwedo, D., Schad, M., & Marston, E. (2011). Predictors of susceptibility to peer influence regarding substance use in adolescence. *Child Development, 83,* 337–350. doi:10.1111/j.1467-8624.2011.01682.x

Allen, J. P., McElhaney, K. B., Land, D. J., Kuperminc, G. P., Moore, C. W., O'Beirne-Kelley, H., & Kilmer, S. L. (2003). A secure base in adolescence: Markers of attachment security in the mother-adolescent relationship. *Child Development, 74,* 292–307. doi:10.1111/1467-8624.t01-1-00536

Atzaba-Poria, N., Meiri, G., Millikovsky, M., Barkai, A., Dunaevsky-Idan, M., & Yerushalmi, B. (2010). Father-child and mother-child interaction in families with a child feeding disorder: The role of paternal involvement. *Infant Mental Health Journal, 31,* 682–698. doi:10.1002/imhj.20278

Aviezer, O., Sagi, A., Joels, T., & Ziv, Y. (1999). Emotional availability and attachment representations in kibbutz infants and their mothers. *Developmental Psychology, 35,* 811–822. doi:10.1037/0012-1649.35.3.811

Bailey, H. N., Moran, G., Pederson, D. R., & Bento, S. (2007). Understanding the transmission of attachment using variable- and relationship-centered approaches. *Development and Psychopathology, 19,* 313–343. doi:10.10170S0954579407070162

Bakermans-Kranenburg, M. J., Van IJzendoorn, M. H., & Juffer, F. (2003). Less is more: Meta-analyses of sensitivity and attachment interventions in early childhood. *Psychological Bulletin, 129*(2), 195–215. doi:10.1037/0033-2909.129.2.195

Bakermans-Kranenburg, M. J., Van IJzendoorn, M. H., & Kroonenberg, P. M. (2004). Differences in attachment security between African-American and white children: Ethnicity or socio-economic status?. *Infant Behavior & Development, 27,* 417–433. doi:10.1016/j.infbeh.2004.02.002

Barlow, J., Davis, H., McIntosh, E., Jarrett, P., Mockford, C., & Stewart-Brown, S. (2007). Role of home visiting in improving parenting and health in families at risk of abuse and neglect: Results of a multicentre randomised controlled trial and economic evaluation. *Archives of Disease in Childhood, 92,* 229–233. doi:10.1136/adc.2006.095117

Barnett, M. A., Deng, M., Mills-Koonce, W. R., Willoughby, M., & Cox, M. (2008). Interdependence of parenting of mothers and fathers of infants. *Journal of Family Psychology, 22,* 561–573. doi:10.1037/0893-3200.22.3.561

Behrens, K. Y., Hart, S. L., & Parker, A. C. (2012). Maternal sensitivity: Evidence of stability across time, contexts, and measurement instruments. *Infant and Child Development, 21,* 348–355. doi:10.1002/icd.1747

Behrens, K. Y., Parker, A. C., & Haltigan, J. D. (2011). Maternal sensitivity assessed during the Strange Situation Procedure predicts child's attachment quality and reunion behaviors. *Infant Behavior & Development, 34*, 378–381. doi:10.1016/j.infbeh.2011.02.007

Bell, B. G., & Belsky, J. (2008). Parents, parenting and children's sleep problems: Exploring reciprocal effects. *British Journal of Developmental Psychology, 26*, 579–593. doi:10.1348/026151008X285651

Berger, L. E., Jodl, K. M., Allen, J. P., McElhaney, K. B., & Kuperminc, G. P. (2005). When adolescents disagree with others about their symptoms: Differences in attachment organization as an explanation of discrepancies between adolescent-, parent-, and peer-reports of behavior problems. *Development & Psychopathology, 17*, 489–507. doi:10.1017/S0954579405050248

Bernier, A., Carlson, S. M., & Whipple, N. (2010). From external regulation to self-regulation: Early parenting precursors of young children's executive functioning. *Child Development, 81*, 326–339. doi:10.1111/j.1467-8624.2009.01397.x

Biringen, Z. (2008). *Emotional Availability (EA) Scales manual (4th ed.): Part 1. Infancy/Early Childhood version (child aged 0–5 years)*. Unpublished manuscript.

Biringen, Z., & Easterbrooks, M. A. (2012). Emotional availability: Concept, research, and window on developmental psychopathology. *Development and Psychopathology, 24*, 1–8. doi:10.1017/S0954579411000617

Biringen, Z., Robinson, J. L., & Emde, R. N. (1998). Appendix B: The Emotional Availability Scales (3rd ed.; an abridged infancy/early childhood version). *Attachment and Human Development, 2*, 256–270. doi:10.1080/14616730050085626

Bradley, R. H., & Corwyn, R. F. (2008). Infant temperament, parenting, and externalizing behavior in first grade: A test of the differential susceptibility hypothesis. *Journal of Child Psychology and Psychiatry, 49*, 124–131. doi:10.1111/j.1469-7610.2007.01829.x

Bretherton, I. (2010). Fathers in attachment theory and research: A review. *Early Child Development and Care, 180*, 9–23. doi:10.1080/03004430903414661

Brown, L. (2007). Heart rate variability in premature infants during feeding. *Biological Research for Nursing, 8*, 283–293. doi:10.1177/1099800406298542

Bystrova, K., Ivanova, V., Edhborg, M., Matthiesen, A. S., Ransjö-Arvidson, A. B., Mukhamedrakhimov, R., … Widström, A. M. (2009). Early contact versus separation: Effects on mother-infant interaction one year later. *Birth, 36*, 97–109. doi:10.1111/j.1523-536X.2009.00307.x

Campbell, S. B., Matestic, P., Stauffenberg, C., Mohan, R., & Kirchner, T. (2007). Trajectories of maternal depressive symptoms, maternal sensitivity, and children's functioning at school entry. *Developmental Psychology, 43*, 1202–1215. doi:10.1037/0012-1649.43.5.1202

Clark, R. (1985). *Early parent-child relationship assessment*. Madison, WI: Department of Psychiatry.

Clark, R., Tluczek, A., & Brown, R. (2008). A mother-infant therapy group model for postpartum depression. *Infant Mental Health Journal, 29*, 514–536. doi:10.1002/imhj.20189

Colonnesi, C., Wissink, I. B., Noom, M. J., Asscher, J. J., Hoeve, M., Stams, G. J. J. M., Kellaert-Knol, M. G. (2013). Basic trust: An attachment-oriented intervention based on mind-mindedness in adoptive families. *Research on Social Work Practice, 23*, 179–188. doi:10.1177/1049731512469301

Coppola, G., Cassibba, R., & Costantini, A. (2007). What can make the difference? Premature birth and maternal sensitivity at 3 months of age: The role of attachment organization, traumatic reaction and baby's medical risk. *Infant Behavior & Development, 30*, 679–684. doi:10.1016/j.infbeh.2007.03.004

Crittenden, P. M. (2001). *CARE-index manual*. Miami, FL: Family Relations Institute.

Dallaire, D. H., & Weinraub, M. (2005). Predicting children's separation anxiety at age 6: The contributions of infant-mother attachment security, maternal sensitivity, and maternal separation anxiety. *Attachment & Human Development, 7*, 393–408. doi:10.1080/14616730500365894

Davidov, M., & Grusec, J. E. (2006). Untangling the links of parental responsiveness to distress and warmth to child outcomes. *Child Development, 77*, 44–58. doi:10.1111/j.1467-8624.2006.00855.x

De Wolff, M. S., & Van IJzendoorn, M. H. (1997). Sensitivity and attachment: A meta-analysis on parental antecedents of infant attachment. *Child Development, 68*, 571–591. doi:10.1111/j.1467-8624.1997.tb04218.x

Del Carmen, R., Pedersen, F. A., Huffman, L. C., & Bryan, Y. E. (1993). Dyadic distress management predicts subsequent security of attachment. *Infant Behavior and Development, 16*, 131–147. doi:10.1016/0163-6383(93)80014-Y

Edelstein, R. S., Weede Alexander, K., Shaver, P. R., Schaaf, J. M., Quas, J. A., Lovas, G. S., Goodman, G. S. (2004). Adult attachment style and parental responsiveness during a stressful event. *Attachment & Human Development, 6*, 31–52. doi:10.1080/146167303100001659584

Egeland, B., Erickson, M. F., Clemenhagen-Moon, J., Hiester, M. K., & Korfmacher, J. (1990). *24 months tools coding manual: Project steep – revised 1990 from Mother-Child Project scales.* Minneapolis, MN: University of Minnesota, Institute of Child Development.

Eiden, R. D., Edwards, E. P., & Leonard, K. E. (2006). Children's internalization of rules of conduct: Role of parenting in alcoholic families. *Psychology of Addictive Behaviors, 20*, 305–315. doi:10.1037/0893-164X.20.3.305

Emde, R. N., & Easterbrooks, M. A. (1985). Assessing emotional availability in early development. In W. Frankenburg, R. N. Emde, & J. Sullivan (Eds.), *Early identification of children at risk. An international perspective* (pp. 79–101). New York, NY: Plenum Press.

Erickson, M. F., Sroufe, L. A., & Egeland, B. (1985). The relationship between quality of attachment and behavior problems in preschool in a high-risk sample. In I. Bretherton & E. Waters (Eds.), *Growing points of attachment: Theory and research. Monographs of the Society for Research in Child Development, 50*, 147–166.

Evans, G. W., Kim, P., Ting, A. H., Tesher, H. B., & Shannis, D. (2007). Cumulative risk, maternal responsiveness, and allostatic load among young adolescents. *Developmental Psychology, 43*, 341–351. doi:10.1037/0012-1649.43.2.341

Fearon, R. M. P., Van IJzendoorn, M. H., Fonagy, P., Bakermans-Kranenburg, M. J., Schuengel, C., & Bokhorst, C. L. (2006). In search of shared and non-shared environmental factors in security of attachment: A behavior-genetic study of the association between sensitivity and attachment security. *Developmental Psychology, 42*, 1026–1040.

Feeley, N., Zelkowitz, P., Shrier, I., Stremler, R. Westreich, R. Dunkley, D. Papageorgiou, A. (2012). Follow-up of the cues and care trial: Mother and infant outcomes at 6 months. *Journal of Early Intervention, 34*, 65–81. doi:10.1177/1053815112453767

Feldman, R. (1998). *Coding Interactive Behavior (CIB) manual.* Unpublished manuscript. Bar-Ilan University.

Feldman, R. (2010). The relational basis of adolescent adjustment: Trajectories of mother-child interactive behaviors from infancy to adolescence shape adolescents' adaptation. *Attachment & Human Development, 12*, 173–192. doi:10.1080/14616730903282472

Feldman, R., & Eidelman, A. I. (2007). Maternal postpartum behavior and the emergence of infant-mother and infant-father synchrony in preterm and full-term infants: The role of neonatal vagal tone. *Developmental Psychobiology, 49*, 290–302. doi:10.1002/dev.20220

Feldman, R., Granat, A., Pariente, C., Kanety, H., Kuint, J., & Gilboa-Schechtman, E. (2009). Maternal depression and anxiety across the postpartum year and infant social engagement, fear regulation, and stress reactivity. *Journal of the American Academy of Child and Adolescent Psychiatry, 48*, 919–927. doi:10.1097/CHI.0b013e3181b21651

Feldman, R., Keren, M., Gross-Rozval, O., & Tyano, S. (2004). Mother-child touch patterns in infant feeding disorders: Relation to maternal, child, and environmental factors. *Journal of the American Academy of Child and Adolescent Psychiatry, 43*, 1089–1097. doi:10.1097/01.chi.0000132810.98922.83

Feldman, R., & Klein, P. S. (2003). Toddlers' self-regulated compliance to mothers, caregivers, and fathers: Implications for theories of socialization. *Developmental Psychology, 39*, 680–692. doi:10.1037/0012-1649.39.4.680

Feldman, R., & Masalha, S. (2010). Parent-child and triadic antecedents of children's social competence: Cultural specificity, shared process. *Developmental Psychology, 46*, 455–467.

Feldman, R., Weller, A., Sirota, L., & Eidelman, A. I. (2003). Testing a family intervention hypothesis: The contribution of mother-infant skin-to-skin contact (kangaroo care) to family interaction, proximity, and touch. *Journal of Family Psychology, 17*, 94–107. doi:10.1037/0893-3200.17.1.94

Fish, M., Belsky, J., & Stifter, C. A. (1991). Conditions of continuity and discontinuity in infant negative emotionality: Newborn to five months. *Child Development, 62*, 1525–1537. doi:10.2307/1130824

Flykt, M., Punamäki, R.-L., Belt, R., Biringen, Z., Salo, S., Posa, T., & Pojulo, M. (2012). Maternal representations and emotional availability among drug-abusing and nonusing mothers and their infants. *Infant Mental Health Journal, 33*, 123–138. doi:10.1002/imhj.21313

Fuertes, M., Lopes-dos-Santos, P., Beeghly, M., & Tronick, E. (2009). Infant coping and maternal interactive behavior predict attachment in a Portuguese sample of healthy preterm infants. *European Psychologist, 14*, 320–331. doi:10.1027/1016-9040.14.4.320

Gonzalez, A., Jenkins, J. M., Steiner, M., & Fleming, A. S. (2012). Maternal early life experiences and parenting: The mediating role of cortisol and executive function. *Journal of the American Academy of Child and Adolescent Psychiatry, 51*, 673–682. doi:10.1016/j.jaac.2012.04.003

Goodman, G., Aber, J. L., Berlin, L., & Brooks-Gunn, J. (1998). The relations between maternal behaviors and urban preschool children's internal working models of attachment security. *Infant Mental Health Journal, 19*, 378–393. doi:10.1002/(SICI)1097-0355(199824)19:4378::AID-IMHJ2>3.3.CO;2-A

Grant, K.-A., McMahon, C., Reilly, N., & Austin, M.-P. (2010). Maternal sensitivity moderates the impact of prenatal anxiety disorder on infant responses to the still-face procedure. *Infant Behavior & Development, 33*, 453–462. doi:10.1016/j.infbeh.2010.05.001

Grossman, K., Grossman, K. E., Fremmer-Bombik, E., Kindler, H., Scheuerer-Englisch, H., & Zimmermann, P. (2002). The uniqueness of the child-father attachment relationship: Fathers' sensitive and challenging play as pivotal variable in a 16-year longitudinal study. *Social Development, 11*, 307–331. doi:10.1111/1467-9507.00202

Grossman, K., Grossman, K. E., Spangler, G., Suess, G., & Unzner, L. (1985). Maternal sensitivity and newborns' orientation responses as related to quality of attachment in northern Germany. In I. Bretherton & E. Waters (Eds.), *Growing points in attachment theory and research. Monographs of the Society for Research in Child Development, 50*(1–2, serial no 209), 223–256.

Grossmann, K., Grossmann, K. E., Kindler, H., & Zimmermann, P. (2008). A wider view of attachment and exploration: The influence of mothers and fathers on the development of psychological security from infancy to young adulthood. In J. Cassidy & P. R. Shaver (Eds.), *Handbook of attachment: Theory, research, and clinical applications* (pp. 857–879). New York, NY: Guilford Press.

Hirsch-Pasek, K., & Burchinal, M. (2006). Mother and caregiver sensitivity over time: Predicting language and academic outcomes with variable- and person-centered approaches. *Merrill-Palmer Quarterly, 52*, 449–485. doi:10.1353/mpq.2006.0027

Hobson, R. P., Patrick, M., Crandell, L., García-Pérez, R., & Lee, A. (2005). Personal relatedness and attachment in infants of mothers with borderline personality disorder. *Development and Psychopathology, 17*, 329–347. doi:10.10170S0954579405050169

Jaffari-Bimmel, N., Juffer, F., Van IJzendoorn, M. H., Bakermans-Kranenburg, M. J., & Mooijaart, A. (2006). Social development from infancy to adolescence: Longitudinal and concurrent factors in an adoption sample. *Developmental Psychology, 42*, 1143–1153.

John, A., Morris, A. S., & Halliburton, A. L. (2012). Looking beyond maternal sensitivity: Mother-child correlates of attachment security among children with intellectual disabilities in urban India. *Journal of Autism and Developmental Disorders, 42*, 2335–2345. doi:10.1007/s10803-012-1479-y

Kärtner, J., Keller, H., & Yovsi, R. D. (2010). Mother-infant interaction during the first 3 months: The emergence of culture-specific contingency patterns. *Child Development, 81*, 540–554. doi:10.1111/j.1467-8624.2009.01414.x

Kelley, M. L., Smith, T. S., Green, A. P., Berndt, A. E., & Rogers, M. C. (1998). Importance of fathers' parenting to African-American toddler's social and cognitive development. *Infant Behavior & Development, 21*, 733–744. doi:10.1016/S0163-6383(98)90041-8

Keown, L. J. (2012). Predictors of boys' ADHD symptoms from early to middle childhood: The role of father–child and mother–child interactions. *Journal of Abnormal Child Psychology, 40*, 569–581. doi:10.1007/s10802-011-9586-3

Keren, M., Feldman, R., & Tyano, S. (2001). Diagnoses and interactive patterns of infants referred to a community-based infant mental health clinic. *Journal of the American Academy of Child and Adolescent Psychiatry, 40*, 27–35. doi:10.1097/00004583-200101000-00013

Kim, E. S., & Kim, B. S. (2009). The structural relationships of social support, mother's psychological status, and maternal sensitivity to attachment security in children with disabilities. *Asia Pacific Education Review, 10*, 561–573. doi:10.1007/s12564-009-9043-y

Kim, P., Feldman, R., Mayes, L. C., Eicher, V., Thompson, N., Leckman, J. F., & Swain, J. E. (2011). Breastfeeding, brain activation to own infant cry, and maternal sensitivity. *Journal of Child Psychology and Psychiatry, 52*, 907–915. doi:10.1111/j.1469-7610.2011.02406.x

Kivijärvi, M., Voeten, M. J. M., Niemelä, P., Räihä, H., Lertola, K., & Piha, J. (2001). Maternal sensitivity behavior and infant behavior in early interaction. *Infant Mental Health Journal, 22*, 627–640. doi:10.1002/imhj.1023

Klein, P. S., & Feldman, R. (2007). Mothers'and caregivers' interactive and teaching behavior with toddlers. *Early Child Development and Care, 177*, 383–402. doi:10.1080/03004430600551682

Kochanska, G., Kim, S., Barry, R. A., & Philibert, R. A. (2011). Children's genotypes interact with maternal responsive care in predicting children's competence: Diathesis–stress or differential susceptibility?. *Development and Psychopathology, 23*, 605–616. doi:10.1017/S0954579411000071

Künster, A. K., Fegert, J. M., & Ziegenhain, U. (2010). Assessing parent-child interaction in the preschool years: A pilot study on the psychometric properties of the toddler CARE-index. *Clinical Child Psychology and Psychiatry, 15*, 379–389. doi:10.1177/1359104510367585

Lewis, C., & Lamb, M. E. (2003). Fathers' influences on children's development: The evidence from two-parent families. *European Journal of Psychology of Education, 18*, 211–228. doi:10.1007/BF03173485

Lindhiem, O., Bernard, K., & Dozier, M. (2011). Maternal sensitivity: Within-person variability and the utility of multiple assessments. *Child Maltreatment, 16*, 41–50. doi:10.1177/1077559510387662

Lohaus, A., Keller, H., Ball, J., Elben, C., & Voelker, S. (2001). Maternal sensitivity: Components and relations to warmth and contingency. *Parenting: Science and Practice, 1*, 267–284. doi:10.1207/S15327922PAR0104_1

Lohaus, A., Keller, H., Ball, J., Voelker, S., & Elben, C. (2004). Maternal sensitivity in interactions with three- and 12-month-old infants: Stability, structural composition, and developmental consequences. *Infant and Child Development, 13*, 235–252. doi:10.1002/icd.351

Lovas, G. S., (2005). Gender and patterns of emotional availability in mother-toddler and father-toddler dyads. *Infant Mental Health Journal, 26*, 327–353. doi:10.1002/imhj.20056

Lucassen, N., Tharner, A., Van IJzendoorn, M. H., Bakermans-Kranenburg, M. J., Volling, B. L., Verhulst, F. C., … Tiemeier, H. (2011). The association between paternal sensitivity and infant-father attachment security: A meta-analysis of three decades of research. *Journal of Family Psychology, 25*, 686–992. doi:10.1037/a0025855

MacDonald, K. (1992). Warmth as a developmental construct: An evolutionary analysis. *Child Development, 63*, 753–773. doi:10.2307/1131231

McElwain, N. L., & Booth-LaForce, C. (2006). Maternal sensitivity to infant distress and nondistress as predictors of infant-mother attachment security. *Journal of Family Psychology, 20*, 247–255. doi:10.1037/0893-3200.20.2.247

McElwain, N. L., Cox, M., Burchinal, M. R., & MacFie, J. (2003). Differentiating among mother-infant insecure attachment classifications: A focus on child-friend interaction and exploration during solitary play at 36 months. *Attachment & Human Development, 5*, 136–164. doi:10.1080/1461673031000108513

Mesman, J. (2010). Maternal responsiveness to infants: Comparing micro- and macro-level measures. *Attachment & Human Development, 12*, 143–149. doi:10.1080/14616730903484763

Mesman, J., Oster, H., & Camras, L. (2012). Parental sensitivity to distress: What do discrete negative emotions have to do with it? *Attachment & Human Development, 14*, 337–348. doi:10.1080/14616734.2012.691649

Mesman, J., Van IJzendoorn, M. H., & Bakermans-Kranenburg, M. J. (2012). Unequal in opportunity, equal in process: Parental sensitivity promotes positive child development in ethnic minority families. *Child Development Perspectives, 6*, 239–250. doi:10.1111/j.1750-8606.2011.00223.x

Moss, E., Dubois-Comtois, K., Cyr, C., Tarabulsy, G. M., St.-Laurent, D., & Bernier, A. (2011). Efficacy of a home-visiting intervention aimed at improving maternal sensitivity, child attachment, and behavioral outcomes for maltreated children: A randomized control trial. *Development and Psychopathology, 23*, 195–210. doi:10.1017/S0954579410000738

Murray, L., Fiori-Cowley, A., Hooper, R., & Cooper, P. (1996). The impact of postnatal depression and associated adversity on early mother-infant interactions and later infant outcome. *Child Development, 67*, 2512–2526. doi:10.2307/1131637

NICHD Early Child Care Research Network. (2000). Factors associated with fathers' caregiving activities and sensitivity with young children. *Journal of Family Psychology, 14*, 200–219. doi:10.1037//D893-3200.14.2.200

NICHD Early Child Care Research Network. (2006). Infant-mother attachment classification: Risk and protection in relation to changing maternal caregiving quality. *Developmental Psychology, 42*, 38–58. doi:10.1037/0012-1649.42.1.38

Oppenheim, D., Koren-Karie, N., Dolev, S., & Yirmiya, N. (2012). Maternal sensitivity mediates the link between maternal insightfulness/resolution and child-mother attachment: The case of children with Autism Spectrum Disorder. *Attachment & Human Development, 14,* 567–584. doi:10.1080/14616734.2012.727256

Oppenheimer, C. W., Hankin, B. L., Jenness, J. L., Young, J. F., & Smolen, A. (2013). Observed positive parenting behaviors and youth genotype: Evidence for gene-environment correlations and moderation by parent personality traits. *Development and Psychopathology, 25,* 175–191. doi:10.1017/S0954579412000983

Owen, M. T. (1992). *The NICHD study of early child care mother–infant interaction scales.* Unpublished manuscript, Timberlawn Psychiatric Research Foundation, Dallas, TX.

Pederson, D. R., & Moran, G. (1995). Appendix B: Maternal behavior Q-set. *Monographs of the Society for Research in Child Development, 60*(2–3), 247–254.

Pederson, D. R., Moran, G., & Bento, S. (1999). *Maternal behaviour Q-sort.* London, ON: University of Western Ontario.

Pederson, D. R., Moran, G., Sitko, C., Campbell, K., Ghesquire, K., & Acton, H. (1990). Maternal sensitivity and the security of infant-mother attachment: A Q-sort study. *Child Development, 61,* 1974–1983. doi:10.1111/j.1467-8624.1990.tb03579.x

Posada, G., Jacobs, A., Carbonell, O. A., Alzate, G., Bustamante, L. R., & Arenas, A. (1999). Maternal care and attachment security in ordinary and emergency contexts. *Developmental Psychology, 35,* 1379–1388. doi:10.1037//0012-1649.35.6.1379

Posada, G., Kaloustian, G., Richmond, M. K., & Moreno, A. J. (2007). Maternal secure base support and preschoolers' secure base behavior in natural environments. *Attachment & Human Development, 9,* 393–411. doi:10.1080/14616730701712316

Ramchandani, P. G., Domoney, J., Sethna, V., Psychogiou, L., Vlachos, H., & Murray, L. (2013). Do early father-infant interactions predict the onset of externalizing behaviours in young children? Findings from a longitudinal cohort study. *Journal of Child Psychology and Psychiatry, 54,* 56–64. doi:10.1111/j.1469-7610.2012.02583.x

Ravn, I. H., Smith, L., Lindemann, R., Smeby, N. A., Kyno, N. M., Bunch, E. H., & Sandvik, L. (2011). Effect of early intervention on social interaction between mothers and preterm infants at 12 months of age: A randomized controlled trial. *Infant Behavior and Development, 34,* 215–225. doi:10.1016/j.infbeh.2010.11.004

Salomonsson, B., & Sandell, R. (2011). A randomized controlled trial of mother-infant psychoanalytic treatment: I. Outcomes on self-report questionnaires and external ratings. *Infant Mental Health Journal, 32,* 207–231. doi:10.1002/imhj.20291

Scher, A. (2001). Mother-child interaction and sleep regulation in one-year-olds. *Infant Mental Health Journal, 22,* 515–528. doi:10.1002/imhj.1015

Schoppe-Sullivan, S. J., Diener, M. L., Mangelsdorf, S. C., Brown, G. L., McHale, J. L., & Frosch, C. A. (2006). Attachment and sensitivity in family context: The roles of parent and infant gender. *Infant and Child Development, 15,* 367–385. doi:10.1002/icd.449

Seifer, R., Schiller, M., Sameroff, A. J., Resnick, S., & Riordan, K. (1996). Attachment, maternal sensitivity, and infant temperament during the first year of life. *Developmental Psychology, 32,* 12–25. doi:10.1037//0012-1649.32.1.12

Selcuk, E., Günaydin, G., Sumer, N., Harma, M., Salman, S., Hazan, C., ... Ozturk, A. (2010). Self-reported romantic attachment style predicts everyday maternal caregiving behavior at home. *Journal of Research in Personality, 44,* 544–549. doi:10.1016/j.jrp.2010.05.007

Shah, P. E., Clements, M., & Poehlmann, J. (2011). Maternal resolution of grief after preterm birth: Implications for attachment security. *Pediatrics, 127,* 284–292. doi:10.1542/peds.2010–1080

Shannon, J. D., Tamis-LeMonda, C. S., & Cabrera, N. (2006). Fathering in infancy: Mutuality and stability between 8 and 16 months. *Parenting, 6,* 167–188. doi:10.1080/15295192.2006.9681304

Shannon, J. D., Tamis-LeMonda, C. S., London, K., & Cabrera, N. (2002). Beyond rough and tumble: Low-income fathers' interactions and children's cognitive development at 24 months. *Parenting, 2,* 77–104. doi:10.1207/S15327922PAR0202_01

Spangler, G., Johann, M., Ronai, Z., & Zimmerman, P. (2009). Genetic and environmental influence on attachment disorganization. *Journal of Child Psychology and Psychiatry, 50,* 952–961. doi:10.1111/j.1469-7610.2008.02054.x

Spinrad, T. L., Eisenberg, N., Silva, K. M., Eggum, N. D., Reiser, M., Edwards, A., ... Gaertner, B. M. (2012). Longitudinal relations among maternal behaviors, effortful control and young children. *Developmental Psychology, 48,* 552–566. doi:10.1037/a0025898

Stams, G.-J. J. M., Juffer, F., Van IJzendoorn, M. H., & Hoksbergen, R. A. C. (2001). Attachment-based intervention in adoptive families in infancy and children's development at age 7: Two follow-up studies. *British Journal of Developmental Psychology, 19*, 159–180. doi:10.1348/026151001166010

Stein, A., Craske, M. G., Lehtonen, A., Harvey, A., Savage-McGlynn, E., Davies, B., … Counsell, N. (2012). Maternal cognitions and mother-infant interaction in postnatal depression and generalized anxiety disorder. *Journal of Abnormal Psychology, 121,* 795–809. doi:10.1037/a0026847

Stolk, M. N., Mesman, J., Van Zeijl, J., Alink, L. R. A., Bakermans-Kranenburg, M. J., Van IJzendoorn, M. H., … Koot, H. M. (2008). Early parenting intervention aimed at maternal sensitivity and discipline: A process evaluation. *Journal of Community Psychology, 36*, 781–797. doi:10.1002/jcop.20280

Tomlinson, M., Cooper, P., & Murray, L. (2005). The mother-infant relationship and infant attachment in a South African peri-urban settlement. *Child Development, 76*, 1044–1054. doi:10.1111/j.1467-8624.2005.00896.x

True, M. M., Pisani, L., & Oumar, F. (2001). Infant-mother attachment among the Dogon of Mali. *Child Development, 72*, 1451–1466.

Valenzuela, M. (1997). Maternal sensitivity in a developing society: The context of urban poverty and infant chronic undernutrition. *Developmental Psychology, 33,* 845–855. doi:10.1037//0012-1649.33.5.845

Van IJzendoorn, M. H., Rutgers, A. H., Bakermans-Kranenburg, M. J., Swinkels, S. H. N., Van Daalen, E., Dietz, C., … van Engeland, H. (2007). Parental sensitivity and attachment in children with Autism Spectrum Disorder: Comparison with children with mental retardation, with language delays, and with typical development. *Child Development, 78*, 597–608. doi:10.1111/j.1467-8624.2007.01016.x

Vereijken, C., Riksen-Walraven, J. M., & Kondo-Ikemura, K. (1997). Maternal sensitivity and infant attachment security in Japan: A longitudinal study. *International Journal of Behavioral Development, 21*, 35–49.

Ward, M. J., & Carlson, E. A. (1995). Associations among adult attachment representations, maternal sensitivity, and infant-mother attachment in a sample of adolescent mothers. *Child Development, 66,* 69–79. doi:10.2307/1131191

Whipple, N., Bernier, A., & Mageau, G. A. (2011). A dimensional approach to maternal attachment state of mind: Relations to maternal sensitivity and maternal autonomy support. *Developmental Psychology, 47,* 396–403. doi:10.1037/a0021310

Yovsi, R. D., Kaertner, J., Keller, H., Lohaus, A. (2009). Maternal interactional quality in two cultural environments German middle class and Cameroonian rural mothers. *Journal of Cross-Cultural Psychology, 40*(4), 701–707. doi:10.1177/0022022109335065

Parental synchrony and nurturance as targets in an attachment based intervention: building upon Mary Ainsworth's insights about mother–infant interaction

Kristin Bernard, EB Meade and Mary Dozier

Department of Psychology, University of Delaware, Newark, DE, USA

As an astute observer of parent–infant interaction, Mary Ainsworth described and assessed facets of maternal sensitivity, including responsiveness to conditions of infant distress and non-distress. This paper considers the importance of distinguishing between parental sensitivity to children's distress cues (which we refer to as nurturance) and parental sensitivity to children's non-distress cues (which we refer to as synchrony). Observations of parents in our intervention, Attachment and Biobehavioral Catch-up (ABC), have led us to believe that distress and non-distress represent distinct contexts in which parents can be differentially sensitive or insensitive in responding. Thus, we have conceptualized nurturance and synchrony as distinct targets of the ABC intervention and, in deciding how to assess parental sensitivity, we have chosen measures that distinguish between nurturance and synchrony. This paper describes the strengths and weaknesses of different approaches we have taken to assess parental sensitivity, including diary methodology that we developed for assessing parental nurturance and global measures that we have used for assessing parental synchrony. Finally, a frequency-based coding system is described that we developed for assessing parental nurturance and synchrony from videotaped intervention sessions.

Following Bowlby's assertions that attachment is shaped by real experience, Mary Ainsworth sought to identify specific characteristics of parenting behavior that were relevant for mother–infant attachment. In her study in Uganda, Ainsworth immersed herself in the lives of 28 babies and their families and recorded detailed observations about everything that seemed to matter: feeding, sleeping arrangements, shared caregiving, quantity of contact with caregivers, etc. (Ainsworth, 1967). Amongst the range of variables she examined, Ainsworth believed that the *quality* of mother–infant interactions was critical to distinguishing between infants who were securely attached from those who were insecurely attached. In her Baltimore study, Ainsworth and colleagues further examined individual differences in the quality of maternal care by visiting 26 families 18 times each (for 4 hours each time) within each baby's first year (Ainsworth, Blehar, Waters, & Wall, 1978). Based on these intensive observations, Ainsworth defined four scales describing facets of maternal responsiveness that she believed to be important to mother–infant attachment: sensitivity-insensitivity, cooperation-interference, availability-ignoring, and acceptance-rejection. Indeed, these global scales proved to be remarkably predictive of infants' attachment classifications. Ainsworth's conceptualization of these key aspects of maternal behavior continues to be central to how we, as a field, measure maternal sensitivity and design interventions that enhance maternal sensitivity.

Since Ainsworth's seminal studies, researchers have continued to examine maternal sensitivity as a key construct. Within the field of developmental psychology, however, we have struggled to consistently demonstrate the strong predictive validity of maternal sensitivity that Ainsworth reported, perhaps in part due to differences in practices for measurement. Ainsworth's findings that maternal sensitivity plays a critical role in predicting attachment quality became an important part of attachment theory when Bowlby incorporated them into his trilogy (1969/1982, 1973). In a meta-analysis of 66 such studies, deWolff and van IJzendoorn (1997) were able to confirm significant associations between parental sensitivity and attachment security, but the correlations were inconsistent and considerably more moderate overall than those reported by Ainsworth. No single measure or approach represented in the meta-analysis stood out as stronger than others in its predictive validity for attachment security. A number of factors may explain why parental sensitivity did not consistently emerge as a strong predictor of attachment quality (see Cassidy et al., 2005; Lindhiem, Bernard, & Dozier, 2011; Pederson, Gleason, Moran, & Bento, 1998). Although we have a gold-standard tool for assessing attachment security (i.e., Strange Situation: Ainsworth et al., 1978), parental sensitivity measures vary the amount of time used for observations, the nature of the tasks (e.g., play, teaching, distress), the instruments used for coding (e.g., global rating scales, micro-level frequency counts, Q-sort methodology), and the characteristics of the child and dyad (e.g., child age).

Sensitivity as a multi-dimensional construct

In Ainsworth's original scale for sensitivity vs. insensitivity to the baby's signals, she defined sensitivity as "the mother's ability to perceive and to interpret accurately the signals and communications implicit in her infant's behavior and, given this understanding, to respond to them appropriately and promptly" (Ainsworth et al., 1978). Ainsworth's definition of maternal sensitivity takes into account how the mother responds to children's signals of distress as well as social cues across contexts of feeding, play, and other daily experiences.

In line with this definition, our lab developed an intervention program that aims to enhance parental sensitivity across these contexts. In our efforts to coach parents to respond more sensitively to children's cues and to measure intervention effectiveness, we have found value in distinguishing parents' sensitivity to children's distress from sensitivity to non-distress. These constructs, which we will refer to as "nurturance" and "synchrony," respectively, are likely separable, may be predicted by different variables, and may show differential effects on children's outcomes (Leerkes, Blankson, & O'Brien, 2009; McElwain & Booth-LaForce, 2006). For example, bids for reassurance from a distressed child may trigger different issues from parents than bids to engage in play. In particular, soothing a distressed child is likely to call up a parent's own attachment experiences to a greater extent than responding to a non-distressed child. We expect that attachment state of mind, or the way in which adults organize and interpret attachment-related experiences, is especially relevant to the way in which parents respond to their child's distress. Attachment state of mind is assessed with the Adult Attachment Interview (George, Kaplan, & Main, 1996; Hesse, 2008). In our view, autonomous parents may be able to respond in a more nurturing way to children's distress than non-autonomous parents. Attachment state of mind may not be especially relevant, however, to parents' ability to respond in synchronous ways to children's non-distress behaviors.

This paper suggests that using definitions of sensitivity that distinguish between sensitivity in distress and non-distress situations will enhance our ability to clearly target these behaviors in early interventions and to delineate potential mechanisms of intervention effectiveness. Below, we define nurturance and synchrony, presenting a rationale for why these constructs represent unique dimensions of parental sensitivity. After describing each construct, we report our attempts at measuring it in this paper. Next, we describe how distinguishing nurturance and synchrony has been useful in our attachment-based intervention (i.e., Attachment and Biobehavioral Catch-up [ABC]: Dozier & The Infant-Caregiver Project Lab, 2012) aimed at enhancing parental responsiveness to infants and toddlers. This paper presents case examples depicting parents with differential strength in the two dimensions of sensitivity, and then describes a frequency-based coding system that was developed to measure these dimensions within intervention sessions.

Nurturance

We define nurturance in terms of how parents respond when children are distressed. Ainsworth et al. (1978) emphasized the importance of the caregiver serving a protective role in the face of threat or danger. Nurturance, as we have defined it, describes the parent's role in providing a "haven of safety" (Bowlby, 1969/1982). Some have argued for a narrow definition of attachment, in which parental protection is the critical component for promoting a secure parent–child relationship (e.g., Goldberg, Grusec, & Jenkins, 1999). Many studies, however, examine parental responsiveness more generally, without differentiating between sensitive responsiveness in distress and non-distress contexts.

Parental nurturance carries particular relevance to children's developing expectations of their parents' availability during times of distress. Using data from the NICHD Study of Early Child Care, McElwain and Booth-LaForce (2006) compared maternal sensitivity to infant distress versus maternal sensitivity to non-distress cues (both coded during the same play interaction task) in predicting attachment security in the Strange Situation. Greater sensitivity to distress at 6 months, but not sensitivity to non-distress, was associated with increased odds of a secure attachment classification at 15 months. Similarly, Leerkes (2011) rated maternal sensitivity in different contexts when infants were 6 months old, using two distress tasks (i.e., fear task using loud remote-control truck, frustration task using arm-restraint procedure) and a non-arousing free play task. Only maternal sensitivity during the distressing tasks predicted attachment security in the Strange Situation. Thus, nurturance to children's distress may be especially important in promoting children's attachment security.

Assessing nurturance

Measuring responsiveness to children's distress can be challenging because it requires very long observation periods allowing multiple occasions for parental response to distress, or, alternatively, a context or paradigm that elicits distress. In her work developing the Strange Situation (Ainsworth et al., 1978), Ainsworth discovered a context that reliably elicits infant distress and reveals stable individual differences in how infants use their parents to manage their distress. The Strange Situation has been a powerful paradigm that made assessment of infant attachment readily accessible. It is hard to imagine a more powerful paradigm.

In our lab, we were interested in changes in attachment behaviors and parent responsiveness during the first weeks and months of a foster placement. Given that the Strange Situation cannot be repeated at frequent intervals because the infant's response likely changes by virtue of repeated exposure and/or it would be ethically questionable, we had to develop an alternative approach to measuring attachment behavior. Thus, we developed a diary method to assess children's response to distress and parent responsiveness on a more frequent basis than is possible with the Strange Situation. Parents' reports tend to be systematically biased (De Los Reyes & Kazdin, 2005; Youngstrom, Izard, & Ackerman, 1999), as are self-reports of generalized behaviors and attitudes (Schwarz, 1999). It was expected that a diary methodology would diminish the influence of such biases if parents were asked to describe *specific* examples from each day.

The Parent Attachment Diary (Dozier & Stovall, 1997) was designed to capture children's attachment behaviors during times of distress and parents' subsequent responses. Parents are asked to complete a diary entry at the end of each day, in which they record incidents when the child is hurt, frightened, and separated. After describing the incident in a brief narrative, the parent completes a checklist of attachment behaviors displayed by the child (e.g., "Cried," "Acted as if nothing was wrong"). Parents record the sequence of the child's behaviors by numbering them in the order that they occur. Parents also record their own behavioral response to the child's distress. In our lab, we used the Parent Attachment Diary for assessing the development of attachment behaviors in new foster care placements (Stovall-McClough & Dozier, 2004). We found that during the first 2 months of a new foster placement, infants placed at younger ages with foster parents assessed as autonomous during the AAI showed higher levels of secure behavior, less avoidant behavior, and more consistent attachment strategies, relative to infants placed with non-autonomous foster parents (Stovall-McClough & Dozier, 2004). Further, we (Stovall & Dozier, 2000) were able to plot the trajectory of change over time in children's attachment behaviors.

Despite some strengths of this diary methodology, we increasingly became concerned about the extent to which reporting of children's attachment behaviors and parents' responses were affected systematically by parental biases. Our concerns were based primarily on anecdotal evidence suggesting that parents were biased in their observations of children's distress. As part of our intervention, for example, we show parents video clips of children during a separation episode and reunion episode of the Strange Situation. Parents vary widely in their interpretations of children's responses, with some noting that a crying child was "not really upset" and others recognizing even subtle signs of child distress, such as diminished quality of play. As we considered the potential biases involved in reporting of attachment situations, we were most concerned that responses were filtered through the lens of the parent's attachment state of mind. For example, an autonomous parent, who is comfortable with her child's distress and values her role in providing support, may be more likely than a non-autonomous parent to report her child's displays of distress and also her subsequent attempts to provide nurturance. In contrast, a parent who has a dismissive state of mind may not interpret her child as in distress even though others would not share that impression. In the diary, she might indicate that her child "appeared fine" after falling down a step and that she did not then do anything to help the child. Thus, findings from our diary studies that indicate that children of dismissing parents show more avoidant behaviors than children of autonomous parents following potentially distressing situations (Stovall-McClough & Dozier, 2004) could be the result of avoidance among such children, or a tendency of dismissing parents to under-report distress. The conflation of these two factors makes this diary method problematic.

In view of the potential biases of self-report, we subsequently decided to rely more on observational measures. For example, we have used the Maternal Behavior Q-Sort (MBQS: Pederson, Moran, & Bento, 1998) in order to assess maternal sensitivity following observations. Ninety items (or 25 in the shortened version: Tarabulsy et al., 2009) that describe various aspects of maternal behavior are sorted into categories from least descriptive to most descriptive of the parent. The items of the resulting forced distribution sorting are scored according to their placement. Scores are correlated with a criterion sort that describes the prototypically sensitive parent. The measure is designed for use following observations during which the parent's attention is divided, usually lasting 1–2 hours. For example, a number of studies have used the Maternal Behavior Q-Sort during research visits in families' homes, while parents are completing questionnaires or being interviewed (van IJzendoorn, Vereijken, Bakermans-Kranenburg, & Riksen-Walraven, 2004). The added challenge on the infant's ability to access the parent and the parent's ability to monitor and respond to child cues in the face of competing demands is expected to enhance the opportunity to observe variability in sensitivity. We have used the 25-item shortened version of the Maternal Behavior Q-Sort as a way to measure global responsiveness across intervention sessions, and found it to work well for this purpose. Specifically, coders observed maternal behavior during videotaped intervention sessions, which lasted approximately 1 hour each. After watching and taking detailed notes of each videotaped intervention session, two independent coders sorted MBQS items and overall sensitivity scores were averaged. In a sample of high-risk mother–infant dyads participating in a 10-session control (non-attachment based) intervention, we examined whether increasing numbers of observations (i.e., more sessions) led to larger effect sizes between MBQS scores and constructs of interest. As expected, we found that as the number of observations increased, the association between state of mind and sensitivity increased (from $r = .37$ to $r = .54$) (Lindhiem et al., 2011).

However, as we have become increasingly interested in distinguishing between parental sensitivity to distress versus sensitivity to non-distress cues, one of the issues with relying on the Maternal Behavior Q-Sort is that it does not distinguish between nurturance and synchrony. Items that describe the prototypically sensitive parent relate both to how parents respond to distress (e.g., "Responds accurately to signals of distress") as well as how parents respond to non-distress cues, such as through contingent responsiveness (e.g., "Builds on the focus of baby's attention"). Although studies have found the Maternal Behavior Q-Sort to be predictive of attachment security, it is not fully satisfactory in helping us parse potentially unique aspects of nurturance versus synchrony.

The challenge of measuring nurturance as a parent's responses to child distress is that distress is a relatively low frequency behavior in typical observation contexts, such as free play, and even in longer home observations. Thus, most recently, we have begun to measure nurturance in situations that elicit distress. For example, as part of a recent study, we pricked preschool-age children's fingers to collect blood spot samples. Consistent with our expectations that this was a good context for assessing nurturance, analyses examining whether parents' attachment state of mind predicted nurturance revealed a large effect size (Simons, Bernard, & Dozier, 2013), with autonomous parents showing higher levels of nurturance than dismissing parents.

Although we have explored the possibility of coding nurturance during the Strange Situation, as others have done (e.g., Behrens, Parker, & Haltigan, 2011), we are cautious for several reasons. First, the Strange Situation instructions themselves are intended to reduce variability in parents' behavior (i.e., by limiting responsiveness). Second, differences in children's attachment strategies are associated with differences in the likelihood that they show distress. For example, an avoidant child is less likely than other children to show distress, perhaps further contributing to how responsive a parent is likely to appear. Thus, opportunities to respond to distress may vary systematically by attachment classification. Finally, if our interest is to examine the association between parental nurturance and infant attachment, it is not ideal to assess both within the same context. Our attempts to identify contexts in which we can specifically assess nurturance parallel efforts by other researchers who distinguish between sensitivity to distress versus sensitivity to non-distress (e.g., Leerkes, Weaver, & O'Brien, 2012).

Our frequency-based coding system, described in more detail in a later section (Evaluating nurturance and synchrony through In the Moment coding), involves coding nurturing parental responses to episodes of child distress that occur naturally during home intervention sessions. Relative to methods that rely on global sensitivity ratings in contexts that may or may not involve child distress, we expect that our frequency-based coding system will provide a stronger measurement of nurturance as it considers how a parent responds to each behavioral indication of child distress as it occurs during an intervention session.

Synchrony

We define synchrony as the parent(s) following the child's lead in interactions, or the parent(s) responding to the child's behavior in ways that maintain the child's perspective and goals, referred to by Blehar, Lieberman, and Ainsworth (1977) as "contingent responsiveness." Shonkoff and Bales (2011) use a "serve and return" metaphor, illustrating the different roles for the parent and child in synchronous interaction, with the child serving and the parent returning the serve. Our definition of synchrony focuses on whether the parent contingently responds to ("returns") a child's bid ("serve"). We believe that this specificity allows us to most effectively target and measure opportunities for synchronous behavior during intervention sessions. However, we recognize that parents may initiate interactions at times, and these initiations are not necessarily incompatible with ongoing synchronous interactions.

Parental synchrony has been linked to a host of physiological and behavioral regulatory outcomes, with early co-regulation of physiology hypothesized as a mediator (Feldman, 2012). Although the field of developmental psychology has conceptualized synchrony in various ways, including as a quality of the dyad, here we highlight work that measured synchrony as parental contingent responsiveness to non-distress cues and linked it to regulatory outcomes. For example, Feldman, Greenbaum, and Yirmiya (1999) found that "infant-leads-mother-follows" synchrony at 3 months was predictive of child self-control at 2 years of age, measured in compliance and delay tasks. The time lag between infant behavior and mother response at 3 months served as an additional predictor of self-control in this study. Bornstein and Tamis-LeMonda (1997) found that maternal responsiveness to non-distress cues at 5 months, measured as the proportion of mother responses to infant non-distress signals, predicted attention span at 13 months, whereas maternal responsiveness to distress did not. Recent findings from our lab even suggest that children in high-risk environments may be buffered from telomere shortening, a marker of cellular aging, if they have mothers who interact synchronously with them (Asok, Bernard, Roth, Rosen, & Dozier, 2013). Thus, whereas nurturance seems particularly important in children's development of attachment security, parent synchrony, in contrast, may be particularly influential in children's development of behavioral and physiological regulation.

Assessing synchrony

Currently, our lab assesses synchrony in ways that relate to Ainsworth's conceptual definition of maternal sensitivity (Ainsworth & Bell, 1969; Blehar et al., 1977). Most overlapping between our and Ainsworth's conceptualizations of this construct is the focus on the attunement and timing/pacing of the mother's responses to her child's social cues. However, Ainsworth's conceptualization of sensitivity is more inclusive than our conceptualization of synchrony as she also considered mothers' responsiveness to distress cues.

We use rating scales from the NICHD's Observational Record of the Caregiving Environment (ORCE: NICHD ECCRN, 1996) to assess various qualities of parent interaction during semi-structured play activities. NICHD studies often use the ORCE to create a composite construct of sensitivity, taking into account several scales, including positive regard and reverse-coded intrusiveness. To assess the specific construct of synchrony, we use the ORCE sensitivity/responsiveness to non-distress scale, and to assess constructs of non-synchrony, we use the intrusiveness scale and the detachment/disengagement scale. The sensitivity/responsiveness to non-distress scale closely matches our definition of synchrony, as it focuses on how the parent "follows the child's lead." The ORCE scales represent global ratings of how the parent tends to respond to specific child behaviors. Although the scales are 4-point scales, we have adapted them to allow greater variability with 5-point ratings. A low score (1) on the sensitivity/responsiveness to non-distress scale reflects a parent who rarely responds appropriately to child cues, and may be predominately detached or intrusive. A high score (5) on the scale reflects a parent who nearly always responds contingently to the child's gestures, vocalizations, and expressions, and maintains "child-centered" interactions. This description of a highly sensitive parent closely matches phrasing used by Ainsworth in her conceptualization: "attuned to B's signals; and responds to them promptly and appropriately," "she makes her responses temporally contingent upon B's signals and communications" (Ainsworth et al., 1978). We have used the ORCE scales to measure parent behavior in various play contexts, including a three box task, and play across ages with toys geared to different developmental levels. We have found preliminary evidence that the scales are sensitive to intervention effects (Dozier, Meade, Wallin, & Bernard, 2013; Wallin, Dozier, Bernard, & Meade, 2013).

Constructs inversely related to synchrony include intrusiveness and detached/unresponsive parenting, which we also code from play interactions using the NICHD ORCE scales. Given that a parent may score low on synchrony by showing either intrusive or detached behavior, we find it useful to code these constructs separately. Intrusiveness is defined as a controlling, overstimulating interactional style in which the parent imposes his or her agenda on the child and does not modulate behavior based on the child's responses. An example of intrusive behavior would be a parent repeatedly asking the child to identify the colors or shapes of blocks, even though the child appears to be trying to build a tower with the blocks instead. Detachment is defined as an uninterested, disengaged interactional style in which the parent fails to respond to the child's bids and behaviors. Both intrusiveness and detachment reflect failures to follow the child's lead in synchronous ways. These conceptualizations of intrusiveness and detachment are similar to Ainsworth's scales of interference (vs. cooperation) and ignoring and neglecting (vs. accessibility), respectively.

Our frequency-based coding system, described in more detail in a later section (Evaluating nurturance and synchrony through In the Moment coding), involves coding parental synchrony as it occurs naturally during home intervention sessions. This provides a complementary method to assessing synchrony during a structured play task, as it captures how the parent interacts with the child when faced with competing demands (e.g., conversation with parent coach).

Attachment and Biobehavioral Catch-up Intervention

"In the Moment" coaching: nurturance and synchrony

As mentioned previously, our rationale for distinguishing between nurturance and synchrony has been driven by experiences with our intervention program. The Attachment and Biobehavioral Catch-up Intervention (ABC: Dozier & The Infant-Caregiver Project Lab, 2012) was developed to target the needs of infants and toddlers who experience early adversity, such as placement in foster care or living with neglecting birth parents. We have found significant ABC intervention effects on both attachment (lower rates of disorganized attachments: Bernard et al., 2012) and biological and behavioral regulation (e.g., more normative diurnal cortisol slope: Bernard, Dozier, Bick, & Gordon, 2013; greater cognitive flexibility: Lewis-Morrarty, Dozier, Bernard, Terraciano, & Moore, 2012).

The ABC intervention is a manualized, 10-session program delivered by a coach in families' homes, and videorecorded with a stationary camera. We see the intervention as following from Mary Ainsworth's seminal work on maternal sensitivity. Two of the primary intervention targets include increasing nurturing behavior in response to children's distress cues and increasing synchronous behavior in response to children's non-distress cues. The primary method of enhancing these behavioral responses is through providing "In the Moment" comments. Opportunities for synchronous or nurturing responses serve as triggers for parent coach comments. The parent coach is expected to comment when such opportunities for nurturance or synchrony occur, highlighting specifically how the parent responded to the child (e.g., "He started to cry and you reached out to pick him up"), labeling the intervention target (e.g., "That's a great example of providing him with nurturance"), and linking the parent's behavior to possible child outcomes (e.g., "That is letting him know that he can trust you when he's upset"). When parents fail to recognize, or respond inappropriately to, opportunities for synchronous or nurturing behavior, the parent coach is expected to support the parent in engaging in synchronous or nurturing behaviors, even though these behaviors may come less naturally to the parent (e.g., "He looks pretty upset. This seems like one of those times when he may need your reassurance").

This In the Moment coaching is expected to make the behavioral targets of the intervention very clear to the parents and support parents in engaging in these behaviors. Thus, In the Moment commenting is similar to video feedback, which we and others (e.g., Circle of Security: Hoffman, Marvin, Cooper, & Powell, 2006) also use to provide feedback about behavior to parents. However, In the Moment comments differ in their frequency, as they are expected to occur at a rate of at least once per minute during the session, and their transactional "in the moment" nature, as they often result in cascades of positive parent behaviors and additional comments. In this respect, In the Moment comments support parents in practicing target behaviors during intervention sessions, and result in increased parental comfort and ease engaging in these behaviors. Comments about parents' positive behaviors vastly outnumber comments about parents' negative behaviors, leading parents to feel effective in their parenting and develop strong rapport with the parent coach. The comments resemble the live coaching of other interventions for parents and children (e.g., Parent Child Interaction Therapy: McNeil & Hembree-Kigin, 1995/2011).

As we have worked to enhance this In the Moment coaching component of the intervention, we have increasingly come to realize the importance of being specific in how we conceptualize and comment on parents' behavior. Specificity, and distinguishing between synchrony and nurturance, allows parent coaches and parents to communicate clearly about how to respond to children in situations of distress and non-distress. Anecdotally, we see that parents who demonstrate strengths in providing nurturance do not necessarily show strengths in synchronous interactions, and vice versa. Although we do not yet have data to examine the frequency of such discrepancies, our current methodology of differentially assessing nurturance and synchrony will allow us to examine this in the future. Here we describe two case examples that help illustrate the distinction.

Case example 1: nurturance as a strength

Joanne was a high-risk birth parent identified by Child Protective Services due to risk of neglect. She was 17 years old and living with her mother when we started seeing her for the ABC intervention. During the first session, Joanne held her 12-month-old baby Arianna in her lap for the full hour. When Arianna fussed, Joanne readjusted her position and quietly whispered, "You okay?" Her responses to Arianna's distress were well timed, and Arianna was easily soothed by her mother. The parent trainer was able to repeatedly point out how nurturing Joanne was to her child's cues of distress. In subsequent sessions, Joanne's nurturing behavior continued, but it became clear that Joanne was less comfortable during interactions that called for her to follow Arianna's lead in play. For example, when playing with a book with pull-out shapes, Joanne asked Arianna questions about the content repeatedly and went at her own pace. For example, she asked Arianna, "Which one is the blue one? Which one is the cat? Oh, you know that. Point to it." She allowed Arianna to pick up and chew on the shapes, but did little to respond contingently to her actions. Throughout the remaining sessions, the parent coach helped Joanne notice opportunities to respond to Arianna in synchronous ways. The parent coach made suggestions about how Joanne could comment on Arianna's behaviors, respond to her vocalizations, and imitate her actions and expressions. Gradually, and with much practice and supportive feedback, Joanne became more comfortable following Arianna's cues.

Case example 2: synchrony as a strength

Donna was a foster parent who had 16-month-old Shawn placed in her care shortly before starting the intervention sessions. Although Shawn did not cry frequently during early sessions, it was clear that Donna struggled to respond to Shawn's cues of distress. For example, during session 1, Shawn tripped over a toy, fell down, and continued playing seemingly unaffected; Donna glanced at Shawn and said "You're okay!" failing to acknowledge that Shawn may have been hurt. During discussions, Donna reported that Shawn "hardly ever cries," noting that "he is a good boy." When asked about her attempts to soothe him, Donna stated that she simply runs through all of his possible needs – "wet diaper, hungry, tired" – until something works. Taken together, her responses suggested that Donna might not easily recognize or be comfortable attending to Shawn's emotional needs. In the subsequent session, there were multiple opportunities to observe Donna's response to Shawn's distress. An older sibling repeatedly took toys from Shawn and played roughly with him, causing Shawn to fuss more frequently. In one instance, Donna said, "Oh stop it – be a big boy," and another time offered items to distract his attention.

She commented to the parent coach, "He's so spoiled." Although Donna struggled to behave in nurturing ways, she was quite attentive and synchronous in non-distress interactions. During conversations with the parent coach, Donna interrupted frequently to respond to Shawn's bids for her attention; she imitated his sounds, took toys as he handed them to her, and clapped her hands as he looked at her with excitement. The parent coach enthusiastically supported Donna's ease with interacting synchronously by using frequent In the Moment comments to talk about these interactions. Given that Donna struggled more with nurturance and given that opportunities for nurturance occurred less frequently than opportunities for synchrony, the parent coach looked for every opportunity during sessions to address this. Even minor fusses that occurred once or twice during the session were used as opportunities to practice how to respond, and celebrate Donna' progress. Throughout the remaining sessions, Donna became more aware of her automatic ways of responding to distress, and she was supported in beginning to respond in a more sensitive manner.

Notably, some parents show strengths in both forms of sensitivity, whereas some struggle with nurturance, synchrony, or both. For this reason, we have found it critical to define these behaviors clearly for our parent coaches as well as for parents. In order to do this, we have developed a measure that allows us to assess nurturance and synchrony behaviorally through frequency-based coding of intervention sessions, which we describe next.

Evaluating nurturance and synchrony through In the Moment coding

In the Moment coaching is considered a key component of the ABC intervention. In order to assess the fidelity of the intervention, we also developed a frequency-based coding system. Coders watch the video-taped intervention sessions in our laboratory and record each opportunity for nurturance or synchrony observed in a portion of the session, as well as the parent coach's response to each behavior (Meade & Dozier, 2012).

We also found In the Moment coding of video-clips from taped sessions to be a unique way to review and measure parent behavior. Coders are required to identify each intervention-relevant behavior as it occurs, which we consider to be a micro-analytic approach to the parent behaviors we target. Coders evaluate each sequential behavior separately and separate the components of mixed behaviors (e.g., picking a crying child up and patting his back, while saying "What are you crying for? You're a big boy"). One benefit to this micro-analytic approach is that patterns and frequencies of parent behaviors can be assessed; for example, two parents rated at the midpoint of a global scale of synchrony (indicating a mix of synchronous and non-synchronous behaviors) may differ greatly in the frequency in which they engage in these behaviors. Sequential coding of events can capture patterns of parent behavior that can be used to tailor subsequent intervention sessions to a parent's specific need; for example, if a parent alternates repeatedly between synchrony and non-synchrony, this pattern may suggest to the parent coach that the parent is unaware of the difference between the two types of behaviors, and may need more support in recognizing this difference.

Assessing parents' behavior from video-recorded intervention sessions at home offers several advantages. The home environment presents competing demands, including other children and adults, pets, telephones, television, and so on. Parents must also divide attention between the child and the parent coach. In this way, intervention sessions present a naturalistic environment in which to assess parent behavior. In addition, because the sessions take place in the parent's home, the parent may be more comfortable than she would be in a laboratory environment, and is more likely to behave as she usually does.

Accordingly, parents' behavior during intervention sessions varies widely, from talking exclusively with the parent coach and attending to the child only when he or she gets into trouble, to repeatedly interrupting the parent coach in order to respond to the child. Most especially, it is of greatest importance to change parental behavior in the home environment, and it is therefore critical that we assess change in this context.

Method of In the Moment coding

The In the Moment coding system assesses several aspects of parent behavior. Based on a child's behavior, coders distinguish between opportunities for synchronous versus nurturing responses. For example, a child falling down and crying would represent an opportunity for a parent to provide a nurturing response (i.e., to a distress cue), whereas a child holding up a toy to show his mother would represent an opportunity to provide a synchronous response (i.e., to a non-distress cue). Thus, the system is set up such that specific child behaviors serve as triggers for the coding of subsequent parent behaviors.

In response to distress cues, parent behaviors are scored as nurturing or non-nurturing. Behaviors that are non-nurturing are further classified as "active" non-nurturance (i.e., inappropriate response) or passive non-nurturance (i.e., absence of response). Similarly, in response to non-distress cues, parent behaviors are scored as synchronous or non-synchronous, with non-synchronous behaviors further classified as active or passive. Further description of these categories and examples are presented below. Although parent coaches do not label insensitive behaviors as "active" or "passive" when providing In the Moment feedback to parents, we decided to make this distinction in our coding system. This specificity in our coding system will allow us to examine whether active versus passive types of insensitive responses are associated with unique child outcomes, predicted by distinct parent characteristics, or differentially amenable to change.

Different instances of parent behaviors are coded on separate lines of an Excel spreadsheet, which automatically tallies the number of instances of different parent behaviors. When two parents are present in the intervention session, a specialized version of the coding sheet is used to separately tally each parent's engagement in the following behaviors. Behaviors are coded sequentially, such that any interruption in a parent behavior (e.g., talking to the parent coach, attending to another child, receiving an In the Moment comment) prompts coding on the subsequent line of the spreadsheet. The total number of parent behaviors in a 5-minute clip can range from 0 to over 30.

Synchrony

An instance of synchronous parent behavior is coded when the parent responds to the child's behavior in a contingent way. The parent may respond to a direct bid from the child, for example, giving the child a toy he was reaching for, taking a toy the child is handing to her, or repeating what the child says to her. The parent may also respond in a contingent way to what the child is doing autonomously, such as commenting on what the child is doing, or mimicking the child's manner of playing with a toy. Parent coaches would consider all of these examples as synchronous behaviors, and would label them as such when providing In the Moment feedback to the parent.

Non-synchrony

An instance of non-synchronous parent behavior is coded when the parent fails to respond to the child in a contingent way. Episodes of passive non-synchrony are distinguished from active non-synchrony. Passive non-synchrony is coded when the parent ignores a child's direct bid or takes longer than 5 seconds to respond to a child's bid. Examples of passive non-synchrony include failure to notice that the child is trying to hand the parent a toy, and responding to the child, who has said "Mama" several times in an attempt to get the parent's attention, after a lengthy delay. Passive non-synchrony is also coded when the parent fails to interact with a child who makes no bids for attention for longer than 60 seconds. We realize that this criterion may seem overly strict, considering that children sometimes engage in independent exploration for periods of time during a typical home visit. In the context of our intervention sessions, however, we encourage parents to remain responsive to their children's behaviors even while engaged in discussions with the parent coach. Parent coaches frequently pause during discussions to encourage parents to attend to their children in ways we consider synchronous, even for just a momentary check-in (e.g., commenting on a child's activity). Additionally, passive non-synchrony is coded less stringently when multiple children are present in the session, placing multiple demands on the parent's attention. When two parents are present in the session, passive non-synchrony is only coded when both parents fail to attend to the child. Importantly, we would not consider a parent insensitive for receiving occasional ratings of passive non-synchrony. Rather, we consider patterns of ratings across sessions to identify areas for improvement. If a parent is consistently being scored for passive non-synchronous behaviors, this may reflect a pattern of detached, unresponsive parenting. Thus, a parent coach would help the parent notice opportunities to attend to the child in ways that followed the child's lead.

Active non-synchrony is coded when the parent responds to the child or initiates interaction with the child in a non-contingent way. Examples of active non-synchrony include correcting the child's speech or way of playing with a toy, and introducing a new toy when the child is already engaged with a toy. Over-stimulating and physically intrusive behavior, such as tickling and poking the child, is coded as a separate category of active non-synchronous behavior. For our purposes, we code any tickling not requested by the child as active non-synchrony. This decision does not account for whether the child appears to enjoy the tickling or whether the tickling is clearly intrusive. We have observed that it can be difficult for parents and parent coaches to know when tickling becomes intrusive, particularly because children's cues may be subtle (e.g., gently turning away) or confusing (e.g., laughing when over-stimulated). Thus, our restricted definition helps parent coaches deliver a simple and clear message to parents.

Notably, there are other important constructs (e.g., autonomy support) that assess how mothers respond to their children's non-distress cues. Although these constructs may differ from our restricted conceptualization of synchrony, we do not consider them incompatible with sensitive parenting more generally. For example, autonomy support is defined as supporting children's goals in a noncontrolling manner; it is often measured in problem-solving tasks, and includes elements of scaffolding, encouragement, perspective taking, flexibility, and allowing the child to set the pace (Grolnick, Gurland, DeCourcey, & Jacob, 2002; Whipple, Bernier, & Mageau, 2011). Our conceptualization of synchrony is more restrictive than autonomy support, with scaffolding and encouragement (to do other than what the child is already doing) not considered behaviors that we would code as synchronous. For example, if a child banged blocks together and the parent said, "Oh, you're banging the blocks together," we would consider the response synchronous, whereas if she said, "Bang them harder, bang them harder" or "I'm going to put one here. What would happen if you put yours on top?" the response would not be considered synchronous (but would be considered encouraging and scaffolding, respectively, in these other systems). Our restricted focus on "synchrony," as we define it, enables us to focus on a limited number of specific, concise behavioral targets in the context of a brief intervention. Although other constructs, such as scaffolding, are compatible with Ainsworth's conceptualization of sensitivity, our very clear and specific definition of synchrony allows us to successfully train parent coaches and communicate to parents about these behaviors.

Nurturance

Nurturing behavior is coded in two types of situations: a parent response to a child's distress and a response to a child's bid for physical affection or closeness. We are not certain whether a response to a child's bid for physical affection truly belongs within the nurturance construct, given that it occurs when a child is not distressed and thus may be less related to attachment state of mind and attachment security than to other constructs. Rather, responding warmly to a bid for physical affection may instead be part of the synchrony construct. These associations remain to be tested and, in order to examine these relationships in the future, we code these two categories of nurturance separately. A nurturing response to distress is coded when the child seems hurt, sad, scared, tired, worried, or sick, and the parent shows the child that she is concerned and available. The parent's behavior may be verbal, such as asking if the child is okay, empathizing with the child's emotions, or making comforting statements like "Aww, honey, Mommy's here." The parent's behavior may also be physical, such as picking the child up, hugging or kissing the child, patting the child's back, and holding or rocking the child. A nurturing response to a child's bid for physical affection is coded when the child approaches the parent looking for physical proximity or affection, and the parent responds in a way that communicates comfort and reciprocity. Because young children sometimes use physical proximity with their parents as a means to an end (e.g., putting a hand on the parent's shoulder as a support while reaching for a toy; sitting in the parent's lap to better view and reach a computer or cell phone), a nurturing response is only coded when it seems that the child just wants to be close to the parent. In addition, we only code times when the child initiates physical affection or proximity. In response to a parent's response to a child's bid for physical affection or to a child's distress cue, the parent coach would provide In the Moment feedback specific to nurturance.

Non-nurturance

Non-nurturing behavior is coded when the parent fails to respond in a nurturing way to the child's distress. As with non-synchronous behavior, active non-nurturing behavior is distinguished from passive non-nurturing behavior. Passive non-nurturing behavior is coded when the parent fails to notice or ignores the child's distress. One example of passive non-nurturing behavior is ignoring a child's cries. Because children who have experienced early adversity do not always signal distress clearly, passive non-nurturing behavior is also coded at times when the child has a high likelihood of being hurt (e.g., falls on face, bangs head on table) but does not show signs of distress, and the parent does not respond to the event. Active non-nurturing behavior is coded when the parent responds to the child's distress in a way that rejects or expresses discomfort with the child's need to be reassured. Examples of verbal non-nurturing behaviors include statements such as, "You're fine," "You're a big boy, don't cry," "I told you not to climb on that chair," and "Ugh! Why are you so whiny today?" Parents may also engage in physical behaviors, such as attempting to distract the child with a toy, or putting a pacifier in the child's mouth without providing any other type of support. Non-nurturing behavior may be communicated simply by tone; for example, a parent may say "Shhhh" in a way that communicates that the parent wants the child to stop crying and be quiet.

Preliminary findings and future directions

Most of our work with the In the Moment coding system has involved coding 5-minute video-clips of intervention sessions, and we have found that this amount of time allows us to successfully measure synchronous interactions. In one study, we found that the number of parent synchronous behaviors increased from session 3 to session 9, and that the number of behaviors in session 9 was predicted by the frequency of parent coach comments in session 3, even when controlling for parent synchrony in session 3 (Meade & Dozier, 2012). Inter-rater reliability for synchrony was acceptable (ICC = .79) and a moderate correlation (r = .40) between synchrony in sessions 3 and 9 suggested some stability. In future work, we plan to assess test-retest reliability using assessments that are closer together in time. In addition, we plan to examine the optimal time needed for coding various behaviors, which is expected to differ for different types of parent behavior. For example, nurturing behavior occurs much less frequently than synchronous and non-synchronous behavior, and will likely require a longer amount of time coded in order to achieve high sensitivity to detecting reliable and valid differences between parents. Future work will also examine the correlation between nurturance and synchrony, and whether these constructs serve as differential predictors of attachment security and physiological/behavioral regulation, respectively, in our sample.

Conclusions

Mary Ainsworth's contributions have forever changed the landscape of developmental psychology. Her ability to observe critical features of parent–child interaction formed the basis of our current understanding of what matters regarding parental responsiveness and child attachment. We relied heavily on our observations of parent–child interactions in the context of our intervention to inform our decisions about how to measure sensitivity.

Our approach to assessing sensitivity builds upon Ainsworth's approach, in which she assessed both responsiveness to distress and non-distress cues in her conceptualization of maternal sensitivity. However, we have come to believe that nurturance and synchrony may differentially contribute to attachment and other outcomes, and have therefore pursued several methods of uniquely assessing nurturance and synchrony. Our current assessment of nurturance includes coding from observations that elicit distress, and our current assessment of synchrony includes semi-structured play interactions. In addition, we have developed a frequency-based coding system to examine nurturing behaviors and synchronous behaviors during intervention sessions. We expect this tool to be important in tailoring the intervention to the unique needs of each parent, in examining the process of change in both dimensions of sensitivity, and in uniquely predicting child outcomes. Given our multi-method approaches to examining nurturance and synchrony, we can also examine whether frequency-based coding during sessions is associated with other more global assessments outside of the intervention context, as well as with other gold-standard attachment instruments (e.g., Adult Attachment Interview and the Strange Situation). We have found it critical to be attentive to issues around defining and assessing sensitivity in ways that will optimize our ability to intervene with families and to evaluate intervention outcomes effectively.

Acknowledgements

This research was supported by National Institutes of Health Grants R01 MH052135, R01 MH074374, and R01 MH084135 to the third author (MD). We thank the children and families who participated in the research.

References

Ainsworth, M. D. S. (1967). *Infancy in Uganda*. Baltimore, MD: Johns Hopkins University.

Ainsworth, M. D. S., & Bell, S. M. (1969). Some contemporary patterns of mother-infant interaction in the feeding situation. In J. A. Ambrose (Ed.), *Stimulation in early infancy* (pp. 133–170). London: Academic Press.

Ainsworth, M. D. S., Blehar, M. C., Waters, E., & Wall, S. (1978). *Patterns of attachment: A psychological study of the strange situation*. Hillsdale, NJ: Erlbaum.

Asok, A., Bernard, K., Roth, T. L., Rosen, J. B., & Dozier, M. (2013). Parental responsiveness moderates the association between early-life stress and reduced telomere length. *Development and Psychopathology, 25*, 577–585.

Behrens, K. Y., Parker, A. C., & Haltigan, J. D. (2011). Maternal sensitivity assessed during the Strange Situation Procedure predicts child's attachment quality and reunion behaviors. *Infant Behavior Development, 34*, 378–381. doi:10.1016/j.infbeh.2011.02.007

Belsky, J., & Fearon, R. P. (2002). Early attachment security, subsequent maternal sensitivity, and later child development: Does continuity in development depend upon continuity of caregiving?. *Attachment & Human Development, 4*, 361–387. doi:10.1080/14616730210167267

Bernard, K., Dozier, M., Bick, J., & Gordon, M. K. (2013). *Normalizing diurnal cortisol production: Effects of an intervention for neglecting birth parents* (Unpublished document). University of Delaware, Newark, DE.

Bernard, K., Dozier, M., Bick, J., Lewis-Morrarty, E., Lindhiem, O., & Carlson, E. (2012). Enhancing attachment organization among maltreated infants: Results of a randomized clinical trial. *Child Development, 83*, 623–636. doi:10.1111/j.1467-8624.2011.01712.x

Blehar, M. C., Lieberman, A. F., & Ainsworth, M. D. S. (1977). Early face-to-face interaction and its relation to later infant-mother attachment. *Child Development, 48*, 182–194.

Bornstein, M. H., & Tamis-Lemonda, C. S. (1997). Maternal responsiveness and infant mental abilities: Specific predictive relations. *Infant Behavior and Development, 20*, 283–296. doi:10.1016/S0163-6383(97)90001-1

Bowlby, J. (1969/1982). *Attachment and loss: Vol. 1. Attachment*. New York, NY: Basic Books.

Bowlby, J. (1973). *Attachment and loss: Vol. 2. Separation*. New York, NY: Basic Books.

Cassidy, J., Woodhouse, S. S., Cooper, G., Hoffman, K., Powell, B., & Rodenberg, M. (2005). Examination of the precursors of infant attachment security: Implications for early intervention and intervention research. In L. Berlin, Y. Ziv, L. Amaya-Jackson, & M. T. Greenberg (Eds.), *Enhancing early attachments: Theory, research, intervention, and policy* (pp. 178–194). New York, NY: Guilford.

De Los Reyes, A., & Kazdin, A. E. (2005). Informant discrepancies in the assessment of childhood psychopathology: A critical review, theoretical framework, and recommendations for further study. *Psychological Bulletin, 131*, 483–509. doi:10.1037/0033-2909.131.4.483

deWolff, M. S., & van IJzendoorn, M. H. (1997). Sensitivity and attachment: A meta-analysis on parental antecedents of infant attachment. *Child Development, 68*, 571–591.

Dozier, M. & The Infant-Caregiver Project Lab. (2012). *Attachment and biobehavioral catch-up* (Unpublished document). University of Delaware, Newark, DE.

Dozier, M., Meade, E., Wallin, A. R., & Bernard, K. (2013, April). *Implementing an evidence-based intervention for high-risk parents in the community: The importance of model fidelity.* Paper presented at the biennial meeting of the Society for Research on Child Development (SRCD), Seattle, WA.

Dozier, M., & Stovall, K. C. 1997. *Parent attachment diary* (Unpublished manuscript). University of Delaware, Newark, DE.

Feldman, R. (2012). Bio-behavioral synchrony: A model for integrating biological and microsocial behavioral processes in the study of parenting. *Parenting, 12*, 154–164. doi:10.1080/15295192.2012.683342

Feldman, R., Greenbaum, C. W., & Yirmiya, N. (1999). Mother–infant affect synchrony as an antecedent of the emergence of self-control. *Developmental Psychology, 35*, 223. doi:10.1037/0012-1649.35.1.223

George, C., Kaplan, N., & Main, M. (1996). *Adult attachment interview* (Unpublished manuscript). University of California, Berkeley.

Goldberg, S., Grusec, J. E., & Jenkins, J. M. (1999). Confidence in protection: Arguments for a narrow definition of attachment. *Journal of Family Psychology, 13*, 475–483. doi:0.1037/0893-3200.13.4.475

Grolnick, W. S., Gurland, S. T., DeCourcey, W., & Jacob, K. (2002). Antecedents and consequences of mothers' autonomy support: An experimental investigation. *Developmental Psychology, 38*, 143–155. doi:10.1037/0012-1649.38.1.143

Hesse, E. (2008). The adult attachment interview: Protocol, method of analysis, and empirical studies. In J. Cassidy & P. R. Shaver (Eds.), *Handbook of attachment: Theory, research, and clinical applications* (2nd ed., pp. 552–598). New York, NY: Guilford.

Hoffman, K. T., Marvin, R. S., Cooper, G., & Powell, B. (2006). Changing toddlers' and preschoolers' attachment classifications: The circle of security intervention. *Journal of Consulting and Clinical Psychology, 74*, 1017–1026. doi:10.1037/0022-006X.74.6.1017

Leerkes, E. M. (2011). Maternal sensitivity during distressing tasks: A unique predictor of attachment security. *Infant Behavior and Development, 34*, 443–446. doi:10.1016/j.infbeh.2011.04.006

Leerkes, E. M., Blankson, A. N., & O'Brien, M. (2009). Differential effects of maternal sensitivity to infant distress and nondistress on social-emotional functioning. *Child Development, 80*, 762–775. doi:10.1111/j.1467-8624.2009.01296.x

Leerkes, E. M., Weaver, J. M., & O'Brien, M. (2012). Differentiating maternal sensitivity to infant distress and non-distress. *Parenting: Science and Practice, 12*, 175–184. doi:10.1080/15295192.2012.683353

Lewis-Morrarty, E., Dozier, M., Bernard, K., Terraciano, S., & Moore, S. (2012). Cognitive flexibility and theory of mind outcomes among foster children: Preschool follow-up results of a randomized clinical trial. *Journal of Adolescent Health, 52*, S17–S22. doi:10.1016/j.jadohealth.2012.05.005

Lindhiem, O., Bernard, K., & Dozier, M. (2011). Maternal sensitivity: Within-person variability and the utility of multiple assessments. *Child Maltreatment, 16*, 41–50. doi:10.1177/1077559510387662

McElwain, N. L., & Booth-LaForce, C. (2006). Maternal sensitivity to infant distress and nondistress as predictors of infant-mother attachment security. *Journal of Family Psychology, 20*, 247–255. doi:10.1037/0893-3200.20.2.247

McNeil, C. B., & Hembree-Kigin, T. L. (2011). *Parent-child interaction therapy.* New York, NY: Springer [Original work published 1995].

Meade, E., & Dozier, M. (2012). *"In the Moment" commenting: A fidelity measurement and active ingredient in a parent training program* (Unpublished manuscript). University of Delaware, Newark, DE.

NICHD Early Child Care Research Network. (1996). Characteristics of infant child care: Factors contributing to positive caregiving. *Early Childhood Research Quarterly, 11*, 269–306. doi:10.1016/S0885-2006(96)90009-5

Pederson, D. R., Gleason, K. E., Moran, G., & Bento, S. (1998). Maternal attachment representations, maternal sensitivity, and the infant-mother attachment relationship. *Developmental Psychology, 34*, 925–933. doi:10.1037/0012-1649.34.5.925

Pederson, D. R., Moran, G., & Bento, S. (1998). *Maternal behavior Q-set* (Version 3.0). Unpublished manuscript. University of Western Ontario, Department of Psychology.

Schwarz, N. (1999). Self-reports: How the questions shape the answers. *American Psychologist, 54*, 93–105. doi:10.1037/0003-066X.54.2.93

Shonkoff, J. P., & Bales, S. N. (2011). Science does not speak for itself: Translating child development research for the public and its policymakers. *Child Development, 82*, 17–32. doi:10.1111/j.1467-8624.2010.01538.x

Simons, C., Bernard, K., & Dozier, M. (2013). *Sensitivity to distress in autonomous vs. nonautonomous caregivers* (Unpublished manuscript). University of Delaware, Newark.

Stovall, K. C., & Dozier, M. (2000). The development of attachment in new relationships: Single subject analyses for 10 foster infants. *Development and Psychopathology, 12*, 133–156. doi:10.1017/S0954579400002029

Stovall-McClough, K. C., & Dozier, M. (2004). Forming attachments in foster care: Infant attachment behaviors during the first 2 months of placement. *Development and Psychopathology, 16*, 253–271. doi:10.1017/S0954579404044505

Tarabulsy, G. M., Provost, M. A., Bordeleau, S., Trudel-Fitzgerald, C., Moran, G., Pederson, D., ... Pierce, T. (2009). Validation of a short version of the maternal behavior Q-set applied to a brief video record of mother-infant interaction. *Infant Behavior and Development, 32*, 132–136. doi:10.1016/j.infbeh.2008.09.006

van IJzendoorn, M. H., Vereijken, C. M. J. L., Bakermans-Kranenburg, M. J., & Riksen-Walraven, J. M. (2004). Assessing attachment security with the Attachment Q-Sort: Meta-analytic evidence for validity of the Observer AQS. *Child Development, 75*, 1188–1213. doi:10.1111/j.1467-8624.2004.00733.x

Wallin, A. R., Dozier, M., Bernard, K., & Meade, E. (2013, April). *Attachment and Biobehavioral Catch-up: Effects on parental positive regard.* Poster presented at the biennial meeting of the Society for Research on Child Development (SRCD), Seattle, WA.

Whipple, N., Bernier, A., & Mageau, G. A. (2011). A dimensional approach to maternal attachment state of mind: Relations to maternal sensitivity and maternal autonomy support. *Developmental Psychology, 47*, 396–403. doi:10.1037/a0021310

Youngstrom, E., Izard, C., & Ackerman, B. (1999). Dysphoria-related bias in maternal ratings of children. *Journal of Consulting and Clinical Psychology, 67*, 905–916. doi:10.1037/0022-006X.67.6.905

Sensitive attunement to infants' internal states: operationalizing the construct of mind-mindedness

Elizabeth Meins

Department of Psychology, University of York, York, UK

This paper focuses on caregiver sensitivity, its relation to mind-mindedness (caregivers' attunement to their infants' internal states), and how well both constructs predict infant attachment security. The seminal Baltimore research on sensitivity and its relation to attachment security is summarized, highlighting the conclusion that mothers in the insecure-resistant and insecure-avoidant categories could not be distinguished on the basis of sensitivity. The contrast between the complex, sophisticated construct detailed in the original studies and the broad-based nature of the sensitivity coding scale is discussed. This paper argues that we should return to Ainsworth, Bell, and Stayton's (1971, 1974) original emphasis on the caregiver's ability to perceive things from the child's point of view in defining a measure of the quality of early infant–caregiver interaction. This approach led to the development of the construct of mind-mindedness. There are two mind-mindedness indices: caregivers' tendency during infant–caregiver interaction to (a) comment appropriately on their infants' putative thoughts and feelings (appropriate mind-related comments), and (b) misread their infants' internal states (non-attuned mind-related comments). Both indices predict independent variance in infant–caregiver attachment security, and together can distinguish between the secure, avoidant, and resistant categories. The specific, multidimensional nature of mind-mindedness complements the global construct of sensitivity.

The observational work of Ainsworth and colleagues in the 1960s and 1970s revolutionized our understanding of early infant–caregiver interaction. Although her name is now synonymous with attachment security and the strange situation (Ainsworth, Blehar, Waters, & Wall, 1978; Ainsworth & Wittig, 1969), Ainsworth's research on the quality of infant–mother interaction in the first year of life has made an equally important contribution to the field of developmental psychology. Even in her early work with Bowlby and Robertson in London in the 1950s, Ainsworth was interested in how individual differences in infant behavior were rooted in the quality of interaction between the infant and mother. This interest took shape in her first empirical studies as an independent researcher, which detailed different patterns of interactional behavior in mothers and infants in Uganda (Ainsworth, 1963, 1967). This ground-breaking work laid the foundations for the research she conducted in Baltimore from which the concept of maternal sensitivity developed (Ainsworth, Bell, & Stayton, 1971, 1974).

This paper will argue that subsequent research had tended to lose focus on Ainsworth's conception of what constitutes sensitivity, and propose that a fuller understanding of how early infant–caregiver interaction predicts children's later development can be achieved by returning to its original definition. Ainsworth's painstaking descriptions of individual differences in mothers' ability to respond sensitively towards their young infants inspired our own research on the construct of maternal mind-mindedness (Meins, 1997). In defining mind-mindedness and developing a scheme for coding caregivers' mind-minded comments, we sought to embody the essence of Ainsworth's sensitivity concept in a new measure of the quality of infant–mother interaction.

Defining maternal sensitivity

Ainsworth's early empirical research in Baltimore involved intensive, home-based observations of 26 infant–mother pairs who participated in 4-hour long observations conducted at 3-weekly intervals throughout the first year of life (Ainsworth & Bell, 1969; Ainsworth et al., 1971, 1974). Detailed narrative transcripts were made to evaluate observed mother–infant behavior and also mothers' spontaneous and interview-based views about their infants. The frequency and scope of these observations remains unsurpassed in the literature and gave Ainsworth and her colleagues a unique insight into individual differences in early mother–infant interaction.

Ainsworth and Bell (1969) rated mothers' behavior in the first 3 months of life according to 22 different scales, although they reported on only six of these: mother's perception of the baby, mother's delight in the baby, mother's acceptance of the baby, appropriateness of mother's interaction with the baby, amount of physical contact, and effectiveness of mother's response to baby's crying. In order to quantify common features of these six maternal behaviors, Ainsworth et al. (1971, 1974) devised a scale for assessing maternal sensitivity, the construct they believed was the core component of the six behaviors that Ainsworth and Bell (1969) reported on. Sensitivity was defined as the mother's "ability to perceive and to interpret accurately the signals and communications implicit in her infant's behaviour, and given this understanding, to respond to them appropriately" (Ainsworth et al., 1974, p. 127). The 9-point sensitivity scale involves five anchor points: (1) highly insensitive, (3) insensitive, (5) inconsistently sensitive, (7) sensitive, and (9) highly sensitive. Behaviors indicative of each anchor point on the scale are described in a paragraph of text. Ainsworth et al. (1971) used this scale to assess maternal sensitivity in the last quarter of the first year of life.

On both the individual scales and the measure of global sensitivity, Ainsworth and colleagues reported wide-ranging variance, highlighting for the first time how differently mothers approach the task of caregiving. As well as describing and assessing these individual differences in interactional behavior, these early studies also explored whether early maternal behavior was able to predict the quality of the subsequent infant–mother attachment relationship. Ainsworth and Bell's (1969) study was the first to suggest a link between maternal behavior in the first year of life and children's later attachment security as assessed in the strange situation procedure.

The original strange situation procedure classifies infants into one of three main categories on the basis of their response to reunion with the caregiver after short periods of separation: secure, insecure-avoidant, and insecure-resistant. These three categories are further sub-divided. There are four sub-groups in the secure category (B1, B2, B3, B4) to identify infants that are securely attached but with differing levels of the two insecure behaviors. For example, B1 infants show evidence of mild avoidance, whereas B4 infants show mild resistance; infants in the B3 category are regarded to be optimally secure. The insecure-avoidant and insecure-resistant categories both have two sub-groups, with groups A1 and C1 indicating the most pronounced avoidance and resistance respectively.

Ainsworth and Bell (1969) reported that on all six of their scales, higher scores distinguished secure-group mothers from their counterparts in the avoidant and resistant groups. However, avoidant- and resistant-group mothers did not differ from one another on any of these indices. Ainsworth et al. (1971) replicated these precise findings using the sensitivity measure to assess the quality of interaction in the final quarter of the first year of life: secure-group mothers were more sensitive than were those in the two insecure groups, but avoidant- and resistant-group mothers could not be distinguished on the basis of sensitivity.

Although this early research is very well known, it is interesting to note that several subtleties in these original findings have tended to be lost in the subsequent literature on infant–caregiver interaction and its association with attachment. The Ainsworth et al. (1971) original figure depicting their results is reproduced in Figure 1. The most obvious thing to note from Figure 1 is that maternal behavior was not only assessed with respect to sensitivity. Ainsworth et al. (1971) developed three additional 9-point scales in an attempt to identify maternal behaviors that might better characterize mothers in the avoidant and resistant groups. These additional scales focused on the dimensions of acceptance–rejection, co-operation–interference, and accessibility–ignoring. As Figure 1 shows, acceptance–rejection was the only scale that appeared to distinguish avoidant- from resistant-group mothers. However, differences between the groups were not analyzed statistically, so it is not possible to establish whether mothers in the two insecure groups differed significantly from one another with respect to this variable.

A second thing to note from Figure 1 is that only the mothers of infants in the optimally secure B3 group scored above 7 and could thus be termed "sensitive". In contrast, mothers of infants in the B1 and B2 groups did not score highly enough even to be classified as "inconsistently sensitive" (i.e., a score of 5). Ainsworth et al. (1971) had no B4 infants in their sample, so their level of sensitivity was unknown. Pooling the group data results in a mean sensitivity score of 5.93 for secure-group mothers which, although higher than those of mothers in the avoidant ($M = 2.63$) and resistant ($M = 2.38$) groups, is well short of the "sensitive" score.

Ainsworth et al. (1971, 1974) thus concluded that mothers in the avoidant and resistant groups could not be differentiated on the basis of sensitivity, and these original findings have been replicated many times. For example, Stifter, Couleham, and Fish (1993) reported that maternal sensitivity failed to predict attachment security at the

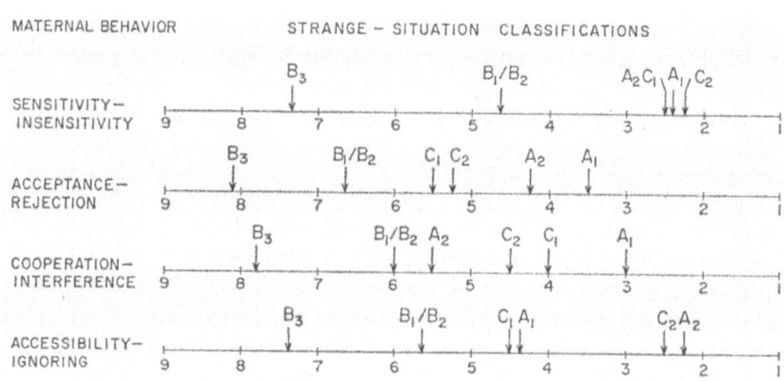

Figure 1. Ainsworth et al. (1971) original figure showing mothers' mean behavior scores as a function of attachment security. Reprinted from Ainsworth et al. (1971), with kind permission of the authors.

three-way (secure, avoidant, resistant) level, as did Egeland and Farber (1984) for the girls in their sample. Isabella (1993) found that maternal sensitivity at 1 month predicted later three-way attachment security (although sensitivity scores of mothers in the avoidant and secure groups did not differ), but the sensitivity measures taken at 4 months and 9 months (the ages most closely matching the infants in the studies of Ainsworth & Bell, 1969, and Ainsworth et al., 1971) did not predict three-way attachment security; indeed the 9-month sensitivity scores did not predict attachment even at the dichotomous (secure/insecure) level. In their meta-analysis of 66 studies, De Wolff and van IJzendoorn (1997) concluded that there was a moderate predictive relation between sensitivity and attachment security, but that, without Ainsworth et al.'s original sample, "the solid scientific fact of a moderately strong causal association between sensitivity and attachment would not have been established" (p. 585). Yet despite providing the strongest evidence for this link, Ainsworth and her colleagues themselves realized that sensitivity could not predict security at anything more fine-grained than a secure/insecure dichotomous split, hence their development of additional scales to assess other aspects of maternal behavior.

One reason why subsequent studies have failed to replicate the strength of association between sensitivity and dichotomous attachment security reported in Ainsworth et al.'s original sample may be the fact that many researchers have assessed sensitivity in the context of a brief, laboratory-based interaction. As discussed above, the sensitivity scale was developed from extensive home-based observations conducted longitudinally, enabling coders to have a much more complete picture of the quality of the interaction between mother and child. To recapture some of this richness, Pederson et al. (1990) developed the Maternal Behavior Q-Sort (MBQS) to assess maternal sensitivity on the basis of a home visit lasting around 2 hours. Research using the MBQS has reported effect sizes of similar magnitude to those found in Ainsworth et al.'s original sample with respect to the relation between sensitivity and dichotomous attachment security (Pederson, Gleason, Moran, & Bento, 1998). The Pederson et al. (1998) study also replicated the Ainsworth et al. (1971) finding that sensitivity could not predict attachment security at the three-way level, although, in this later study, it was mothers in the secure and resistant groups who could not be distinguished on the basis of their MBQS sensitivity scores.

Multiple assessments of caregiver behavior

As discussed above, Ainsworth et al. (1971, 1974) operationalized three scales in addition to sensitivity in order to attempt to distinguish between mothers of infants with insecure-avoidant and insecure-resistant attachments, with acceptance–rejection being the dimension on which secure-, avoidant-, and resistant-group mothers appeared most clearly to differ (see Figure 1). However, scores on the sensitivity and acceptance–rejection scales were highly positively correlated, suggesting that both scales were assessing the same underlying construct. Ainsworth et al. (1971) reported a coefficient of .89 for this correlation, which is remarkably high. These findings thus present something of a paradox in that both scales assess the same aspect of maternal behavior, but the acceptance–rejection scale appears better able to distinguish between the three attachment groups.

While one can debate which of the original scales should have attained prominence, the reason behind the desire to focus on a single dimension of behavior is uncontentious. If one had to assess infant–caregiver interaction using multiple scales, each of which needs to be coded by independent researchers who can demonstrate good levels of reliability, conducting research on a reasonably large sample within a tolerable timescale would become largely untenable. A small number of studies have, however, assessed more atypical forms of parenting (e.g., hostility, intrusion, coercion, withdrawal/disengagement) in addition to traditional sensitivity in order to attempt to predict attachment security at a three-way level. Isabella (1993) found that maternal rejection (a composite measure including hostility, frustration, anger, and interfering manipulation) at age 1 month was associated with insecure-resistant attachment, whereas the exact same measure at age 9 months was associated with insecure-avoidant attachment. Isabella and Belsky (1991) reported that intrusive and ignoring behaviors were characteristic of avoidant-group mothers, whereas resistant-group mothers appeared unable to coordinate their response with the infant's cue. However, these results do not provide compelling evidence for specific differences in the interactional behavior of mothers in the insecure-avoidant and insecure-resistant groups.

More recent studies have investigated how sensitivity and atypical parenting predict attachment security and attachment disorganization. Main and Solomon (1986, 1990) defined a fourth pattern of attachment (insecure-disorganized) to classify infants whose strange situation behavior did not fit with any of three original categories (secure, avoidant, resistant) and appeared to lack any clear strategy for organizing their attachment behaviors. Studies by Tomlinson, Cooper, and Murray (2005) and Moran, Forbes, Evans, Tarabulsy, and Madigan (2008) reported that atypical parenting behavior predicted secure/insecure and organized/disorganized attachment independently of sensitivity, highlighting the utility of including additional assessments of caregiver behavior.

However, including the disorganized category causes further problems for obtaining a clear picture of the predictive relationship between caregiver behavior and attachment security. Rather than establishing how indices of caregiver behavior relate to the four individual categories of attachment security, researchers typically report on how caregiver behavior predicts dichotomous organized/disorganized attachment. Since the organized category includes infants in the secure, avoidant, and resistant groups, this precludes any understanding of differences in caregiver behavior among these three organized forms of attachment. Thus, neither the Tomlinson et al. (2005) nor the Moran et al. (2008) study speaks to the issue of whether multiple assessments of caregiver behavior help to distinguish between infants in the insecure-avoidant and insecure-resistant groups. Consequently, despite decades of research, the picture of the relation between early maternal interactional behavior and the three organized patterns of attachment security is no clearer than when Ainsworth and colleagues first published their results.

Sensitivity: the concept versus the scale

Given Ainsworth and colleagues' original finding that sensitivity could not distinguish between mothers of avoidant and resistant infants (despite these two patterns of attachment being strikingly different), the way in which the sensitivity construct has become inextricably linked with attachment is rather puzzling. Moreover, viewing sensitivity only in terms of its ability to predict attachment security ignores the powerful contribution sensitivity can make to our understanding of early infant–mother interaction. Even if sensitivity had been found to have no predictive utility, it would remain a vitally important index of individual differences in the quality of early infant–caregiver interaction.

It is interesting to note that, from the outset, Ainsworth and her colleagues were aware of the likelihood that subsequent researchers would take shortcuts and use strange situation classifications as proxies for the quality of early infant–mother interaction: "In view of the expensive and very time-consuming nature of longitudinal research, it is an attractive notion that one might in a 20-minute procedure [the strange situation] obtain a reasonably reliable and valid assessment of the nature of the relationship that has developed between an infant and his mother" (Ainsworth et al., 1971, p. 19). Over 40 years later, this statement seems particularly prescient. The strange situation is often the earliest measure taken in longitudinal research, ignoring the richness of interaction in the first year of life that Ainsworth et al.'s research so eloquently described. In an interview conducted in 1994, Ainsworth remarked: "I have been quite disappointed that so many attachment researchers have gone on to do research with the strange situation rather than looking at what happens in the home or in other natural settings" (Ainsworth & Marvin, 1995, p. 12). When earlier sensitivity is assessed, it is often viewed merely as a precursor of full-blown attachment relationships; sensitivity has thus not received the research attention it deserves in its own right.

If, as Ainsworth et al. (1971) suggested, attachment security is a construct whose success is founded on the simple but effective way in which it can be assessed, the exact opposite could be argued of maternal sensitivity. In their early writing, Ainsworth and colleagues described a highly sophisticated construct. Ainsworth et al. (1971) defined the sensitive mother as being "capable of perceiving things from [the child's] point of view" and respecting the child "as a separate person" (p. 43). In contrast, the insensitive mother was characterized as trying to "socialize with the baby when he is hungry, play with him when he is tired, and feed him when he is trying to initiate social interaction" (Ainsworth et al., 1974, p. 129). This highlights how the sensitive mother does not merely respond to cues from her child; she responds in a way that indicates she is able to "read" the cues appropriately and represent the child's needs and wishes. The description of the insensitive mother shows that she does not simply ignore the child's cues, but rather cannot interpret them in terms of the child's underlying needs and so responds in a way that is mismatched to the child's cue. Thus, a sensitive response is possible because the mother has extensive knowledge of the child, accumulated via careful observation of what cues have meant in the past, what responses have been successful in dealing with such cues, and so on. In other words, the sensitive mother recognizes the cue as indicating a particular state in the child, responds in a way that usually satisfies the child's need or desire, and monitors her child's response on this occasion to ensure that she has read the initial cue correctly. Consequently, one can only designate a maternal behavior as sensitive if one views the mother–infant dyad, rather than the individual mother, as the unit of analysis.

The complexity and dyadic nature of sensitivity was not, however, translated effectively into Ainsworth et al.'s (1971, 1974) sensitivity scale. A short narrative description for each of the five anchor points on the scale is all that is provided. These descriptions use a wide range of terms to describe infant cues: "subtle", "minimal", "understated", "clear", "definite", "forceful", "compelling", "intense", "prolonged", and "repeated". The caregiver's perception of the infant's cue is also described in various different ways: "attuned", "appropriate", "accurate", "inappropriate", "inaccurate", and "distorted". Finally, in order to assign a sensitivity score, it is necessary to interpret the motives underlying the mother's response; the scale requires one to calculate whether the caregiver fails to comply with a cue because she feels that the infant "is too excited, over-imperious, or wants something he should not have" (Ainsworth et al., 1974, p. 131) or because "it is inconvenient or she is not in the mood for it, or because she is determined not to 'spoil' him" (Ainsworth et al., 1974, p. 133). The former is a description of the "highly sensitive" mother, whereas the latter describes the "insensitive" mother. No further details or behavioral examples are given to help anyone using the sensitivity scale to distinguish among these different infant cues or the mother's behaviors and underlying motivations. If, like Ainsworth and colleagues, one had spent countless hours observing each dyad and becoming highly familiar with the mother and infant, these fine-grained distinctions would be easier to make. However, researchers who have used the scale in the intervening years have typically assessed sensitivity from short observations that are often conducted only once, which makes correctly interpreting subtle differences in infant cues and the motivations for the mother's behavior considerably more challenging.

The global and interpretative nature of the original scale may be one reason why sensitivity has gradually become an umbrella concept for numerous aspects of early infant–caregiver interaction. For example, over half of the studies included in De Wolff and van IJzendoorn's (1997) meta-analysis on sensitivity and attachment assessed caregiver behavior along dimensions such as the temporal contiguity of the caregiver's response to the infant, or the amount of support or stimulation the caregiver provided. As Meins, Fernyhough, Fradley, and Tuckey (2001) noted, these aspects of caregiver behavior have lost the focus on the appropriateness of the response that was so central to Ainsworth et al.'s (1971, 1974) description of the sensitive caregiver.

Returning to Ainsworth's original conception of what constitutes sensitivity and insensitivity provided the impetus for our own operationalization of the quality of infant–caregiver interaction in the first year of life: mind-mindedness. Mind-mindedness is defined as caregivers' tendency to treat their young children as individuals with minds of their own, and enables caregivers to "tune in" to what their infants may be thinking or feeling. Meins et al. (2001) focused on the core features of sensitivity – awareness and accurate interpretation of the infant's cues, and appropriate and prompt response to them – in developing the construct of mind-mindedness in the first year of life. Our previous research had highlighted individual differences in mothers' attributions of mindful behavior to their children, defining mind-mindedness in terms of mothers' tendency (a) spontaneously to focus on their preschoolers' mental characteristics when given an open-ended invitation to describe their child (Meins, Fernyhough, Russell, & Clark-Carter, 1998), and (b) to interpret their 20-month-olds' non-word utterances as having meaning (Meins, 1998). The first aim of the 2001 study was to establish potential ways in which caregivers could demonstrate mind-mindedness in the first year of life.

Our aim in developing the mind-mindedness coding scheme was to provide researchers with a tool that was suitable for assessing relatively brief, laboratory-based interactions, giving clear descriptions of a number of discrete behaviors that could be quantified. While less naturalistic than the home environment, we reasoned that the laboratory provides the clearest test of whether a caregiver can perceive things from the infant's point of view. In the laboratory, the mother does not have to divide her attention between the infant and other activities, and the infant is likely to be alert and ready to interact – insensitivity to the child's cues when the caregiver's only task is to interact with the child is thus more striking than an insensitive response when the caregiver is attempting to complete tasks around the home in addition to caring for the child.

In order to develop the mind-mindedness measure, Meins et al. (2001) observed mothers and their 6-month-olds interacting in a free-play session in which the only instruction was for the mother to play with her baby as she would if they had spare time together at home. Several behaviors that could index mind-mindedness were identified: (a) response to change in the infant's gaze direction, (b) response to the infant's object-directed activity, (c) imitating the infant, and (d) encouraging autonomy in the infant. These responses indicated that the mother believed her child's behavior was intentional and goal-directed, and thus implied treating the infant as an individual with a mind of their own. For example, a mother would not name or fetch a toy in response to the infant looking at it or gesturing toward it if she did not interpret the child's gaze or gesture as being meaningful. Similarly, a mother would not imitate a child's facial expression or manipulation of a toy, or encourage the child to perform a behavior autonomously, if she did not view the child as being capable of intentional behavior.

These types of maternal response were expected, but the final mind-mindedness category – appropriate mind-related comments – indexed a somewhat more surprising maternal behavior. Despite the fact that the infants were only 6 months of age, the vast majority of mothers commented on what their infants might be thinking or feeling. As well as commenting on likes and desires, mothers talked about their infants' cognitive processes (e.g., memory, recognition, decision-making), emotional reactions (e.g., surprise, excitement, happiness), and some mothers even attributed sophisticated mental states such as joking and teasing to their 6-month-olds.

Mind-related comments focus exclusively on the mother's attributions about the infant's internal state; attributions about the internal states of any other individual are not included in this category. Mind-related comments involve the mother voicing out loud what might be going on in her child's mind, and thus provide the most obvious indication that the mother is representing the infant's thoughts and feelings. To be classified as appropriate, the mind-related comment has to (a) indicate an internal state that appeared consistent with the infant's current behavior (e.g., stating that the infant liked or was interested in a toy with which they were playing), (b) link current behavior with a similar event in the past or future (e.g., "You remember going to the farm" while the child was playing with toy farm animals), or (c) clarify how to proceed after a lull in the interaction (e.g., "You'll like this book"). Comments where the mother "put words into the child's mouth" so that the mother's speech became a dialogue are also classified as appropriate mind-related comments. Caregivers receive scores for each category of mind-mindedness that can be expressed as basic frequency measures or as a proportion of the caregivers' overall amount of speech to control for verbosity.

Mind-mindedness, with its focus on quantifying specific aspects of caregiver behavior, thus complements the global assessment of the interaction as a whole that is provided by Ainsworth et al.'s (1971, 1974) maternal sensitivity scale. In order to establish how the mind-mindedness indices related to traditional sensitivity, Meins et al. (2001) additionally assessed the free-play interactions using Ainsworth et al.'s scale and coding procedure. Sensitivity was positively correlated with all of the mind-mindedness indices apart from encouragement of autonomy. The strongest relations with sensitivity were observed for response to infant gaze and appropriate mind-related comments, suggesting that these variables were tapping into similar aspects of sensitive responsiveness, although the size of the coefficients (rs = .40) indicated that these variables were by no means equivalent.

The final aim of Meins et al.'s (2001) study was to explore whether mind-mindedness predicted attachment security as assessed in the strange situation at age 12 months. Given the relatively small sample size ($N = 71$), attachment security was treated as a dichotomous variable (secure/insecure) in the main analyses. When the five mind-mindedness indices were entered into a logistic regression, only appropriate mind-related comments predicted attachment security. A second regression investigated whether appropriate mind-related comments and maternal sensitivity independently predicted attachment security. Appropriate mind-related comments accounted for 12.7% of the variance in dichotomous attachment security over and above the variance predicted by sensitivity (6.5%). These findings thus showed that, although positively correlated with traditional sensitivity, this index of mind-mindedness was an independent predictor of infant–mother attachment security, providing the first evidence that maternal attunement specifically to infants' internal states facilitates secure attachment.

This link between appropriate mind-related comments and attachment security has been replicated in independent samples (Laranjo, Bernier, & Meins, 2008; Lundy, 2003). However, due to the fact that these studies assessed attachment using the Attachment Q-Sort (Waters, 1995), which does not classify infants into attachment categories, it was not possible to establish whether appropriate mind-related comments could distinguish among infants in the secure, insecure-avoidant, and insecure-resistant groups.

Mind-mindedness as a multi-dimensional construct

The promising results of Meins et al.'s (2001) study prompted us to explore the construct of mind-mindedness and its relation with sensitivity and attachment in greater detail. Ainsworth et al.'s (1971, 1974) four maternal behavior scales were all unidimensional, with the two poles of these original scales – sensitivity–insensitivity, acceptance–rejection, cooperation–interference, accessibility–ignoring – representing opposite ends of the same behavioral dimension. It thus makes no sense to assess both sensitivity and insensitivity, or acceptance and rejection, because one would simply be measuring the same core behavior twice: it is meaningless to assess the sensitivity of a behavior if it has already been classified as insensitive.

In the 2001 study, we similarly treated mind-related comments as a unidimensional construct, focusing solely on mind-related comments that were appropriate attributions of the infant's likely internal state. However, not all mind-related comments were deemed to be appropriate; we also defined criteria for classifying mind-related comments that were not attuned to the infant's internal state. A comment was coded as non-attuned if (a) the attributed internal state appeared at odds with the infant's behavior (e.g., stating the infant disliked or was bored with a toy while the infant was actively playing with it), (b) the internal state relating to the infant's past or future behavior was unrelated to the infant's current behavior (e.g., commenting on a food that the infant loved while the infant was playing with a ring-stack toy), (c) the mother queried what the infant wanted when the infant was already clearly engaged in an activity, or (d) the referent of the internal state was not clear (e.g., stating the infant liked something when there was no obvious object or activity to which this comment could refer). As for appropriate mind-related comments, caregivers receive a score for the total number of non-attuned comments made during the observation, and this can be expressed either as a frequency score or as a proportion of the total amount of maternal speech. If the caregiver makes non-attuned comments, the infant is likely to experience the interaction as disjointed and non-collaborative, whereas infants will experience a sense of partnership and attunement if the caregiver comments appropriately on their internal states.

Meins et al. (2001) did not consider the possibility that appropriate and non-attuned mind-related comments might relate to sensitivity and security in different, independent ways, and none of the analyses in this paper involved non-attuned comments. In retrospect, it seems obvious that we should also have reported on non-attuned comments, but our aim in this first paper was to focus explicitly on the appropriateness of response (the core feature of sensitivity) in defining the mind-mindedness indices. However, subsequent papers reporting on this sample suggested that appropriate and non-attuned mind-related comments do not represent opposite poles of a unidimensional scale.

For example, in a follow-up study investigating relations between early mind-mindedness and children's mentalizing abilities in the preschool years, Meins et al. (2003) reported that the two indices of mind-mindedness were unrelated (r = .08). Moreover, Meins et al. (2003) reported that non-attuned mind-related comments were unrelated to maternal sensitivity as assessed on Ainsworth et al.'s (1971, 1974) scale, in contrast to the positive correlation between appropriate mind-related comments and sensitivity that was observed in this sample (Meins et al., 2001). Given that the two forms of mind-related comments appear to tap into unrelated facets of the caregiver's tendency to treat the infant as an individual with a mind, the assumption that appropriate and non-attuned mind-related comments represent opposite poles of the same behavioral dimension may not be well founded. The potential multidimensional nature of mind-mindedness was thus explored in a larger-scale study, involving an entirely new sample of infants and mothers (Meins et al., 2012). We argued that by assessing caregivers' mind-related comments, and distinguishing between those that were appropriate versus non-attuned to the infant's internal state, it was possible to measure the quality of infant–caregiver interaction along two distinct dimensions within one coding system. Given that appropriate mind-related comments are positively correlated with scores on Ainsworth et al.'s (1971, 1974) sensitivity scale, this index of mind-mindedness can be seen to assess the type of engagement with and responsivity to the child's cues that is the hallmark of traditional sensitivity. In contrast, comments that betray a misreading of the infant's internal state appear to index a form of caregiver behavior that is orthogonal to traditional conceptualizations of sensitivity. Only by taking into consideration what the caregiver says about the infant's internal state can this distinction be made.

Meins et al. (2012) highlighted the fact that non-attuned mind-related comments index subtle failures in caregivers' attunement to their infants' internal states that are likely to be missed by coding schemes that assess more overtly insensitive or atypical caregiving behavior, such as those used by Tomlinson et al. (2005) and Moran et al. (2008). To illustrate the greater clarity in interpreting the quality of caregiver behavior that is afforded by assessing caregivers' mind-related comments, we used the example of a mother who withdraws a toy car when her young infant calmly turns away from it. If one focuses solely on the caregiver's behavior, withdrawing the toy is likely to be coded as a sensitive response. However, suggesting alternative types of mind-related comment that could accompany withdrawing the toy gives a different flavor to the quality of this same caregiver behavior. Imagine that the mother said, "The toy scared you" or "You really don't like playing with me" as she withdrew the toy; here, one would have to conclude that the mother has misrepresented the underlying internal state governing the infant's calm turning away. Conversely, if the mother commented that the infant did not want or was not interested in the toy as she withdrew it, this would appear to be an appropriate attribution of what the infant was thinking or feeling.

The mismatch between sensitivity and the non-attuned nature of the caregiver's speech can also be illustrated by responses to infant distress. An infant in the 2012 study toppled over, hurt his cheek on a toy, and began to cry. The mother promptly picked the infant up and attempted to comfort him, and this response was coded as sensitive. However, while comforting the child, the mother stated repeatedly that the infant was crying because he was "grumpy and tired", thus misattributing the true cause of the infant's distress, despite having witnessed her child injure himself. Conversely, it is possible for a caregiver accurately to read the infant's internal state but be unable to use this information to act in a sensitive manner. For example, Pawlby et al. (2010) investigated mind-mindedness in a sample of mothers who had been hospitalized for a range of severe mental illnesses. They described a mother who accurately commented that her child was "fascinated" by the strap on the baby seat, but said this in a very irritated voice because she wanted the child to look at and interact with her rather than play with the strap.

Meins et al.'s (2012) study involved a new sample of 206 infant–mother pairs who were observed in a free play interaction when the infants were aged 8 months. These interactions were coded for mind-mindedness using Meins et al.'s (2001) scale, yielding scores for appropriate and non-attuned mind-related comments. As reported for our previous sample (Meins et al., 2003), we found that appropriate comments were considerably more frequent than were non-attuned comments. The free play interactions were also assessed for maternal sensitivity using Ainsworth et al.'s (1971, 1974) scale and coding procedure. Meins et al. (2012) replicated previous findings that (a) appropriate and non-attuned mind-related comments are unrelated (r = .07), (b) appropriate mind-related comments are positively correlated with sensitivity (r = .39), and (c) non-attuned mind-related comments are not related to sensitivity (r = .04). Indeed, the correlation coefficients were almost identical to those reported in Meins et al.'s (2001, 2003) previous study.

These subtleties in attunement and lack of attunement to the infant's internal states that are highlighted by coding caregivers' mind-related speech can help explain the pattern of relations observed between the two mind-mindedness indices and sensitivity. Depending on the nature of the accompanying mind-related comment, a seemingly sensitive behavior can be classified as appropriate or non-attuned. Conversely, a seemingly insensitive behavior can potentially be accompanied by an appropriate mind-related comment, as Pawlby et al. (2010) demonstrated in their study on mothers with severe mental illness. The lack of association between traditional sensitivity and non-attuned mind-related comments, and the relatively modest strength of the relation between sensitivity and appropriate mind-related comments – particularly in contrast to the extremely high positive correlations among Ainsworth et al.'s (1971) original scales – are thus not surprising.

Mind-mindedness and attachment security

Considering the possibility that the two indices of mind-mindedness might independently predict the quality of the caregiver–child relationship also provided grounds for hypothesizing ways in which the multidimensional nature of mind-mindedness might help predict attachment security across all four categories (secure, avoidant, resistant, disorganized). Meins et al. (2012) hypothesized that different combinations of high versus low scores for appropriate and non-attuned mind-related comments could help distinguish among caregivers in the four attachment groups. We expected to replicate Meins et al.'s (2001) finding that secure-group mothers scored highly for appropriate mind-related comments. With respect to non-attuned comments, Ainsworth et al.'s (1971) characterization of secure-group mothers as being highly sensitive, accepting, cooperating, and accessible led to the prediction that secure attachment would be associated with low levels of non-attuned mind-related comments.

Ainsworth et al.'s (1971) results indicated that rejection characterized mothers of insecure-avoidant infants. We thus predicted that avoidant-group mothers would score low on appropriate mind-related comments due to their inability or unwillingness to engage with or respond to the child's needs. Avoidant-group mothers were also predicted to score highly on non-attuned mind-related comments because of their documented tendency to follow their own agenda rather than respond to cues from the child. For example, Ainsworth et al. (1971) described avoidant-group mothers as "quite unable … to be guided by the baby's display of initiative [discounting] the baby's communications … as relevant guidelines" (p. 44). One could thus imagine that these mothers would be more likely to make non-attuned comments due to the fact that they imposed their own thoughts or feelings on the child, rather than recognizing that the infant may be thinking or feeling something entirely different. For example, a mother might comment that her infant no longer wanted a toy, despite the fact that the infant was still actively engaged in playing with it, because she herself wished the child to move onto another activity.

Mothers of resistant infants were predicted to have a third profile of appropriate and non-attuned mind-related comments. Ainsworth et al. (1971) described the caregiving of resistant-group mothers as being inconsistent, although these mothers "had a strong emotional investment in the maternal role … [and] gloried in being mothers" (p. 44). These mothers scored moderately highly with respect to acceptance of the child's cues, but nevertheless scored low on sensitivity, cooperation, and accessibility. Meins et al. (2012) thus predicted that resistant-group mothers might score highly on both indices of mind-mindedness because acceptance is likely to be accompanied by appropriate mind-related comments, whereas their tendency to interfere and ignore the child's cue will lead to them commenting in a non-attuned manner on the infant's internal state.

Meins et al. (2012) also explored relations between mind-mindedness and insecure-disorganized attachment. Obviously, Ainsworth et al.'s (1971) descriptions of maternal behavior cannot provide guidance for the types of caregiving behavior that may be involved in disorganization because this form of attachment was first identified in 1986. However, more recent research has indicated that atypical caregiving behaviors may play a role in disorganization. Lyons-Ruth, Bronfman, and Parsons (1999) devised the AMBIANCE scheme to assess behaviors such as withdrawal, negative-intrusion (e.g., mocking the infant), and affective errors, and reported that mothers of disorganized infants engaged in higher levels of these atypical behaviors. Hesse and Main (2000, 2006) identified maternal frightening or fearful behaviors as predicting insecure-disorganized attachment. Bernier and Meins (2008) argued that these atypical behaviors were likely to be related to the caregiver's inability to read the infant's internal states appropriately; thus, disorganized attachment might be associated with high levels of non-attuned comments. Due to the fact that infants classified as disorganized are given an additional "forced choice" classification to indicate their underlying attachment strategy (secure, avoidant, or resistant), Meins et al. did not make directional predictions for the mind-mindedness profile of mothers of disorganized infants.

Meins et al.'s (2012) results on the relation between infant–mother interaction at age 8 months and attachment security at age 15 months are summarized in Figure 2. In a series of multinomial regression analyses, we explored whether the two mind-mindedness indices and sensitivity could distinguish among mothers in the four attachment groups. The first analysis focused on the issue of whether the early interaction variables could predict infant attachment according to Ainsworth's original three categories (secure, avoidant, resistant). Secure group mothers attained higher scores for appropriate mind-related comments and lower scores for non-attuned mind-related comments than their counterparts in the both the avoidant and resistant groups. With respect to distinguishing between mothers in the two insecure groups, resistant-group mothers scored more highly than avoidant-group mothers on non-attuned mind-related comments, but there was no difference between the two groups' scores for appropriate mind-related comments.

The fact that avoidant- and resistant-group mothers could be distinguished on the basis of non-attuned mind-related comments is noteworthy, given that this index of mind-mindedness differs most obviously from previous scales for assessing the quality of infant–caregiver interaction. As discussed above, non-attuned comments are not related to traditional sensitivity, nor are they sufficiently extreme to fall within the scope of schemes assessing atypical caregiving behaviors. Considering non-attuned comments in combination with appropriate mind-related comments can thus help explain our success in distinguishing

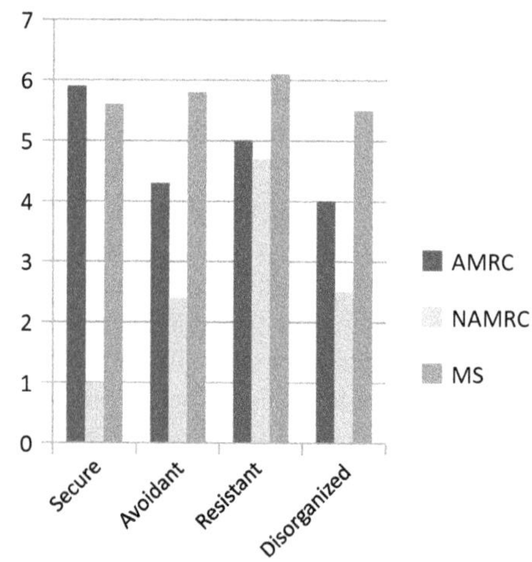

Figure 2. Mean scores for mind-mindedness and sensitivity as a function of attachment security. Notes: AMRC = appropriate mind-related comments; NAMRC = non-attuned mind-related comments; MS = maternal sensitivity. Scores on the y-axis represent percentages of appropriate or non-attuned mind-related comments, or the score on Ainsworth et al.'s (1974) sensitivity scale.

among mothers in the secure, avoidant, and resistant groups. Meins et al. (2012) highlighted how non-attuned comments were particularly rare in secure-group mothers, with scores of less than 2% for 90% of the mothers in this group. Supplementing the data presented in the 2012 paper, 35% of secure-group mothers did not make any non-attuned comments during the observation, with a further 21% making only a single non-attuned comment. In contrast, all of the mothers in the insecure-resistant group made at least one non-attuned comment, as did 92% of the mothers in the avoidant group.

A follow-up analysis that additionally included the disorganized group showed that secure-group mothers achieved higher scores for appropriate mind-related comments and lower scores for non-attuned mind-related comments compared with their disorganized-group counterparts. However, no differences were observed between the disorganized group and those in the avoidant and resistant groups, except for the elevated level of non-attuned comments in the resistant-group mothers (see Figure 2).

In contrast to the clear differences among the attachment groups with respect to appropriate and non-attuned mind-related comments, Figure 2 shows that Meins et al.'s (2012) study could not predict attachment security from mothers' sensitivity scores. Indeed, sensitivity did not predict attachment even at a dichotomous secure/insecure level. Although at odds with Ainsworth et al.'s (1971) original findings and those of our own initial study (Meins et al., 2001), this lack of association between sensitivity and dichotomous attachment is consistent with a number of null findings on wide-ranging populations (e.g., Goldberg, Perrotta, & Minde, 1986; Isabella, 1993; Lyons-Ruth, Connell, Zoll, & Stahl, 1987; Seifer, Schiller, Sameroff, Resnick, & Riordan, 1996).

The results of Meins et al.'s (2012) study thus show that, although it was not possible to predict infant–mother attachment security on the basis of scores on the original sensitivity scale, by returning to Ainsworth et al.'s (1971, 1974) emphasis on appropriateness and perceiving the world from the child's perspective as key components of sensitive caregiving, it is possible to distinguish secure-group infants from their counterparts in each of the three insecure groups, and to distinguish insecure-avoidant infants from those who are insecure-resistant. The two indices of mind-mindedness focus on a very specific caregiving behavior – mind-related comments – and the coding scheme (Meins & Fernyhough, 2012; Meins et al., 2001) gives criteria and examples to help researchers classify such comments as appropriate or non-attuned. The scheme is also tailored to assess caregivers' attunement to their infants in the context of a single, relatively short observation in the developmental laboratory. Consequently, mind-mindedness is operationalized much more precisely than was sensitivity, while maintaining clear links with Ainsworth's theoretical construct.

A new analysis of Meins et al.'s (2001) data

Despite the success of caregivers' mind-related comments in predicting attachment security at the fine-grained level, operationalizing mind-mindedness purely in terms of caregivers' speech presents one obvious conundrum: why is what caregivers *say* to their infants a more important predictor than how caregivers *respond* to their infants? As discussed above, our original 2001 paper on mind-mindedness in the first year of life suggested various caregiver behaviors that might index the ability to treat the infant as an individual with a mind, whereas our more recent research has moved to an exclusive focus on mind-related comments as the index of mind-mindedness in the first year of life. While Meins et al. (2001) reported that none of the behavioral indices of mind-mindedness (response to infant gaze or object-directed activity, imitation, encouragement of autonomy) were predictors of attachment security, it is possible that a measure that includes both mind-minded behavior and mind-related comments may predict later patterns of attachment.

Meins et al.'s (2001) data were reanalyzed to investigate whether (a) appropriate and non-attuned comments independently predicted attachment security, and (b) a composite score involving behavioral and speech-based indices of mind-mindedness predicted dichotomous attachment security. To address (a), Meins et al.'s (2001) original binary logistic regression was rerun including non-attuned mind-related comments in addition to the original variables (infant cognitive ability, maternal education, maternal sensitivity, appropriate mind-related comments). With all variables entered into the regression equation, the two mind-mindedness indices were the only independent predictors of dichotomous (secure/insecure) attachment: non-attuned comments, Wald = 7.06, $p < .01$, $R^2 = .17$; appropriate comments, Wald = 4.70, $p < .05$, $R^2 = .09$. Non-attuned mind-related comments were lower for secure group mothers ($M = 0.81$, $SD = 1.35$) compared with their insecure group counterparts ($M = 3.13$, $SD = 2.63$), $t(69) = 4.22$, $p < .001$. These findings thus replicate the precise pattern of findings reported by Meins et al. (2012) in a separate sample: when both indices of mind-mindedness are included in the analysis, maternal sensitivity does not account for independent variance in attachment security, and non-attuned mind-related comments predict attachment security more strongly than do appropriate mind-related comments.

To investigate the comparative strength of a composite score involving behavioral and speech-based indices of mind-mindedness in predicting attachment security, the internal reliability of a number of potential composites was first explored. Meins et al. (2001) reported that three of the five original indices of mind-mindedness were robustly positively correlated: appropriate mind-related comments, response to infant gaze, and response to infant object-directed activity. The internal reliability for the composite measure of these three variables was acceptable, $\alpha = .69$. The binary logistic regression analysis described above was rerun, with this three-variable composite replacing appropriate mind-related comments. The independent variables were thus: infant cognitive ability, maternal education, maternal sensitivity, non-attuned mind-related comments, and the mind-mindedness behavior/speech composite. In this analysis, only non-attuned mind-related comments predicted dichotomous attachment security, Wald = 7.50, $p < .01$, $R^2 = .21$, with the behavior/speech composite failing to predict independent variance, Wald = 1.27, $p = .259$, $R^2 = .02$.

This reanalysis shows the independent role of both appropriate and non-attuned mind-related comments in predicting later attachment security, and is in line with the argument that mind-mindedness is a multidimensional construct. Moreover, these new analyses involving the original behavioral mind-mindedness scales most strongly related to appropriate mind-related comments suggest that speech-based indices of mind-mindedness are more successful in predicting attachment security than a composite index based on both behavior- and speech-based indicators of mind-mindedness.

Caregiver speech and caregiver behavior

Despite the fact that reanalysis of Meins et al.'s (2001) data showed that a measure incorporating a behavioral dimension of mind-mindedness was worse in predicting attachment security than were the speech-based measures of mind-mindedness, this does not rule out the possibility that behavioral manifestations of mind-mindedness play a role. In a new conceptualization of infant–caregiver interaction, Shai and Belsky (2011) focused on caregivers' kinesthetic behaviors as a marker of their ability to recognize their infants' internal states (so-called *parental embodied mentalization*). These kinesthetic behaviors are coded entirely independently of caregivers' speech; indeed, the soundtrack to the observation is muted so as not to influence the coder's interpretation of the caregiver's kinesthetic response to the child.

The main strength of Shai and Belsky's (2011) work is its focus on the infant–caregiver dyad as the unit of analysis. Thus, assessing parental embodied mentalization and the appropriateness of mind-related comments both require one to consider the parent's response in light of the infant's ongoing behavior. This commonality suggests that parental embodied mentalization may be a behavioral index of mind-mindedness, a suggestion that we are currently testing by coding the same infant–mother interactions for both mind-related comments and parental embodied mentalization. This research will further develop the construct of mind-mindedness by elaborating its potential behavioral dimensions.

Alternatively, combining laboratory-based assessments of mind-mindedness with extensive home-based assessments of maternal sensitivity may provide the most complete picture of the quality of early caregiver–child interaction. In previous research, mind-mindedness and sensitivity have been assessed from the same free-play observation (Meins et al., 2001, 2012). If mind-mindedness is assessed in a different context to that in which maternal sensitivity is measured, different findings may emerge. For example, it may be that the positive correlation between appropriate mind-related comments and sensitivity will not be as robust when assessed from different observations.

The results of Laranjo et al. (2008), who assessed maternal sensitivity using the MBQS and appropriate mind-related comments from a free play interaction, are in line with this suggestion. The measures of mind-mindedness in this study were somewhat different (frequency scores of specific sub-categories of appropriate mind-related comments) from those used in Meins et al.'s longitudinal studies, but the correlation coefficients for relations between mind-mindedness and sensitivity ranged from .14 to .28, in contrast to coefficients of .40 and .39 reported respectively by Meins et al. (2001, 2012). However, Laranjo et al.'s (2008) free play interaction was conducted in the home, meaning that this study cannot provide a definitive answer to how appropriate mind-related comments in a laboratory setting relate to sensitivity in the home environment. It may also be the case that non-attuned mind-related comments in free play relate more strongly to insensitivity in the home environment than in the laboratory. For example, it seems reasonable to hypothesize that caregivers who tend to misinterpret their infants' internal states in the relatively low-stress context of a laboratory-based free play session are likely to be insensitive when they have to deal with the additional demands on their time that occur in the home environment.

It is also possible, though, that what caregivers say is genuinely more important in predicting attachment security than what they actually do. The wealth of literature showing that caregivers' representations of attachment relationships in the Adult Attachment Interview relate strongly to infant–caregiver attachment (e.g., van IJzendoorn, 1995) is testament to the influence of "offline" attachment representations on the quality of actual relationships. Research on the caregiving system has also shown how caregivers' representations of the child and themselves in the caregiving role as assessed in the Parent Development Interview (Slade, Aber, Berger, Bresgi, & Kaplan, 2003) or Caregiving Interview (George & Solomon, 1998) relate to infant–caregiver attachment security.

Secure attachment is associated with having a caregiver who is capable of reflecting on how parenting involves a complex interplay between the internal states of the caregiver and child (Slade, Grienenberger, Bernbach, Levy, & Locker, 2005), and who represents caregiving in a flexible, balanced, and integrated fashion (see George & Solomon, 2008). Moreover, research has failed to provide convincing evidence for infant–caregiver interactional behaviors mediating the relation between caregivers' interview-based representations and caregiver–infant attachment security (Goldberg, Benoit, Blokland, & Madigan, 2003; Grienenberger, Kelly, & Slade, 2005; Lyons-Ruth, Yellin, Melnick, & Atwood, 2005; Madigan, Pederson, & Moran, 2006; Schuengel, Bakermans-Kranenburg, & van IJzendoorn, 1999; van IJzendoorn, 1995), leading to van IJzendoorn's conclusion that there is a "transmission gap" in the intergenerational transfer of attachment. These findings thus highlight the important association between what caregivers say about their close relationships and the security of the infant–caregiver attachment relationship. In light of this seminal research, it is less surprising that we found caregivers' mind-related comments during actual interactions with their infants predicted attachment security more strongly than did behavioral measures of the quality of infant–mother interaction.

While several studies have explored the relation between mind-mindedness and infant–caregiver attachment, research has not fully investigated how mind-mindedness relates to representational measures of attachment. Arnott and Meins' (2007) results suggested that mind-mindedness in infant–caregiver interaction was associated with caregivers' attachment representations in the Adult Attachment Interview, but the sample size in this study was very small, precluding any firm conclusions from being drawn. No study has yet investigated how mind-mindedness during infant–caregiver interaction relates to parents' caregiving representations during the Parent Development Interview or Caregiving Interview. Investigating these relations is thus an interesting avenue for future research. As well as exploring the relation between mind-mindedness and caregivers' representations of attachment and caregiving, future studies should establish whether mind-mindedness – and its focus on caregivers' attunement specifically to their infants' internal states – can help bridge the transmission gap, and thus shed light on the potential mechanisms involved in the intergenerational transfer of attachment security.

Final reflections

Mary Ainsworth has had an influence on my entire research career. Her work on early infant–mother interaction first sparked my interest in individual differences and inspired me to pursue academic research in developmental psychology. Three aspects of her approach have acted as constant guides in my own work: (a) start every new piece of research with careful observation, (b) do not be afraid to define new constructs that may initially be seen to be at odds with accepted theories, and (c) be open-minded to alternative ideas that can refine and extend your research.

If Ainsworth had not taken an empirical approach to attachment and actually observed infants interacting with their mothers, we would not have the concept of attachment security or realize that the patterns of attachment behavior were much more varied than Bowlby (1958) originally believed. Ainsworth's early empirical research was thus instrumental in Bowlby's (1969/1982) revision of attachment theory and his move to describing attachment as a goal-corrected system. Of course, Ainsworth herself was equally willing to embrace the findings of other researchers in revising her own research ideas. For example, she readily accepted the insecure-disorganized pattern of attachment (Main & Solomon, 1986, 1990) as an important refinement of her original strange situation classification system. Indeed, when asked how she would react if someone discovered a new pattern of insecure behavior, Ainsworth replied, "That would not be all that surprising; there are many more possible ways of organizing behavioral strategies for coping with an insecure relationship" (Ainsworth & Marvin, 1995, p. 14). She was also willing to revise her own ideas if she believed they could be improved: when it was discovered that the maternal sensitivity construct could not distinguish between mothers of infants in the avoidant and resistant attachment categories, Ainsworth et al. (1971, 1974) invented new scales to assess other aspects of interactional behavior that might prove more discriminating.

I hope that, in our research on mind-mindedness, I have managed to continue Ainsworth's spirit of discovery through careful observation. In all of this work, we have sought to use the core features of Ainsworth's original concept of sensitivity as our guiding principle, with the aim of defining specific interactional behaviors that best fit the criteria for appropriate interpretation of the infant's cues. If our research has been critical of the concept of sensitivity, then this criticism is not of the construct itself but of the assessment scale and its misinterpretation and misuse over the intervening years. In giving clear-cut criteria and detailed examples for coding mind-related comments as appropriate or non-attuned, we hope to provide researchers with a useful, freely-available tool for assessing infant–caregiver interaction in the developmental laboratory. Moreover, our goal was to make the coding scheme sufficiently detailed that it could be used without the requirements for researchers undergoing labor-intensive training and reliability procedures. Feedback on the mind-mindedness coding scheme is actively encouraged, and researchers who are independently using the scheme in their work continually make valuable suggestions for its adaptation and improvement. I believe that Ainsworth would approve of our adaptation of her concept of sensitivity: the precision of the mind-mindedness coding scheme and its utility in assessing brief, laboratory-based observations perfectly complements the sensitivity scale as an index of the global quality of extensive observation in the home.

Had we not observed – and more importantly, listened to – mothers interacting with their young infants, keeping an open mind about the ways in which caregivers might demonstrate their attunement to their young infants, we may not have recognized the importance of mothers voicing out loud what their infants might be thinking or feeling. With their specific focus on caregivers' attunement to their infants' mental and emotional states, appropriate mind-related comments are likely to facilitate not only secure attachment, but also children's own subsequent understanding of other people's perspectives and internal states. In support of this proposal, research has shown that mothers' appropriate mind-related comments in the first year of life have been found to predict children's mentalizing abilities throughout the preschool years (Laranjo, Bernier, Meins, & Carlson, 2010; Meins, Fernyhough, Arnott, Leekam, & de Rosnay, 2013; Meins et al., 2002, 2003). This research thus highlights how individual differences in the quality of early infant–caregiver interaction are able to predict core developmental abilities well beyond the establishment of the attachment relationship.

Mind-mindedness is a construct at the interface between behavioral and representational measures of the quality of the infant–caregiver relationship. To be mind-minded, the caregiver must first accurately represent the infant's thoughts and feelings and then actually voice this representation. Mind-mindedness provides an index of how caregivers represent their infants' internal states "online" while interacting with the child. As such, this construct complements both purely behavioral and purely representational (interview-based) assessments of the infant–caregiver relationship. I hope that our research has thus followed the advice Ainsworth gave in 1994: "I believe that we must continue to rely on direct observation – on what I've called 'fieldwork' – in gathering more information on what actually happens in different contexts in different relationships. But moving to *also* study internal attachment-related events is certainly appropriate and necessary to get at the 'rules' and processes … As long as this trend doesn't become an 'either/or' thing – either you observe, or you probe for internal events – but remains rather a matter of balance between the two, I think it will serve us well" (Ainsworth & Marvin, 1995, p. 21, original emphasis).

Acknowledgements

I am very grateful to Inge Bretherton for her generosity in sharing her first hand experience of Ainsworth's original research, and to the editors for giving me the honor of contributing to this special issue.

Funding

The research discussed in this paper was supported by Staffordshire University and the Economic and Social Research Council [R000239456].

References

Ainsworth, M. D. (1963). The development of infant–mother interaction among the Ganda. In B. M. Foss (Ed.), *Determinants of infant behaviour* (Vol. 2). London: Methuen.

Ainsworth, M. D. S. (1967). *Infancy in Uganda: Infant care and the growth of love*. Baltimore, MD: Johns Hopkins University Press.

Ainsworth, M. D. S., & Bell, S. M. (1969). Some contemporary patterns of mother–infant interaction in the feeding situation. In A. Ambrose (Ed.), *Stimulation in early infancy* (pp. 133–163). London: Academic Press.

Ainsworth, M. D. S., Bell, S. M., & Stayton, D. J. (1971). Individual differences in strange situation behavior of one year olds. In H. R. Schaffer (Ed.), *The origins of human social relations* (pp. 17–52). London: Academic Press.

Ainsworth, M. D. S., Bell, S. M., & Stayton, D. J. (1974). Infant–mother attachment and social development: Socialisation as a product of reciprocal responsiveness to signals. In M. P. M. Richards (Ed.), *The introduction of the child into a social world* (pp. 99–135). London: Cambridge University Press.

Ainsworth, M. D., Blehar, M. C., Waters, E., & Wall, S. (1978). *Patterns of attachment: A psychological study of the strange situation*. Hillsdale, NJ: Erlbaum.

Ainsworth, M. D. S., & Marvin, R. S. (1995). On the shaping of attachment theory and research: An interview with Mary D. S. Ainsworth (Fall 1994). *Monographs of the Society for Research in Child Development, 60*, 3–21.

Ainsworth, M. D. S., & Wittig, B. A. (1969). Attachment and exploratory behaviour in one year olds in a strange situation. In B. M. Foss (Ed.), *Determinants of infant behaviour* (Vol. 4). New York, NY: Barnes & Noble.

Arnott, B., & Meins, E. (2007). Links between antenatal attachment representations, postnatal mind-mindedness, and infant attachment security: A preliminary study of mothers and fathers. *Bulletin of the Menninger Clinic, 71*, 132–149.

Bernier, A., & Meins, E. (2008). A threshold approach to understanding the origins of attachment disorganization. *Developmental Psychology, 44*, 969–982.

Bowlby, J. (1958). The nature of the child's tie to his mother. *International Journal of Psycho-Analysis, 39*, 350–373.

Bowlby, J. (1969/1982). *Attachment and loss, Vol. 1. Attachment* (2nd ed.). New York, NY: Basic Books.

De Wolff, M. S., & van IJzendoorn, M. H. (1997). Sensitivity and attachment: A meta-analysis on parental antecedents of infant attachment. *Child Development, 68*, 571–591.

Egeland, B., & Farber, E. A. (1984). Infant–mother attachment: Factors related to its development and expression over time. *Child Development, 55*, 753–771.

George, C., & Solomon, J. (1998). *The caregiving interview: Caregiving representation rating manual*. Unpublished manuscript. Mills College, Oakland, CA.

George, C., & Solomon, J. (2008). The caregiving system: A behavioral systems approach to parenting. In J. Cassidy & P. R. Shaver (Eds.), *Handbook of attachment: Theory, research, and clinical applications* (2nd ed.). New York, NY: The Guildford Press.

Goldberg, S., Benoit, D., Blokland, K., & Madigan, S. (2003). Atypical maternal behavior, maternal representations, and infant disorganized attachment. *Development and Psychopathology, 15*, 239–257.

Goldberg, S., Perrotta, M., & Minde, K. (1986). Maternal behavior and attachment in low-birth-weight twins and singletons. *Child Development, 57*, 34–46.

Grienenberger, J., Kelly, K., & Slade, A. (2005). Maternal reflective functioning, mother–infant affective communication, and infant attachment: Exploring the link between mental states and observed caregiving behavior in the intergenerational transmission of attachment. *Attachment & Human Development, 7*, 299–311.

Hesse, E., & Main, M. (2000). Disorganized infant, child, and adult attachment: Collapse in behavioral and attentional strategies. *Journal of the American Psychoanalytic Association, 48*, 1017–1127.

Hesse, E., & Main, M. (2006). Frightened, threatening, and dissociative parental behavior in low-risk samples: Description, discussion, and interpretations. *Development and Psychopathology, 18*, 309–343.

Isabella, R. A. (1993). Origins of attachment: Maternal interactive behavior across the first year. *Child Development, 64*, 605–621.

Isabella, R. A., & Belsky, J. (1991). Interactional synchrony and the origins of infant–mother attachment: A replication study. *Child Development, 62*, 373–384.

Laranjo, J., Bernier, A., & Meins, E. (2008). Associations between maternal mind-mindedness and infant attachment security: Investigating the mediating role of maternal sensitivity. *Infant Behavior & Development, 31*, 688–695.

Laranjo, J., Bernier, A., Meins, E., & Carlson, S. M. (2010). Early manifestations of children's theory of mind: The roles of maternal mind-mindedness and infant security of attachment. *Infancy, 15*, 300–323.

Lundy, B. L. (2003). Father– and mother–infant face to face interactions: Differences in mind-related comments and infant attachment? *Infant Behavior & Development, 26*, 200–212.

Lyons-Ruth, K., Bronfman, E., & Parsons, E. (1999). Maternal frightened, frightening, or atypical behavior and disorganized infant attachment patterns. *Monographs of the Society for Research in Child Development, 64*, 67–96.

Lyons-Ruth, K., Connell, D. B., Zoll, D., & Stahl, J. (1987). Infants at social risk: Relations among infant maltreatment, maternal behavior, and infant attachment behavior. *Developmental Psychology, 23*, 223–232.

Lyons-Ruth, K., Yellin, C., Melnick, S., & Atwood, G. (2005). Expanding the concept of unresolved mental states: Hostile/helpless states of mind on the Adult Attachment Interview are associated with disrupted mother–infant communication and infant disorganization. *Development and Psychopathology, 27*, 1–23.

Madigan, S., Pederson, D., & Moran, G. (2006). Unresolved states of mind, disorganized attachment relationships, and disrupted mother–infant interactions of adolescent mothers and their infants. *Developmental Psychology, 42*, 293–304.

Main, M., & Solomon, J. (1986). Discovery of an insecure-disorganized/disoriented attachment pattern. In T. B. Brazelton & M. W. Yogman (Eds.), *Affective development in infancy* (pp. 95–124). Westport, CT: Ablex.

Main, M., & Solomon, J. (1990). Procedures for identifying infants as disorganized/disoriented during the Ainsworth strange situation. In M. T. Greenberg, D. Cicchetti, & E. M. Cummings (Eds.), *Attachment in the preschool years: Theory, research, and intervention* (pp. 121–160). Chicago, IL: University of Chicago Press.

Meins, E. (1997). *Security of attachment and the social development of cognition*. Hove: Psychology Press.

Meins, E. (1998). The effects of security of attachment and maternal attribution of meaning on children's linguistic acquisitional style. *Infant Behavior & Development, 21*, 237–252.

Meins, E., & Fernyhough, C. (2012). *Mind-mindedness coding manual, Version 2.1*. Unpublished manuscript. Durham University, Durham.

Meins, E., Fernyhough, C., Arnott, B., Leekam, S. R., & de Rosnay, M. (2013). Mind-mindedness and theory of mind: Mediating roles of language and perspectival symbolic play. *Child Development, 84*, 1777–1790.

Meins, E., Fernyhough, C., de Rosnay, M., Arnott, B., Leekam, S. R., & Turner, M. (2012). Mind-mindedness as a multidimensional construct: Appropriate and non-attuned mind-related comments independently predict infant–mother attachment in a socially diverse sample. *Infancy, 17*, 393–415.

Meins, E., Fernyhough, C., Fradley, E., & Tuckey, M. (2001). Rethinking maternal sensitivity: Mothers' comments on infants' mental processes predict security of attachment at 12 months. *Journal of Child Psychology and Psychiatry, 42*, 637–648.

Meins, E., Fernyhough, C., Russell, J., & Clark-Carter, D. (1998). Security of attachment as a predictor of symbolic and mentalising abilities: A longitudinal study. *Social Development, 7*, 1–24.

Meins, E., Fernyhough, C., Wainwright, R., Clark-Carter, D., Das Gupta, M., Fradley, E., & Tuckey, M. (2003). Pathways to understanding mind: Construct validity and predictive validity of maternal mind-mindedness. *Child Development, 74*, 1194–1211.

Meins, E., Fernyhough, C., Wainwright, R., Das Gupta, M., Fradley, E., & Tuckey, M. (2002). Maternal mind-mindedness and attachment security as predictors of theory of mind understanding. *Child Development, 73*, 1715–1726.

Moran, G., Forbes, L., Evans, E., Tarabulsy, G. M., & Madigan, S. (2008). Both maternal sensitivity and atypical maternal behavior independently predict attachment security and disorganization in adolescent mother–infant relationships. *Infant Behavior & Development, 31*, 321–325.

Pawlby, S., Fernyhough, C., Meins, E., Pariante, C. M., Seneviratne, G., & Bentall, R. P. (2010). Mind-mindedness and maternal responsiveness in infant–mother interactions in mothers with severe mental illness. *Psychological Medicine, 40*, 1861–1869.

Pederson, D. R., Gleason, K. E., Moran, G., & Bento, S. (1998). Maternal attachment representations, maternal sensitivity, and the infant–mother attachment relationship. *Developmental Psychology, 34*, 923–933.

Pederson, D. R., Moran, G., Sitko, C., Campbell, K., Ghesquire, K., & Acton, H. (1990). Maternal sensitivity and the security of infant–mother attachment: A Q-sort study. *Child Development, 61*, 1974–1983.

Schuengel, C., Bakermans-Kranenburg, M. J., & van IJzendoorn, M. H. (1999). Attachment and loss: Frightening maternal behaviour linking unresolved loss and disorganized infant attachment. *Journal of Consulting and Clinical Psychology*, *67*, 54–63.

Seifer, R., Schiller, M., Sameroff, A. J., Resnick, S., & Riordan, K. (1996). Attachment, maternal sensitivity, and infant temperament during the first year of life. *Developmental Psychology*, *32*, 12–25.

Shai, D., & Belsky, J. (2011). When words just won't do: Introducing parental embodied mentalizing. *Child Development Perspectives, 5*, 173–180.

Slade, A., Aber, J., Berger, B., Bresgi, I., & Kaplan, M. (2003). *The parent development interview – R*. Unpublished protocol. The City University of New York, New York.

Slade, A., Grienenberger, J., Bernbach, E., Levy, D., & Locker, A. (2005). Maternal reflective functioning, attachment, and the transmission gap: A preliminary study. *Attachment & Human Development*, *7*, 283–298.

Stifter, C. A., Couleham, C. M., & Fish, M. (1993). Linking employment to attachment: The mediating effects of maternal separation anxiety and interactive behavior. *Child Development*, *64*, 1451–1560.

Tomlinson, M., Cooper, P., & Murray, L. (2005). The mother–infant relationship and infant attachment in a South African peri-urban settlement. *Child Development*, *76*, 1044–1054.

van IJzendoorn, M. H. (1995). Adult attachment representations, parental responsiveness, and infant attachment: A meta-analysis on the predictive validity of the Adult Attachment Interview. *Psychological Bulletin*, *117*, 1–17.

Waters, E. (1995). The attachment Q-Set, Version 3.0. (Appendix A). *Monographs of the Society for Research in Child Development*, *60*, 234–246.

The insightfulness assessment: measuring the internal processes underlying maternal sensitivity

David Oppenheim and Nina Koren-Karie

University of Haifa, Haifa, Israel

In her description of sensitive mothers, Ainsworth described not only maternal behaviors but also the internal processes underlying such behavior, including the capacity to "see things from the child's point of view". Ainsworth assessed this capacity from her extensive observations of mothers interacting with their infants, from records of mothers' talk *to* the babies, and from brief interviews *about* their babies. Attachment researchers following Ainsworth focused primarily on observations of maternal sensitive behavior, however, and the processes underlying such behavior were mostly inferred from the mothers' behavior. The Insightfulness Assessment (IA), a video replay procedure in which mothers are interviewed regarding their children's thoughts and feelings after they watch brief video clips of their children, was developed to assess systematically and directly the mother's ability to take the child's perspective. This paper uses examples from the IA to show how it captures many of the internal processes underlying caregiving behavior which Ainsworth described. Data supporting the IA's validity is reviewed, which suggest that the IA can complement observations of mothers' caregiving behavior in order to obtain a more comprehensive assessment of maternal sensitivity.

As is well known, maternal sensitivity is assessed from observations of mother–infant interactions and particularly by observing maternal caregiving behavior toward the infant (Ainsworth, Blehar, Waters, & Wall, 1978). In her description of sensitivity, Ainsworth did not only refer to observed maternal behavior, however, but also made frequent references to the internal processes underlying sensitive behavior (Ainsworth, 1969). She described "seeing things from the child's point of view" as a necessary condition for sensitivity to infant signals and cooperation with ongoing behavior, and distortions in the mother's perceptions of the child as leading to insensitive behavior (Ainsworth, 1969). In both her Uganda and Baltimore studies (Ainsworth, 1967; Ainsworth et al., 1978), Ainsworth learned about these internal processes from her extensive observations of mothers interacting with their infants, from records of mothers' talk *to* the babies, and from brief interviews *about* their babies (Bretherton, personal communication, April 13, 2013). Attachment researchers following Ainsworth focused primarily on observations of maternal sensitive behavior, however, and the mothers' ability to take the child's perspective, a key component of sensitivity for Ainsworth, was mostly inferred from mothers' behavior and not directly studied (e.g., by interviewing mothers).

In order to address this gap – that is, to assess the capacity of the parent to "see things from the child's point of view" – we developed the Insightfulness Assessment (IA: Oppenheim &

Koren-Karie, 2009). In the IA, mothers are interviewed regarding their children's thoughts and feelings after they watch short videotaped vignettes of their children interacting with them. Insightfulness is revealed in the mothers' capacity to talk coherently about the motives that underlie the child's behavior, accept these motives, provide a multi-dimensional portrait of the child, and be open to the information gleaned from the video segments. In this paper we will first review Ainsworth's scales of maternal behavior, highlight Ainsworth's references to internal processes that support or impede sensitive maternal behavior, and show how the IA can capture these processes. We will review not only the well-known Sensitivity vs. Insensitivity to the baby's signals scale, but also the other three scales of maternal behavior: Cooperation vs. Interference, Physical and Psychological Availability vs. Ignoring and Neglecting, and Acceptance vs. Rejection (Ainsworth, Bell, & Stayton, 1971, 1974). The first goal of the paper is to illustrate how the IA can directly and systematically assess the internal aspect of maternal sensitivity. The second goal of this paper is to review the empirical evidence that supports the IA's validity.

Ainsworth's scales of maternal behavior: references to internal processes

Ainsworth's scales of maternal behavior were designed to assess the quality of behavior observed in the home during the last quarter of the infants' first year. In our discussion of the scales we rely on direct quotes from Ainsworth's original coding manual (Ainsworth, 1969) because it captures so well the way Ainsworth blended behaviorally based coding with references to internal processes. In fact, using current terminology, Ainsworth's scales presuppose mothers' quality of mentalization (Fonagy et al., 1995; Main, 2000) or "mind-mindedness" (Meins, Fernyhough, Wainwright, Gupta, & Tuckey, 2002) about their children. These concepts refer to the capacity to envision both one's own and others' intentions, thoughts, feelings, and desires, and the recognition of the separateness and interconnectedness of minds (Slade, 2007). As we will describe below, these concepts are embedded, more or less explicitly, in Ainsworth's scales.

Parenthetically, Ainsworth's attention to what now would be referred to as mentalization is also evident in a lesser known but very interesting scale developed in her Uganda study called "Mother's excellence as an informant" (Ainsworth, 1967). This was coded based on interviewing the mothers about their infants, and Ainsworth described excellent informants as those who "show interest in their baby, are free from preoccupations and anxieties of their own, are sensitively perceptive of the baby's idiosyncratic ways of behaving and of the ways he expresses his needs, wishes, and preferences, and take enough interest and pleasure to want to talk about the baby, volunteering information about him rather than talking about other things" (Ainsworth, 1969, pp. 397–398). Ainsworth found that mothers who were rated higher on this scale were more likely to have securely attached children. Thus even in this early stage of her research, in which Ainsworth focused primarily on observations of infants and mothers, she already noted that careful attention to the way mothers talked about their infants reveal important aspects of caregiving that are related, in turn, to infants' security. We will now review each of the four Ainsworth scales.

Sensitivity vs. insensitivity to the baby's signals scale

Ainsworth used an information processing framework to describe the steps involved in generating a sensitive response. These included detection of the baby's signals, interpreting them as meaningful, interpreting them correctly, generating an appropriate response, and delivering the response in a timely manner. Ainsworth further emphasized that correct interpretation of the baby's signals includes empathy and freedom from distortion. For Ainsworth, being aware of the baby's distress or demands and even understanding them correctly is not sufficient, if such awareness and understanding are not accompanied by empathy. Additionally, Ainsworth emphasized the sensitive mother's accurate reading of the *entire spectrum* of the baby's signals and emotional needs, including both distress and social signals. Finally, Ainsworth described sensitive mothers as not only empathic toward the baby but also as having insight toward their own wishes and moods. She argued that such insight "leads to a more realistic judgment of the infant's behavior", probably because it enables the mother to separate her own feelings from the infants' emotional signals.

Cooperation vs. interference with baby's ongoing behavior

Similar references to internal processes are also present in the Cooperation vs. Interference with baby's ongoing behavior scale. Ainsworth describes highly interfering mothers as those who have "no respect for the baby as a separate, active, and autonomous person, whose wishes and activities have a validity of their own". She describes various "underlying dynamics" to such an attitude, including an obsessive-compulsive mother who needs to control her baby's behavior to squelch her own anxiety, or a mother who sees the baby as a "narcissistic extension of herself".

Physical and psychological availability vs. ignoring and neglecting

In her description of this scale, Ainsworth also talks about the "dynamics" underlying maternal behavior, particularly with regard to mothers who are imperceptive or unaware of the baby's signals. She describes some mothers as "teetering on the brink of depression and/or fragmentation and disintegration" and "finding the demands implicit in the baby's signals an intolerable threat to their precarious balance". It is necessary for them, therefore, to tune out the baby's signals, or to change their meaning profoundly (e.g., "perceiving crying as happy noises").

Ainsworth describes an additional dynamic leading to lack of accessibility, when the mother "creates a barrier against the babies demands". She describes these mothers as "preoccupied with their own activities … ruminating, lost in their own thoughts and worries". Other inaccessible mothers are described as "perfectly well aware of the baby's signals and interpreting them correctly" but who nonetheless deliberately ignore these signals. Ainsworth argues that these mothers are "not sufficiently able to see things from the baby's point of view – or perhaps to feel things from the baby's point of view – to want to intervene".

Acceptance vs. rejection of the baby's needs

Finally, in discussing the Acceptance vs. Rejection of the Baby's needs scale, Ainsworth describes acceptance as dependent not only on love overriding frustrations and limitations, but on the positive feelings toward the baby encompassing and defusing negative feelings. Negative components are not so much absent as they are subsumed within the context of the positive relationship. At the other side of the continuum, rejection is not the complete lack of positive feelings but the absence of integration with the negative components resulting in primarily negative feelings and even resentment toward the baby.

Although Ainsworth's descriptions of the four rating scales include many references to internal processes, as shown above, the bulk of the text describing each scale provide behavioral, observational descriptors. Consider the sensitivity scale as an example: "In the last analysis", Ainsworth writes, "the appropriateness and promptness of the mother's responses to communications are the hallmark of sensitivity". Ainsworth emphasizes observable qualities such as the quality of the mother's interaction with the baby, the appropriateness of her responses, and the degree to which they are well resolved and well rounded. Similar behavioral descriptions are abundant in the other scales as well. This behavioral emphasis notwithstanding, it appears that for Ainsworth the internal processes underlying caregiving behavior are an inseparable part of understanding maternal behavior and its impact on the infant's sense of being understood and accepted – and ultimately, the infant's sense of security in his or her attachment relationship.

Interestingly, Ainsworth's insights regarding the mental processes underlying sensitivity (and insensitivity) are consistent with the literature on parent–infant clinical work. Fraiberg's classic "Ghosts in the Nursery" paper (Fraiberg, Adelson, & Shapiro, 1975) describes how past traumas distort maternal perceptions of the child's behavior, and how resolution of the trauma frees the child from these distortions and enables the mother to respond appropriately to the infant's signals. Similarly Lieberman, who was one of Ainsworth's students, describes how maternal negative attributions with regard to the infant or young child become self-fulfilling prophecies leading to maternal behavior that exacerbates the child's negative behavior (e.g., Silverman & Lieberman, 1999). These clinical examples show remarkable parallels with Ainsworth's descriptions of the dynamics underlying maternal behavior.

The *research* use of the sensitivity scales, however, has focused on coding based on observed behavior. This research has proven to be very productive and has yielded a large corpus of studies regarding the sequalae of maternal sensitivity (e.g., De Wolff & van IJzendoorn, 1997; Weinfield, Sroufe, Egeland, & Carlson, 1999). However, Ainsworth's insights regarding the importance of "seeing things from the child's point of view" as the basis for sensitive behavior have by and large not been examined by subsequent researchers and, as mentioned earlier, we developed the IA (Oppenheim & Koren-Karie, 2009) to address this gap.

Our work on insightfulness was based on the "move to the level of representation" within the attachment paradigm (Main, Kaplan, & Cassidy, 1985). Most importantly it has its roots in Main's Adult Attachment Interview (Hesse, 1999), particularly in its emphasis on the primacy of the organization of maternal thought and speech over the content of maternal memories. For example, organization is reflected in the consistency between the general characterization of the relationship with the parent and specific episodic memories that are brought as support for this characterization. Also influential were attachment researchers who followed Main's path and developed maternal interviews that focused on the "internal working model" of the child (e.g., Bretherton, Biringen, Ridgeway, Maslin, & Sherman, 1989; Fonagy, Steele, Steele, Moran, & Higgit, 1991; George & Solomon, 1999; Slade, Belsky, Aber, & Phelps, 1999; Zeanah, Benoit, Hirshberg, Barton, & Regan, 1994). This line of research made headway in studying mothers' representations of their children. The contribution of the IA is in examining how such representations are applied in order to understand the child's behavior in a specific moment. The parent uses what they know about the child from past experience and what the child's behavior means for him or her in order to understand the child's behavior and figure out the thoughts and feelings on which it may be based. The meeting between parental representations and "reality" – that is, the behavior of the child as observed by the parent – may reinforce, modify, or change what the parent knows and feels about the child, and this reciprocal process is at the heart of the IA.

The insightfulness assessment procedure

Insightfulness is assessed using a video replay procedure in which parents and children are first videotaped in three interactional contexts representing different aspects of the parent–child relationship, such as caregiving, play, and teaching (Oppenheim & Koren-Karie, 2009). Subsequently, parents are shown the first two minutes of each of the video segments, and after each one are asked what they believe their child was thinking or feeling in the segment and where on the video they could see that the child was thinking or feeling in that particular way. They are asked whether the behaviors they saw on the video are typical of their child; finally they are asked about the way they felt when they were watching the video. Specifically, we inquire whether their child's behaviors surprised them, concerned them, or made them happy. At the end of the interview, parents are asked two general questions: first, to list their child's main characteristics and, second, to describe what best characterizes their relationship. The IA has been used with parents of children as young as 6 months and up to 18 years.

The interview transcripts are analyzed based on *how* the parents talk about the child more than on the specific descriptions they provide. In particular, we look at the capacity of the parent to talk about the motives underlying the child's behavior in a complex, accepting, and open way while anchoring their statements in the video segments. Note that the accuracy of parental statements vis-à-vis the video segments is not assessed and that the assessment is based solely on reading the transcripts of the interview, without looking at the video segments the mothers observed. As mentioned above, our emphasis on the organization of parental speech and thought process is based on Main's insights about parental states of mind regarding their childhood histories as revealed in the Adult Attachment Interview (Main, 2000). Main discovered that how the parents talked about their past – particularly the coherence of their speech and thought – was more critical to the prediction of their infants' attachments to them than the specific memories that were evoked in the interview (Main et al., 1985). In a parallel fashion we emphasize *how* the parents talk about the thoughts and feelings that underlie their children's behavior more than on the specific thoughts and feelings they attribute to their children or the accuracy of these attributions.

The interview transcripts are rated on 10 scales (Insight into child's motives, Openness, Complexity in description of child, Maintenance of focus on child, Richness of description of child, Acceptance, Anger, Worry, Separateness from child, Coherence of thought; see Table 1) and subsequently classified into one of four groups based on the profiles of the scales (Koren-Karie & Oppenheim, 2001). The first of the four groups indicates the capacity for insightfulness while the remaining three indicate a lack of insightfulness. The groups are:

(1) *Positively Insightful (PI):* The main characteristic of these parents is their attempt to understand the motives underlying their child's behavior and their acceptance of these motives. Additionally, they talk openly about a wide spectrum of child behaviors, both positive and negative.
(2) *One-sided (Os):* One-sided parents seem to have a preset conception of the child that they impose on the video-taped segments, and this conception does not appear open to

Table 1. Insightfulness assessment scales.

IA scale	Low	High
Insight into child's motives	Mother[1] does not talk about possible motives for her child's behavior	Mother tries to understand the thoughts and feelings that may underlie her child's behavior; she moves freely between the videotaped observations and her knowledge about her child, draws parallels between the two, and tries to gain deeper understanding
Openness	Mother is not open to the information of the videotaped observations, but rather speaks about her fixed and preset ideas about the child; the observation may be dismissed as not typical of the child	Mother is open to the information arising from the videotaped observations; she compares what she knows about her child with the video observations and modifies her perceptions if needed
Complexity in description of child	Mother describes the child in a uni-dimensional, one-sided way, emphasizing either only positive or only negative aspects of the child	Mother provides a believable description of the child in which the child is described as a "whole" with both positive and negative aspects
Maintenance of focus on child	The child is not the focus of discussion; rather, the focus is on the mother and her feelings and thoughts or other irrelevant issues	The child is the focus of discussion; if mother talks about herself, it will be when she is asked to do so or regarding her maternal role
Richness of description of child	Limited responses that lack substance or full responses with mostly irrelevant details	Mother responds to the interview questions in a full, comprehensive, and vivid way
Acceptance	Mother expresses dissatisfaction or disappointment in the child or talks about the child in a derogatory way	Mother accepts the full range of her child's behaviors and shows tolerance and understanding toward challenging aspects; she is open about difficulties in her child's behavior and conveys a deep acceptance of the child
Anger	Mother's speech does not include current anger even though she can talk about behaviors that caused her to feel angry in the past	Current anger toward the child is a central feature of mother's talk; the child is described as having many irritating traits, and many of his behaviors on the videotaped observation elicit anger in mother
Worry	Mother expresses belief in herself and her child's capacity to cope with challenges	Mother's worry regarding the child, her maternal behavior, or their relationship is a central, repetitive theme throughout the interview
Separateness from child	Mother finds it difficult to talk about the child with a sense of clear boundaries; she may talk about the child's thoughts as if spoken out loud or refers to ideas regarding what the child *might* think or feel as facts	Mother sees the child as a separate person and accepts that the child may sometimes have needs and wishes that are different or even contradictory to hers
Coherence of thought – Overall Scale	Mother's speech does not convey a consistent and clear picture, and it is difficult to understand what she means; responses may contain digressions and contradictions, or mother may ignore the videotaped observations	Mother is focused on the videotaped segments, and in her answer she develops ideas in a consistent, connected, and relaxed way; her speech forms an integrated and clear picture linked both to the videotaped segments and the child as a whole

Note: [1]Scales apply to fathers or other caregivers as well.

change. Some One-sided parents find it difficult to maintain the focus of their speech on the child, and others overemphasize the child's positive qualities without being able to support their statements with examples. Still others may describe the child as "all negative" and talk only about his/her faults and misbehaviors.

(3) *Disengaged (De)*: Disengaged parents are characterized by their lack of emotional involvement during the interview. Their answers are short and limited, and they do not use the observation as an opportunity to reflect upon their child's and their own behavior. It seems that attempts for understanding what is on their child's mind are novel to them. Disengaged parents talk very little about their children's emotions, and talk more about their behavior.

(4) *Mixed (Mx):* This category involves parents who do not show one type of speech as defined in the above categories. Rather, such parents may respond to one video segment in one style, and to another segment with a different style. For example, a parent may sound overwhelmed, unfocused, or hostile in the responses to the three video segments, but insightful, complex, and open in the response to the two general questions that follow.

The validity of the claim that the IA captures mothers' capacity to "see things from the child's point of view", that is, the processes underlying sensitivity, ultimately rests on empirical findings. We will review these later, but first we return to Ainsworth's scales and show how the IA captures the references to internal processes they include. Obviously, the similarity between the IA and Ainsworth's description of sensitivity is not a coincidence, because our work was inspired by Ainsworth. What the IA adds is a systematic, direct way to assess the capacity to "see things from the child's point of view" and the thought processes that can impede or derail this capacity.

The internal processes underlying maternal behavior: how are they expressed in the IA?

Sensitivity vs. insensitivity to the baby's signals scale

One of the main features of insensitive mothers, according to Ainsworth, is their misinterpretation of their child's signals because "their perception is distorted by projection, denial, or other marked defensive operations" and they "tend to bias their 'reading' of their babies according to their own wishes, moods and fantasies". Such biases can be captured in the IA, as the following example illustrates.

In a study of mothers who were sexually abused as children, a mother who was molested by her father described her 11-year-old daughter as very decisive, independent, and assertive. She talked supportively about these characteristics but, as the following excerpt shows, other behaviors or characteristics of the child which were not consistent with assertiveness and strength were dismissed. After watching a video clip in which she played with her child a separation-reunion scenario using doll figures, the mother said that her child looked very stressed by the separation but continued by saying:

> "She was just pretending here. In reality she has no fears at all. She is really very brave. We can leave her for a weekend, and actually even for a week or more, and she won't be stressed because she knows that nothing would harm her".

In this example we can see how the mother's need to see her daughter as brave and invulnerable prevented her from accepting her child's distress around separation and possible need for closeness and protection. In order to maintain this perception, expressions of the child's neediness are described as not representing her "real" capacities and feelings. The mother "knows" the "real" child, the child who has no fears, and stresses these characteristics while ignoring characteristics that are inconsistent with this preconception. Importantly, the mother's lack of insight is not based on judging her description of the child as "just pretending" as inaccurate. Rather, lack of insightfulness is evident in her inability to support her claims regarding her child's lack of distress with behavior from the video segment. In fact, there is a contradiction between the behavior the mother describes (i.e., distress) and the conclusion she draws (i.e., her child has "no fears"), and it is this contradiction that reveals her bias or "distortion", in Ainsworth's terms.

Cooperation vs. interference with baby's ongoing behavior

According to Ainsworth, cooperative parenting is based on the mother's ability to see her child as a separate person. In the IA this is reflected in the stance of "active observation": the mother observes her child's behaviors, tries to understand their meaning (e.g., is the child withdrawn because he is embarrassed? Is he cooperative because he likes the specific toy?), while at the same time speaking about her child as having needs and wishes that may be quite different from her own (e.g., the child likes noisy toys that she finds irritating). The opposite of cooperation, interference is described by Ainsworth as the mother "having no respect for the baby as a separate, active, and autonomous person, whose wishes and activities have a validity of their own". In the IA this is reflected in responses that show lack of respect of their child's autonomy and distinctiveness.

For example, the mother of an 8-year-old boy was shown a video segment in which she played a competitive game with her son. When asked about her son's thoughts and feelings during that clip, she said that he hates losing and described her son as very competitive and showing excessive emotional reactions when he loses. When asked for an everyday example of this behavior she described the day in which her son got a letter in which he was told that he was not accepted to a program for gifted children. She told the interviewer that the child read the letter and a few minutes later went outside to play football with his friends, a common afternoon activity for him. When he came back home for dinner he looked calm and content and did not mention the rejection letter. The mother added that she had waited anxiously for a positive letter of acceptance, and was very disappointed when the rejection letter arrived. She said:

> "Such a program could open so many options for him. I think that is why he was so upset when he heard the news. It was such a heart break for both of us. It could have been a wonderful and unique opportunity that we were so sorry to have missed".

Note that this mother's statement that "It was such a heart break for both of us" is inconsistent with her earlier description of the child's calm response. In her mind, *her* wishes and feelings become *the child's* experience. The child's behavior is interpreted according to the mother's preset concept of him which reflects her own wishes and, by so doing, there is no room left for seeing the child as an autonomous person with wishes and goals that may be different or even opposite to those of the mother.

Maternal interference can also be expressed in the IA in lack of acceptance. Ainsworth describes the interfering mother as "… feeling that the baby is hers and that she has a perfect right to impose her will on him". A mother who feels that she "has the right" to have a specific child may focus on specific characteristics of the child that are in line with her sense of her "right" and dismiss or reject behaviors and characteristics with which they are not in line. For example, when referring to the child's wish to play football with his friends, the same mother described above said:

> "it is such a waste of time. A bunch of boys who just don't know what to do with their spare time ... just running and running, as if that will bring them somewhere ... it will bring him nowhere! He should listen to me and exercise his brain muscles instead of his leg muscles in chasing this ball". Thus, this mother's feeling of her "right" to have a gifted child is expressed in her positive way of talking about the child's academic pursuits and her rejection of her child's wish to play.

Availability vs. ignoring and neglecting

Ainsworth describes ignoring and neglecting mothers as "preoccupied with their own activities ... lost in their own thoughts and worries. While they are thus preoccupied, the baby may go unnoticed". Paralleling this description of preoccupation we see in the IA mothers who find it difficult to keep their answers focused on their child's thoughts and feelings. They may begin by focusing on the child but soon thereafter they drift to other, unrelated, issues with no reflection on this drift.

For example, a mother of a 4.5-year-old child was shown a video segment in which she assisted her child with the construction of a house according to a model that was given to the mother and the child. She was asked "What do you think was going on in your child's mind while you were building the house together?" and answered:

> "The funny thing is that I was startled by the whole thing. I wasn't really sure how to understand the instructions. I turned over the house, organized the blocks but I wasn't really sure if I'm doing the right thing. After all, it's so simple to do it once you understand. Really, not a big deal. But that's only afterwards, once I built it I saw how simple it was. But in the beginning I was really scared and I felt like I was in some kind of test. That you are testing me, you know, as if it's some kind of intelligence test, and that reminded me the test anxieties I had as a student. Really, my hands were sweating and I became so thirsty. I used to come to the exam room with 2 or 3 bottles of waters".

This mother's preoccupation with herself is evident in her response: instead of focusing on her child's thoughts and feelings as she was requested, she focused on her own thoughts, feelings, and memories. The central issue in her response was her, not the child. The importance of such drift is that by losing the focus on the child, the child becomes unnoticed in the mother's mind, paralleling Ainsworth's description of ignoring and neglecting mothers.

Acceptance vs. rejection of the baby's needs

Finally, this scale also has parallels in the IA, particularly in the parent's ability to portray a complex, multidimensional picture of the child. Ainsworth described the Acceptance vs. Rejection of the baby's needs scale as dealing "with the balance between the mother's positive and negative feelings about her baby". A mother with complex speech in the IA is characterized by her capacity to portray a full and integrated picture of her child that includes both positive and rewarding behaviors as well as more challenging and less rewarding behaviors. Complex speech means that the mother is able to talk about positive dimensions of the child even in the case of a very challenging child (e.g., a child with autism), and at the same time is able to describe less favorable and rewarding moments when talking about a very easy going and competent child.

Balanced, complex descriptions do not imply that each positive description is followed by a negative description or vice versa. In fact, at least in normative samples, it is quite common for positive descriptions to outweigh the negative ones. The balance is expressed in the mothers' ability to mention, alongside the positive descriptions, the possibility that the child is not always easy and that parenting is not always rewarding, and to not show insistence on portraying a "perfect" picture.

For example, a mother of 3-year-old described her child as follows:

> She is pretty independent. She is good in entertaining herself, at taking an ordinary situation and making it something fun for herself. She is really creative and she is a happy and easygoing child. As I said earlier, she also likes taking charge. She has her own timing and her own will about things. I appreciate her being focused on the things she wants and I think this is good, but sometimes it's a negative thing, because we have a large family, and we have to do certain things at certain times. She hasn't yet understood that, of course it is related to her age, that she's not comfortable with "no".

This mother described positive characteristics of her child (e.g., "creative", "easygoing") together with less positive characteristics ("likes taking charge") and by so doing created a balanced and complex picture of her child. In addition, the mother did not talk about her child's need to be in charge as representing negative qualities or difficult personality traits, but rather was able to put child's behavior into a developmental context by taking her age into consideration.

Empirical support for the IA

Up to this point we have shown how the IA captures some of the internal processes underlying sensitive (and insensitive) parenting that Ainsworth described in her scales. If the IA captures this aspect of sensitivity, it is expected that it would be associated with secure attachment in a way that parallels the findings regarding observed maternal sensitivity. We review studies that support this hypothesis next. These studies attempted to not only match the IA with infant attachment patterns at the dichotomous level (i.e., insightful/non-insightful with secure/insecure) but to match each of the four IA classifications (Positive Insightfulness, One-sided, Disengaged, Mixed) with each of the four infant attachment classifications (Secure, Ambivalent, Avoidant, Disorganized: Ainsworth et al., 1978; Main & Solomon, 1990), respectively. These specific concordances were important because a core concept in attachment theory involves the specific adaptations (i.e., types of secure and particularly insecure attachment) children make to specific types of sensitive and particularly insensitive parental care.

We hypothesized that parents classified as *Positively Insightful* will be likely to have children classified as secure, because their insightfulness would facilitate correct interpretations and empathic responses to their infants' signals, as well as open examination of the appropriateness (or inappropriateness) of their caregiving behavior based on their children's reactions. Such caregiving is likely to be experienced by the child as matched to his or her emotional needs and therefore to contribute to a secure infant–mother attachment (Ainsworth et al., 1978).

We further expected that the *One-sided IA* classification would be associated with the insecure-ambivalent attachment pattern. The reasoning was that the uni-dimensional view of the child is likely to be associated with inconsistent care: when the child's behavior is congruent with the mother's expectations she may respond appropriately, whereas when the child's behavior is not congruent with mother's expectations she may ignore or respond in a way that is not matched to the child's needs. Another scenario involving the one-sided classification involves understanding without empathy: some mothers in this classification show understanding of the motives underlying the child's behavior combined with a rejection of those motives. Both expressions of the one-sided stance may be experienced by the child as frustrating and confusing – the kind of caregiving presumed to lead to ambivalent attachment (Cassidy & Berlin, 1994).

We expected that parents classified as *Disengaged* would be most likely to have children classified as avoidant. Here the reasoning was that the lack of emotional engagement characteristic of these parents may lead to minimizing or even ignoring the child's bids for closeness and protection which may be experienced by the child as rejection (Main, 2000). Perhaps more than any of the other IA classifications, the Disengaged orientation may leave children with the feeling that while their external behavior may be acknowledged, as emotional and mental beings they are not known by their caregivers (Slade, 1999). These experiences are likely to lead to a shutting off of the child's emotional expression, particularly of negative affect and emotional needs, and therefore be associated with an avoidant attachment (Zeanah et al., 1994).

Finally, we expected that parents classified as *Mixed* would be most likely to have children classified as having an insecure-disorganized attachment. We argued that the lack of a coherent strategy while speaking about the child will be reflected in competing or contradictory caregiving behaviors when interacting with the child (Hesse & Main, 2000). Such strategies have been described by Lyons-Ruth and colleagues (Lyons-Ruth, Bronfman, & Atwood, 1999; Madigan et al., 2006) as being expressed in disruptive parental affective communication and leading to disorganized attachment.

Studies with low-risk families

Two studies of low-risk families that focused on the links between the IA and infant–mother attachment assessed using the Strange Situation Procedure provided support for these associations (Koren-Karie, Oppenheim, Dolev, Sher, & Etzion-Carasso, 2002; Oppenheim, Koren-Karie, & Sagi, 2001). In both studies mothers classified Positively Insightful were most likely to have securely attached children, mothers classified One-sided were most likely to have insecure/ambivalent children, and mothers classified Mixed were most likely to have children classified insecure/disorganized: 4 × 4 concordance in the Koren-Karie et al. (2002) study was 64%, kappa = .39, $p < .01$; in the Oppenheim et al. (2001) study 4 × 4 concordance was 56%, kappa = .33, $p < .001$. Unexpectedly, no associations were found between the Disengaged classification and children's attachment, perhaps because our samples (like all those based on studies conducted in Israel: van IJzendoorn & Sagi, 1999) included very few children classified Avoidant. However, the Disengaged classification received support because mothers classified as Disengaged were observed to be the least sensitive (Koren-Karie et al., 2002) and showed low levels of appropriate "Mind-minded" comments (Meins et al., 2002) while interacting with their babies (Fridman, 2005). In addition, children of mothers classified as Disengaged had the lowest Theory of Mind scores 3 years later (Oppenheim, Koren-Karie, Etzion-Carasso, & Sagi-Schwartz, 2005). Taken together, the findings regarding the Disengaged classification support the notion that it reflects emotional distance.

The IA studies reviewed heretofore all involved *maternal* insightfulness, but in a recent family study with 18-month-old toddlers *paternal* insightfulness was also assessed (Marcu, 2013). The goal of the study was to extend the dyadic findings linking insightfulness to observed interaction to the triadic level. Specifically, the study examined the contribution of parental insightfulness to triadic, mother–father–child play interactions (assessed using the Lausanne Trilogue Play [LTP] procedure: Fivaz-Depeursinge, Frascarolo, & Corboz-Warnery, 1996), hypothesizing that parental insightfulness would contribute to coordinated and cooperative family interactions. In order to capture the joint contribution of the insightfulness of both parents we formed three groups: the most optimal group in which both parents were insightful, a middle group in which one parent was insightful and the other non-insightful, and a least optimal group in which neither parent was insightful. The results showed that when both parents were insightful the triadic interactions were rated as coordinated, the most optimal LTP classification; when only one parent was insightful the triadic interactions were rated as conflictual, the mid-range LTP classification; and when both parents were non-insightful the triadic interactions were classified as disordered, the least optimal LTP classification. The results of this study provide additional support for the importance of insightfulness in promoting synchronized interactions between parents and children, and extend the primarily dyadic context of insightfulness research to the triadic context. In addition the study supports the use of the IA with fathers, and it would valuable in future research to parallel the research done with mothers and establish the links between insightfulness, sensitivity, and security in samples of fathers and their children.

Studies with high-risk children

Support for the link between the IA and child attachment was also obtained in two samples of atypically developing children, including children with Autistic Spectrum Disorder (Oppenheim, Koren-Karie, Dolev, & Yirmiya, 2009) and children with Intellectual Disability (Feniger-Shaal & Oppenheim, 2012; Oppenheim, Feniger-Shaal, & Koren-Karie, 2010). The samples in both studies were too small to examine the four insightfulness classifications separately; rather, mothers were grouped as either insightful or non-insightful. In both studies, mothers who were Insightful were more likely to have children who were securely attached as assessed using the Strange Situation Procedure, and mothers who were non-insightful were more likely to have children who were insecurely attached: 2×2 concordance in the Oppenheim et al. (2009) study was 69%, Likelihood Ratio = 6.99, $p < .03$; in the Oppenheim et al. (2010) study concordance was 73%, kappa = .46, $p < .05$. Importantly, in both studies insightfulness was not related to the severity of children's disability or their IQ, suggesting that insightfulness (or lack thereof) is not merely a reflection of the level of challenge the child represents to the parent. In other words, it is possible to reveal insightfulness toward a child whose diagnosis is severe and whose functioning is low. This finding regarding insightfulness is consistent with the theorizing about maternal sensitivity that emphasizes the adaptation of the parent to the child's specific and unique characteristics, and that stresses that the challenge the child presents, such as having a developmental disability or even milder developmental variations including a difficult temperament, does not preclude the parent from showing sensitivity.

Because the IA was designed to assess mental processes underlying sensitive (or insensitive) behavior, another important research question involved the associations between the IA and maternal observed sensitivity. In support of the IA we found in one study (Koren-Karie et al., 2002) that mothers classified as positively insightful were more sensitive in their interactions with their infants in both home and laboratory observations than those not so classified. As mentioned above, attachment (coded for this analysis as secure vs. insecure) was also assessed in this study, and we found that sensitivity did not account for all of the shared variance between maternal insightfulness (coded for this analysis as insightful vs. non-insightful) and child attachment. In other words, insightfulness explained variance in attachment beyond the variance accounted for by sensitivity. While this could be due to limitations in the assessment of sensitivity, which was coded based on relatively brief laboratory and home observations, this finding could also point to the way insightfulness adds to the assessment of sensitivity from observation alone.

The association between insightfulness and maternal sensitivity was also demonstrated in the Autism Spectrum Disorder (Oppenheim et al., 2009, 2012) and the Intellectual Disability samples mentioned above (Oppenheim et al., 2010). Mothers classified as insightful were rated as more sensitive than those classified non-insightful. In fact, the mean sensitivity score of the mothers classified as insightful was high – above the cutoff score defining the threshold for sensitive maternal behavior. Similar results have been reported by Hutman, Siller and Sigman (2009), who found that mothers of children with Autism Spectrum Disorder classified as insightful were more synchronous in their interactions with their children than mothers classified non-insightful. Thus it appears that even when children's input into the interaction with the parent is severely limited and atypical, as is the case in Autism, insightfulness is possible and is associated with more sensitive caregiving behavior.

A study with older children in a foster group home setting (Koren-Karie, Oppenheim, Yuval-Adler, & Mor, 2013) also showed links between insightfulness and sensitive caregiver behavior. In this study the foster caregivers were observed with two of several children that were under their care, one nominated by an independent rater as the most challenging child and the other nominated as the least challenging child. The caregivers and the children were asked to jointly construct narratives about past emotional experiences of the child, such as when the child felt happy, mad, sad, scared, or safe. The caregivers' sensitive guidance of the conversations was coded from the transcripts of mother–child dialogues, based on their ability to co-construct emotionally open, well-regulated, and organized narratives that stressed the child's capacity to cope with challenges (Koren-Karie et al., 2013), and their insightfulness toward each of the two children with whom they were observed was assessed. The results showed similarity in the insightfulness the foster caregivers showed toward each of the two children, indicating that insightfulness appears to capture a relatively stable characteristic of the caregivers (Yuval-Adler, 2010). In addition, caregivers who were insightful guided their conversations with the children more sensitively than those who were non-insightful, although this was only true with the least challenging children. Perhaps with the challenging children additional factors, such as high levels of emotional and behavioral dysregulation, were more influential with regard to how the conversations evolved.

Intervention studies

Finally, three intervention studies provided additional support for the IA. The first study (Oppenheim, Goldsmith, & Koren-Karie, 2004) included preschoolers referred due to a wide range of behavioral and emotional problems to a therapeutic preschool in which the entire environment was designed to address the children's emotional and behavioral challenges (Goldsmith, 2007). In parallel, their mothers participated in therapy sessions focusing on parenting issues. The findings showed that prior to treatment only 9% of the mothers were classified as insightful, and that following 7 months of treatment 50% were so classified. Additional findings linked improvements in mothers with improvements in children. The preschool teachers' reports regarding children's behavior problems indicated that following treatment there was a significant drop in both internalizing and externalizing problems, but only for children of mothers who shifted from non-insightfulness prior treatment to insightfulness following the treatment. While the design of the study does not permit us to determine whether changes in mothers led to changes in children or vice versa, they do show that reduction in children's behavior problem was associated with increases in insightfulness, suggesting that insightfulness may play an important role in enhancing children's emotional and behavioral regulation and/or maintaining children's gains in these domains once they are achieved.

The second intervention study using the IA employed the Circle of Security (Powell, Cooper, Hoffman, & Marvin, 2007) group intervention in order to enhance the insightfulness and sensitivity of mothers with a trauma history and increase the security of children's attachments (Muzik et al., 2012). IA and attachment assessments were obtained prior to treatment, following the 12 week intervention, and at a 6 month follow-up. Results showed improvements in mothers' insightfulness following treatment (but no additional improvements in the follow-up). In particular, the IA scales on which improvements were found were insight, acceptance, openness, richness, and coherence. The results also showed that mothers who were insightful following the intervention had children who were more secure at the follow-up assessment (as measured by the Strange Situation – Preschool version), suggesting that improvements in maternal insightfulness promoted security in children's attachments. Interestingly the time lag between the assessments suggests that there may be some delay between the gains in maternal insightfulness and those in children's attachment. Both of the intervention studies we reviewed were limited due to small sample sizes and the lack of a control group, but provide promising preliminary results supporting the importance of insightfulness for children's therapeutic gains and the potential for enhancing insightfulness using interventions.

A final intervention study involved a randomized clinical trial designed to increase responsive parental behaviors and child communication in young children with Autism Spectrum Disorder (Siller, Hutman, & Sigman, 2013). The intervention involved 12 home visits, in each of which in the first part mothers and children as well as the interventionist play, and in the second part the interventionist and the mother discuss strategies for enhancing parental responsiveness using a range of learning techniques such as workbooks, review of video material, and discussion of homework assignments. Maternal insightfulness was assessed prior to treatment, and the study's results showed gains in the responsiveness of the mothers in the treatment group, but only in the mothers who were classified as insightful prior to treatment. In other words, insightfulness moderated the treatment effectiveness, perhaps because insightful mothers, who are more open to modify their views of their child and who are more flexible and balanced in their thinking about the child's experience, could more readily and rapidly learn additional or alternative interactional strategies. These findings are intriguing because they suggest that the effectiveness of interventions in other similar studies (e.g., Green et al., 2010) may have been underestimated. Maybe the results of such studies reflect a strong intervention effect for insightful mothers with weak or no effect for non-insightful mothers.

Conclusion

Following Ainsworth (1969) we conceptualized insightfulness as "seeing – and feeling – things from the child's point of view". In developing the IA, we set out to complement the observable aspect of coding sensitivity with the internal aspect that is more difficult to code from observation because it requires information regarding thoughts and feelings in the parent. In other words, the IA builds on Ainsworth's insights regarding the importance of internal processes as integral parts of caregiving that promote – or in some cases inhibit – the establishment of a secure attachment between the child and the parent. The main contribution of the IA is in offering a direct and systematic method to assess these processes.

The empirical findings reviewed above provide a network of associations around the IA that support its validity. Insightfulness was found to be associated with maternal sensitivity and secure attachment in both typically developing children and those with atypical development. Additionally, insightfulness was found to be relatively independent of the level of challenge presented by the child, and thus appears to be more a reflection of parental efforts to understand the motives for the child's behavior than of the child's characteristics. Finally, intervention studies have shown that insightfulness may play an important moderating role in such interventions. Taken together, our findings suggest that the IA provides a valuable complement to the observational assessment of parental sensitivity pioneered by Ainsworth.

References

Ainsworth, M. D. S. (1967). *Infancy in Uganda: Infant care and the growth of love*. Baltimore, MD: Johns Hopkins University Press.

Ainsworth, M. D. S. (1969). *Maternal sensitivity scales*. Retrieved from http://www.psychology.sunysb.edu/attachment/measures/content/ainsworth_scales.html

Ainsworth, M. D. S., Bell, S. M., & Stayton, D. J. (1971). Individual differences in the strange situation behavior of one-year-olds. In H. R. Schaffer (Ed.), *The origins of human social relations* (pp. 17–58). San Diego, CA: Academic Press.

Ainsworth, M. D. S., Bell, S. M., & Stayton, D. J. (1974). Infant-mother attachment and social development: Socialisation as a product of reciprocal responsiveness to signals. In M. J. M. Richards (Ed.), *The integration of a child into a social world* (pp. 99–135). London: Cambridge University Press.

Ainsworth, M. D. S., Blehar, M. C., Waters, E., & Wall, S. (1978). *Patterns of attachment: A psychological study of the strange situation*. Hillsdale, NJ: Erlbaum.

Bretherton, I., Biringen, Z., Ridgeway, D., Maslin, C., & Sherman, M. (1989). Attachment: The parental perspective. *Infant Mental Health Journal, 10*, 203–221.

Cassidy, J., & Berlin, L. (1994). The insecure/ambivalent pattern of attachment: Theory and research. *Child Development, 65*, 971–991. doi:10.2307/1131298

De Wolff, M. S., & van IJzendoorn, M. H. (1997). Sensitivity and attachment: A meta-analysis on parental antecedents of infant attachment. *Child Development*, *68*, 571–591.

Feniger-Shaal, R., & Oppenheim, D. (2012). Resolution of the diagnosis and maternal sensitivity among mothers of children with intellectual disability. *Research in Developmental Disabilities*, *34*, 306–313.

Fivaz-Depeursinge, E., Frascarolo, F., & Corboz-Warnery, A. (1996). Assessing the triadic alliance between fathers, mothers, and infants at play. In J. McHale & P. Cowan (Eds.), *Understanding how family-level dynamics affect children's development: Studies of two parent families (New Directions for Child Development, Vol. 74)*. San Francisco, CA: Jossey-Bass.

Fonagy, P., Steele, M., Steele, H., Leigh, T., Kennedy, R., Mattoon, G., & Target, M. (1995). Attachment, the reflective self, and borderline states: The predictive specificity of the Adult Attachment Interview and pathological emotional development. In S. Goldberg, R. Muir, & J. Kerr (Eds.), *Attachment theory: Social, developmental, and clinical perspectives* (pp. 233–278). Hillsdale, NJ: The Analytic Press.

Fonagy, P., Steele, M., Steele, H., Moran, G. S., & Higgit, A. C. (1991). The capacity for understanding mental states: The reflective self in parent and child and its significance for security of attachment. *Infant Mental Health Journal*, *13*, 200–217.

Fraiberg, S., Adelson, E., & Shapiro, V. (1975). Ghosts in the nursery: A psychoanalytic approach to the problems of impaired infant-mother relationships. *Journal of the American Academy of Child Psychiatry*, *14*, 387–421. doi:10.1016/S0002-7138(09)61442-4.

Fridman, A. (2005). *Maternal mind-mindedness: Relations with maternal insightfulness and infant behavior at one year* (Unpublished master's thesis). University of Haifa, Israel.

George, C., & Solomon, J. (1999). Attachment and caregiving: The caregiving behavioral system. In J. Cassidy & P. Shaver (Eds.), *Handbook of attachment: Theory, research, and clinical applications* (pp. 649–670). New York, NY: Guilford.

Goldsmith, D. F. (2007). Challenging children's negative internal working models: Utilizing attachment based strategies in a therapeutic preschool. In D. Oppenheim & D. F. Goldsmith (Eds.), *Attachment theory in clinical work with children: Bridging the gap between research and practice* (pp. 203–225). New York, NY: Guilford.

Green, J., Charman, T., McConachie, H., Aldred, C., Slonims, V., Howlin, P., … PACT Consortium. (2010). Parent-mediated communication-focused treatment in children with autism (PACT): A randomised controlled trial. *The Lancet*, *375*(9732), 2152–2160.

Hesse, E. (1999). The Adult Attachment Interview: Historical and current perspectives. In J. Cassidy & P. Shaver (Eds.), *Handbook of attachment: Theory, research, and clinical applications* (pp. 395–433). New York, NY: Guilford.

Hesse, E., & Main, M. (2000). Disorganized infant, child, and adult attachment: Collapse in behavioral and attentional strategies. *Journal of the American Psychoanalytic Association*, *48*(4), 1097–1127.

Hutman, T., Siller, M., & Sigman, M. (2009). Mothers' narratives regarding their child with autism predict maternal synchronous behavior during play. *Journal of Child Psychology and Psychiatry*, *10*, 1255–1263. doi:10.1111/j.1469-7610.2009.02109.x.

Koren-Karie, N., & Oppenheim, D. (2001). *Insightfulness procedure coding manual* (Unpublished manual). University of Haifa, Israel.

Koren-Karie, N., Oppenheim, D., Dolev, S., Sher, E., & Etzion-Carasso, A. (2002). Mothers' empathic understanding of their infants' internal experience: Relations with maternal sensitivity and infant attachment. *Developmental Psychology*, *38*, 534–542. doi:10.1037/0012-1649.38.4.534.

Koren-Karie, N., Oppenheim, D., Yuval-Adler, S., & Mor, H. (2013). Emotion dialogues of foster caregivers with their children: The role of the caregivers, above and beyond child characteristics, in shaping the interactions. *Attachment & Human Development*, *15*(2), 175–188.

Lyons-Ruth, K., Bronfman, E., & Atwood, G. (1999). A relational diathesis of hostile-helpless states of mind: Expressions in mother-infant interaction. In J. Solomon & C. George (Eds.), *Attachment disorganization* (pp. 33–70). New York, NY: Guilford.

Madigan, S., Bakermans-Kraneneburg, M., Van IJzendoorn, M. H., Moran, G., Pederson, D. R., & Benoit, D. (2006). Unresolved states of mind, anomalous parental behavior, and disorganized attachment: A review and meta-analysis of a transmission gap. *Attachment & Human Development*, *8*, 89–111.

Main, M. (2000). The organized categories of infant, child, and adult attachment: Flexible vs. inflexible attention under attachment-related stress. *Journal of the American Psychoanalytic Association*, *48*, 1055–1096.

Main, M., Kaplan, N., & Cassidy, J. (1985). Security in infancy, childhood, and adulthood: A move to the level of representation. In I. Bretherton & E. Waters (Eds.), Growing points in attachment theory and research. *Monographs of the Society for Research in Child Development*, *50*(1–2, Serial No. 209), 66–104. Retrieved from http://www.wiley.com/bw/journal.asp?ref=0037-976x .

Main, M., & Solomon, J. (1990). Procedures for identifying infants as disorganized/disoriented during the Ainsworth Strange Situation. In M. T. Greenberg, D. Cicchetti, & E. M. Cummings (Eds.), *Attachment in the preschool years: Theory, research, and intervention* (pp. 121–160). Chicago, IL: University of Chicago Press.

Marcu, I. (2013). *Parental insightfulness regarding the child's inner world: Its contribution to the family alliance in families with toddlers* (Unpublished doctoral dissertation). Department of Psychology, University of Haifa, Israel.

Meins, E., Fernyhough, C., Wainwright, R., Gupta, M. D., & Tuckey, M. (2002). Maternal mind-mindedness and attachment security as predictors of theory of mind understanding. *Child Development*, *73*, 1715–1726. doi:10.1111/1467-8624.00501.

Muzik, M., Rosenblum, K., Marcus, S., Richardson, P., Barnett, D., Koren-Karie, N., ... Marvin, R. (2012). *Circle of security parent course: An attachment-based intervention for risk-mothers*. Paper presented at the World Association for Infant Mental Health Congress, Cape Town, South Africa.

Oppenheim, D., Feniger-Shaal, R., & Koren-Karie, N. (2010). *Insightfulness of mothers of young children with intellectual disability*. Unpublished raw data.

Oppenheim, D., Goldsmith, D., & Koren-Karie, N. (2004). Maternal insightfulness and preschoolers' emotion and behavior problems: Reciprocal influences in a day-treatment program. *Infant Mental Health Journal, 25*, 352–367. doi:10.1002/imhj.20010

Oppenheim, D., & Koren-Karie, N. (2009). Parents' insightfulness regarding their children's internal worlds: Assessment, research, and clinical implications. In C. Zeanah (Ed.), *Handbook of infant mental health* (3rd ed., pp. 266–280). New York, NY: Guilford.

Oppenheim, D., Koren-Karie, N., Dolev, S., & Yirmiya, N. (2009). Maternal insightfulness and resolution of the diagnosis are related to secure attachment in preschoolers with Autism Spectrum Disorder. *Child Development, 80*, 519–527. doi:10.1111/j.1467-8624.2009.01276.x.

Oppenheim, D., Koren-Karie, N., Dolev, S., & Yirmiya, N. (2012). Maternal Sensitivity mediates the link between maternal insightfulness/resolution and child-mother attachment: The case of children with Autism Spectrum Disorder. *Attachment & Human Development, 14*, 567–584.

Oppenheim, D., Koren-Karie, N., Etzion-Carasso, A., & Sagi-Schwartz, A. (2005, April). *Maternal insightfulness but not infant attachment predicts 4-year-olds' theory of mind*. Poster session presented at the biennial meeting of the Society for Research in Child Development, Atlanta, GA.

Oppenheim, D., Koren-Karie, N., & Sagi, A. (2001). Mother's empathic understanding of their preschoolers' internal experience: Relations with early attachment. *International Journal of Behavioral Development, 25*, 16–26. doi:10.1080/01650250042000096.

Powell, B., Cooper, G., Hoffman, K., & Marvin, R. (2007). The circle of security project: A case study "it hurts to give that which you did not receive." In D. Oppenheim & D. F. Goldsmith (Eds.), *Attachment theory in clinical work with children: Bridging the gap between research and practice* (pp. 172–202). New York, NY: Guilford Press.

Siller, M., Hutman, T., & Sigman, M. (2013). A parent-mediated intervention to increase responsive parental behaviors and child communication in children with ASD: A randomized clinical trial. *Journal of Autism and Developmental Disorders, 43*, 540–555.

Silverman, R. C., & Lieberman, A. F. (1999). Negative maternal attributions, projective identification, and intergenerational transmission of violent relational patterns. *Psychoanalytic Dialogues, 9*, 161–186.

Slade, A. (1999). Representation, symbolization, and affect regulation in the concomitant treatment of a mother and a child: Attachment theory and child psychotherapy. *Psychoanalytic Inquiry, 19*, 797–830. doi:10.1080/07351699909534277.

Slade, A. (2007). Reflective parenting programs: Theory and development. *Psychoanalytic Inquiry, 26*(4), 640–657.

Slade, A., Belsky, J., Aber, J. L., & Phelps, J. (1999). Maternal representations of their relationship with their toddlers: Links to adult attachment and observed mothering. *Developmental Psychology, 35*, 611–619.

van IJzendoorn, M. H., & Sagi, A. (1999). Cross-cultural patterns of attachment: Universal and contextual determinants. In J. Cassidy & P. R. Shaver (Eds.), *Handbook of attachment: Theory, research, and clinical applications* (pp. 713–734). New York, NY: Guilford.

Weinfield, N. S., Sroufe, L. A., Egeland, B., & Carlson, E. A. (1999). The nature of individual differences in infant-caregiver attachment. In J. Cassidy & P. Shaver (Eds.), *Handbook of attachment: Theory, research, and clinical applications* (pp. 68–88). New York, NY: Guilford Press.

Yuval-Adler, S. (2010). *Emotion dialogues between challenging and easy foster children and their mothers: Associations with maternal insightfulness* (Unpublished master's thesis). University of Haifa, Israel.

Zeanah, C. H., Benoit, D., Hirshberg, L., Barton, M. L., & Regan, C. (1994). Mothers' representations of their infants are concordant with infant attachment classifications. *Developmental Issues in Psychiatry and Psychology, 1*, 9–18.

Parsing the construct of maternal insensitivity: distinct longitudinal pathways associated with early maternal withdrawal

Karlen Lyons-Ruth[a], Jean-Francois Bureau[b], M. Ann Easterbrooks[c], Ingrid Obsuth[a], Kate Hennighausen[a] and Lauriane Vulliez-Coady[a]

[a]*Department of Psychiatry, Harvard Medical School, Boston, USA;* [b]*Department of Psychology, University of Ottawa, Ottawa, Canada;* [c]*Eliot Pearson Department of Child Development, Tufts University, Medford, USA*

The current paper expands on Ainsworth's seminal construct of maternal sensitivity by exploring the developmental pathways associated with one particular form of insensitivity: maternal withdrawal. Drawing on longitudinal data from infancy to age 20 in a high-risk cohort, we highlight how maternal withdrawal over the first eight years of life is associated with child caregiving behavior and with maternal role confusion, as well as with features of borderline and antisocial personality disorders. We also present evidence for the specificity of this pathway in relation to other aspects of maternal insensitivity and other aspects of child adaptation. To illuminate these pathways we both review recent published work and report new findings on the middle childhood and adolescent components of these trajectories. Finally, we consider the implications for assessment of maternal behavior in high-risk samples and indicate directions for productive future work.

Maternal hostility and intrusiveness in infancy have been repeatedly confirmed as important risk factors for child maladaptation, both as a correlate of disorganized attachment behavior in infancy (Lyons-Ruth, Bronfman, & Parsons, 1990; Lyons-Ruth, Connell, Grunebaum, & Botein, 1999) and as a predictor of later child hostile behavior towards peers in kindergarten (Fearon, Bakermans-Kranenburg, van IJzendoorn, Lapsley, & Roisman, 2010; Lyons-Ruth, Alpern, & Repacholi, 1993; van IJzendoorn, Schuengel, & Bakermans-Kranenburg, 1999) and middle childhood (Lyons-Ruth, Easterbrooks, & Cibelli, 1997). However, in recent analyses of our longitudinal data on outcomes for at-risk infants in late adolescence, the predictive power of early hostile-intrusive maternal behavior has been considerably attenuated, and early maternal withdrawal has emerged as the single strongest predictor of an array of psychopathology in the transition to young adulthood (Dutra, Bureau, Holmes, Lyubchik, & Lyons-Ruth, 2009; Lyons-Ruth, Bureau, Holmes, Easterbrooks, & Brooks, 2013; Pechtel, Woodman, & Lyons-Ruth, 2012; Shi, Bureau, Easterbrooks, Zhao, & Lyons-Ruth, 2012). Therefore, it becomes a priority to understand the developmental pathways that lead from these early withdrawing interactions to disturbed later outcomes. The aim of this paper is first, to expand on Ainsworth's seminal construct of sensitivity-insensitivity by exploring the developmental pathways associated with one particular form of insensitivity, namely, maternal withdrawal, and second, to contrast the relational adaptations linked to withdrawal with outcomes associated with maternal hostility.

We will first consider why Ainsworth's construct of sensitivity has been a robust predictor of child attachment security in lower risk samples but has not been a strong predictor of disorganized attachment patterns in high-risk samples. We will then review our recent findings relating maternal withdrawal in infancy to antisocial behavior, borderline features, and recurrent suicidality in adolescence. Subsequently, we will present an overview of the relations between maternal withdrawal and child attachment behavior in infancy and middle childhood from our longitudinal data. In the final section, we report new data on maternal role confusion at age 20, assessed by both interview and self-report measures, and its relation to earlier maternal withdrawal and concurrent adolescent role-confused/caregiving behavior at age 20, using a recently validated measure of attachment disorganization in adolescence (Obsuth, Brumariu, Hennighausen, & Lyons-Ruth, 2013). Finally, we will draw these strands together to describe pathways over time and to indicate gaps in our knowledge and fruitful directions for further work.

Ainsworth's construct of sensitivity-insensitivity

Ainsworth (1969) beautifully described the essence of sensitive caregiving behavior, in the preamble of her scale by the same name:

> The sensitive caregiver responds socially to [the baby's] attempts to initiate social interaction, playfully to his attempts to initiate play. She picks him up when he seems to wish it, and puts him down when he wants to explore. When he is distressed, she knows what kinds and degree of soothing he requires to comfort him – and she knows that sometimes a few words or a distraction will be all that is needed. On the other hand, the mother who responds inappropriately tries to socialize with the baby when he is hungry, play with him when he is tired, or feed him when he is trying to initiate social interaction (Ainsworth, 1969, p. 2; see also Ainsworth, Bell, & Stayton, 1974).

She identified the following components of sensitivity: "Sensitivity requires being aware of and correctly interpreting the infant's signals, and responding appropriately and promptly. A mother also needs to follow through with her responses, such as holding her infant long enough that he is comforted and does not immediately seek to be picked up again after being set down" (Ainsworth et al., 1974, p. 129).

It is less well known that Ainsworth also considered and created scales to assess aspects of maternal Cooperation versus Interference, Acceptance versus Rejection, and Accessibility versus Ignoring and Neglecting (Ainsworth, 1969; summarized in Ainsworth, Bell, & Stayton, 1971). In her own words, a cooperative mother "seeks to guide rather than control the infant's actions whereas an interfering or intrusive caregiver may interrupt the infant's activity, and thus cause dysregulation" (Ainsworth, 1969, p. 3). Particularly relevant to the focus of this paper, the Acceptance-Rejection scale deals with the balance between the mother's positive and negative feelings about her baby and her ability to integrate or resolve conflicting feelings, whereas the Accessibility versus Ignoring and Neglecting scale, at the low end, reflects mothers who are too self-absorbed to pay meaningful attention to infants' signals.

Ainsworth paid particular attention to the difficulty in trying to distinguish rejection from ignoring and neglecting. She described rejection as consisting of maternal retaliation by deliberate ignoring of infant signals, although she noted that highly defended mothers who seem bland or emotionally detached may show no signs of either positive acceptance or hostility. This contrasts with the definition of ignoring and neglecting in which Ainsworth captures key elements of maternal withdrawal: "She [the mother] finds the demands implicit in the baby's signals an intolerable threat to her precarious balance. It is necessary, in order to hold herself together, to 'tune out' the baby's signals" (Ainsworth, 1969, p. 9).

Findings presented in the classic volume on Patterns of Attachment (Ainsworth, Blehar, Waters, & Wall, 1978) indicated that the Sensitivity scale applied to five 4-hour observations from 9–12 months strongly distinguished mothers of children classified as secure and insecure in the Strange Situation Procedure (SSP). She had expected the other three scales to differentiate mothers of avoidant infants from those of ambivalent infants, but all four scales differentiated secure from avoidant and secure from ambivalent at or above the .01 level. In addition, Stayton, Hogan, & Ainsworth (1971) published a factor analysis on three of the scales, including sensitivity, acceptance, and cooperation, and found that a single factor defined those scales. Only in an exploratory analysis of the subgroups of the insecure classifications did notable differences emerge in maternal behavior, with mothers of A1 infants by far the most rejecting, and those of C2 infants the most ignoring or withdrawing. No attempt has ever been made to replicate these results on the insecure subgroups. However, this work suggested the utility of making further differentiations among insecure infants and Main and Solomon (1990) subsequently described a fourth classification for disorganized patterns of attachment behavior.

Following two decades of studies validating Ainsworth's construct of sensitivity, the NICHD Early Child Care Research Network (NICHD-ECCRN) conducted the largest investigation to date of sensitivity in mother–child relationships, assessing sensitivity repeatedly from infancy to age 15. A composite measure of maternal sensitivity was used at each age. At 6 and 15 months, the sensitivity composite included ratings for maternal sensitivity to child non-distress, intrusiveness [reversed], and positive regard. At older ages, the sensitivity composite reflected the sum of ratings for supportive presence, respect for autonomy, and hostility [reversed] (NICHD ECCRN, 1997, 2001a). This composite was used in analyses because factor analyses of the maternal behavior scales at each age yielded a single main factor, with the scales for sensitivity to child non-distress, positive regard, supportive presence, and respect for autonomy anchoring the positive pole of the factor and hostility and intrusiveness anchoring the negative pole (unpublished data; Margaret Tresch Owen, personal communication, 9 August 2013). In support of Ainsworth's initial work, this sensitivity composite has been consistently related to security of attachment assessed at 15 and 36 months (NICHD ECCRN, 1997, 2001a), as well as to a variety of later child outcomes (e.g. NICHD ECCRN, 2001b, 2004, 2006). Notably, the sample recruited by the NICHD ECCRN was largely middle income, as was Ainsworth's original sample.

As attachment researchers began to investigate children at high-risk for disorder due to serious maternal and family risk factors, the development of more differentiated scales for maternal behavior that would better distinguish among varieties of disturbed parenting became increasingly important. Most importantly, as disorganized attachment classifications were identified and related to a number of later deviations in development (Lyons-Ruth & Jacobvitz, 2008), the assessment of maternal sensitivity-insensitivity did not prove specific and differentiated enough to be a robust predictor of disorganized infant attachment. This was noted in a meta-analysis by van IJzendoorn and colleagues (1999), as well as in the large NICHD Study of Early Child Care and Youth Development (SECCYD) study (NICHD ECCRN, 1997). In the SECCYD, the effect size relating sensitivity and disorganization was $r = .06$, n.s., and for 11 studies of sensitivity and disorganization in the meta-analysis by van IJzendoorn and colleagues (1999) the combined effect size was also small, $r = .10$, $p = .004$.

The puzzling finding that sensitivity is a stronger correlate of attachment security than of attachment disorganization has not received a great deal of discussion. However, the positive pole of sensitivity captures a coherent and integrated parental stance of responding promptly and appropriately to infant signals, a stance that is particularly prevalent and thus is easily recognizable and codable. In addition, based on the factor analyses cited above, coders seem to spontaneously rate hostile and intrusive parental responses as the most insensitive opposite of the construct of sensitivity (NICHD ECCRN, 1997, 2001a). Thus, a sensitive-to-hostile factor seems well captured in current studies.

Yet, among parents exposed to traumatic experiences, disturbed caregiving can be manifested in a number of very different ways that many coders are unlikely to have encountered through general life experience and, more importantly, for which no separate scales have been available. When sensitive or responsive behaviors become mixed with indicators of fear, threat, disorientation, role confusion, or withdrawing behavior, it becomes necessary to create assessments that capture these behaviors. However, since Ainsworth developed her scales, few developmental researchers have taken up the challenge of developing assessments of these other forms of caregiving disturbance and their potential associations with later child outcomes. Conceptually, we regarded it as very likely that the effects of maternal withdrawal, disorientation, or role confusion would be different from the effects associated with hostile and interfering behavior. However, the potential for such differential outcomes associated with different forms of parenting disturbance has been surprisingly under-conceptualized and under-studied in work with high-risk samples (but see Bailey, Moran, Pederson, & Bento, 2007).

In one notable exception using a high-risk sample of adolescent mothers, Bailey et al. (2007) conducted a Q-factor analysis on items of their Maternal Behavior Q-Set (Pederson, Moran, & Bento, 1998) that yielded three factors: (1) Sensitive; (2) Disengaged; (3) Nonsynchronous. Strong associations were found between mothers' Disengaged interaction and infant disorganized attachment. This work supports the need for a much more differentiated coding system for capturing varieties of "insensitive" parenting in a high-risk cohort.

Assessment of maternal behavior associated with infant disorganization

Observations of the disturbed interactions engaged in by mothers of disorganized infants led Main and Hesse (1990) to hypothesize that parental frightened or frightening behavior was etiologically tied to infant disorganization. Subsequently, Lyons-Ruth, Bronfman, and Parsons (1999) advanced a somewhat broader hypothesis that infant fear that is not directly provoked by the parent's frightened or frightening behavior may still lead to infant disorganization if the parent fails to respond to the infant's need for comfort. These failures to comfort can occur in a variety of ways. For instance, the parent can give contradictory responses to the infant's cues or give self-referential responses that focus on the parent's needs rather than the infant's needs. The parent also can withdraw and respond in a cursory or reluctant manner or fail to respond altogether.

To operationalize this broader conceptualization and capture the variety of ways that disturbed parenting can manifest in high-risk samples, the Atypical Maternal Behavior Instrument for Assessment and Classification (AMBIANCE; Bronfman, Madigan, &

Table 1. Elements of the AMBIANCE coding system.

Maternal Disrupted Affective Communication Atypical Maternal Behavior Instrument for Assessment and Classification (AMBIANCE)
A. Overall disrupted communication scaled score (1–7) B. Frequencies for five dimensions of disrupted communications 1. Negative-Intrusive Behavior e.g. mocks or teases infant. 2. Role Confusion e.g. draws attention to self when infant is in need. 3. Contradictory Affective Communication e.g. talks in inviting voice but physically blocks infant's access. 4. Disorientation e.g. shows confused, frightened, or odd affect with infant. 5. Withdrawal e.g. interacts from a distance; interacts silently; walks around infant.

Note: Adapted from Lyons-Ruth, Bronfman, and Parsons (1999).

Lyons-Ruth, 1992–2009) was developed. It included not only the Main and Hesse (1992) inventory of frightened or frightening behaviors but also a wider range of parental behaviors observed in high-risk samples, including contradictory communications and withdrawing behavior as well as a broader array of negative-intrusive and role-confused behaviors. The five dimensions of disturbed maternal behavior assessed by the coding system are shown in Table 1. In subsequent sections of this paper, we will review our longitudinal findings associated with this coding system, drawing together the now numerous converging threads that paint a picture of the developmental pathway associated with early maternal withdrawing behavior.

The family pathways study

The developmental patterns summarized in this report emerged in analyses of data from the Family Pathways Study, a multi-wave, multi-method study of the development of infants at social risk, with assessments from the first year of life to age 20. Given the large number of measures mentioned here, in what follows readers are referred to the relevant publications for detailed descriptions of methods. Here we include only a brief description of the participants and attachment assessments.

The infant sample consisted of 76 infant–mother dyads from low-income families. To participate in the study, all families were required to be below the official federal poverty level. Of those dyads, approximately half ($N = 41$; 18 girls) were clinically referred to the study for home visiting services by health or social service agency staff because of concerns about the quality of the parent–infant relationship. The remaining families ($N = 35$; 15 girls) were recruited from the same low-income communities and closely matched to referred families on demographic risk factors. Families in the community group did not have documented psychiatric histories, history of abuse or neglect of children, or obvious parenting difficulties during a 1-hour home observation. The sample was 81% Caucasian, 40% of mothers were not high school graduates, and 49% were single parents (Lyons-Ruth et al., 1990).

At the middle childhood follow-up (ages 7 and 8), 56 families were relocated and contacted (74%). Fifty-one agreed to participate (67%), and five refused participation. Of the 51 participating families, eight families' videotapes were not available due to equipment failure, scheduling difficulties, or having moved too far from the research lab. Thus, 43 families contributed to the middle childhood data in this report. The families who participated in the study in middle childhood were similar to those who did not participate on all demographic, maternal, and infancy measures reported on here except for clinical referral, with clinically referred families somewhat less likely to come back for the middle childhood follow-up (Bureau, Easterbrooks, & Lyons-Ruth, 2009).

For the adolescent follow-up (age 20) the retention rate from infancy was again 74% (56). Of the 76 families seen in infancy, 14% (11) could not be located, 11% (7) refused, and 3% (2) lived overseas. Families assessed in adolescence did not differ from families not assessed on any infancy or childhood outcome measure (effect sizes (φ, η, or τ) = −.15 to .16) (Lyons-Ruth, Bureau, et al., 2013; Obsuth et al., 2013).

Except where noted below, all observations of maternal disrupted communication and infant attachment patterns or child attachment behavior took place in the laboratory. In infancy the standard Strange Situation Procedure (SSP) was used (Lyons-Ruth et al., 1990) and in middle childhood the Modified SSP was used following the procedure suggested by Main and Cassidy (1988), consisting of a 1-hour mother–child separation followed by a 5-minute reunion. The laboratory assessment of attachment-related interaction between adolescent and parent, using a new coding system for Goal-Corrected Partnership in Adolescence (GPACS), is described later in this report. In infancy, construct validity of the AMBIANCE was assessed in relation to mother–infant interaction assessed during a 40-minute unstructured observation in the home (see Lyons-Ruth et al., 1990, for description of home coding system).

Adolescent psychopathology associated with early maternal withdrawal

In a series of recent papers, we examined maternal behavior in the lab in infancy as a predictor of antisocial personality disorder, borderline features, suicidality, and substance abuse in late adolescence (Figure 1; Lyons-Ruth, Bureau, et al., 2013; Pechtel et al., 2012; Shi et al., 2012). In each publication, all five dimensions of maternal behavior in infancy were evaluated as predictors of later psychopathology. However, only early maternal withdrawal was predictive of disorder in late adolescence. In addition, in relation to dissociation in young adulthood, the overall AMBIANCE score was a robust predictor of dissociation, and maternal lack of involvement at home, but not hostile-intrusive

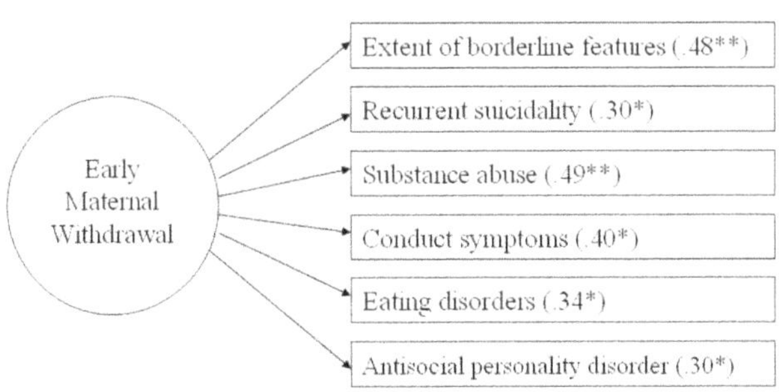

Figure 1. Maternal withdrawal and adolescent outcomes on the SCID in late adolescence. Effect sizes shown are beta for continuous outcomes or eta for dichotomous outcomes. From Pechtel et al. (2012), Shi et al. (2012) and Lyons-Ruth, Bureau, et al. (2013); Eating disorders and Conduct symptoms unpublished.
Note: $*p < .05$ and $**p < .01$.

Table 2. Characteristics of a withdrawing profile of maternal behavior in infancy.

Withdrawing Profile
A. Lack of parental initiative around attachment e.g. does not initiate greeting; does not initiate comforting; does not initiate interaction with the infant.
B. Delayed Responding
C. Cursory Responding e.g. "hot potato" pickup and putdown; moves away quickly.
D. Directs infant away from self to toys
E. Distanced Interaction e.g. walks around infant; interacts from across the room.
F. Little or no hostility or intrusion.

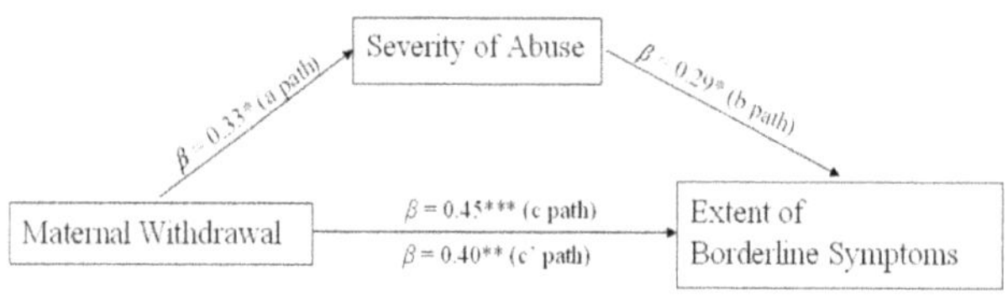

Figure 2. Severity of abuse does not mediate the effect of early maternal withdrawal on later borderline symptoms.
Note: Preacher and Hayes bootstrapping test for mediation not significant. See Lyons-Ruth, Bureau, et al. (2013). **p* < .05; ***p* < .01; ****p* < .001.

behavior at home, predicted additional variance in dissociation (Dutra et al., 2009; see also Ogawa, Sroufe, Weinfield, Carlson, & Egeland, 1997). Table 2 delineates the withdrawing profile as seen at 18 months.

Furthermore, the reports examining longitudinal predictors of borderline features, suicidality, dissociation, and antisocial symptoms all evaluated the potential mediation of this longitudinal prediction by experiences in later childhood, in particular severity of emotional, sexual, and physical abuse which occurred at high rates in this cohort and was also related to adolescent psychopathology (see Lyons-Ruth & Block, 1996; Lyons-Ruth, Yellin, Melnick, & Atwood, 2005). However, severity of childhood abuse did not mediate the prediction from early maternal withdrawal to any of these later psychopathologies. Instead, maternal withdrawal at 18 months remained a significant and strong independent predictor of all outcomes. Figure 2 displays the mediation analysis linking both maternal withdrawal and childhood abuse to the extent of borderline personality disorder features at age 20. Similar analyses are presented in other papers regarding suicidality, antisocial personality disorder, and dissociation.

We also examined whether the child's disorganized attachment classification might mediate the prediction associated with early maternal withdrawal. Attachment disorganization in infancy was not a strong predictor of outcomes in any of these analyses. In middle childhood, the extent of disorganized/controlling attachment behavior, as rated on 7-point scales from a 5-minute reunion after a 1-hour separation (Bureau et al., 2009), *was* predictive of both borderline features and antisocial behavior by age 20 (Lyons-Ruth, Bureau, et al., 2013; Shi et al., 2012). However, again mediation analyses indicated that the effects of early maternal withdrawal were independent of the extent of later child disorganized/controlling behavior.

In summary, strong and significant relations emerged in our data between early maternal withdrawal and an array of young adult psychopathologies associated with borderline and antisocial personality disorders in the standard psychiatric diagnostic system. In subsequent sections of the paper, we explore the child developmental pathways that are associated with this early maternal stance. In order to have a contrast point, at times we will compare aspects of development associated with withdrawal to aspects associated with maternal negative-intrusive behavior. Because other types of maternal behavior in infancy did not have the predictive strength of these two forms, we will not treat them further here. These comparisons between withdrawal and negative-intrusive behavior indicate that we can now move beyond simply documenting that negative early interactions are associated with negative later outcomes. Instead, the study of developmental psychopathology has matured to the point where we can examine the differential effects of different types of early interaction on the child's development.

Separating longitudinal pathways associated with maternal withdrawal and maternal hostility during infancy

Construct and discriminant validity of maternal withdrawal and maternal hostility during infancy

In the initial report on the AMBIANCE (Lyons-Ruth, Bronfman, & Parsons, 1999), maternal negative-intrusive behavior and maternal withdrawal were assessed for construct validity in relation to similar aspects of mother–infant interaction assessed during a 40-minute unstructured observation in the home. Table 3 displays the significant associations between maternal behavior observed at home and in the lab. Validity has also been demonstrated in relation to clinical referral by service providers (Lyons-Ruth, Bureau, et al., 2013). The relative risk for clinical referral by outside service providers predicted from maternal withdrawal in the lab was odds ratio (OR) = 1.5. This indicates that for *each additional withdrawing behavior* displayed by mothers in relation to their infant's attachment cues in the SSP, the likelihood of clinical referral by service providers was increased by 50%. These data lend both ecological validity and clinical urgency to the need for better identification of withdrawing forms of maternal behavior in infancy.

Table 3. Discriminant validity of maternal withdrawal and maternal negative intrusiveness across assessment settings.

	Laboratory assessment (AMBIANCE)	
	Maternal withdrawal (18 months)	Maternal negative intrusiveness (18 months)
Maternal behavior in the home		
Maternal lack of involvement (Home, 18 months)	$r = .30^{*}$ (64)	$r = .16$ (64)
Maternal hostility (Home, 18 months)	$r = .10$ (64)	$r = .33^{**}$ (64)
Clinical judgment		
Clinical referral (0–18 months)	*eta* = .38** (65)	*eta* = .19 (65)

Notes: In part, from Lyons-Ruth, Bronfman, and Parsons (1999). *N*s shown in parentheses. For two continuous variables, *r* is shown; for one categorical variable, *eta* is shown. $^{+}p < .10$; $^{*}p < .05$; $^{**}p < .01$.

Table 4. Characteristics of disorganized-approach and disorganized-avoidant/ambivalent attachment behavior in infancy.

Disorganized-Approach	Disorganized-Avoidant/Ambivalent
• Disorganized behaviors • Little avoidance or resistance • Distress to separation • Seeks proximity to parent	• Disorganized behaviors • Avoidance, resistance, or both • Often appears quite conflicted • May combine separation distress with marked avoidance at reunion
• Calms to contact with parent • May appear passive, depressed, aimless, hesitant, or apprehensive	• May show no separation distress

Infant attachment classifications associated with maternal withdrawal and negative-intrusive behavior

It is not widely recognized that 52% of disorganized infants continue to approach the caregiver, seek comfort, and cease their distress without clear ambivalent or avoidant behavior (Main & Solomon, 1990; NICHD Study of Early Child Care and Youth Development, K. McCartney, personal communication, 13 October 2003). This occurs despite the presence of pronounced conflict behavior, such as stopping and starting on the way to the parent (Table 4). This pattern has traditionally been labeled D-Secure behavior but we use the term D-Approach for greater clarity, because we regard the secure term as misleading (see below). The other 48% of disorganized infants *do show* avoidant or ambivalent behaviors, in addition to disorganized behaviors (Table 4). This group has traditionally been labeled D-Insecure. For greater clarity, here we will refer to this group as D-Avoidant/Ambivalent. To date, few hypotheses have been advanced regarding the mechanisms underlying this striking difference among infants who display disorganized behavior.

In the initial infancy findings from our study, differences in maternal behavior in the lab were associated with whether disorganized infants continued to approach their mothers (D-Approach). Mothers of D-Approach infants were significantly more withdrawing but had low rates of negative-intrusive behaviors. In contrast, mothers of D-Avoidant/Ambivalent infants displayed significantly more negative-intrusive and self-referential behavior (Lyons-Ruth, Bronfman, & Atwood, 1999; Figure 3).

In addition, and important to the study of high-risk samples, David and Lyons-Ruth (2005) found that as maternal withdrawal in the SSP became more pronounced, infant approach behaviors during the SSP also became more pronounced. This resulted in the unexpected finding that as maternal withdrawal became more extreme, the infant's approach behavior became more likely to fit the coding criteria for the secure (and non-disorganized) classification. Thus, among clinically referred infants, both those classified D-Approach and those classified fully Secure had mothers with significantly higher levels of withdrawing behavior compared to all other infants. Maternal withdrawal means: Secure = 5.50 (SD = 4.93), D-Approach = 5.25 (SD = 2.82), Avoidant = 1.33 (SD = 1.21), D-Avoidant/Ambivalent = 2.92 (SD = 2.40), $F(3,33) = 2.89$, $p = .05$. This tendency to approach a withdrawing mother was seen regardless of infant gender (David & Lyons-Ruth, 2005).

Therefore, a different theoretical lens may be needed for understanding responses to the attachment threat embodied in maternal withdrawal compared to that involved in maternal hostile or threatening behavior. When maternal behavior is more frightening,

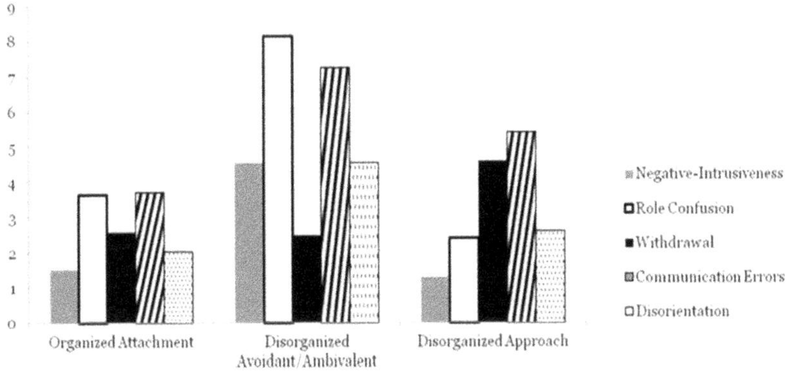

Figure 3. Maternal behavior profiles associated with disorganized-approach and disorganized-avoidant/ambivalent infant classification at 18 months.
Notes: Mothers of infants with D-Avoidant/Ambivalent attachment behavior exhibited significantly more negative-intrusive behavior ($F(1,28) = 6.42$, $p = .02$, $R^2 = .19$) and role confusion ($F(1,28) = 4.53$, $p = .04$, $R^2 = .14$). Mothers of infants with D-Approach behavior exhibited significantly more withdrawal ($F(1,28) = 5.23$, $p = .04$, $R^2 = .14$). Maternal communication errors and disorientation were core features that significantly discriminated between mothers of disorganized infants and mothers of non-disorganized infants across both subtypes (see Lyons-Ruth, Bronfman, & Parsons, 1999).

negative, or intrusive, infants exhibit the more flagrant approach and avoidance conflict behaviors that are particularly prominent in the D-Avoidant/Ambivalent subgroup. However, when the mother withdraws from attachment cues, infants may activate contact-seeking behavior and suppress or control the experience or expression of fearful or hostile affects that would lead them to fight or flee from the parent. In evolutionary terms, this makes adaptive sense, because the infant cannot afford to allow the parent to withdraw from providing care.

In a related line of thought, Taylor et al. (2000) contended that the activation of affiliative or attachment behaviors may also be an adaptive response to fear and threat, theorizing that females would be more prone to activate "tend or befriend" responses in the face of threat, while males would be more likely to activate fight or flight responses, but we found no support for gender differences in infant response to maternal withdrawal (David & Lyons-Ruth, 2005).

Here we contend that rather than being gender-related, "tend or befriend," and "fight or flight" behaviors are activated by different classes of threat. Specifically, we advance the view that the response to the threat of loss or abandonment is to suppress negative affect toward the abandoning attachment figure and to increase the display of attachment behavior. In contrast, the threat of physical attack implicit in hostile or physically intrusive behavior activates fight or fright behavior.

In support of the view that approach behavior can be a response to the threat of abandonment, we also found that D-Approach was predictive of long-term psychopathology. In relation to later suicidality, D-Approach at 18 months of age was significantly predictive of recurrent suicidality or self-injury at 20 years of age (Lyons-Ruth, Bureau, et al., 2013). Disorganized avoidant or ambivalent behavior was not predictive. This longitudinal prediction from D-Approach infant behavior to suicidality in adolescence underscores the serious consequences associated with this subtype of infant disorganized attachment behavior.

This longitudinal prediction of recurrent suicidality or self-injury also enlarges our view of the parent–infant dynamics that may be set in motion by early maternal withdrawal from the infant's attachment cues, as coded in the SSP at 18 months of age. The model that emerges is of a mother who withdraws from close contact coupled with an infant who continues to approach the mother for soothing, setting the stage for a potentially escalating transactional process in which the infant's need for soothing may provoke parental withdrawal, which in turn increases the child's distress and need to involve the parent. Such a developmental trajectory could lead to profound child distress and hopelessness culminating in recurrent suicidal thoughts and self-injury as one way of magnifying affective signals and attempting to elicit care from unavailable attachment figures.

These findings, then, raise concern that if maternal withdrawal intrinsically activates more pronounced approach behavior, current assessments of infant attachment may misjudge the security of infants of very withdrawing mothers in high-risk samples, as noted by David and Lyons-Ruth (2005). This would further produce a pattern of results in which assessments of the mother's behavior in high-risk samples would be much stronger predictors of later outcomes than assessments of infant attachment behavior, due to the error introduced by the secure-appearing nature of some infant approach behavior.

Maternal withdrawal in infancy and maternal and child behavior in middle childhood

As disorganized infants and toddlers make the transition into the preschool years, the signs of conflict, apprehension, or helplessness characteristic of disorganized attachment strategies in infancy often give way to various forms of controlling behavior toward the parent when assessed in a Modified SSP (Main & Cassidy, 1988; Moss, Cyr, Bureau, Tarabulsy, & Dubois-Comtois, 2005; NICHD SECCYD, 2001a; Wartner, Grossmann, Fremmer-Bombik, & Suess, 1994). Controlling behaviors are manifest in either a caregiving or a punitive fashion. Children classified as Controlling-Punitive use "authoritarian" behavior with the caregiver that may include harsh commands, verbal threats, and occasional physical aggression toward the parent. Children classified as Controlling-Caregiving direct the parent's activities and conversational exchanges by structuring interactions in a helpful and/or emotionally positive manner. Solomon, George, and De Jong (1995) suggested that such behaviors function to control a parent who is the source of unintegrated fears thereby regulating the child's own internal state and behavior. Based on the two subtypes of disorganized behavior observed in infancy and their differential relations to withdrawing maternal behavior, Lyons-Ruth, Lyubchik, Wolfe, and Bronfman (2002) further hypothesized that child controlling-caregiving attachment patterns might be differentially associated with a more helpless and withdrawing maternal stance in infancy, while child controlling-punitive classifications might be associated with a more hostile and intrusive maternal stance.

In two recent papers, we have now assessed this hypothesis, and our earlier prediction that infants of withdrawing mothers might develop controlling-caregiving attachment strategies was indeed borne out in the middle childhood data (Bureau et al., 2009). As shown in Table 5, maternal withdrawal in the SSP at 18 months was a robust predictor of controlling-caregiving attachment in middle childhood, as assessed in the standard Modified SSP. Contrary to prediction, early maternal negative-intrusive behavior alone was not a strong predictor of controlling-punitive attachment behavior in middle childhood. However, *overall* disrupted maternal behavior in infancy did significantly predict controlling-punitive attachment behavior in middle childhood. In contrast to the prediction

Table 5. Middle childhood attachment behavior associated with early maternal withdrawal and negative-intrusiveness.

	Middle childhood attachment behavior			
Maternal behavior in infancy	Child caregiving	Child disoriented	Child punitive	Overall disorganized/ controlling behavior
Maternal withdrawal (Lab, 18 months)	.43**	.19	–.13	.31^{+}
Maternal negative-intrusiveness (Lab, 18 months)	–.15	–.15	.15	–.07
Overall maternal disrupted communication (Lab, 18 months)	.07	.15	.39*	.38*

Notes: N = 34. Table shows β statistics after controlling for overall socioeconomic status. See Bureau et al. (2009). $^{+}p < .10$; $*p < .05$; $**p < .01$.

based on maternal behavior, the *infant's* disorganized attachment classification or subtype was not a strong predictor of controlling or disorganized attachment behavior by middle childhood.

Maternal and child behavior in middle childhood

The concurrent relations between maternal emotional availability and child attachment behavior in middle childhood were also assessed (Easterbrooks, Bureau, & Lyons-Ruth, 2012). The Emotional Availability Scales (Biringen, Robinson, & Emde, 1993) yield assessments of three aspects of maternal interaction: overall sensitivity, hostility, and passive-withdrawn behavior.

Again, when specific forms of insensitivity were examined, differential relations to forms of child attachment behavior emerged. Children of hostile mothers were significantly more likely to show punitive behavior, but child punitive behavior showed no significant relation to maternal passive-withdrawn behavior. In contrast, child caregiving behavior was robustly associated with maternal passive-withdrawn interaction in middle childhood (r = .35, $p < .05$), as in infancy. In addition, maternal passive-withdrawn interaction was marginally associated with child behavioral disorganization (r = .31, $p < .06$), suggesting that children of passive-withdrawing mothers were more disorganized as well as more caregiving. In addition, in middle childhood, child caregiving behavior was robustly associated with concurrent maternal hostility (Easterbrooks et al., 2012). However, as noted earlier, if the mother was hostile *in infancy* there was no tendency for the child to become caregiving (Table 5). Thus, controlling-caregiving behavior in middle childhood was preceded by maternal withdrawal in infancy, but by middle childhood was mixed with behavioral disorganization and was accompanied by both maternal passive-withdrawal and maternal hostility.

Also notably, when teacher reports of total child behavior problems on the Child Behavior Checklist were examined, overall maternal insensitivity in middle childhood was associated with total behavior problems (r = .35, $p < .05$). However, when the two different forms of insensitivity were distinguished, only maternal passive-withdrawal was associated with behavior problems (r = .41, $p < .01$), while maternal hostility was not significantly related (r = .17, n.s.). The same pattern occurred in relation to externalizing problems alone ($r = .38$, $p < .05$ vs. $r = .06$, n.s.). There were no significant relations between maternal emotional availability and teacher-reported internalizing problems on the CBCL (Easterbrooks et al., 2012).

Early maternal withdrawal and parental role confusion

Given the specificity of these relations between maternal passive-withdrawal and child controlling-caregiving behavior, we conducted an additional series of analyses examining predictors of adolescent–mother role confusion at age 20. Participants at age 20 included the 56 families from the longitudinal cohort on which earlier findings were based, as well as an additional 65 families from low-to-moderate income families from the community (see Obsuth et al., 2013).

An important focus of the adolescent study was to develop and validate an observational measure of attachment in adolescence. Adolescent–parent interaction was observed during a 5-minute reunion episode and a 10-minute conflict discussion. Ten rating scales were developed to code both collaborative and disorganized aspects of parent and adolescent behavior (Goal-Corrected Partnership in Adolescence Coding System [GPACS]; Obsuth et al., 2013). A Confirmatory Factor Analysis (CFA) on the 10 rating scales of the GPACS yielded the four dyadic factors shown in Figure 4, including one factor for collaborative interaction and three factors indexing the three aspects of disorganized/controlling behavior seen among younger children. Reliability and validity data on these factors are available in Obsuth et al. (2013). Models that specified only one factor

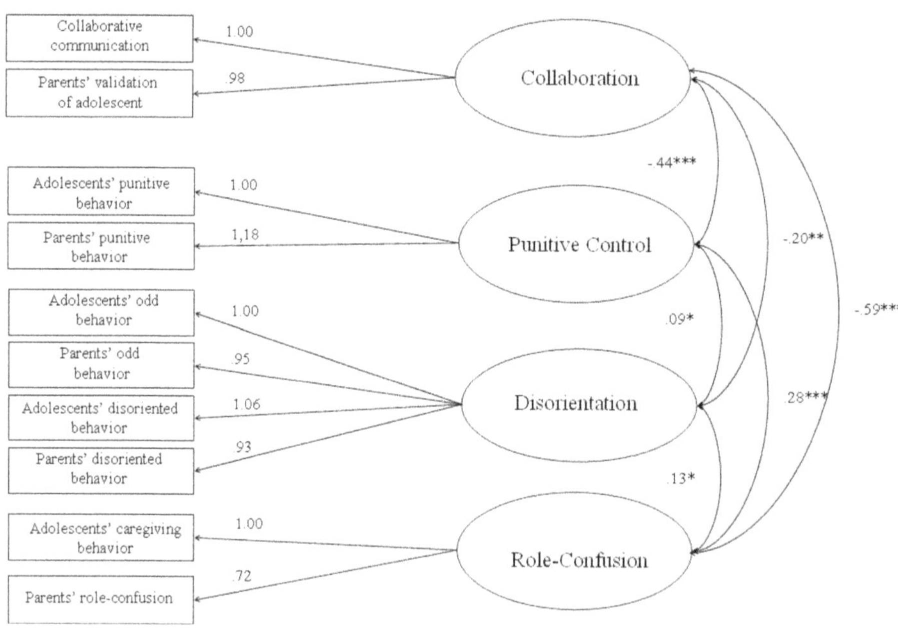

Figure 4. Confirmatory factor analysis: four-factor model of adolescent–parent interaction.
Note: $N = 120$. Coefficients with asterisks indicate covariances among the latent factors, with associated significance levels (*$p < .05$; **$p < .01$; ***$p < .001$); coefficients without asterisks indicate the item loadings for the 10 measurement scales on the four latent factors (all were significant at $p < .001$). Reprinted with permission from Obsuth et al. (2013).

(collaborative/non-collaborative) or two factors (collaborative/disorganized) resulted in a significantly poorer fit to the data.

As shown in Figure 4, the CFA indicated that adolescent and parental behaviors were related in a coherent fashion. Specifically, collaborative behaviors by parent and adolescent were correlated with one another, punitive behavior by parent and adolescent were correlated, and disoriented behavior by parent and adolescent were correlated. However, adolescent caregiving behavior was associated with the parent's abdication of a parental role, and not with parental collaborative behavior toward the adolescent. So the first important finding of the study was that adolescent and parent behavior exhibited several distinct patterns of underlying dyadic structure.

Mothers in the longitudinal group were also administered two interview/self-report measures of maternal role confusion in the adolescent follow-up. The first measure was the Caregiving Helplessness Questionnaire (CHQ; George & Solomon, 2011), a structured maternal self-report measure assessing mothers' experienced helpless in relation to the demands of parenting. The second was the Experiences of Caregiving Interview (ECI; George & Solomon, 1996), coded with a newly developed coding system for the degree of maternal role confusion on the ECI (Parental Assessment of Role Confusion [PARC]; Vulliez-Coady, Obsuth, Torreiro Casal, Ellertsdottir, & Lyons-Ruth, 2013).

We first explored the concurrent associations between the interview/self-report measures of maternal role confusion and role confusion as directly observed in the dyadic interaction between mother and adolescent. Both indices of maternal role confusion were significantly correlated with dyadic role confusion in observed interaction, but not with punitive or disoriented forms of interaction (Table 6).

Table 6. Mother–child interaction over time and interview assessments of maternal role confusion at age 20.

	Parental Assessment of Role Confusion (PARC)	Caregiving Helplessness Questionnaire (CHQ)
	B	*β*
Model 1. Disrupted affective communication with infant (AMBIANCE)		
Role/boundary confusion	.31*	.05
Withdrawal	.34**	.46**
Negative–intrusive behavior	.04	–.08
Affective communication errors	–.23^{+}	–.06
Disorientation	.09	.09
Model 2. Maternal emotional availability in middle childhood		
Maternal passive–withdrawal (7 years)[a]	.25	.31
Maternal hostility (7 years)	–.11	–.29
Maternal lack of sensitivity (7 years)	.11	.21
Model 3. Observed mother–adolescent interaction (GPACS)		
Collaboration	.08	-.22
Caregiving/role confusion	.27*	.29*
Punitive behavior	.09	.14
Disorientation	–.19	.10

Notes: For infancy and adolescence, $n = 51$; for middle childhood, $n = 32$. SES controlled in all analyses. PARC coded from Experiences of Caregiving Interview. $^{+}p < .10$; $^{*}p < .05$; $^{**}p < .01$. Data in part from Vulliez-Coady et al. (2013).

We then examined longitudinal predictions from maternal behavior in infancy and middle childhood to the measures of role confusion in late adolescence. Maternal withdrawal in infancy was a significant and specific predictor of maternal role confusion on both the PARC and the CHQ, with medium to large effect sizes over a 20-year period (Table 6). Maternal role confusion in interaction in infancy, also coded with the AMBIANCE, was also a significant predictor of maternal role confusion in adolescence as coded by the PARC, but did not predict self-reported caregiving helplessness by the mother on the CHQ. In contrast, maternal hostility in infancy was unrelated to the mother's later role confusion on either measure (Table 6).

When maternal behavior in middle childhood was examined, the same pattern of associations emerged, but did not reach significance with the smaller sample in middle childhood. Maternal passive-withdrawal was the strongest predictor of maternal role confusion on both measures at age 20, with medium effect sizes. Maternal hostility in middle childhood did not predict maternal role confusion and, in fact, showed a negative correlation with both measures (Table 6).

Thus, a strikingly coherent construct of maternal role confusion emerges across 20 years of multi-wave, multi-method assessments. In addition, these results underscore the specificity of the relation between early withdrawal and the mother's continued role-confused stance in adolescence, which is further related to the adolescent's controlling-caregiving behavior toward the parent.

Adolescent–parent role confusion and adolescent psychopathology

Finally, recent analyses further underscore the critical importance of adolescent–parent role confusion in pathways to disturbed functioning. Role confusion in parent–adolescent interaction was significantly related to overall borderline features in adolescence and was particularly strongly related to recurrent suicidality or self-injury (Lyons-Ruth, Brumariu, Bureau, & Holmes, 2013). In addition, role confusion in parent–adolescent interaction accounted for independent prediction in both borderline features and suicidality beyond variance in these outcomes accounted for by abuse experiences (Lyons-Ruth, Brumariu, et al., 2013).

Disorientation in interaction during adolescence was also associated with both borderline features and suicidality (Lyons-Ruth, Brumariu, et al., 2013). However, these relations were weaker and disorientation was also related to severity of abuse. Punitive adolescent–parent interaction was unrelated to borderline psychopathology.

Summary and discussion

The depth of the multi-wave, multi-method longitudinal assessments examined here yields a clear picture of a coherent developmental pathway related to early maternal withdrawal, with maternal withdrawal at every age associated with concurrent child caregiving and maternal role confusion. Further, both maternal withdrawal and adolescent caregiving emerged as contributors to the pathways toward adolescent borderline and antisocial psychopathologies.

The overall pattern of results from all waves of the study is presented in Figure 5. The first important implication of the distinct developmental pathways emerging from these longitudinal analyses is that specially tailored scales are required to assess different forms of insensitivity. The positive pole of sensitivity describes a coherent and integrated internal working model of attachment relationships that allows the parent to hold both

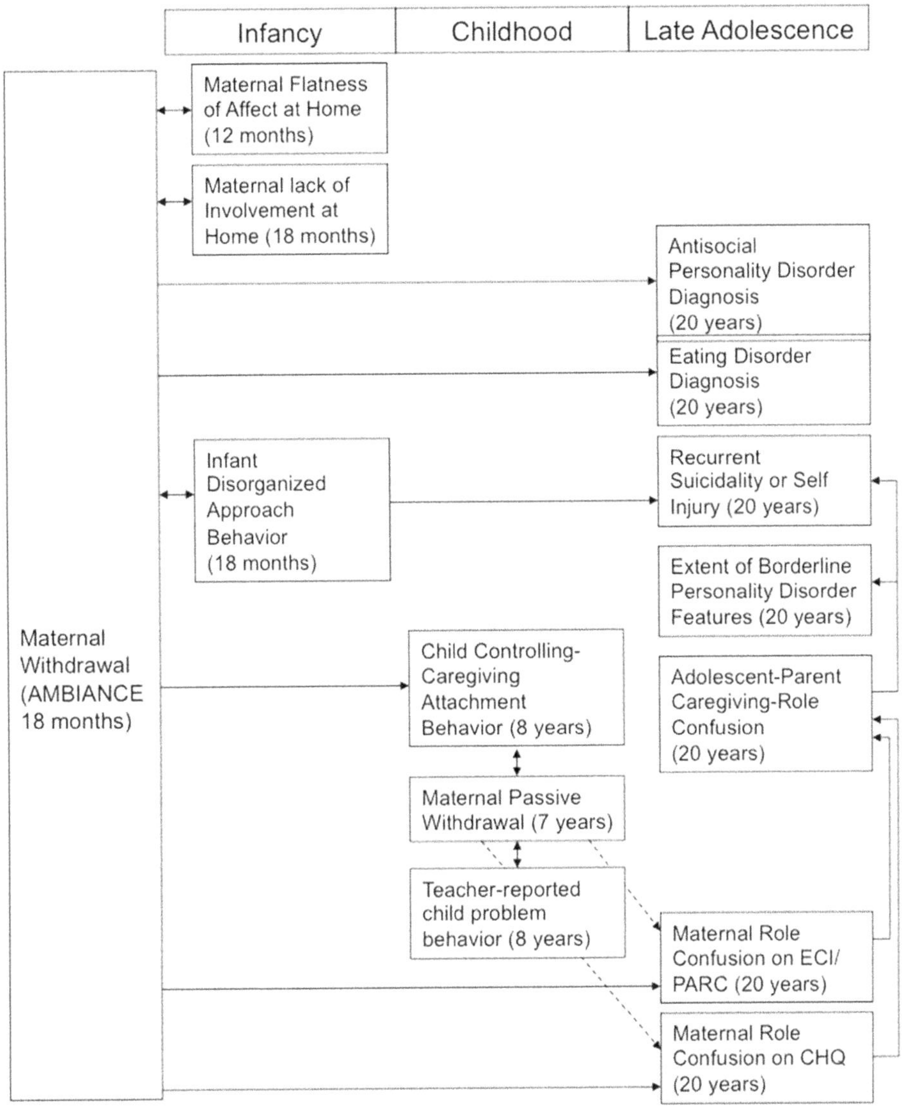

Figure 5. Summary of outcomes associated with maternal withdrawal.

her own and her child's needs in mind and flexibly attend to both. However, the current work describes at least two, and possibly three, discriminable patterns of insensitive maternal behavior that have quite different correlates in infant, child, and adolescent adaptation. Thus, the implication of these findings is that it is helpful to elaborate our descriptions of the varied deviations observed in parental responses to infant and child attachment behavior, in order to further understand how they may be linked to distinct child adaptations and distinct forms of psychopathology in later development.

Maternal withdrawal may have been under-assessed in previous work that has relied on global sensitivity scales that include multiple forms of insensitivity at the lower end of the scale. One problem that arises in assessing maternal withdrawal, in particular, is that it is more difficult to create scales for coding *absences* of expected behavior. Thus, rating scales need to include very specific descriptions of the types of structuring and responsive behaviors that are normative and expected for a given age group in a particular assessment context, so that any absence is noted and appropriately weighted.

A number of structuring and engaging parental behaviors were noted to be missing in infancy, and their absences were coded as part of the withdrawing dimension. These included not initiating interaction with the infant, not initiating comforting behavior, moving away rather than toward the infant while interacting, or interacting silently with the infant. However, in addition to such failures to structure and engage, mothers often responded but in a hesitant, delayed, or cursory manner, as shown in Table 2. Finally, mothers who failed to initiate such interactions often *did* respond once the infant initiated, and their infants often initiated relatively quickly. Thus, the mother's abdication of a structuring role in the interaction was often subtle and not equivalent to a failure to respond to the infant entirely. Additional description is available in Lyons-Ruth, Bronfman, and Atwood (1999). This was also true in middle childhood and adolescence, so that it was very important to carefully attend to whether parent or child was responsible for initiating, sustaining, and repairing any difficulties in the interaction over time.

Given the strength of early maternal withdrawal in predicting pathways associated with self-damaging behavior, more research is needed to examine the biological consequences of early withdrawal for the infant's regulation of stressful arousal. Self-injuring individuals are known to experience states of intense arousal, so that the long-term prediction associated with maternal withdrawal may be mediated in part through effects on the child's stress response system. Randomized animal models have shown that inattentive care in infancy can produce sustained enhancement of biological stress responses (Barr et al., 2004; Francis, Szeqda, Campbell, Martin, & Insel, 2003). Among human children, Bugental, Martorell, and Barraza (2003) found an association between maternal withdrawal and higher child cortisol levels. In young adulthood, lack of perceived parental protection, but not lack of confiding, is associated with increased baseline cortisol levels (Lyons-Ruth, Choi-Kain, Pechtel, Bertha, & Gunderson, 2011). Further work is clearly needed to assess stress responsiveness among children and adolescents in role-confused, caregiving relationships with parents.

An important caveat is that we cannot judge, based on correlational data, whether disturbances in parent–child relations are child adaptations to disturbances in parenting or parental adaptations to emerging child disturbance or both. Given the links between borderline and antisocial symptoms and genetic factors (Anguelova, Benkelfat, & Turecki, 2003; Lyons-Ruth et al., 2007; Torgerson et al., 2000), it is possible that a more stress-reactive child genotype would produce more persistent child contact-seeking which could lead in turn to increased caregiver withdrawal, particularly if parents themselves are genetically vulnerable to stress (White, Gunderson, Zanarini, & Hudson, 2003). One potential model that emerges is of a genetically stress-sensitive and contact-seeking infant coupled with a parent who withdraws from close contact, setting the stage for an escalating transactional process in which the infant's need for soothing may provoke parental withdrawal, which in turn increases the child's distress and need to involve and control the parent.

The analyses presented here rely on a relatively small sample, particularly in middle childhood, so these results should be viewed as generating, rather than confirming, important hypotheses about developmental pathways. However, the data set is unusual in including observational assessments of child attachment behavior both in middle childhood and in adolescence in the context of a multi-wave, multi-method study. In addition, despite its small size, attachment-related findings from this cohort have replicated well across both low- and high-risk groups in two meta-analytic reviews (Madigan et al., 2006; van IJzendoorn et al., 1999). Given the coherence of the data over a number of diverse assessments spanning 20 years of development, we expect that these patterns will also prove robust in other studies of young children at risk.

Acknowledgments

This paper is dedicated with much warmth and gratitude to Mary Ainsworth for her encouragement to the first author, as a graduate student, to pursue how attachment relationships may be configured in high-risk and clinical samples. I know she would be deeply satisfied that the field she pioneered continues to deepen our understanding of the complex adaptations in attachment relationships that occur in response to more extreme conditions of deprivation and adversity. We would also like to thank our most important collaborators who are the families who have so generously given their time to this study over a lifetime. We would also like to acknowledge the invaluable contributions of Nancy Hall Brooks, the study coordinator, and many additional students and staff to the study over time.

Funding

This work was supported by grants to Dr. Lyons-Ruth from the National Institute of Mental Health [R01MH35122 and R01MH06030], the Smith-Richardson Foundation, the Borderline Foundation, the FH Leonhardt Foundation, and the Milton Fund of Harvard University; by a Social Sciences and Humanities Research Council of Canada Postdoctoral Research Fellowship to Dr. Bureau; by a Social Sciences and Humanities Research Council of Canada Postdoctoral Research Fellowship to Dr. Obsuth; by a Clinical Research Training Fellowship through NIH Grant [T32 MH 16259-32] to Dr. Hennighausen; by a grant from Tufts University to Dr. Easterbrooks; and by grants from the Foundation de France, Bourse Sacks Harvard, and Groupement d'Etudes et Prevention du Suicide to Dr. Vulliez-Coady.

References

Ainsworth, M. D. S. (1969). *Ainsworth maternal scales.* Retrieved (as Maternal Sensitivity Scales) from http://www.psychology.sunysb.edu/attachment/measures/content/ainsworth_scales.html

Ainsworth, M. D. S., Bell, S. M., & Stayton, D. J. (1971). Individual differences in strange-situation behavior of one-year-olds. In H. R. Schaffer (Ed.), *The origins of human social relations* (pp. 17–58). London and New York: Academic Press.

Ainsworth, M. D. S., Bell, S. M., & Stayton, D. J. (1974). Infant-mother attachment and social development: Socialisation as a product of reciprocal sensitivity to signals. In M. P. M. Richards (Ed.), *Introduction of the child into a social world* (pp. 99–135). Cambridge, UK: Cambridge University Press.

Ainsworth, M. D. S., Blehar, M. C., Waters, E., & Wall, S. (1978). *Patterns of attachment: A psychological study of the strange situation.* Hillsdale, NJ: Erlbaum.

Anguelova, M., Benkelfat, C., & Turecki, G. (2003). A systematic review of association studies investigating genes coding for serotonin receptors and the serotonin transporter: II. Suicidal behavior. *Molecular Psychiatry, 8*(7), 646–653.

Bailey, H. N., Moran, G., Pederson, D. R., & Bento, S. (2007). Understanding the transmission of attachment using variable- and relationship-centered approaches. *Development and Psychopathology, 19*(2), 313–343.

Barr, C. S., Newman, T. K., Shannon, C., Parker, C., Dvoskin, R. L., Becker, M. L., … Higley, J. D. (2004). Rearing condition and rh5-HTTLPR interact to influence limbic hypothalamic-pituitary-adrenal axis response to stress in infant macaques. *Biological Psychiatry, 55*(7), 733–738.

Biringen, Z., Robinson, J., & Emde, R. N. (1993). *The emotional availability scales* (*2nd ed.*) (Unpublished manual). Department of Human Development and Family Studies, Colorado State University, Fort Collins, Colorado.

Bronfman, E., Madigan, S., & Lyons-Ruth, K. (1992–2009). *Atypical maternal behavior instrument for assessment and classification* (*AMBIANCE*). Manual for coding disrupted affective communication (Unpublished manual). Department of Psychiatry, Harvard Medical School, Cambridge, Massachusetts.

Bugental, D. P., Martorell, G. A., & Barraza, V. (2003). The hormonal costs of subtle forms of infant maltreatment. *Hormones and Behavior, 43*, 237–244.

Bureau, J., Easterbrooks, A., & Lyons-Ruth, K. (2009). Attachment disorganization and role-reversal in middle childhood: Maternal and child precursors and correlates. *Attachment & Human Development, 11*(3), 265–284.

David, D. H., & Lyons-Ruth, K. (2005). Differential attachment responses of male and female infants to frightening maternal behavior: Tend or befriend versus fight or flight? *Infant Mental Health Journal, 26*, 1–18.

Dutra, L., Bureau, J., Holmes, B., Lyubchik, A., & Lyons-Ruth, K. (2009). Quality of early care and childhood trauma: A prospective study of developmental pathways to dissociation. *Journal of Nervous Mental Disease, 197*(6), 383–390.

Easterbrooks, M. A., Bureau, J.-F., & Lyons-Ruth, K. (2012). Developmental correlates and predictors of emotional availability in mother-child Interaction: A longitudinal study from infancy to middle childhood. *Development & Psychopathology, 24*, 65–78.

Fearon, R. M. P., Bakermans-Kranenburg, M. J., van IJzendoorn, M. H., Lapsley, A., & Roisman, G. I. (2010). The significance of insecure attachment and disorganization in the development of children's externalizing behavior: A meta-analytic study. *Child Development, 81*(2), 435–456.

Francis, D. D., Szeqda, K., Campbell, G., Martin, W. D., & Insel, T. R. (2003). Epigenetic sources of behavioral difference in mice. *Nature Neuroscience, 6*(5), 445–446.

George, C., & Solomon, J. (1996). Representational models of relationships: Links between caregiving and attachment. In C. George & J. Solomon (Eds.), Special issue: Defining the caregiving system. *Infant Mental Health Journal, 17*, 198–216.

George, C., & Solomon, J. (2011). Caregiving helplessness: The development of a screening measure for disorganized maternal caregiving. In J. Solomon & C. George (Eds.), *Disorganized attachment and caregiving* (pp. 133–166). New York, NY: Guilford Press.

Lyons-Ruth, K., Alpern, L., & Repacholi, B. (1993). Disorganized infant attachment classification and maternal psychosocial problems as predictors of hostile-aggressive behavior in the pre-school classroom. *Child Development, 64*, 572–585.

Lyons-Ruth, K., & Block, D. (1996). The disturbed caregiving system: Relations among childhood trauma, maternal caregiving, and infant affect and attachment. *Infant Mental Health Journal, 17* (3), 257–275.

Lyons-Ruth, K., Bronfman, E., & Atwood, G. (1999). A relational diathesis model of hostile-helpless states of mind: Expressions in mother-infant interaction. In J. Solomon & C. George (Eds.), *Attachment disorganization* (pp. 33–69). New York, NY: Guilford Press.

Lyons-Ruth, K., Bronfman, E., & Parsons, E. (1999). Maternal frightened, frightening, or atypical behavior and disorganized infant attachment patterns. In J. I. Vondra & D. Barnett (Eds.), A typical patterns of infant attachment: Theory, research, and current directions. *Monographs of the society for research in child development, 64*(3, Serial No. 258), 67–96.

Lyons-Ruth, K., Brumariu, L., Bureau, J.-F., & Holmes, B. (2013). *Observed quality of young adult-parent interaction among individuals with borderline traits or suicidality/self-injury.* Manuscript submitted for publication.

Lyons-Ruth, K., Bureau, J.-F., Holmes, B., Easterbrooks, M., & Brooks, N. H. (2013). Borderline symptoms and suicidality/self-injury in late adolescence: Prospectively observed relationship correlates in infancy and childhood. *Psychiatry Research, 206*, 273–281. doi:10.1016/j.psychres.2012.09.030.

Lyons-Ruth, K., Choi-Kain, L., Pechtel, P., Bertha, E., & Gunderson, J. (2011). Perceived parental protection and cortisol responses among young females with borderline personality disorder and controls. *Psychiatry Research, 189*, 426–432.

Lyons-Ruth, K., Connell, D., Grunebaum, H., & Botein, D. (1990). Infants at social risk: Maternal depression and family support services as mediators of infant development and security of attachment. *Child Development, 61*, 85–98.

Lyons-Ruth, K., Easterbrooks, M., & Cibelli, C. (1997). Disorganized attachment strategies and mental lag in infancy: Prediction of externalizing problems at age seven. *Developmental Psychology, 33*, 681–692.

Lyons-Ruth, K., Holmes, B., Sasvari-Szekely, M., Ronai, Z., Nemoda, Z., & Pauls, D. (2007). Serotonin transporter polymorphism associated with borderline and antisocial features. *Psychiatrics Genetics, 17*, 339–343.

Lyons-Ruth, K., & Jacobvitz, D. (2008). Attachment disorganization: Genetic factors, parenting contexts, and developmental transformation from infancy to adulthood. In J. Cassidy & P. R. Shaver (Eds.), *Handbook of attachment* (2nd ed) (pp. 666–697). New York: Guilford.

Lyons-Ruth, K., Lyubchik, A., Wolfe, R., & Bronfman, E. (2002). Parental depression and child attachment: Hostile and helpless profiles of parent and child behavior among families at risk. In S. Goodman & I. Gotlib (Eds.), *Children of depressed parents: Alternative pathways to risk for psychopathology* (pp. 89–121). Washington, DC: American Psychological Association Press.

Lyons-Ruth, K., Yellin, C., Melnick, S., & Atwood, G. (2005). Expanding the concept of unresolved mental states: Hostile/helpless states of mind on the Adult Attachment Interview are associated with disrupted mother-infant communication and infant disorganization. *Development and Psychopathology, 17*(1), 1–23.

Madigan, S., Bakermans-Kranenburg, M. J., van IJzendoorn, M. H., Moran, G., Pederson, D. R., & Benoit, D. (2006). Unresolved states of mind, anomalous parental behavior, and disorganized attachment: A review and meta-analysis of a transmission gap. *Attachment & Human Development, 8*, 89–111.

Main, M., & Cassidy, J. (1988). Categories of response to reunion with the parent at age six: Predictable from infant attachment classifications and stable over a one-month period. *Developmental Psychology, 24*, 415–426.

Main, M., & Hesse, E. (1990). Parents' unresolved traumatic experiences are related to infant disorganized attachment status: Is frightened and/or frightening parental behavior the linking mechanism? In M. T. Greenberg, D. Cicchetti, & E. M. Cummings (Eds.), *Attachment in the preschool years: Theory, research, and intervention* (pp. 161–182). Chicago, IL: University of Chicago Press.

Main, M., & Hesse, E. (1992). *Frightening, frightened, dissociated, or disorganized behavior on the part of the parent: A coding system for parent–infant interactions* (Unpublished manuscript). University of California at Berkeley, Berkeley, CA.

Main, M., & Solomon, J. (1990). Procedures for identifying infants as disorganized/disoriented during the Ainsworth strange situation. In M. Greenberg, D. Cicchetti, & M. Cummings (Eds.), *Attachment in the preschool years* (pp. 121–160). Chicago, IL: University of Chicago Press.

Moss, E., Cyr, C., Bureau, J. F., Tarabulsy, G. M., & Dubois-Comtois, K. (2005). Stability of attachment during preschool period. *Developmental Psychology, 41*(5), 773–783.

NICHD Early Child Care Research Network. (1997). The effects of infant child care on infant-mother attachment sevcuirty: Results of the NICHD study of early child care. *Child Development, 68*(5), 860–879.

NICHD Early Child Care Research Network. (2001a). Child-care and family predictors of preschool attachment and stability from infancy. *Developmental Psychology, 37*, 847–862.

NICHD Early Child Care Research Network. (2001b). Child care and children's peer interaction at 24 and 36 months: The NICHD Study of Early Child Care. *Child Development, 72*(5), 1478–1500.

NICHD Early Child Care Research Network. (2004). Trajectories of physical aggression from toddlerhood to middle childhood: Predictors, correlates, and outcomes. *Monographs of the Society for Research in Child Development, 69*(4), vii, 1–129.

NICHD Early Child Care Research Network. (2006). Infant-mother attachment classification: Risk and protection in relation to changing maternal caregiving quality. *Developmental Psychology, 42*(1), 38–58.

Obsuth, I., Brumariu, L., Hennighausen, K., & Lyons-Ruth, K. (2013). Disorganized behavior in adolescent-parent interactions: Relations to attachment state of mind, partner abuse, and psychopathology. *Child Development.* Advance online publication. doi: 10.1111/cdev.12113

Ogawa, J. R., Sroufe, L. A., Weinfield, N. S., Carlson, E. A., & Egeland, B. (1997). Development and the fragmented self: Longitudinal study of dissociative symptomatology in a nonclinical sample. *Development and Psycholopathology, 9*(4), 855–879.

Pechtel, P., Woodman, A., & Lyons-Ruth, K. (2012). Early maternal withdrawal and non-verbal childhood IQ as precursors for substance abuse diagnosis in young adulthood: Results of a 20-year prospective study. *International Journal of Cognitive Therapy, 5*, 316–329.

Pederson, D. R., Moran, G., & Bento, S. (1998). *Maternal Behavior Q-set ~Version 3.0* (Unpublished manuscript). University of Western Ontario, Department of Psychology.

Shi, Z., Bureau, J.-F., Easterbrooks, M. A., Zhao, X., & Lyons-Ruth, K. (2012). Childhood maltreatment and prospectively observed quality of early care as predictors of antisocial personality disorder. *Infant Mental Health Journal, 33*, 1–14.

Solomon, J., George, C., & De Jong, A. (1995). Children classified as controlling at age six: Evidence of disorganized representational strategies and aggression at home and at school. *Development and Psychopathology, 7*, 447–463.

Stayton, D. J., Hogan, R., & Ainsworth, M. D. S. (1971). Infant obedience and maternal behavior: The origins of socialization reconsidered. *Child Development*, *42*, 1057–1069.

Taylor, S. E., Klein, L. C., Lewis, B. P., Gruenewald, T. L., Gurung, R. A., & Updegraff, J. A. (2000). Biobehavioral responses to stress in females: Tend-and-befriend, not fight-or-flight. *Psychological Review*, *107*, 411–429.

Torgersen, S., Lygren, S., Oien, P. A., Skre, I., Onstad, S., Edvardsen, J., Tambs, K., & Kringlen, E. (2000). A twin study of personality disorders. *Comprehensive Psychiatry*, *41*(6), 416–425.

van IJzendoorn, M., Schuengel, C., & Bakermans-Kranenburg, M. (1999). Disorganized attachment in early childhood: Meta-analysis of precursors, concomitants, and sequelae. *Development and Psychopathology*, *11*(2), 225–249.

Vulliez-Coady, L., Obsuth, I., Torreiro Casal, M., Ellertsdottir, L., & Lyons-Ruth, K. (2013). Maternal role-confusion: Relations to maternal attachment and mother-child interaction from infancy to adolescence. *Infant Mental Health Journal*. Advance online publication. doi:10.1002/imhj

Wartner, U. G., Grossmann, K., Fremmer-Bombik, E., & Suess, G. (1994). Attachment patterns at age six in South Germany: Predictability from infancy and implications for preschool behavior. *Child Development*, *65*, 1014–1027. doi:10.1111/j.1467-8624.1994.tb00799.x

White, C. N., Gunderson, J. G., Zanarini, M. C., & Hudson, J. I. (2003). Family studies of borderline personality disorder: A review. *Harvard Review of Psychiatry*, *11*(1), 8–19.

How does microanalysis of mother–infant communication inform maternal sensitivity and infant attachment?

Beatrice Beebe[a] and Miriam Steele[b]

[a]*New York State Psychiatric Institute, New York, NY, USA;* [b]*New School for Social Research, New York, NY, USA*

Microanalysis research on 4-month infant–mother face-to-face communication operates like a "social microscope" and identifies aspects of maternal sensitivity and the origins of attachment with a more detailed lens. We hope to enhance a dialogue between these two paradigms, microanalysis of mother–infant communication and maternal sensitivity and emerging working models of attachment. The prediction of infant attachment from microanalytic approaches and their contribution to concepts of maternal sensitivity are described. We summarize aspects of one microanalytic study by Beebe and colleagues published in 2010 that documents new communication patterns between mothers and infants at 4 months that predict future disorganized (vs. secure) attachment. The microanalysis approach opens up a new window on the details of the micro-processes of face-to-face communication. It provides a new, rich set of behaviors with which to extend our understanding of the origins of infant attachment and of maternal sensitivity.

Microanalysis research on 4-month infant–mother face-to-face communication can contribute to our understanding of maternal sensitivity and the development of infant internal working models in the origins of infant–parent attachment (Ainsworth, Blehar, Waters, & Wall, 1978). Microanalysis operates like a "social microscope," identifying "subterranean" rapid communications, which are often not quite perceptible in real time. This approach offers the possibility of identifying aspects of maternal sensitivity and the origins of attachment with a more detailed lens.

In this paper we review two research paradigms, the microanalytic approach to mother–infant face-to-face communication (dubbed "microanalysis approach") and maternal sensitivity and emerging working models of attachment, in the spirit of an enhanced dialogue between the two. Ainsworth and colleagues set the stage for relating 4-month infant–mother communication to 12-month attachment by coding mother–infant face-to-face interaction and predicting outcomes in the Strange Situation in a study by Blehar, Lieberman, and Ainsworth (1977).

The prediction of infant attachment from microanalytic approaches and their contribution to concepts of maternal sensitivity are presented. We describe one microanalytic study by Beebe and colleagues (Beebe et al., 2010) which documents new communication patterns between mothers and infants at 4 months that predict future disorganized (vs. secure) attachment. These findings provide one basis for describing emerging infant-with-mother working models of disorganized attachment, procedurally organized expectancies of action sequences, as early as 4 months. In describing the nature of the mother's communication with her infant on a moment-to-moment basis, microanalysis research can also refine our understanding of maternal sensitivity.

These two approaches, maternal sensitivity and microanalysis of face-to-face communication, share a central underlying construct: that the patterning of mother–infant interaction is central to infant social-emotional development. However, the theory, terminology, methods of behavioral coding, and statistical approaches differ considerably.

Ainsworth's construct and assessment of maternal sensitivity

Maternal sensitivity is one of the central constructs of attachment theory and research. Ainsworth's sensitivity construct derives from observations of 26 mother–infant dyads who participated in the Baltimore study and were visited at home for 4 hours every 3 weeks from 3 to 54 weeks. The visitor-observers took detailed notes of the infants' interactions with their mothers and anyone else present. The notes were subsequently audio-recorded and transcribed into narrative records. Based on the 9–12 month narrative records, Ainsworth developed a Maternal Sensitivity Scale and three additional scales (cooperation, accessibility, and acceptance). Each scale provides an extensive definition of the underlying construct as well as descriptions of each scale-point.

The definition of Maternal Sensitivity has four essential components: awareness of infant signals, accurate interpretation, appropriate response, and prompt response. In the scale, awareness of infant signals is described as follows: "In play and social interaction, the mother responds appropriately to her child, does not over-stimulate him by interacting in too intense, too vigorous, too prolonged or too exciting manner. She can perceive and accurately interpret the signs of over-excitement, undue tension, or incipient distress and shift the tempo or intensity before things have gone too far. Similarly, she is unlikely to under-stimulate the child, because she picks up and responds to the signals he gives when he is bored or when he wants more interaction than has heretofore been forthcoming" (Ainsworth, Bell, & Stayton, 1974, p. 128). The coder has to learn the gestalt of Ainsworth's formulations concerning sensitivity. Maternal sensitivity ratings were strongly correlated with infants' classifications in the Strange Situation at 1 year (Ainsworth et al., 1978).

Subsequent empirical studies more broadly connecting global measures of maternal sensitivity to infant attachment security/insecurity have not been as robust as would be predicted from Ainsworth's findings. The meta-analysis by De Wolff and Van IJzendoorn (1997) found that maternal sensitivity and infant–mother attachment were related but with a modest effect size, concluding that "sensitivity is important but not an exclusive condition of attachment security" (p. 571). Thus despite important recent progress in understanding the origins of 12-month attachment, a full understanding of the mechanisms of attachment formation prior to 12 months is still lacking (Hofer, 1994; Lyons-Ruth, Bronfman, & Parsons, 1999; Madigan et al., 2006; Tarabulsy, Tessier, & Kappas, 1996).

Less well known, Blehar et al. (1977) also used the Baltimore narrative transcripts described above to analyze early face-to-face interactions. As the authors explained: "little attention has been given to the behavior of mothers when in face-to-face interaction with their infants" (Blehar et al., 1977, p. 183). Citing Daniel Stern (1974), they suggested "the possibility that individual differences in the patterning of maternal behavior [that] might lead to distinctive patterns of infant behavior, especially as the goal of these interactions is the regulation of stimulation so that an affectively positive level of arousal in the infant is maintained" (Blehar et al., 1977, p. 183). Stern (1974, p. 402) had argued: "By providing a more fine-grained view of the instant-by-instant interactive events which make up the mother–infant relationship, we may be in a better position to modify and expand current working theories on the nature of developing object relations or attachments."

Blehar et al. (1977) reported on 732 episodes of face-to-face interaction extracted from the narrative records of the home visits at 6, 9, 12, and 15 weeks. Coders were blind to the infant's subsequent attachment classifications. Both maternal and infant behaviors were coded; most codes required qualitative judgments (such as maternal pacing in line with the infant's state of arousal) rather than pure counts of behavior. While broader and less specific, these codes convey some of the essence of the more detailed codes used in microanalysis, as we will see below.

At 12 months, infants identified as securely (vs. insecurely) attached to their mothers in the SSP had been more responsive in early face-to-face encounters, and their mothers had been more contingently responsive and encouraging of interaction (Blehar et al., 1977). Contingent responsivity was judged coding from the narrative records. Infants later identified as anxiously (vs. securely) attached were more unresponsive and their mothers were more likely to be impassive or abrupt. Securely (vs. insecurely) attached infants were more positively responsive to their mothers than to unfamiliar figures in face-to-face interactions. Blehar et al. (1977, p. 193) concluded: "It would be good to replicate this study using recording methods that permit more fine-grained measures than those we could employ." The microanalysis research reported in this paper, now nearly 50 years later, is in this tradition.

Theory and research informing a microanalysis approach to mother–infant face-to-face communication

Microanalysis of mother–infant face-to-face communication in the first months of life is concerned with the communication process itself: how does it work, how does it facilitate development, and what are the early communication disturbances and their developmental consequences? This approach has been used to document the effects of maternal distress, such as depression and anxiety, on mother–infant communication and to predict infant social, cognitive, and attachment outcomes. Compared to an attachment approach, there are important differences in theory as well as in the approach to coding and data analysis.

Brazelton, Trevarthen, and Stern all began fine-grained studies of mother–infant face-to-face communication around the same time. Daniel Stern published his first paper in 1971; Colwyn Trevarthen in 1974; and T. Berry Brazelton, Barbara Kozlowski, and Mary Main in 1974. Edward Tronick, Brazelton's student, soon became a leading figure, as did Lynne Murray, Trevarthen's student; as well as Alan Fogel, Tiffany Field, Michael Lewis, Jeffrey Cohn, among others. Beatrice Beebe was Daniel Stern's student. Currently Ruth Feldman and Daniel Messinger (Alan Fogel's student) have become prominent in this field. Although Louis Sander did not study face-to-face communication, his systems view of self- and mutual regulation, informed by biological systems views (particularly those of Van Bertalanffy and Weiss) were extremely influential. Sander (1977) argued that both partners generate complexly organized behavior that must be coordinated in a bi-directional process of mutual modification. Ethology, the study of behavior in its natural habitat, also influenced the careful, descriptive, microanalytic approach. Three figures in this field have also been psychoanalysts: Sander, Stern, and Beebe. Lyons-Ruth is also active in psychoanalysis. Psychoanalysis has a longstanding interest in the mother–infant relationship, and together the two fields of infant research and psychoanalysis have generated a creative synergy enriching to both (see for example Beebe & Lachmann, 2002; Stern et al., 1998).

In the study of face-to-face communication, mother and infant are seated face-to-face. Two cameras, one on each partner's face, generate a split screen view. The mother is instructed to play with her baby as she would at home, but without toys. Interactions videotaped when infants are approximately 4 months old have generated the majority of the research. This research spans infant ages 2–9 months. Earlier than 3–4 months, infants have difficulty regulating their arousal sufficiently to sustain face-to-face engagement. They easily become fussy, or they go to sleep. By 3–4 months, infants become easier subjects and sustain face-to-face engagement. Moreover, 3–4 months marks the flowering of infant social expressive display. Although all of the facial expressions are myelinated before birth, the full open-mouth "gape smile," the apex of positive affect, is not routinely seen until this age. Long periods of sustained, mutual gaze also become reliable at this age.

Face-to-face communication is extremely rapid. Much of it is out of awareness. Moreover, in real time, it is often extremely difficult to discern the exact sequence of behaviors. For example, watching a particular mother–infant pair in real time, Beebe's students often insist that the infant broke eye-contact and looked down at the moment he did because the mother had moved her finger in toward the infant's belly, about to poke; the interpretation is that the mother's movement in to poke influenced the infant's gaze down. But microanalysis reveals the opposite order: the infant broke eye-contact and looked down first, the mother reacted with some facial tensing, and then she lightly poked the infant's belly, as if to say, "Come back" (see Beebe & Lachmann, 2013). In this viewing, the infant looking down influenced the mother to poke.

This vignette illustrates a central proposal in the face-to-face interaction literature, that communication is reciprocal and two-way. Each individual affects the behavior of the other, moment-by-moment. The data analysis attempts to pry apart each person's effect on the other, to see if this two-way communication is in fact operating.

Coding approach

Compared to coding from narrative records, the microanalysis coder's task is entirely different. Behavior is coded with a small time unit, generally one second (or smaller). The coder has to learn to see or hear very small shifts and subtle nuances in behavior. For example, in coding infant vocal affect, Beebe et al. (2010, 2011) distinguished high positive, neutral/positive, no-vocalization, fuss-whimper, angry-protest, and cry. Many of the qualities of behavior being coded, such as affectionate vs. static touch vs. jiggle, require repeated viewings in slowed time. Much of what is coded cannot be accurately grasped with the naked eye, a key difference between microanalysis of behavior vs. coding maternal and infant behavior, let alone global sensitivity, from narrative records. Careful judgment is involved in both. However, the behavioral referent is very narrow in microanalysis, such as the judgment as to whether gaze is on or off the partner's face. The judgment in coding from narrative records usually has a broader referent, such as the determination of appropriate maternal pacing of the interaction. Thus, microanalytic second-to-second assessments reveal new information.

Communication as "process" and as "content"

The *process* of communication (the moment-to-moment temporal process of behavior across time) is distinct from its *content* or qualitative features (such as affective valence, rates of gaze aversion, or intrusive touch). Microanalysis research considers both. In contrast, most attachment research is based on coding of qualitative features of behavior, such as infant resistance to the parent manifested by fussing or crying, without being able to be comforted.

Mutual regulation

Using a "wide-angle lens," both paradigms construe mother and infant as each influencing the other, a bi-directional, reciprocal, mutual regulation process. Although Ainsworth focused more on the mother's influence, she also addressed aspects of mutual adaptation.

Mutual regulation is not necessarily equal or similar. The mother brings her own genetic and temperamental variations, her attachment history, and states of mind, such as depression or anxiety. The infant brings variations in regulatory capacity and temperament factors such as sensory sensitivities.

Using a "narrow-angle lens," the definition of mutual regulation shifts. Microanalysis approaches generally define mutual regulation in terms of how each partner may "influence" the other moment-to-moment. "Influence" is defined as the degree to which one individual's prior behavior predicts the partner's current behavior. The terms regulation, influence, coordination, and contingency are used here interchangeably. Greater emphasis on infant coordination with mother, as well as maternal coordination with infant, has been important in the longitudinal prediction of infant attachment outcomes from microanalysis of mother–infant interaction (Feldman, 2007; Fogel, 1992; Jaffe, Beebe, Feldstein, Crown, & Jasnow, 2001; Tarabulsy et al., 1996). This focus on both partner's contribution with micro-analytic second-to-second assessments reveals new information that narrative records cannot capture, whether globally rated or behaviorally coded.

The term "contingency" is central in both paradigms, but defined very differently, an important source of confusion. Perhaps because Ainsworth was criticized for the value-laden implications of the term sensitivity, Blehar et al. (1977) used contingent responsivity as a synonym. In Ainsworth's approach, the global maternal measure of contingent responsivity (sensitivity) incorporated aspects of the infant's response to determine whether the mother is sensitive and was measured by ratings of the narrative transcripts of behavior.

In contrast, the definition of contingency and contingent responsiveness in the micro-analytic face-to-face interaction literature rests on statistical analyses of correlations between the moment-to-moment processes of the two partners' streams of behavior. This definition of contingency is neutral; its interpretation depends on its relation to other constructs, such as maternal depression or attachment security. This approach requires separate coding of each individual, across time, followed by computation of the degrees of correspondence between the two behavioral streams (Kenny, Kashy, & Cook, 2006; Moore et al., 2013). A central approach to the analysis of contingent coordination is that of time-series analysis, a sophisticated method built on correlation, which revolutionized the study of social interaction in the 1980s. Interactive contingency indexes degree of correspondence by assessing moment-to-moment adjustments that each individual makes to the partner's prior behavior. Metaphorically it measures expectancies of "how I affect you" and "how you affect me." Self-contingency indexes the degree to which an individual's behavior is predictable from her "just prior" behavior. It assesses degree of stability/lability within the individual's stream of behavior.

In calculating an individual's interactive contingency, her own self-contingency is statistically removed. Thus the analysis identifies whether, over and above the predictability in the individual's behavior, there is any further variation in her behavior that is predicted by the prior behavior of the partner. Similarly, in calculating an individual's self-contingency, the individual's interactive contingency is removed (see Beebe et al., 2010 for details).

Contingency (coordination) as used in the microanalysis literature, and defined by time-series approaches, is a complex construct. Contingency as used here is not to be confused with maternal sensitivity or maternal contingent responsivity as used in the attachment literature.

The time-series measure of contingency rests on the infant's perceptual capacity. The infant is a remarkable "contingency detector" from birth (DeCasper & Carstens, 1980; Papousek, 1992). Infants detect predictable consequences of their actions, by estimating probabilities of "if-then" sequences (Saffran, Aslin, & Newport, 1996; Tarabulsy et al., 1996).

By 3–4 months, mothers and infants participate in an interactive "dance": contingently coordinating gaze patterns, yielding mutual gaze; facial affect, often termed facial mirroring; vocal rhythms, such as speech rate and turn-taking; orientation patterns, such as mutual approach or approach-avoid; and touch patterns (Beebe et al., 2010; Feldman, 2007; Jaffe et al., 2001; Malatesta, Culver, Tesman, & Shepard, 1989; Messinger, 2002; Stern, 1985; Tronick, 1989).

Self-regulation

From an attachment perspective, the regulation of affect is a central aspect of the attachment process as well as one of its most significant outcomes (Cassidy, 1994). The developmental trajectory proceeds from the establishment of internal working models (with significant caregivers) by the second half of the first year to the child's increasing ability to regulate affect. The infant's "lived" experiences are represented at various levels of specificity within the mind, serving as guides to perception of the self and others, including strategies for how to interpret and manage negative emotions. Although affect regulation is an aspect of functioning which resides in the child, it also reflects qualities of interactions with a specific caregiver. Infant management of negative affect in the Ainsworth Strange Situation reflects this process. For example, infants classified as avoidant tend to show minimal affect, while those classified as resistant maximize the affect they display, often showing distress without diminution in the caregiver's presence. Self- and interactive regulation patterns over the first year of life, however, have not been as systematically described in attachment research as they have in microanalytic research.

Within the face-to-face interaction literature, a sophisticated understanding of interactive regulation emerged with little attention to self-regulation (for an exception see Tronick, 1989). But the infant's experience is shaped not only by the parent's patterns of behavior, but also by his own. Increasingly, microanalysis researchers consider self-processes to be as important as interactive processes (Beebe et al., 2010, 2011; Chow, Haltigan, & Messinger, 2010; Feldman, Greenbaum, Yirmiya, & Mayes, 1996; Messinger, Ruvolo, Ekas, & Fogel, 2011). Fogel (1992) described all behavior as *unfolding in the individual*, while at the same time continuously modifying and being modified by the changing behavior of the partner.

One common definition of self-regulation is the down-regulation of negative affect. Another definition is based on the temporal patterning of social behaviors, and the degree to which current action is influenced by prior action, analyzed by time-series methods. This definition indexes the relative stability vs. variability of each person's own behaviors over time and is fundamental to an understanding of social competence (Beebe et al., 2010, 2011; Messinger et al., 2011). We term this process "self-contingency" to distinguish it from more common definitions of self-regulation. It is so basic that it may seem invisible, like breathing. Because self-contingency provides the individual with continuous information about the likelihood of staying in the same state, it indexes the person's ability to anticipate, in the procedural mode, her own behavior from moment-to-moment.

Beebe et al. (2010) define each person's moment-to-moment adjustments to her own prior behavior as *self-contingency*, and to her partner's prior behavior as *interactive contingency*. These measures address self- and interactive contingency processes across the entire segment of the play session analyzed, rather than specific sequences of behaviors, such as maternal smile follows infant smile. For example, Beebe et al. (2010) measure maternal facial affect *interactive contingency* by how closely mothers coordinate (correlate) their entire range of facial affect changes, from positive to negative, with infant prior facial affect changes. That is, how closely does the mother follow or correspond to the infant's just previous direction of affective change, as the infant becomes more positive or negative? *Self-contingency* with respect to maternal facial affect measures how predictably degrees of positive to negative maternal facial affect unfold from moment-to-moment. For example, when mothers are overly stable in their facial affect from moment-to-moment, they may become "inscrutable" (see Beebe et al., 2010).

Infant procedural representation and the origins of attachment

The literature on internal working models of attachment, based on expectancies of actual experiences (Bowlby, 1969; Bretherton & Munholland, 1999; Main, Kaplan, & Cassidy, 1985), and a parallel literature on the origins of procedural, presymbolic forms of representations, also based on expectancies of actual experiences (for reviews see Beebe & Lachmann, 2002; Bornstein, 1985; Stern, 1985), have proceeded in parallel. An integration of these two literatures facilitates our ability to conceptualize the origins of attachment patterns.

As noted, infants are intrinsically motivated to detect pattern and order, to perceive contingency and degree of contingency, to anticipate when events will occur, to generate procedural expectancies, and to act on these expectancies (Haith, Hazan, & Goodman, 1988). Infants estimate probabilities of "if-then" sequences (Saffran et al., 1996), and engage in an active process of ordering and re-ordering information. This allows them to develop ongoing expectancies of sequences of events within the self, within the partner, and between the two. This procedural form of representation is based on the predictability of events and the perception of degree of contingent "control" over events (Stern, 1985; Tarabulsy et al., 1996). Infant procedural representational capacities in the first 3–4 months are already extensive (Bornstein, 1985; Haith et al., 1988; Shields & Rovee-Collier, 1992). Infants are highly sensitive to ways that their behaviors are contingently responded to (Beebe et al., 2010; DeCasper & Carstens, 1980; Haith et al., 1988; Jaffe et al., 2001; Muir & Hains, 1993; Murray & Trevarthen, 1985; Stern, 1985; Tarabulsy et al., 1996; Watson, 1985).

Procedural expectancies can be seen as the building blocks of infant internal working models of attachment as early as 4 months (Beebe et al., 2010; Stern, 1985). Microanalysis of 4-month face-to-face interactions may help us characterize in more detail what infants come to expect from interactions with their parents. Specifically, 4-month infant procedural expectancies of self- and interactive patterns provide ways of defining processes by which patterns of intimate relating and attachment security are constructed. Expectancies of interactive contingency include the degree to which each person's changes correspond to the partner's direction of change; that is, how tightly mothers contingently coordinate with infants, how tightly infants contingently coordinate with mothers, and how stable/labile each partner's pattern of self-contingency may be. Expectancies of interactive contingency include the degree to which each person's changes correspond to the partner's direction of change. These are also expectancies of specific behavioral qualities, such as rates of looking away, or rates of intrusive touch. These patterns offer a more detailed perspective on the origins of infant working models of attachment as well as on forms of maternal sensitivity/insensitivity.

The optimal mid-range model

Contingency as used here is a neutral term. It acquires meaning only in relation to some other construct, such as attachment security. Mother–infant face-to-face interaction literature tends to assume that "more is better": more contingency, more coordination, more attunement, and more synchrony (see Tarabulsy et al., 1996; Van Egeren, Barratt, & Roach, 2001). But the role of degree of tightness/looseness of interpersonal coordination in infant development has been unclear (Jaffe et al., 2001; Keller, Lohaus, Volker, Cappenberg, & Chasiotis, 1999). High coordination (high interactive contingency) has been seen as more optimal for development (Chapple, 1970) or as an index of stress (Gottman, 1979).

A number of studies now converge on an "optimum midrange model" of interactive contingency for attachment and social outcomes, in which poles of higher and lower degrees of contingent coordination are both problematic. Maternal overstimulation, intrusiveness, inconsistency, and particularly high *or* low levels of maternal stimulation, maternal responsiveness, or infant responsiveness, predict insecure outcomes (Hane, Feldstein, & Dernetz, 2003; Isabella & Belsky, 1991; Jaffe et al., 2001; Lewis & Feiring, 1989; Leyendecker, Lamb, Fracasso, Scholmerich, & Larson, 1997; Malatesta et al., 1989).

The prediction of attachment from microanalytic studies

Relatively few studies have predicted 12-month attachment using detailed microanalytic coding of videotaped mother–infant interaction and contingency assessed with mathematical approaches. In this section a half dozen of such studies are briefly described, selected with the criteria of split-screen videotaping of mother–infant face-to-face play, the coding of behavior on a 1 s time base, and infant age 4 months (except where noted). Attachment may be assessed through classifications or through interaction scales (contact-initiating, contact-maintaining, resistance, avoidance). In such studies, the ways in which mother and infant jointly regulate communication at 4 months generates a trajectory in development that has been shown to predict attachment at 12 months. Communication modalities such as vocalization, attention, affect, head orientation, and touch are examined. Thus aspects of attachment patterns are already in place at 4 months, in subtle processes of face-to-face communication.

Langhorst and Fogel (1982) found that maternal stimulation (such as facial, vocal, or touch) during periods of infant gazing at mother, and holding back on stimulation during infant gaze aversion, was negatively correlated with avoidance in the Strange Situation. Maternal tendency to increase stimulation following negative infant cues was positively correlated with infant avoidance. Infant gaze aversion and postural "avoid" were also positively correlated with avoidance. Stimulating while infants gaze (and holding back while infants look away) identifies one aspect of maternal *sensitivity*; conversely, maternal tendency to increase stimulation following infant distress identifies an aspect of maternal *insensitivity*. These findings are consistent with Brazelton, Kozlowski, and Main (1974), who proposed that mothers who reserve their stimulation for periods of infant gazing facilitate the infant's ability to use gaze aversion as a coping mechanism to down-regulate arousal as needed. These findings are consistent with Field's (1981) documentation that infants use periods of looking away from mother to down-regulate arousal and return to a comfortable baseline arousal level.

At 2.5, 5, and 7.5 months, Malatesta et al. (1989) analyzed maternal facial responsivity to infant facial affect, defined as maternal changes contingent within 1 s on infant changes (but did not analyze infant contingent on mother). Mothers of future secure infants showed moderate contingency, whereas those of future avoidant infants showed high levels of contingency. That is, mothers of secure infants followed the infant's direction of affective change to a moderate degree, whereas mothers of future avoidant infants followed more tightly. This finding is an early example of the optimal midrange model: the highest coordination is not necessarily optimal for secure attachment. A moderate level of maternal contingent facial coordination emerges as a dimension of maternal sensitivity.

Slade et al. (1995) used contingency measurements of mother and infant social engagement with findings similar to those of Malatesta et al. (1989), and Tobias (1995) used the Adult Attachment Interview (AAI) administered in the last trimester of the mother's pregnancy to predict mother–infant interaction. Mothers who were Free-Autonomous/secure on the AAI showed moderate degrees of contingency when interacting with their infants at 4 months, whereas mothers classified as Preoccupied/Entangled showed higher degrees of contingency. Strikingly, the infants' level of contingency matched that of their mothers. Again, a moderate level of maternal contingent coordination emerged as an aspect of maternal sensitivity. This study also shows that the mother's state of mind with respect to attachment, visible in pregnancy, predicts maternal communication at 4 months, providing one of the first links between maternal states of mind and face-to-face communication.

The still-face paradigm (Tronick, 1989) introduces a brief interruption into mother–infant face-to-face play. Following regular play, the mother is instructed to hold a completely still face for 2 minutes. Thereafter the play resumes normally. Tronick (1989) found that infants who experienced more repairs of mismatches in an ongoing interaction, and who used more adaptive methods of coping with the still-face experiment (such as continuing to signal the mother), were more likely to have secure attachments. Using the still-face paradigm, Cohn, Campbell, and Ross (1991) showed that 6-month future secure, but not avoidant, infants displayed positive signaling/eliciting behaviors while mother maintained a still face. Infants who continue to signal their mothers, in a positive fashion, are more likely to become securely attached.

Braungart-Rieker, Garwood, Powers, and Wang (2001) analyzed 4-month infant facial/vocal affect and self-regulation (self-touch/focus on something other than mother) during the still-face episode, and maternal sensitivity (coded on 5-point scale every 10 s epoch) during free-play. Greater 4-month maternal sensitivity predicted 12-month security. Future avoidant infants showed higher levels of 4-month self-regulation; future secure infants showed midrange levels; and future resistant infants showed low levels, again pointing to an optimal mid-range model.

Jaffe et al. (2001) predicted 12-month disorganized, resistant, and avoidant attachment, compared to secure, from degree of 4-month vocal rhythm coordination, coded on a ¼ s time base. Vocal rhythm coordination assesses the degree each individual "matches" (correlates) the *durations* of vocal sounds and silences with that of the partner. Particularly salient was the vocal turn-taking coordination, as each partner may match the duration of the "switching" pause as partners switch vocal turns. Time-series methods were used to determine degree of contingent coordination. Again, a midrange degree of interactive contingency (coordination) predicted security: a moderate degree of correspondence with the partner's rhythms of turn taking. Higher and lower degrees predicted disorganized/resistant and avoidant attachment, respectively. Higher coordination increases the predictability of the interaction and was here interpreted as excessive monitoring, "trying too hard," or "vigilance," a coping strategy elicited by novelty, interactive challenge, or threat. Lower coordination was interpreted as inhibition of monitoring, or withdrawal. Midrange coordination may leave more "space," more room for uncertainty, initiative, and flexibility within the experience of correspondence and contingency, optimal for secure attachment. Thus one aspect of maternal sensitivity from an attachment perspective may be moderate levels of maternal contingent coordination.

Working with the Jaffe et al. (2001) data set, Koulomzin et al. (2002) predicted 12-month secure vs. avoidant attachment from infant behavior during face-to-face interaction. Unusual in microanalysis studies, mother behavior was not coded. What is particularly interesting in this study is that attachment was predicted by the infant's behavior alone. Future secure (vs. avoidant) infants looked at mother more, with a more stable pattern; and showed greater range of positive and negative facial signaling, more sustained gaze, and more coordinated gaze/head orientation (yielding a stable focus of attention to mother's face), regardless of self-touch/mouthing. Future avoidant infants showed more frequent and variable tactile behaviors, more looking away, and looking at mother with a wandering head. Future avoidant infants maintained a level of stable gaze at mother equal to that of future secure infants only if involved in self-touch/mouthing.

From these studies, the following aspects of maternal sensitivity emerge in relation to infant attachment outcomes: (1) stimulating while infants gaze at mother, and holding back on stimulating while infants gaze avert, facilitates infant ability to use looking away as a coping mechanism to down-regulate arousal; (2) maternal tendency to increase stimulation following infant distress is an aspect of maternal insensitivity; (3) contingent maternal coordination with infant behavior that is "midrange" in degree, neither very high or very low, predicts attachment security; and (4) maternal facilitation of repair following disruptions predicts attachment security.

Beebe et al. (2010): the origins of disorganized attachment at 4 months

We turn to a study by Beebe et al. (2010) that predicted 12-month attachment outcomes from 2.5 minutes of mother–infant face-to-face communication at 4 months. We summarize here the prediction of 12-month disorganized attachment from 4-month behavior, contrasting secure (B), $N = 47$, vs. disorganized (D), $N = 17$. Attachment classifications were coded by Elizabeth Carlson. For details of method, statistical analyses, and results, see Beebe et al. (2010).

The mother was instructed to play with her 4-month infant as she would at home, but without toys, for 10 minutes. The first 2.5 uninterrupted continuous minutes of videotaped interaction were coded on a 1 s time base by coders blind to attachment status. Analysis of only a few minutes of video footage is consistent with the microanalysis literature

(Ambady & Rosenthal, 1992; Cohn & Tronick, 1989; Messinger, 2002) and yields robust session-to-session consistency (Cohn & Tronick, 1989; Weinberg & Tronick, 1991; Zelner, Beebe, & Jaffe, 1982).

In this study, unlike many other microanalytic studies cited above, many communication modalities were examined simultaneously (rather than one modality, such as vocalization or gaze). Attention, emotion, orientation, and touch were coded. Moreover, both self-regulation and interactive regulation were assessed.

Mothers and infants were coded independently as follows. For mothers: gaze, facial affect, touch, and spatial orientation; for infants: gaze, facial affect, vocal affect, touch, and head orientation. Two types of measures were generated: *frequencies of behavioral qualities*, such as gaze aversion or intrusive touch; and the *process of relating across time*, measured by self- and interactive contingency.

Interactive contingency is defined as adjustments of one individual's behavior that are correlated with the partner's prior behavior. *Self-contingency* is defined as adjustments of an individual's behavior that are correlated with his or her own prior behavior (in the context of a particular partner). Self-contingency refers to the degree of predictability (stability/lability) within an individual's own rhythms of activity; it provides the individual with continuous information about the likelihood of staying in the same state.

Beebe et al. (2010) asked whether 4-month infants and mothers who were classified as disorganized at 12 months ("future" disorganized at 4 months) differed from those classified as secure ("future" secure). Regarding contingency measures, they asked which partner (mother or infant) in future disorganized dyads might show 4-month degree of contingency that differs from that of future secure dyads; whether contingency is increased, or decreased, relative to secure dyads; the type of contingency that is altered, self- or interactive; and the communication modality in which contingency is altered.

Antecedents of disorganized (vs. secure) attachment were found: both in frequencies of behavioral qualities and in contingencies; in both mothers and infants; in self-contingency as well as interactive contingency; in both increased and decreased contingencies relative to secure dyads; and in all communication modalities assessed (attention, emotion, orientation, and touch).

Mothers of future disorganized infants bring their own difficult attachment history to their interactions with their infants. They are likely to suffer from unresolved loss, abuse, or trauma (Lyons-Ruth et al., 1999; Main & Hesse, 1990; Main et al., 1985). Difficulties with their own distress are likely to disturb their responses to distress in their infants.

Despite important recent progress in understanding disorganized attachment, we still lack a full understanding of how disorganized attachment is formed prior to 12 months (Leyendecker et al., 1997; Madigan et al., 2006; Main & Hesse, 1990; Main & Solomon, 1990). Maternal behavior within the Ainsworth Strange Situation has been found to be frightened and/or frightening (Jacobvitz, Hazen, & Riggs, 1997; Lyons-Ruth et al., 1999; Schuengel, Bakermans-Kranenburg, & Van IJzendoorn, 1999). Lyons-Ruth et al. (1999) suggested that the degree of communicative derailment seen in disorganized dyads "should be fear-arousing in itself because the infant will have little sense of influence over the caregiver at times of heightened fear or stress" (p. 69).

In our analyses, infants' diminished sense of influence is translated into lowered maternal contingent coordination with infant behavior: the mother does not predictably follow the direction of the infant's prior behavior (such as becoming more positive as the infant does so, and dampening to concern as the infant becomes distressed). When the infant has difficulty predicting what the mother will do next, his expectation that he can influence her is lowered, impairing a sense of agency. We also hypothesized that future disorganized (vs. secure) infants use more discrepant affect (simultaneous positive and negative facial and/or vocal affect), based on the frequently observed simultaneous approach and avoidance behavior shown by infants classified as disorganized in the Strange Situation.

Summary of future disorganized (vs. secure) dyads at 4 months

Four-month infants who will be classified disorganized (vs. secure) at 12 months were more likely to be male and to show complex forms of dysregulation:

- more vocal distress, and more combined facial and/or vocal distress;
- more *discrepant* facial and vocal affect in the same second;
- lowered engagement self-contingency, an emotional destabilization;
- more failure to touch, less touching one's own skin, and greater likelihood of continuing in a "no touch" state, all of which compromise infant access to arousal regulation through touch, in the context of increased distress.

Mothers of 4-month infants who will be classified disorganized (vs. secure) at 12 months were more likely to show the following patterns:

- extensive (20% of the time or more) gazing away from infant's face (14.9% of mothers of future B and 35% of mothers of future D infants met this criterion), and less predictable self-contingency patterns of gazing at and away from the infant, compromising infant ability to expect and rely on predictable maternal visual attention;
- extensive (20% of the time or more) "looming" head movements, which were relatively unpredictable, interpreted as potentially threatening;
- greater likelihood of positive and/or surprise expressions while infants were distressed, interpreted as maternal emotional "denial" of infant distress;
- lowered emotional (facial-visual engagement) coordination with infant emotional ups and downs, interpreted as maternal emotional withdrawal from distressed infants;
- heightened maternal facial self-contingency, an overly stable face leading to a "closed-up" inscrutable face;
- lowered maternal contingent touch coordination with infant touch, a form of withdrawal.

Infant distress and discrepant affect

Compared to future secure infants, future disorganized infants at 4 months show more vocal distress, and combined facial and/or vocal distress. They also show more discrepant affect within the same second, such as smile with whimper. These are painful moments to watch. Because of discrepant affect, it may be difficult for future disorganized infants eventually to recognize what they feel, or know how to make sense of their contradictory feelings. Contradictory positive and negative infant affect at 4 months is strikingly similar to contradictory infant approach and withdrawal behavior at 12 months in the Strange Situation, a key feature of disorganized attachment.

Dyadic affective conflict: maternal smile or surprise to infant distress

Not only the infant but also the dyad was in affective conflict. Mothers of future disorganized (vs. secure) infants were more likely to show smile and/or surprise faces specifically following infant facial/vocal distress: a maternal emotional "denial" of infant distress. Thus these mothers "opposed" or "countered" infant distress, literally going in the opposite affective direction, as if attempting to "ride negative into positive." The infant's expectation of matching and being matched in the direction of affective change, which lays the groundwork for feeling "attuned to" or "on the same wavelength," is disturbed. We propose that unresolved fears about intimate relating in these mothers trigger complex "defensive" maneuvers and contradictory behavioral tendencies that derail their infants. Smiling and surprise faces in response to infant distress can be seen as a disturbance in maternal sensitivity. We infer that these infants come to *expect* that their mothers do not empathically share their distress.

Dyadic conflict: attention dysregulation

Despite greater distress in future disorganized infants, as noted above, their mothers showed extensive gazing away from the infant's face. Moreover, these mothers showed less self-predictability in patterns of gazing at and away from the infant's face. This pattern may lead to infant feelings of being too visually "separate" from their mothers, of not being "seen," and of being confused about mother's visual presence and availability. Thus infant ability to rely on a predictable maternal pattern of visual attention is compromised.

Extensive maternal looking away may reflect maternal discomfort with intimate engagement through mutual gaze, or it may reflect moments of maternal dissociation. Maternal dissociation fits the literature on the adult attachment interview in which forms of dissociation such as lapses in attention, dysfluencies, or entertaining contradictory facts are characteristic of mothers classified as "unresolved," who are likely to have disorganized infants (Main, Hesse, & Goldwyn, 2008). Extensive maternal looking away can also be seen as a disturbance in maternal sensitivity.

Maternal intermodal discordance

Mothers of future disorganized infants exhibited an intermodal discordance between extensive gazing away, thus "too far away," and extensive looming into the infant's face, thus "too close in." Both gazing away and looming in disturb the potential for mutual gaze. Because eye contact is arousing, we conjecture that both these maternal behaviors reflect her concerns about visual intimacy, which may be over-arousing.

Both maternal gaze away and maternal loom occurred in the context of lowered maternal visual and spatial self-predictability. Not only is there a maternal intermodal discordance (looming in/gazing away), but these discordant behaviors unfold in relatively unpredictable ways. This constellation defines a disturbance in maternal sensitivity.

Dyadic conflict: lowered maternal engagement coordination

A third form of dyadic conflict was seen when, despite infant distress, mothers of future disorganized infants lowered their facial-visual engagement coordination with infant engagement: an emotional-attentional withdrawal from contingently coordinating with infant positive as well as distress moments. These mothers did not join the infant's attentional and emotional direction, disturbing the likelihood of shared affective processes, consistent with our hypothesis. Although the prevalence of *behavioral qualities* of positive or negative facial affect did not differ in mothers of future disorganized vs. secure infants, the ways that mothers *contingently coordinated* their facial-visual behavior with that of the infants differed. Thus the disturbance is found in the *process* of relating over time, rather than the mere frequency of behaviors, defining another dimension of disturbance in maternal sensitivity.

Maternal withdrawal makes it difficult for future disorganized infants to come to expect that their behaviors can influence mothers to coordinate with them, to join their distressed or their positive states. In short, infants are relatively helpless to affect mothers with their facial-visual engagement processes, which disturbs the infant's sense of interactive efficacy.

Lowered maternal facial coordination with infant facial or vocal affect, or lowered maternal gaze coordination with infant gaze, was not found in mothers of future disorganized infants when these communication modalities were analyzed separately. Thus mothers of future disorganized infants *perceive* infant affect and gaze and in many ways are adequately responsive. Instead, it is only when the overall *gestalt* of infant facial-visual *engagement* (which includes infant head orientation and vocal affect as well) is considered that we find lowered maternal coordination. Thus, although facial-mirroring seems intact, maternal mirroring of the entire infant facial-vocal-visual-head-orientation gestalt is not.

We theorize that mothers of future disorganized infants cannot coordinate with infant emotional ups and downs, and cannot acknowledge moments of infant distress, because they cannot bear to pay attention to their own emotional distress. The infant's distress may evoke the mother's own distress, and her ensuing efforts to manage it. We interpret the mother's lowered emotional responsivity (lowered contingent engagement coordination with infant engagement), as well as maternal smile or surprise to infant distress, as maternal emotional "denial" of infant distress. Although minimization of distress has been associated with avoidant attachment (Cassidy, 1994), the forms of maternal denial of distress documented here are different from minimization. Lowered emotional coordination communicates to the infant: "You can't affect me." Showing the opposite (positive) emotion to the infant's negative emotion constitutes an "opposing" of the infant's emotion, communicating: "I'm not going there." We propose that the infant represents these maternal responses to his distress through procedurally organized expectancies of action sequences. Moreover, one aspect of this representation is the infant's own distress and potential alarm.

Heightened maternal facial self-contingency: "closing up one's face"

Lowered maternal engagement coordination was accompanied by mothers remaining overly facially stable or too "steady-state," like a momentary "still-face" (Tronick, 1989). We interpret this finding as mothers "closing up their faces"; another way of not being available to the "play of faces" and another way of saying "you can't affect me." To remain empathic to infant distress might re-evoke aspects of the mother's own original traumatized state. This facial over-stabilization provides another dimension of disturbance in maternal sensitivity. Ainsworth also described mothers of some avoidant infants as inexpressive/"poker-faced" (Inge Bretherton, personal communication, 8 June 2013).

The constellation of momentarily closing her face, lowering her ongoing coordination with the infant's emotional shifts, and extensive looking away from her infant's face, may be ways of shutting herself down in a self-protective effort, possibly dissociative. This pattern disturbs the infant's ability to feel sensed. We infer that future disorganized infants come to expect that their mothers do not "join" their distress with acknowledgments such as maternal "woe face," an empathic form of maternal facial mirroring. Instead they come to expect that their mothers are happy, surprised, or "closed" when they are distressed.

Lowered infant engagement self-predictability: Infant "destabilization"

In the context of lowered maternal engagement coordination, future disorganized (vs. secure) infants lowered their facial-visual engagement self-predictability. That is, from moment-to-moment the future disorganized (vs. secure) infant's level of facial-visual engagement is less predictable from the immediately prior state. This finding indicates a more variable process in which the infant's ability to anticipate his own moment-to-moment action tendencies is lowered. Infants are metaphorically "destabilized."

Dyadic touch dysregulation

Mothers of future disorganized (vs. secure) infants not only lowered their contingent engagement coordination with infant engagement, disturbing infant interactive efficacy in the facial-visual realm, but they also lowered contingent touch coordination with infant touch, disturbing infant interactive efficacy in the touch realm. These mothers were less able than mothers of secure infants to acknowledge increasing frequency of infant touch as a cue for more affectionate, tender touch. This pattern provides another dimension of disturbance in maternal sensitivity. We infer that future disorganized infants come to expect that their mothers will be unavailable to help modulate states of affective distress through maternal touch coordination with their own touch behavior: an interpersonal touch dysregulation. Infants are left too alone, too separate, in the realm of touch.

Simultaneously, future disorganized infants showed an intrapersonal touch dysregulation: less touch overall, specifically less touching of their own skin, and greater likelihood of continuing in states of "no touch," metaphorically "getting stuck in states of no-touch." Lowered infant access to his own touch further disturbs infant regulation of distress through touch (self-soothing, fingering an object or his mother). Together, future disorganized infants and their mothers thus showed a dyadic touch dysregulation.

If their procedural experience could be put into words, we imagine future disorganized infants might experience: "I'm so upset and you're not helping me. I'm smiling at you and whimpering; don't you see I want you to love me? When I'm upset, you smile or close up or look away. You make me feel worse. I feel confused about what I feel and about what you feel. I can't predict you. I don't know what is going on. What am I supposed to do? I feel helpless to affect you. I feel helpless to help myself. I feel frantic. I feel unsafe."

In an effort to understand further mothers of future disorganized infants, we note that a facial expression produced by one person tends to evoke a similar expression in the partner, out of awareness (Dimberg, Thunberg, & Elmehed, 2000), a powerful way of participating in the state of the other. This is such a robust phenomenon that some researchers dub it an "automatic" facial mimicry (Hatfield, Cacioppo, & Rapson, 1993). But as we have seen, mothers of future disorganized infants do not match or empathically join the facial distress of their infants. We conjecture that mothers of future disorganized infants cannot process and respond to emotional information in the moment because they are flooded by their experience of the infant's distress, which may re-evoke earlier traumatic states of their own. They may shut down their own emotional processing, and be unable to use the infant's distress behaviors as communications, in a momentary dissociative process.

Emerging internal working models of future disorganized infants at 4 months

The proposal of this research is that future disorganized infants represent these individual and dyadic patterns as emerging internal working models of self-with-mother in the form of procedural representations, based on expectancies of self- and interactive patterns. These expectancies bias the trajectory of how experience is organized, activating certain pathways and inhibiting others, ultimately limiting the range, flexibility, and *coherence* of experience. The findings show many forms of intrapersonal and interpersonal conflict, intermodal discordance, or contradiction, leading to confusion and incoherent working models in future disorganized infants. Our results provide one response to the Madigan et al. (2006) call for better identification of the details of the elusive behaviors of anomalous parenting directly implicated in the development of disorganized attachment.

Emerging internal working models of future disorganized infants with their mothers are characterized by expectancies of intense infant emotional distress and inability to obtain comfort. In many ways, future disorganized infants are alone with their facial/vocal distress and helpless to affect their mothers with their frantic distress. At critical moments they are opposed by their mothers. A second feature is an expectancy of difficulty predicting what will happen, both within the self and within the partner. A third feature is difficulty in knowing what the self feels and what the partner feels: a form of emotional incoherence. A fourth feature is a disturbance in experiences of recognition, leading to the expectation of not feeling "sensed" or "known," particularly when distressed. These profound experiences of non-recognition may disturb the infant's core sense of safety. A further critical feature of these expectancies of future disorganized infants is the experience of intrapersonal and dyadic contradictory communications, conflict, and remarkable intermodal discrepancies. These contradictions disturb the coherence of the infant's emerging internal working model.

In sum, many fundamental disturbances in the processes through which future disorganized infants may come to feel known and can recognize being recognized, through which infants may come to know their mothers, and through which infants come to sense their own states, can be elucidated with a microanalytic approach. This picture provides detailed behavioral mechanisms that could result in the lack of a consistent strategy of dealing with negative emotions, characteristic of disorganized infants in the Strange Situation by 12 months (Van IJzendoorn, Schuengel, & Bakerman-Kranenburg, 1999). The disturbance in individual and dyadic emotional coherence in future disorganized infants and their mothers offers a striking parallel to the contradictory and unintegrated affects of disorganized infants in the Ainsworth Strange Situation, and to the contradictory evaluations of attachment relationships in the findings of their mothers in the Adult Attachment Interview.

Conclusion

The microanalysis approach opens up a new window on the micro-processes of face-to-face communication and attachment formation, revealing aspects of the origins of attachment with a more detailed lens. By coding rapid communications which are often not quite perceptible in real time, it provides a remarkable "social microscope."

The purpose of this paper is not to suggest microanalysis as a method for mainstream attachment research. Instead, we illustrated the kinds of detailed information regarding the origins of disorganized attachment that the microanalysis approach can generate. This approach provides a new, rich set of behaviors and self- and interactive patterns that extend our understanding of the origins of infant disorganized attachment, and of patterns of maternal sensitivity and insensitivity.

Acknowledgements

Beatrice Beebe thanks Joseph Jaffe (in memoriam), Karlen Lyons-Ruth, Jude Cassidy, Mary Sue Moore, and John Kerr; and her lab assistants Daisy Bear, Dhru Desai, Allison Dorf, Robert Frashure, Daniel Friedman, Caroline Kazlow, Meghan Mak, Zachary Neumann, Jane Roth, Maeva Schlienger, Sara Van Hoose, Daniel Vigliano, Kaitlin Walsh, and Ella Bandes (in memoriam).

References

Ainsworth, M., Bell, S., & Stayton, D. (1974). Individual differences in the development of some attachment behaviors. *Merrill-Palmer Quarterly of Behavior and Development*, *18*(2), 123–143.

Ainsworth, M., Blehar, M., Waters, E., & Wall, S. (1978). *Patterns of attachment: A psychological study of the strange situation*. Hillsdale, NJ: Lawrence Erlbaum Associates.

Ambady, N., & Rosenthal, R. (1992). Thin slices of expressive behavior as predictors of interpersonal consequences: A meta-analysis. *Psychological Bulletin*, *2*, 256–274.

Beebe, B., Jaffe, J., Markese, S., Buck, K., Chen, H., Cohen, P., ... Feldstein, S. (2010). The origins of 12-month attachment: A microanalysis of 4-month mother-infant interaction. *Attachment & Human Development*, *12*(1–2), 1–135.

Beebe, B., & Lachmann, F. (2002). *Infant research and adult treatment: Co-constructing interactions*. Hillsdale, NJ: The Analytic Press.

Beebe, B., & Lachmann, F. (2013). *The origins of attachment: Infant research and adult treatment*. London: Routledge.

Beebe, B., Steele, M., Jaffe, J., Buck, K., Chen, H., Cohen, P., ... Feldstein, S. (2011). Maternal anxiety and 4-month mother-infant self- and interactive contingency. *Infant Mental Health Journal*, *32*(2), 174–206.

Blehar, M., Lieberman, A., & Ainsworth, M. (1977). Early face-to-face interaction and its relation to later infant-mother attachment. *Child Development*, *48*, 182–194.

Bornstein, M. (1985). Infant into adult: Unity to diversity in the development of visual categorization. In J. Mehler & R. Fox (Eds.), *Neonate cognition* (pp. 115–138). Hillsdale, NJ: Lawrence Erlbaum Associates.

Bowlby, J. (1969). *Attachment and loss*. New York, NY: Basic Books.

Braungart-Rieker, J., Garwood, M., Powers, B., & Wang, X. (2001). Parental sensitivity, infant affect, and affect regulation: Predictors of later attachment. *Child Development*, *72*(1), 252–270.

Brazelton, T., Kozlowski, B., & Main, M. (1974). The origins of reciprocity. In M. Lewis & L. Rosenblum (Eds.), *The effects of the infant on its caregiver* (pp. 137–154). New York, NY: Wiley-Interscience.

Bretherton, I., & Munholland, K. (1999). Internal working models in attachment: A construct revisited. In J. Cassidy & P. R. Shaver (Eds.), *Handbook of attachment theory* (pp. 89–111). New York, NY: Guilford Press.

Cassidy, J. (1994). Emotion regulation: Influences of attachment relationships. *Monographs of the Society for Research in Child Development*, *59*(2–3 Serial No. 240), 2228–2249.

Chapple, E. (1970). *Culture and biological man*. New York, NY: Hold, Rinehart & Winston.

Chow, S., Haltigan, J., & Messinger, D. (2010). Dynamic infant–parent affect coupling during the face-to-face/still-face. *Emotion*, *10*(1), 101–114.

Cohn, J., Campbell, S., & Ross, S. (1991). Infant response in the still-face paradigm at 6 months predicts avoidant and secure attachments at 12 months. *Development and Psychopathology, 3*, 367–376.

Cohn, J., & Tronick, E. (1989). Mother-infant face-to-face interaction: The sequence of dyadic states at 3, 6, 9 months. *Developmental Psychology, 23*, 68–77.

De Wolff, M., & Van Ijzendoorn, M. (1997). Sensitivity and attachment: A meta-analysis on parental antecedents of infant attachment. *Child Development, 68*, 571–591.

DeCasper, A., & Carstens, A. (1980). Contingencies of stimulation: Effects on learning and emotion in neonates. *Infant Behavior and Development, 9*, 19–36.

Dimberg, U., Thunberg, M., & Elmehed, K. (2000). Unconscious facial reactions to emotional facial expressions. *Psychological Science, 11*(1), 86–89.

Feldman, R. (2007). Parent-infant synchrony and the construction of shared timing; physiological precursors, developmental outcomes and risk conditions. *Journal of Child Psychology and Psychiatry, 48*(3–4), 329–354.

Feldman, R., Greenbaum, C., Yirmiya, N., & Mayes, L. (1996). Relations between cyclicity and regulation in mother-infant interaction at 3 and 9 months and cognition at 2 years. *Journal of Applied Developmental Psychology, 17*, 347–365.

Field, T. (1981). Infant gaze aversion and heart rate during face-to-face interactions. *Infant Behavior and Development, 4*, 307–315.

Fogel, A. (1992). Co-regulation, perception and action. *Human Movement Science, 11*, 505–523.

Gottman, J. (1979). *Marital interactions*. New York, NY: Academic Press.

Haith, M., Hazan, C., & Goodman, G. (1988). Expectation and anticipation of dynamic visual events by 3.5 month old babies. *Child Development, 59*, 467–479.

Hane, A., Feldstein, S., & Dernetz, V. (2003). The relation between coordinated interpersonal timing and maternal sensitivity in four-month-old infants. *Journal of Psycholinguistic Research, 32*, 525–539.

Hatfield, E., Cacioppo, J., & Rapson, R. (1993). Emotional contagion. *Current Directions in Psychological Science, 2*, 96–99.

Hofer, M. (1994). Hidden regulators in attachment, separation and loss. *Monographs of the Society for Research in Child Development, 59*(2–3, Serial No. 240), 192–207.

Isabella, R., & Belsky, J. (1991). Interactional synchrony and the origins of infant-mother attachment: A replication study. *Child Development, 62*, 373–384.

Jacobvitz, D., Hazen, N., & Riggs, S. (1997, April). *Disorganized mental processes in mothers: Frightening/frightened caregiving and disoriented, disorganized behavior in infancy.* Paper presented at the biennial meeting of the Society for Research in Child Development, Washington, DC.

Jaffe, J., Beebe, B., Feldstein, S., Crown, C., & Jasnow, M. (2001). Rhythms of dialogue in infancy. *Monographs of the Society for Research in Child Development, 66*(2, Serial No. 264), 1–132.

Keller, H., Lohaus, A., Volker, S., Cappenberg, M., & Chasiotis, A. (1999). Temporal contingency as an independent component of parenting behavior. *Child Development, 70*, 474–485.

Kenny, D., Kashy, D., & Cook, W. (2006). *Dyadic Data Analysis*. New York, NY: Guilford Press.

Koulomzin, M., Beebe, B., Anderson, S., Jaffe, J., Feldstein, S., & Crown, C. (2002). Infant gaze, head, face, and self-touch at four months differentiate secure vs. avoidant attachment at one year: A microanalytic approach. *Attachment & Human Development, 4*, 3–24.

Langhorst, B., & Fogel, A. (1982, March). *Cross validation of microanalytic approaches to face-to-face play.* Presented at International conference on Infant Studies, Austin, TX.

Lewis, M., & Feiring, C. (1989). Infant, mother and mother-infant interaction behavior and subsequent attachment. *Child Development, 60*, 831–837.

Leyendecker, B., Lamb, M., Fracasso, M., Scholmerich, A., & Larson, D. (1997). Playful interaction and the antecedents of attachment: A longitudinal study of Central American and Euro-American mothers and infants. *Merrill Palmer Quarterly, 43*, 24–47.

Lyons-Ruth, K., Bronfman, E., & Parsons, E. (1999). Maternal disrupted affective communication, maternal frightened or frightening behavior, and disorganized infant attachment strategies. *Monographs of the Society for Research in Child Development, 64*(3 Serial No. 258), 67–96.

Madigan, S., Bakermans-Kranenburg, M., Van IJzendoorn, M., Moran, G., Pederson, D., & Benoit, D. (2006). Unresolved states of mind anomalous parental behavior, and disorganized attachment: A review and meta-analysis of a transmission gap. *Attachment & Human Development, 8*, 89–111.

Main, M., & Hesse, E. (1990). Parents' unresolved traumatic experiences are related to infant disorganized attachment status: Is frightened and/or frightening parental behavior the linking mechanism? In M. Greenberg, D. Cicchetti, & E. Cummings (Eds.), *Attachment in the preschool years: Theory, research, and intervention* (pp. 161–182). Chicago, IL: University of Chicago Press.

Main, M., Hesse, E., & Goldwyn, R. (2008). Studying differences in language usage in recounting attachment history: An introduction to the AAI. In H. Steele & M. Steele (Eds.), *Clinical application of the adult attachment interview* (pp. 31–68). New York, NY: The Guilford Press.

Main, M., Kaplan, N., & Cassidy, J. (1985). Security in infancy, childhood, and adulthood: A move to the level of representation. *Monographs of the Society for Research in Child Development, 50* (Serial No. 209), 66–104.

Main, M., & Solomon, J. (1990). Procedures for identifying infants as disorganized/disoriented during the Ainsworth Strange Situation. In M. Greenberg, D. Cicchetti & E. Cummings (Eds.), *Attachment in the preschool years* (pp. 121–160). Chicago, IL: University of Chicago Press.

Malatesta, C., Culver, C., Tesman, J., & Shepard, B. (1989). The development of emotion expression during the first two years of life. *Monographs of the Society for Research in Child Development, 54*(Serial No. 219, Nos. 1–2), 1–136.

Messinger, D. (2002). Positive and negative: Infant facial expressions and emotions. *Current Directions in Psychological Science, 11*, 1–6.

Messinger, D., Ruvolo, P., Ekas, N., & Fogel, A. (2011). "Are you interested, baby?" Young infants exhibit stable patterns of attention during interaction. *Infancy, 17*(2), 233–244.

Moore, G., Powers, C., Bass, A., Cohn, J., Propper, C., Allen, N., & Lewinsohn, P. (2013). Dyadic interaction: Greater than the sum of its parts? *Infancy, 18*(4), 490–515.

Muir, D., & Hains, S. (1993). Infantile sensitivity to perturbations in adult facial, vocal, tactile, and contingent stimulation during face-to-face interaction. In B. DeBoysson-Bardies, S. DeSchonen, P. Jusczyk, P. McNeilage, & J. Morton (Eds.), *Developmental neurocognition: Speech and face processing in the first year of life* (pp. 171–185). Dordrecht: Kluwer Academic Publications.

Murray, L., & Trevarthen, C. (1985). Emotional regulation of interactions between two-month-olds and their mothers. In T. Field & N. Fox (Eds.), *Social perception in infants* (pp. 177–197). Norwood, NJ: Ablex.

Papousek, M. (1992). Early ontogeny of vocal communication in parent-infant interaction. In H. Papousek, U. Juergens, & M. Papousek (Eds.), *Nonverbal vocal communication* (p. 230) New York, NY: Cambridge University Press.

Saffran, J., Aslin, R., & Newport, E. (1996). Statistical learning by 8-month-old infants. *Science, 274*, 1926–1928.

Sander, L. (1977). The regulation of exchange in the infant-caretaker system and some aspects of the context-content relationship. In M. Lewis & L. Rosenblum (Eds.), *Interaction, conversation, and the development of language* (pp. 133–156). New York, NY: Wiley.

Schuengel, C., Bakermans-Kranenburg, M., & Van IJzendoorn, M. (1999). Frightening maternal behavior linking unresolved loss and disorganized infant attachment. *Journal of Consulting and Clinical Psychology, 67*, 54–63.

Shields, P., & Rovee-Collier, C. (1992). Long-term memory for context-specific category information at six months. *Child Development, 63*, 245–259.

Slade, A., Dermer, M., Gerber, J., Gibson, L., Graf, F., Siegel, N., & Tobias, K. (1995, March). *Prenatal representation, dyadic interaction and quality of attachment.* Paper presented at the meeting of the Society for Research in Child Development, Indianapolis, IN.

Stern, D. (1971). A microanalysis of the mother-infant interaction. *Journal of the American Academy of Child Psychiatry, 10*, 501–507.

Stern, D. (1974). Mother and infant at play: The dyadic interaction involving facial, vocal and gaze behaviors. In M. Lewis & L. Rosenblum (Eds.), *The effect of the infant on its caregiver* (pp. 187–213). New York, NY: Wiley.

Stern, D. (1985). *The interpersonal world of the infant.* New York, NY: Basic Books.

Stern, D., Sander, L., Nahum, J., Harrison, A., Bruschweiler-Stern, N., & Tronick, E. (1998). Non-interpretative mechanisms in psychoanalytic therapy. *International Journal of Psycho-Analysis, 79*, 903–921.

Tarabulsy, G., Tessier, R., & Kappas, A. (1996). Contingency detection and the contingent organization of behavior interactions: Implications for socioemotional development in infancy. *Psychological Bulletin, 120*, 25–41.

Tobias, K. (1995). *The relation between maternal attachment and patterns of mother-infant interaction at four months* (Unpublished doctoral dissertation). City University of New York, New York, NY.

Trevarthen, C. (1974). The psychobiology of speech development. In E. Lenneberg (Ed.), *Language and brain: Developmental aspects. Neurosciences Research Program Bulletin, 12*, 570–585.

Tronick, E. (1989). Emotions and emotional communication in infants. *American Psychologist, 44*, 112–119.

Van Egeren, L., Barratt, M., & Roach, M. (2001). Mother-infant responsiveness: Timing, mutual regulation, and interactional context. *Developmental Psychology, 37*(5), 684–697.

Van IJzendoorn, M., Schuengel, C., & Bakerman-Kranenburg, M. (1999). Disorganized attachment in early childhood: Meta-analysis of precursors, concomitants and sequelae. *Development and Psychopathology, 11*, 225–250.

Watson, J. (1985). Contingency perception in early social development. In T. Field & N. Fox (Eds.), *Social perception in infants* (pp. 157–176). Norwood, NJ: Ablex.

Weinberg, K., & Tronick, E. (1991). *Stability of infant social and coping behaviors and affective displays between 6 and 15 months: Age-appropriate tasks and stress bring out stability.* Paper presented at the Society for Research in Child Development, Seattle, Washington, DC.

Zelner, S., Beebe, B., & Jaffe, J. (1982, April). *The organization of vocalization and gaze in early mother-infant interactive regulation*. Presented at the International conference on Infant Studies, New York, NY.

One doll fits all: validation of the Leiden Infant Simulator Sensitivity Assessment (LISSA)

Alexandra Voorthuis, Dorothée Out, Rixt van der Veen, Ritu Bhandari, Marinus H. van IJzendoorn and Marian J. Bakermans-Kranenburg

Centre for Child and Family Studies, Leiden University, Leiden, The Netherlands

Children vary hugely in how demanding of their caregivers they are. This creates differences in demands on parents during observation, making the comparison of sensitivity *between* parents difficult. It would therefore be of interest to create standard situations in which all caregivers are faced with the same level of demand. This study developed an ecologically valid but standardized setting using an infant simulator with interactive features, the Leiden Infant Simulator Sensitivity Assessment (LISSA). The infant simulator resembles a real infant in appearance and it produces crying sounds that are life-like. The simulator begins with fussing and progresses to more intense crying in case of no care or inappropriate care. It responds by being calm again if appropriate care is given. One hundred and eighty-one female participants took care of the infant simulator for two evenings and in a 30 min lab session with increasing competing demands. Sensitive parenting behavior during the lab session was coded with the Ainsworth Sensitivity Scale. Sensitivity ratings covered the whole range of the scale (1–9), and were stable across settings (free play, competing demands). Sensitivity was related to an increase of positive affect during caretaking, and insensitivity was related to intended harsh caregiving response during a computerized cry paradigm. Sensitivity was unrelated to social desirability and self-reported quality of care given to the infant simulator. We discuss the potentials of the infant simulator for research on sensitive parenting, for preventive interventions, and for clinical practices.

Mary Ainsworth defined maternal sensitivity as "the mother's ability to perceive and to interpret accurately the signals and communications implicit in her infant's behavior and, given this understanding, to respond to them appropriately and promptly" (Ainsworth, Bell, & Stayton, 1974, p. 127). Sensitivity is an important aspect of the parent–child relationship and is causally related to the child's attachment security (e.g., Ainsworth et al., 1974; Bakermans-Kranenburg, van IJzendoorn, & Juffer, 2003). However, evidence for the strength of this association is inconsistent (De Wolff & van IJzendoorn, 1997). Varying associations between caregiver sensitivity and infant attachment security may be due to differences in operational definitions of the sensitivity construct or to methodological variations in the observation of sensitivity. The aim of this study is to introduce a standardized experimental setting for the assessment of sensitive parenting.

The Ainsworth Sensitivity Scale was originally used for naturalistic observations during a number of four-hour home visits (Ainsworth et al., 1974). While extensive naturalistic observations are still used and may be the optimum (Higley & Dozier, 2009; van IJzendoorn & Hubbard, 2000), more time-efficient methods that could be used in different settings have established themselves as alternatives for long naturalistic observations. In particular, play sessions have grown popular (e.g., Coppola, Vaughn, Cassibba, & Costantini, 2006; Jin, Jacobvitz, Hazen, & Jung, 2012; McElwain, Cox, Burchinal, & Macfie, 2003; Vereijken, Riksen-Walraven, & Kondo-Ikemura, 1997). For example, of all published papers in *Attachment & Human Development* (1999–2012) that reported on observed sensitivity (k = 30), sensitivity ratings were based on observations of free play in 50% of the studies, while only 9% of the studies involved rating caregiver sensitivity in situations eliciting distress. However, play sessions may provide fewer opportunities for observing responsiveness to infant distress signals. This presents an important limitation as responsiveness to infant distress appears to be an essential dimension of sensitivity and crucial to the prediction of attachment security (Bowlby, 1969; 1984; Goldberg, Grusec, & Jenkins, 1999; Thompson, 1997). Earlier studies showed that responses to infant distress signals were more predictive of attachment security than sensitivity during non-distress (McElwain & Booth-LaForce, 2006).

To enable the observation of parental sensitivity to infant distress, some studies use stress-inducing paradigms such as the Still Face Paradigm (SFP; Tronick, Als, Adamson, Wise, & Brazelton, 1978). When infants get distressed due to the break in normal social interaction during the "still-face" episode, the caregiver's ability to sooth the infant in the following episode can be observed. However, the level of infant distress to the still face differs considerably between dyads (Mesman, van IJzendoorn, & Bakermans-Kranenburg, 2009), hampering the comparison of parental sensitivity across dyads. This is of course true for any setting inducing stress to the infant or the infant–parent dyad, since the variability in infant reactivity to a stressor (both within and between infants) creates dissimilar challenges to the caregiver. It could be argued that the ability of the caregiver to adjust to the infant's state is a part of parental sensitivity. However, experienced coders know that even when longer observations are used, as with the Maternal Behavior Q-Sort (MBQS; Pederson & Moran, 1995), in a number of cases sensitivity to distress cannot be observed. In those cases, the caregiver's ability to deal with infant distress has to be inferred from his or her ability to deal with a cheerful infant.

Caregiver responses to standardized infant cues in experimental paradigms may offer an alternative. One such paradigm is the infant cry paradigm, with exposure to audiotaped infant crying varying in pitch of the cry sound (Frodi et al., 1978; Out, Pieper, Bakermans-Kranenburg, & van IJzendoorn, 2010; Zeskind, 1980, 1983). Caregivers are asked to indicate their intended caregiving response after listening to infant cries (Frodi et al., 1978; Out, Pieper, Bakermans-Kranenburg, Zeskind, & van IJzendoorn, 2010) or after watching a videotape of a crying baby (Zeifman, 2004). These studies have shown that listening to high-pitched cry sounds makes individuals less willing to interact with the infant (Frodi et al., 1978) and more likely to indicate harsh caregiving responses (Out, Pieper, Bakermans-Kranenburg, Zeskind, & van IJzendoorn, 2010). The suggested relation between high-pitched crying and less optimal caregiving is in line with studies showing that high-pitched cry sounds are characteristic of infants with medical or neurological conditions or prenatal and perinatal complications (Soltis, 2004; Wasz-Höckert, Michelsson, & Lind, 1985), and that these same infants are also known to be at increased risk for abuse and neglect. However, these paradigms do not take the caregivers' behavioral responses into account, i.e., they provide no information on observed sensitive parenting.

The Leiden Infant Simulator Sensitivity Assessment (LISSA) is a standardized test to assess sensitivity in an experimental setting using a "life-like" infant simulator with prerecorded cry sounds. The infant simulator (Realityworks, Eau Claire, WI, USA) was developed as a parenting teaching aid for high school students with the aim to prevent teenage pregnancies. Two experimental studies with the infant simulator showed that, after caring for the infant simulator, high school students had significantly more realistic attitudes to parenting and were also more realistic and understanding about dealing with an infant that persistently cried (Roberts & McCowan, 2004; Strachan & Gorey, 1997).

Earlier research on adults' responses to crying using the infant simulator showed that young women who were exposed to the crying infant simulator reported increased negative affect and state anxiety, and they had more negative perceptions of the infant's temperament (Bruning & McMahon, 2009). Testosterone levels in men increased when listening to baby cries, but decreased when the cry was coupled with caretaking responses for the infant simulator (Van Anders, Tolman, & Volling, 2012). Our study is the first in which sensitivity to the infant simulator was observed, including caregiving sensitivity in response to its standardized signals of distress.

Current study

The aim of this study was to introduce a standardized experimental setting for the assessment of sensitive parenting, and test the validity of this measure. We examined the measure's reliability both in terms of its internal consistency across different settings and the possibility to reach high standards of intercoder reliability. We tested whether the participants experienced caretaking of the infant simulator as realistic (face-validity), and we hypothesized that those who reported talking to the infant simulator and using its name when unobserved would be more sensitive during observed caregiving (criterion validity). We expected observed sensitivity to be related to intended caregiving in response to the cry paradigm, a computerized task with exposure to infant cry sounds varying in pitch (convergent validity). We expected higher sensitivity to be related to more positive and less negative mood after taking care of the infant simulator (convergent validity), since negative mood is associated with lower levels of sensitivity (Musser, Ablow, & Measelle, 2012) and positive mood is related to active problem solving (Moskowitz, Folkman, Collette, & Vittinghoff, 1996). The inclination to comply with the experimenter's expectations could lead to the participants' attempt to provide sensitive care of the infant simulator while being observed, and thus we hoped to find no relation between social desirability and sensitivity (discriminant validity). Lastly, because self-report assessments of parenting and attachment have no good credentials in terms of validity (Driscoll & Easterbrooks, 2007; Fitzgerald, Shipman, Jackson, McMahon, & Hanley, 2005; van IJzendoorn, Vereijken, Bakermans-Kranenburg, & Riksen-Walraven, 2004) or association with expert ratings (Roisman et al., 2007; van IJzendoorn et al., 2004), we expected no relation between self-reported quality of care of the infant simulator and observed sensitivity (discriminant validity).

Method

Participants

A total of 353 undergraduate students from the departments of education and child studies, and psychology at Leiden University participated in the first phase of the study. In this phase, the participants completed online questionnaires on temperament, caregiving experiences, traumatic childhood experiences, and some demographic details. One participant was excluded due to random responses. Ten male participants and five females with children of their own were excluded to avoid effects of gender and parental experience on the outcomes. The remaining 337 participants were then invited for the second phase of the study where they had to take care of a "life-like" infant simulator for two evenings and during a 30 min lab session with increasing competing demand. One hundred and eighty-six participants (55.2%) were willing to participate; they did not differ from the non-participants on demographic characteristics (all $p > .05$). Due to technical problems, data from the lab sessions were not available for five participants, resulting in a total of 181 female participants, aged between 17 and 28 years (M = 19.83, SD = 1.53). More than 95% of the participants were born in the Netherlands. The majority (81%) had lived with both biological parents up until 16 years of age and, at the time of the study, 51% of the participants were still living with both biological parents. One hundred and thirty-three participants (74%) had caretaking experiences with a child younger than two years of age. Fourteen participants (8%) reported to have a chronic illness, a physical handicap, or a psychiatric disorder (such as asthma or Attention Deficit Hyperactivity Disorder).

Procedure

Participants were asked to take care of an infant simulator for two evenings at their home (5 pm–10 pm) and during a lab session as if it were their own baby. During the two evenings, the simulator was programmed with various cry episodes. The participants used a hand held computer to answer questions about their perception of the crying after each cry and caretaking episode (Bhandari et al., 2013). After taking care of the infant simulator for two evenings, the participants were asked to fill in a questionnaire about their experiences with the infant simulator.

Following the two evenings, the participants took care of the infant simulator in a 30 minute lab session with increasing competing demands. The lab room was decorated as a living room with a dresser with a changing mat, a baby cot, an infant carrier, a desk with a chair, an easy chair, magazines, children's books, and toys. The participants were told that they were allowed to use all materials in the room while taking care of the simulator as if it was a real infant. In the first 10 minutes (part A), the participants were given no further instructions. In the next 10 minutes (part B), they were asked to fill in a questionnaire while taking care of the simulator (competing demand 1). In the final period of 10 minutes (part C), the participants were asked to perform a computer task (Tower of London) as fast as they could while taking care of the simulator (competing demand 2). Participants were told that those who performed the computer task fastest would receive an additional reward of five Euros, to increase the potential pressure of the competing demand. Before and after taking care of the infant simulator, the participants filled in the Positive Affect Negative Affect questionnaire (PANAS; Crawford & Henry, 2004; Watson, Clark, & Tellegen, 1988) to indicate their current mood. Sessions were videotaped and coded for sensitivity. After caring for the infant simulator, the cry paradigm was administered. The procedure was approved by the Departmental Ethics Committee and informed consent was obtained from all participants.

Measures

Infant simulator

The infant simulator (RealCare Baby II-Plus; Realityworks, Eau Claire, WI, USA) is a doll resembling a real infant in physical appearance, size, and weight (2.95 kg). The physical features of the infant simulator are modeled in a way that requires taking care like a real infant. For example, it has a lifelike neck that falls back if not supported. The doll is programmed as an infant with realistic cry sounds (beginning with mild fussing eventually increasing to full-blown crying) as well as breathing, burping, giggling, and suckling sounds. Moreover, cry episodes are programmed for which specific caregiving activity is required, such as feeding, burping, diaper change, and rocking. Starting with fussing, the cry sounds progressively become more intense in case of no care or inappropriate care. The infant simulator responds with a short giggle or by being calm again if the appropriate care is provided. Special inbuilt sensors in combination with external sensors (in diapers and feeding bottles) register whether correct caregiving was provided or not. The schedules (cry frequencies, gap between cry episodes, etc) are based on diaries kept by parents of real infants. For the home sessions, a "difficult baby" schedule was used in order to have sufficient cry episodes. During the lab session, the infant simulator was programmed to be nonresponsive to the given care, and as a result it would cry for approximately five minutes ($M = 4.72$, $SD = 0.35$) of each of the three 10 min observations (free play, competing demand 1, competing demand 2). After about four minutes, the infant started with 30 seconds of whining, followed by three minutes of intense crying, five seconds quiet, one minute crying, eight seconds quiet, one minute crying, and finally one minute silent. The doll used in our study was a Caucasian female infant.

Sensitivity during the lab session

Sensitivity during the lab session was assessed using the Ainsworth Sensitivity scale (Ainsworth et al., 1974). Using this scale we evaluated (1) the caregivers' awareness of the signals (i.e., is she aware of the infant simulator's signals? Does she note the more subtle signals of the simulator or does she only notice obvious distress of the simulator?), (2) the caregivers' interpretation of the signals (i.e., does she understand that the infant needs care or does she interpret the signal as something else, e.g., the infant is just grumpy? Is she showing empathy rather than, for example, ignoring the simulator, mocking it, or caring for it without any friendly vocalization and/or empathic facial expressions?), (3) the appropriateness of the response (i.e., does the caregiver try different soothing strategies when one does not work or does she persist with a strategy that appears to be not effective? While trying to sooth the simulator, does she try all methods to sooth the baby, including carrying it in various ways, feeding, changing diaper, distracting, and gentle rocking? Does she show well-rounded interactions, i.e., taking the time and without sudden interruptions?), and (4) promptness of the response (i.e., does the caregiver respond immediately when the simulator starts being fussy or does she wait till the simulator is full-blown crying?).

Scores ranged from 1 (insensitive) to 9 (sensitive), and three scores were assigned for each participant (Free Play, Competing Demand 1, and Competing Demand 2). For each participant, the three parts were rated independently by nine different trained coders. Intercoder reliability was high, mean intra-class coefficient (single measure, absolute agreement) was .85 (range .80–.92, $n = 20$).

Experiences with the infant simulator at home

A 10-item questionnaire was administered after the two home sessions to assess the participants' experience and perception of their caretaking of the infant simulator (see e.g., Bath, Cunningham, & McIntosh, 2000). Four items were used for this study. One item ("Do you think taking care of the baby was a realistic experience?") was used to indicate how realistic they found their experience on a 10-point scale (1 = *not realistic* and 10 = *realistic*). On average, participants found the experience realistic (M = 6.21, SD = 1.74). Two items (*yes* or *no*) assessed how they interacted with the doll: "Did you notice yourself talking to the baby?" and "Did you use the baby's name?" One item ("How would you rate the quality of your caregiving for the baby?") was used as self-report measure of their caretaking qualities on a 10-point rating scale (1 = *no good care* and 10 = *really good care*).

Mood

The Positive Affect Negative Affect Scale (PANAS; Crawford & Henry, 2004; Watson et al., 1988) was used during the lab session to assess the transient mood of the participant before they took care of the doll and after they had taken care of the doll. These items included 10 items for positive affect (e.g., alert, enthusiastic, determined) and 10 items for negative affect (e.g., upset, irritable, nervous). Each item was rated on a 5-point scale ranging from 1 = *not at all* to 5 = *a lot*. Two scales, Positive affect (α before = .79, α after = .83) and Negative affect (α before = .73, α after = .80) were constructed indicating positive mood and negative mood before and after care for the infant simulator.

Social desirability

Eighteen social desirability items from the Child Abuse Potential Inventory (CAPI; Milner, 1986) were used for assessing participants' social desirability tendencies. Cronbach's α was .64.

Cry paradigm

The cry paradigm (Crowe & Zeskind, 1992; Out, Pieper, Bakermans-Kranenburg, & van IJzendoorn, 2010) was administered using a laptop with E-prime software. Participants listened to three blocks of three cry sounds each that varied in fundamental frequency within each block. Cry stimuli were derived from the spontaneous crying of a healthy two-day old, full birth-weight and full term female infant while she was in a supine position in her bassinette, midway between scheduled feedings. A 10 s portion of the sustained period of crying, containing seven expiratory sounds, was selected for presentation. To provide cry stimuli with a wide range of fundamental frequencies, the original cry (averaging approximately 500 Hz) was digitally altered to increase the fundamental frequency while holding temporal and other spectral aspects of the cry constant. Two new 10 s cry stimuli were thus created, resulting in two new cry sounds of 700 Hz and 900 Hz (see Crowe & Zeskind, 1992; Out, Pieper, Bakermans-Kranenburg, & van IJzendoorn, 2010). Each of the three blocks of cry sounds contained each of the three cry sounds (i.e., 500 Hz, 700 Hz, 900 Hz) presented in a random order. The cry stimuli were presented at a constant volume through Sennheiser HD202 headphones.

Following a practice trial in which the 500 Hz cry was presented, participants listened to the three blocks of three cry sounds each. Following every presented cry, participants indicated their perception (not included here) and intended caregiving response on 5-point rating scales. They were asked to indicate how likely they would respond to each of the cry sounds with the following behaviors: pick up, cuddle, wait and see, give pacifier, feed (Zeskind, 1980, 1983), focus on something else than on the crying baby, and firm handling (Out, Pieper, Bakermans-Kranenburg, & van IJzendoorn, 2010). To cover more forms of insensitive and harsh parenting behavior, the following three items were added: slap, shake, and reprimand. Two scales were constructed based on the mean of the standardized item scores; *Sensitive Response* ($\alpha = .73$), including pick up, cuddle, feed, wait and see (reversed), and focus on something else (reversed) (similar to Out, Pieper, Bakermans-Kranenburg, & van IJzendoorn, 2010), and *Harsh Response* ($\alpha = .78$), including firm handling, slap, shake, and reprimand.

Data analysis

Distributions of all variables of interest were checked for normality. The distribution of the PANAS negative mood scale scores was skewed and transformed using a Log transformation (Tabachnick & Fidell, 2007). After transformation, the distribution showed significant improvement and the transformed scale scores were used for further analyses. Inspection of the data showed that there was one missing value for the reality question (0.6%), one missing value for caretaking behavior during the home sessions (0.6%), and three missing values for the intended care in the cry paradigm (1.7%). Missing values were replaced by the overall mean. Minor variations in the doll's cry duration during the lab session were not related to caregiver sensitivity ($r = .10$, $p = .19$).

The internal consistency of the sensitivity scores over settings (free play, competing demand 1, competing demand 2) was computed, and associations with background variables were examined. We related behavior to the doll during the home sessions and self-reported quality of care during the home sessions to observed sensitivity in the lab session using analyses of covariance and (partial) correlations. To examine the effect of taking care of the infant simulator on participants' mood, a multivariate repeated measures analysis of variance on positive and negative mood before and after taking care of the doll in the lab session was performed with sensitivity (less or more, median split) as between-subjects factor. Lastly, associations between observed sensitivity and intended caregiving in response to the cry bouts of the cry paradigm were established using Pearson's correlation coefficients.

Results

Descriptives and bivariate correlations

Table 1 shows the means and standard deviations of the sensitivity scores, the affect scores, and correlations with age and reality value. Sensitivity scores during free play and competing demands were positively correlated (r between .39–.58), showing that caregivers who were more sensitive during free play were also more sensitive during competing demands. The internal consistency of the sensitivity scores over settings was alpha = .74. A repeated-measures analysis with setting (free play, competing demand 1, and competing demand 2) as within-subjects factor and age of the participant and reality

Table 1. Means, standard deviations, and range of sensitivity and affect: correlations with age, reality value, and social desirability.

	Range	*M (SD)*	1	2	3	4	5	6	7	8	Age	Reality
1. Sensitivity Free play	1 to 9	6.23 (1.47)									.09	.19*
2. Sensitivity Competing demand 1	1 to 9	5.03 (1.66)	.48**								.16*	.13
3. Sensitivity Competing demand 2	1 to 9	4.41 (1.86)	.39**	.58**							.12	.10
4. Mean sensitivity score	1 to 9	5.22 (1.35)	.74**	.85**	.84**						.16*	.17*
5. Positive affect before doll	1 to 5	2.65 (0.48)	.09	.11	.15*	.15*					.02	.14
6. Positive affect after doll	1 to 5	2.65 (0.56)	.21**	.22**	.24**	.28**	.57**				−.01	.19*
7. Negative affect before doll	1 to 5	1.33 (0.31)	−.04	.06	.10	.06	.15*	.18*			−.01	.02
8. Negative affect after doll	1 to 5	1.37 (0.38)	−.04	−.01	.06	.01	.11	−.05	.47**		.01	.11
9. Social desirability	1 to 14	5.09 (2.83)	−.06	.03	.03	.01	.09	−.03	−.12	−.05	.02	−.11

Note: $n = 181$; $^{*}p < .05$; $^{**}p < .01$.

value as covariates showed no significant effect of setting, $F(2, 177) = 1.33$, $p = .27$, $\eta^2 = .02$.

There was no difference in sensitivity between the participants who had lived with both their biological parents up until they were 16 and those who had not, $t(179) = 0.03$, $p = .98$, $d = 0.01$, or for those with and without a chronic illness, physical handicap, or psychiatric disorder, $t(14$, unequal variance$) = –0.23$, $p = .82$, $d = –0.07$. Sensitivity scores were not different for participants with and without experience in taking care of young children, $t(179) = –0.28$, $p = .79$, $d = –0.05$. However, participants who were older were on average somewhat more sensitive ($r = .16$, $p < .05$), and higher sensitivity scores were modestly correlated with higher reality values ($r = .17$, $p < .05$). Social desirability was not related to sensitivity scores (Table 1). Thus, age and reality value were included as covariates when necessary in subsequent analyses.

Associations with caregiving during the home sessions

The majority of the participants (81%) reported that they talked to the infant simulator during the home sessions as if it were a real baby, and half of them used its name (50%). Sensitivity was not related to self-reported talking to the infant simulator (controlling for reality value), $F(1,178) = 2.09$, $p = .15$, $\eta^2 = .01$, but participants using the doll's name were significantly more sensitive during the lab session ($M = 5.49$, $SD = 1.30$) than participants who did not ($M = 4.96$, $SD = 1.36$), $F(1, 178) = 5.14$, $p = .03$, $\eta^2 = .03$. Participants rated the quality of their care for the infant simulator during the home sessions quite high, with a mean rating of 7.34 ($SD = 0.97$) on a scale ranging from 1 to 10. However, no relation between self reported quality of care and observed sensitivity was found (controlling for reality value), $r = .08$, $p = .26$.

Associations with mood and with intended caregiving in the cry paradigm

Positive and negative affect

A multivariate repeated measures analysis of variance with positive and negative mood before and after the lab session was performed with sensitivity (less or more, median split) as between-subjects factor. We found a significant difference between less sensitive and more sensitive caregivers, $F(2, 178) = 3.83$, $p = .02$, $\eta^2 = .04$. The univariate effects for negative affect were not significant, but positive affect showed a significant main effect for sensitivity, $F(1, 179) = 7.68$, $p = .01$, $\eta^2 = .04$, and a significant interaction effect between sensitivity and time, $F(1, 179) = 5.16$, $p = .02$, $\eta^2 = .03$. After caring for the infant simulator, positive mood in the more sensitive individuals increased while positive mood in the less sensitive individuals decreased (Figure 1).

Intended caregiving in the cry paradigm

After listening to the bouts of cry sounds, participants indicated how likely they would respond with sensitive care behavior or with more harsh caregiving behaviors. Intended sensitive care was not significantly related to observed sensitivity ($r = -.06$, $p = .45$), but more intended harsh care was related to lower observed sensitivity ($r = -.17$, $p = .03$).

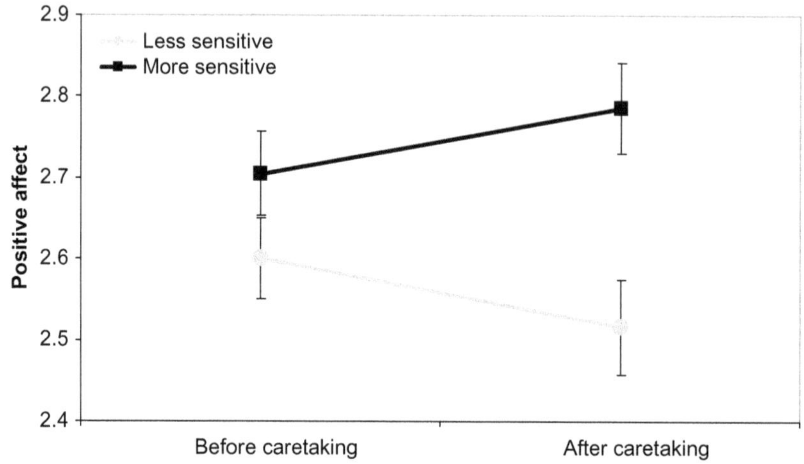

Figure 1. Mean positive affect before and after caretaking. Vertical bars represent standard errors.

Discussion

One of the key advantages of the Leiden Infant Simulator Sensitivity Assessment (LISSA) is that it provides a standardized setting for the observation of caregiver sensitivity with controlled infant stimuli. The results of this study show that, with the use of an infant simulator with interactive features, sensitivity could be reliably assessed. Furthermore, both convergent and discriminant validity were substantiated.

Sensitivity as observed in different contexts (free play and competing demands) showed high internal consistency. These findings are in line with Mary Ainsworth's, who was the first to show that mothers who were sensitive in response to crying were also sensitive during face-to-face interaction (Blehar, Lieberman, & Ainsworth, 1977), and with more recent research showing that sensitivity is rather consistent across various settings (Behrens, Hart, & Parker, 2012; Joosen, Mesman, Bakermans-Kranenburg, & van IJzendoorn, 2012) and stable over distressing and non-distressing contexts (Leerkes, Nayena Blankson, & O'Brien, 2009). Notably, we were able to establish high intercoder reliability for all nine coders, which points to the strengths of training sensitivity coding in a standardized setting.

Participants reported that they found the experience fairly realistic. The majority of the caregivers talked to the infant simulator and those who used the doll's name during the home sessions, which may indicate their feelings of emphatic engagement with the doll, were more sensitive during the lab session than those who did not, which supports the measure's criterion validity. In previous studies the infant simulator was also taken seriously by eighth graders (Barnett & Hurst, 2004), but not considered realistic by medical students (Bath et al., 2000). An important difference with our study is, however, that these studies used an earlier version of the infant simulator in which the simulator stopped crying when a key was inserted, while in our study the simulator was comforted by real caregiving activities such as rocking, feeding, and changing the diaper, adding substantially to the reality value of the caretaking. However, the observed behavior in our study was not limited to these specific caregiving activities as we observed also the more fine-grained behaviors that allowed us to see not only basic competence but also low, medium, or high levels of sensitivity. Although the nature of the caretaker–infant interaction is of course limited by the inability of the simulator to respond to the caregiver in a more differentiated way (moving, facial expression, etc) we were able to observe a broad range of care taking behavior during 30 minutes of observation. It may be critical that in our study the participants had cared for the doll for two evenings to get attuned to it before the observation of sensitivity took place. This might be an essential part of the procedure.

After taking care of the infant simulator, positive mood increased in the more sensitive participants while it decreased in the less sensitive participants. Intended harsh caregiving in response to cry sounds was related to lower sensitivity, providing evidence for the measure's convergent validity. These findings also indicate that sensitivity is not so much influenced by the initial positive mood as it is influenced by the ability to maintain positive mood even if the crying does not stop. Lastly, as expected, self reported caregiving and social desirability were unrelated to observed sensitivity, supporting the discriminant validity of the measure. Our results are in line with the earlier research that showed that self reported parenting is not strongly related to observed parenting (e.g., Fitzgerald et al., 2005) indicating that how individuals *feel* about their parenting is not the same as how they actually behave as a parent. In addition, the absence of a relation between social desirability and observed sensitivity may indicate that our results are not biased by the participants' tendency to make a positive impression while being observed.

Although earlier studies showed that attachment security was better predicted by sensitivity in response to infant distress compared to sensitivity with a non-distressed infant (McElwain & Booth-LaForce, 2006), support for exploration in non-distress situations is also part of caregiver sensitivity. In the current study the infant simulator was distressed during approximately 15 out of 30 minutes, providing the participants with ample opportunity to try and reduce infant distress. The 15 minutes of non-distress provided an opportunity to engage in more positive interactions with the simulator. Substantial differences in parenting behavior were observed. Whereas some participants read a book with the infant, played with the toys, or walked around the room showing the infant the materials, others put the infant aside and continued with their own activities, glancing through a magazine or checking their e-mail.

The current study has some limitations to consider. First, we could not compare sensitivity in interaction with the infant simulator to observed sensitivity with the own infant. We are currently collecting data on mothers who are observed interacting with their own infant and with the infant simulator. Second, using an infant simulator to assess sensitivity yields the risk that for some individuals the experience is not sufficiently realistic. Although in our study participants reported to find the experience in general realistic, as is also evident from their talking to the infant simulator and using its name, we suggest that a reality value check should be routinely included in order to exclude those participants who consider the caregiving experience as highly unrealistic. Finally, future research should examine the association between caregiver's attachment representations as assessed with the Adult Attachment Interview (George, Kaplan, & Main, 1984, 1985, 1996) or the Secure Base Script approach (Waters & Waters, 2006), and the observed sensitivity with the infant simulator (van IJzendoorn, 1995). This also enables testing the relation between adult attachment and sensitivity for adults who do not (yet) have children of their own.

An important issue in attachment research is the direction of effects between child characteristics and parenting (e.g., Del Vecchio & Rhoades, 2010; Parsons et al., in press). The LISSA provides an opportunity to test for causality in parent–infant relationships since infant variables related to, e.g., infant temperament or soothability are standardized and can be manipulated. Thus sensitivity and its physiological correlates can be examined in a standardized setting with controlled infant characteristics. Moreover, the LISSA can be used to measure caregiver sensitivity in individuals without children of their own. This may shed light on (biological) processes affecting parenting that result from early caregiving experiences (Cicchetti, Rogosch, & Toth, 2006) without the interfering (biological) effects of pregnancy, giving birth, and specific infant characteristics.

The LISSA may be of crucial importance in clinical practice as it can be used as a measure for screening, or for the evaluation of intervention programs. Individuals at risk for child abuse due to their own experiences of child abuse or psychopathology may profit from interventions aiming at sensitive parenting before starting a family and, using the measure as a screening instrument, those individuals may be targeted before their own child is born. The LISSA might complement assessments of child abuse or neglect potential with the more conventional means of self-report questionnaires like the CAPI (Milner, 1986). In addition, the LISSA can be used to monitor progress and evaluate the effectiveness of preventive intervention programs, and as a training tool for specific groups such as individuals with mental disabilities who want to become parents (e.g., Toone & McLaren, 2003).

In conclusion, we found evidence for the reliability and validity of the Leiden Infant Simulator Sensitivity Assessment. Ainsworth and her colleagues developed the Strange Situation Procedure in order to make sense of the myriad of observations of parent–infant interactions conducted at home. The laboratory procedure was meant to standardize parental behavior to a certain extent, and to have a closer look at variations in infant secure base behavior (Ainsworth, Blehar, Waters, & Wall, 1978). Inspired by the groundbreaking discoveries Mary Ainsworth made with the Strange Situation Procedure, we propose here to standardize the behavioral repertoire of the infant, and to observe variations in parenting responses to the infant simulator. The LISSA is a means of standardizing the assessment of the assumed cause of children's attachment quality, whereas the SSP is a test of its effect. Compared to the validation of the SSP, the validation of the LISSA is only in its infancy but we hope she may grow up in the next few decades and, in the spirit of Mary Ainsworth, add to our knowledge of parenting and attachment in the years to come.

Acknowledgements

DO, MJBK, and MHvIJ were supported by awards from the Netherlands Organization for Scientific Research (DO: Rubicon grant; MJBK: VICI grant; MHvIJ: SPINOZA prize). The authors do not have nor intend to acquire any shares or other commercial interests in Realityworks, Inc., Virtual Parenting, Coffs Harbour, NSW, although it might become profitable in the near future.

References

Ainsworth, M. D. S., Bell, S. M., & Stayton, D. J. (1974). Infant mother attachment and social development; Socialization as a product of reciprocal responsiveness to signals. In M. P. M. Richards (Ed.), *The integration of a child into a social world* (pp 99–135). Cambridge: Cambridge University Press.

Ainsworth, M. D. S., Blehar, M. C., Waters, E., & Wall, S. (1978). *Patterns of attachment: A psychological study of the strange situation*. Hillsdale, NJ: Erlbaum.

Bakermans-Kranenburg, M. J., van IJzendoorn, M. H., & Juffer, F. (2003). Less is more: Meta-analyses of sensitivity and attachment interventions in early childhood. *Psychological Bulletin, 129*(2), 195–215. doi:10.1037/0033-2909.129.2.195

Barnett, J. E., & Hurst, C. S. (2004). Do adolescents take "Baby Think It Over" seriously? *Adolescence, 39*, 65–75.

Bath, L. E., Cunningham, S., & McIntosh, N. (2000). Medical students' attitudes to caring for a young infant – can parenting a doll influence these beliefs? *Archives of Disease in Childhood, 83*(6), 521–523. doi:10.1136/adc.83.6.521

Behrens, K. Y., Hart, S. L., & Parker, A. C. (2012). Maternal Sensitivity: Evidence of stability across time, contexts, and measurement instruments. *Infant and Child Development, 21*(4), 348–355. doi:10.1002/Icd.1747

Bhandari, R., Voorthuis, A., Van der Veen, R., Out, D., Bakermans-Kranenburg, M. J., & van IJzendoorn, M. H. (2013). Temperamental sensitivity moderates the effects of maternal love-withdrawal on perception of infant crying. *Family Science, 3*, 246–254. doi:10.1080/19424620.2013.789977

Blehar, M. C., Lieberman, A. F., & Ainsworth, M. D. S. (1977). Early face-to-face interaction and its relation to later infant-mother attachment. *Child Development, 48*, 182–194.

Bowlby, J. (1969). *Attachment and loss: Vol. 1. Attachment.* London: Random House.

Bowlby, J. (1984). *Attachment and loss: Vol 1. Attachment* (Rev. ed). London: Pelican.

Bruning, S., & McMahon, C. (2009). The impact of infant crying on young women: A randomized controlled study. *Journal of Reproductive and Infant Psychology, 27*(2), 206–220. doi:10.1080/02646830802350856

Cicchetti, D., Rogosch, F. A., & Toth, S. L. (2006). Fostering secure attachment in infants in maltreating families through preventive interventions. *Development and Psychopathology, 18* (3), 623–649. doi:10.1017/S0954579406060329

Coppola, G., Vaughn, B. E., Cassibba, R., & Costantini, A. (2006). The attachment script representation procedure in an Italian sample: Associations with adult attachment interview scales and with maternal sensitivity. *Attachment & Human Development, 8*(3), 209–219. doi:10.1080/14616730600856065

Crawford, J. R., & Henry, J. D. (2004). The positive and negative affect schedule (PANAS): Construct validity, measurement properties and normative data in a large non-clinical sample. *British Journal of Clinical Psychology, 43*, 245–265. doi:10.1348/0144665031752934

Crowe, H. P., & Zeskind, P. S. (1992). Psychophysiological and perceptual responses to infant cries varying in pitch – comparison of adults with low and high scores on the child-abuse potential inventory. *Child Abuse & Neglect, 16*(1), 19–29. doi:10.1016/0145-2134(92)90005-C

Del Vecchio, T., & Rhoades, K. A. (2010). Bidirectional influences in mother-toddler dyads: An examination of the relative influence of mothers' and children's behaviours. *Infant and Child Development, 19*(5), 516–529. doi:10.1002/Icd.674

De Wolff, M. S., & van IJzendoorn, M. H. (1997). Sensitivity and attachment: A meta-analysis on parental antecedents of infant attachment. *Child Development, 68*(4), 571–591.

Driscoll, J. R., & Easterbrooks, M. A. (2007). Young mothers' play with their toddlers: Individual variability as a function of psychosocial factors. *Infant and Child Development, 16*(6), 649–670. doi:10.1002/Icd.515

Fitzgerald, M. M., Shipman, K. L., Jackson, J. L., McMahon, R. J., & Hanley, H. M. (2005). Perceptions of parenting versus parent-child interactions among incest survivors. *Child Abuse & Neglect, 29*(6), 661–681. doi:10.1016/j.chiabu.2004.10.012

Frodi, A. M., Lamb, M. E., Neff, C., Sherry, D., Leavitt, L. A., & Donovan, W. L. (1978). Fathers and mothers responses to faces and cries of normal and premature-infants. *Developmental Psychology, 14*(5), 490–498. doi:10.1037/0012-1649.14.5.490

George, C., Kaplan, N., & Main, M. (1984). *Adult attachment interview protocol.* Unpublished manuscript. University of California, Berkeley, CA.

George, C., Kaplan, N., & Main, M. (1985). *Adult attachment interview protocol.* [2nd]. Unpublished manuscript. University of California, Berkeley, CA.

George, C., Kaplan, N., & Main, M. (1996). *Adult attachment interview protocol.* [3rd]. Unpublished manuscript. University of California, Berkeley, CA.

Goldberg, S., Grusec, J. E., & Jenkins, J. M. (1999). Confidence in protection: Arguments for a narrow definition of attachment. *Journal of Family Psychology, 13*(4), 475–483. doi:10.1037/0893-3200.13.4.475

Higley, E., & Dozier, M. (2009). Nighttime maternal responsiveness and infant attachment at one year. *Attachment & Human Development, 11*(4), 347–363. doi:10.1080/14616730903016979

Jin, M. K., Jacobvitz, D., Hazen, N., & Jung, S. H. (2012). Maternal sensitivity and infant attachment security in Korea: Cross-cultural validation of the Strange Situation. *Attachment & Human Development, 14*(1), 33–44. doi:10.1080/14616734.2012.636656

Joosen, K. J., Mesman, J., Bakermans-Kranenburg, M. J., & van IJzendoorn, M. H. (2012). Maternal sensitivity to infants in various settings predicts harsh discipline in toddlerhood. *Attachment & Human Development, 14*(2), 101–117. doi:10.1080/14616734.2012.661217

Leerkes, E. M., Nayena Blankson, A., & O'Brien, M. (2009). Differential effects of maternal sensitivity to infant distress and nondistress on social-emotional functioning. *Child Development, 80*(3), 762–775. doi:10.1111/j.1467-8624.2009.01296.x

McElwain, N. L., & Booth-LaForce, C. (2006). Maternal sensitivity to infant distress and nondistress as predictors of infant-mother attachment security. *Journal of Family Psychology, 20*(2), 247–255. doi:10.1037/0893-3200.20.2.247

McElwain, N. L., Cox, M. J., Burchinal, M. R., & Macfie, J. (2003). Differentiating among insecure mother-infant attachment classifications: A focus on child-friend interaction and exploration during solitary play at 36 months. *Attachment & Human Development, 5*(2), 136–164. doi:10.1080/1461673031000108513

Mesman, J., van IJzendoorn, M. H., & Bakermans-Kranenburg, M. J. (2009). The many faces of the Still-Face Paradigm: A review and meta-analysis. *Developmental Review, 29*(2), 120–162. doi:10.1016/J.Dr.2009.02.001

Milner, J. S. (1986). *The child abuse potential inventory: Manual* (2nd ed.). Webster, NC: Psytec.

Moskowitz, J. T., Folkman, S., Collette, L., & Vittinghoff, E. (1996). Coping and mood during AIDS-related caregiving and bereavement. *Annals of Behavioral Medicine, 18*(1), 49–57.

Musser, E. D., Ablow, J. C., & Measelle, J. R. (2012). Predicting maternal sensitivity: The roles of postnatal depressive symptoms and parasympathetic dysregulation. *Infant Mental Health Journal, 33*(4), 350–359. doi:10.1002/imhj.21310

Out, D., Pieper, S., Bakermans-Kranenburg, M. J., & van IJzendoorn, M. H. (2010). Physiological reactivity to infant crying: A behavioral genetic study. *Genes, Brain, and Behavior, 9*(8), 868–876. doi:10.1111/j.1601-183X.2010.00624.x

Out, D., Pieper, S., Bakermans-Kranenburg, M. J., Zeskind, P. S., & Van IJzendoorn, M. H. (2010). Intended sensitive and harsh caregiving responses to infant crying: The role of cry pitch and perceived urgency in an adult twin sample. *Child Abuse & Neglect, 34*(11), 863–873. doi:10.1016/j.chiabu.2010.05.003

Parsons, C. E., Young, K. S., Bhandari, R., van IJzendoorn, M. H., Bakermans-Kranenburg, M. J., Stein, A., et al. (in press). The Bonnie baby: Experimentally manipulated temperament affects perceived cuteness and motivation to view infant faces. *Developmental Science.*

Pederson, D. R., & Moran, G. (1995). A categorical description of infant-mother relationships in the home and its relation to Q-sort measures of infant-mother interaction. *Monographs of the Society for Research in Child Development, 60*(2–3), 111–132. doi:10.2307/1166174

Roberts, S. W., & McCowan, R. J. (2004). The effectiveness of infant simulators. *Adolescence, 39* (155), 475–487.

Roisman, G. I., Holland, A., Fortuna, K., Fraley, R. C., Clausell, E., & Clarke, A. (2007). The adult attachment interview and self-reports of attachment style: An empirical rapprochement. *Journal of Personality and Social Psychology, 92*(4), 678–697. doi:10.1037/0022-3514.92.4.678

Soltis, J. (2004). The signal functions of early infant crying. *Behavioral and Brain Sciences, 27*(4), 443–490.

Strachan, W., & Gorey, K. M. (1997). Infant simulator lifespan intervention: Pilot investigation of an adolescent pregnancy prevention program. *Child and Adolescent Social Work Journal, 14*(3), 171–180.

Tabachnick, B. G., & Fidell, L. S. (2007). *Using multivariate statistics*. Boston, MA: Pearson Education.

Thompson, R. A. (1997). Sensitivity and security: New questions to ponder. *Child Development, 68* (4), 595–597. doi:10.1111/j.1467-8624.1997.tb04220.x

Toone, D., & McLaren, P. (2003). Insight into parenthood. *Learning Disability Practice, 6*(6), 12–15.

Tronick, E., Als, H., Adamson, L., Wise, S., & Brazelton, T. B. (1978). Infants response to entrapment between contradictory messages in face-to-face interaction. *Journal of the American Academy of Child and Adolescent Psychiatry, 17*(1), 1–13. doi:10.1016/S0002-7138 (09)62273-1

Van Anders, S. M., Tolman, R. M., & Volling, B. L. (2012). Baby cries and nurturance affect testosterone in men. *Hormones and Behavior, 61*(1), 31–36. doi:10.1016/j.yhbeh.2011.09.012

van IJzendoorn, M. H. (1995). Adult attachment representations, parental responsiveness, and infant attachment: A meta-analysis on the predictive validity of the Adult Attachment Interview. *Psychological Bulletin, 117*(3), 387–403.

van IJzendoorn, M. H., & Hubbard, F. O. (2000). Are infant crying and maternal responsiveness during the first year related to infant-mother attachment at 15 months? *Attachment & Human Development, 2*(3), 371–391. doi:10.1080/14616730010001596

van IJzendoorn, M. H., Vereijken, C. M. J. L., Bakermans-Kranenburg, M. J., & Riksen-Walraven, J. M. (2004). Assessing attachment security with the attachment Q sort: Meta-analytic evidence for the validity of the observer AQS. *Child Development, 75*(4), 1188–1213. doi:10.1111/j.1467-8624.2004.00733.x

Vereijken, C. M. J. L., Riksen-Walraven, J. M., & Kondo-Ikemura, K. (1997). Maternal sensitivity and infant attachment security in Japan: A longitudinal study. *International Journal of Behavioral Development, 21*(1), 35–49.

Wasz-Höckert, O., Michelsson, K., & Lind, J. (1985). Twenty-five years of Scandinavian cry research. In B. M. Lester & C. F. Z. Boukydis (Eds.), *Infant crying: Theoretical and research perspectives* (pp. 83–104). New York, NY: Plenum Press.

Waters, H. S., & Waters, E. (2006). The attachment working models concept: Among other things, we build script-like representations of secure base experiences. *Attachment & Human Development, 8*(3), 185–197. doi:10.1080/14616730600856016

Watson, D., Clark, L. A., & Tellegen, A. (1988). Development and validation of brief measures of positive and negative affect: The PANAS scales. *Journal of Personality and Social Psychology, 54*(6), 1063–1070.

Zeifman, D. M. (2004). Acoustic features of infant crying related to intended caregiving intervention. *Infant and Child Development, 13*(2), 111–122. doi:10.1002/Icd.344

Zeskind, P. S. (1980). Adult responses to cries of low and high risk infants. *Infant Behavior and Development, 3*, 167–177.

Zeskind, P. S. (1983). Cross-cultural differences in maternal perceptions of cries of low-risk and high-risk infants. *Child Development, 54*(5), 1119–1128. doi:10.1111/j.1467-8624.1983.tb00533.x

Maternal anxiety, maternal sensitivity, and attachment

Joan Stevenson-Hinde[a], Rebecca Chicot[a], Anne Shouldice[a] and Camilla A. Hinde[b]

[a]*Sub-Department of Animal Behaviour, University of Cambridge, Cambridge, UK;* [b]*Department of Animal Sciences, Behaviour Ecology Group, University of Wageningen, Wageningen, The Netherlands*

Previous research has related maternal anxiety to insecurity of attachment. Here we ask whether different aspects of maternal sensitivity mediate this link. From a community sample of intact families with 1–3 children, mothers with 4.5-year-olds were selected for low, medium, or high anxiety levels ($N = 98$). Following Mary Ainsworth's lead, our maternal sensitivity measures were primarily based on ratings of direct observations. Six sets of measures were obtained: positive maternal style at home (a mean of four different ratings); providing a sensitive framework, limit setting, allowing autonomy, criticizing/cutting in (each a mean over two laboratory joint tasks); and tension-making (a mean of three different ratings in a fear-inducing task). Regression analyses showed firstly that maternal anxiety rather than behavioral inhibition or sex of child was the significant predictor of each maternal sensitivity measure; and secondly that these measures rather than maternal anxiety or sex were the significant predictors of security of attachment. Finally, ANOVA's indicated which sets of maternal ratings were associated with each pattern of attachment (Avoidant, Secure, Ambivalent, or Controlling).

Introduction

This paper focuses on maternal sensitivity as a mediator between two major constructs – maternal anxiety and insecurity of attachment. Each may be regarded as risk factors for the development of childhood anxiety (e.g., for maternal anxiety: McClure, Brennan, Hammen, & LeBrocque, 2001; Shamir-Essakow, Ungerer, & Rapee, 2005; and for insecure attachment: Bar-Haim, Dan, Eshel, & Sagi-Schwartz, 2007; Warren, Huston, Egeland, & Sroufe, 1997).

Furthermore, maternal anxiety has been related to attachment insecurity (Manassis, Bradley, Goldberg, Hood, & Swinson, 1995), particularly an Ambivalent pattern (Scher & Mayseless, 2000). In the present community sample of mothers and their 4.5-year-olds, maternal anxiety was significantly related to insecurity of attachment ratings as well as to an Ambivalent and a Controlling pattern (Stevenson-Hinde, Shouldice, & Chicot, 2011). Here we go on to ask whether aspects of sensitivity mediate this link. In selecting which maternal interactions to observe, we were guided by Mary Ainsworth's concept of "sensitivity". Based on extensive home observations of mothers and infants over the first year of life, she defined sensitivity as being aware of infant's signals, interpreting them accurately, and responding promptly and appropriately (Ainsworth, Blehar, Waters,

& Wall, 1978). Her 9-point maternal sensitivity-insensitivity scale was significantly related to year-old infants' security of attachment in the Strange Situation. In order to distinguish between mothers of insecure infants – classed as Avoidant or Ambivalent – Ainsworth developed three additional scales for assessing maternal interactions at home in the fourth quarter. These were acceptance-rejection, co-operation-interference, and accessible-ignoring. Correlations with sensitivity-insensitivity were high: .89, .86, and .83, respectively (Ainsworth, Bell, & Stayton, 1971), suggesting that these other qualities of maternal behavior may reflect an underlying sensitive responsiveness. This may be one reason why various assessments of sensitivity were significantly associated with security of attachment (e.g., De Wolff & van IJzendoorn, 1997), with intervention studies indicating a causal link between the two (Bakermans-Kranenburg, van IJzendoorn, & Juffer, 2003).

Although originally based on home observations of mothers with infants (Ainsworth et al., 1978), the concept of maternal sensitivity lends itself to different contexts as well as to different ages. For example in previous research with preschool children, the concept of sensitivity guided our choice of which maternal interactions to assess at home and in the lab over three successive samples: (1) an unselected sample at 42 and 48 months (Simpson & Stevenson-Hinde, 1985); (2) an unselected sample at 2.5, 3.5, and 4.5 years (Stevenson-Hinde & Shouldice, 1990, 1995a); and (3) a sample selected for low, medium, and high behavioral inhibition (Stevenson-Hinde & Glover, 1996; Stevenson-Hinde & Marshall, 1999).

Mary Ainsworth also provided a guide for what might be called "sensitive assessment" of direct observations. Her rating scales relied upon careful observation and interpretation of the whole context, in contrast to so-called "more objective" frequency counts or durations of behavior. In spite of such widespread acceptance of Ainsworth's methods and concepts nowadays, one should not forget the fact that for some years her presentations and attempts at journal publication "were quite often received with hostility or even ridicule by established figures in the field" (Bretherton, 2003, p. 328).

Maternal anxiety has been related to a variety of maternal "insensitive" interactions. In a study involving 3–12-year-olds, mothers with a current primary diagnosis of an anxiety disorder were less sensitive than controls in a social task, but not in a cognitive one (Kertz, Smith, Chapman, & Woodruff-Borden, 2008). Moreover, in both clinical and community samples, anxious mothers have been observed to be less warm and positive, less granting of autonomy, more intrusive, more critical, and more catastrophizing in comparison with normal mothers of young children (e.g., Creswell, Apetroaia, Murray, & Cooper, 2013; Moore, Whaley, & Sigman, 2004; Whaley, Pinto, & Sigman, 1999; Woodruff-Borden, Morrow, Bourland, & Cambron, 2002). Although over-control has sometimes been associated with maternal anxiety, recent studies and meta-analyses do not support this (McLeod, Wood, & Weisz, 2007; van der Bruggen, Bögels, & van Zeilst, 2010; van der Bruggen, Stams, & Bögels, 2008).

After identifying interactions that characterize anxious mothers in the present sample of 4.5-year-olds, we shall ask how these relate to security ratings as well as to patterns of attachment. In previous studies the Avoidant pattern has been associated with mothers averse to both physical contact and expressing emotions (reviewed in Weinfield, Sroufe, Egeland, & Carlson, 2008), leading to the development of a child's maintenance of neutrality (Stevenson-Hinde & Shouldice, 1995a). Maternal behavior associated with the development of an Ambivalent pattern of attachment includes interactions possibly reflecting maternal anxiety – interfering, inconsistent, and unpredictable. This may imply "*uncertain* maternal availability" in times of stress, in contrast to the "*certain* maternal unavailability" experienced by Avoidant infants (Cassidy & Berlin, 1994). Such uncertainty gives rise to chronic vigilance over the caregiver's availability, as well as anger (Weinfield et al., 2008). A Controlling pattern has been related to maternal "lack of resolution of mourning" on the Adult Attachment Interview (reviewed in Lyons-Ruth & Jacobvitz, 2008). George and Solomon (1996) found a relation between Controlling and a maternal "helpless stance" on their Caregiving Interview, which in some cases involved a failure to provide reassurance. This too could be associated with maternal anxiety.

In an earlier study with an unselected "normal" sample of preschool children, home observations at 3.5 years showed that mothers of children later classified "Secure" (at 4.5 years) were rated higher than mothers of Insecure children on positive mood, meshing, enjoyment of child, and providing a relaxed home atmosphere. In a laboratory joint task at 4.5 years, mothers of Secure children showed a higher frequency of monitoring, planning, and affirming, and higher ratings for providing a sensitive framework. Compared with all other mothers, mothers of Avoidant children monitored less and planned less, mothers of Ambivalent children had the lowest rating of observed meshing with child, and mothers of Controlling children affirmed less, enjoyed the task less, and provided a less sensitive framework (Stevenson-Hinde & Shouldice, 1995a).

The present study applies similar methods to a community sample of 4.5-year-olds with mothers spread evenly over low, medium, and high anxiety levels. We shall pose three main questions: How does maternal anxiety relate to observed aspects of maternal sensitivity in different situations? Does maternal sensitivity mediate the previously established link between maternal anxiety and security of attachment? How do the different aspects of maternal sensitivity relate to the different patterns of attachment (Avoidant, Secure, Ambivalent, or Controlling)?

Further considerations

The sample used in this study was selected from a large community sample, in order to reflect normative development and to carry implications for preventive intervention. From the large sample we selected fairly equal groups of mothers with low, medium, or high levels of anxiety (using the Hospital Anxiety & Depression Scale: Snaith & Zigmond, 1994; see Methods). This spread may serve as a magnifying glass to illuminate effects of anxiety that may otherwise be obscured in a non-clinical sample.

Given the transactional nature of mother/child interactions (e.g., Murray et al., 2012; van der Bruggen et al., 2010), a temperamental characteristic of the child as well as maternal anxiety will be considered here. Behavioral inhibition (BI) has been related to anxiety in families (reviewed in Degnan, Almas, & Fox, 2010), and is a risk factor for anxiety later in childhood (e.g., Degnan & Fox, 2007; Hirshfeld-Becker et al., 2003). In our "normative" or unselected sample, "shyness" (assessed by a temperament interview to mothers) was correlated with maternal interactions differently for boys vs girls, in the direction of "negative" interactions with shy boys but "positive" ones with shy girls (Simpson & Stevenson-Hinde, 1985; Stevenson-Hinde & Hinde, 1986). However, *unselected* samples such as the above contain approximately only 10% of children with truly high inhibition. In order to overcome this, a sample was selected to have inhibition ratings spread as evenly as possible over three groups: Low (1–3); Medium (4–6); and High (7–9) (Stevenson-Hinde & Glover, 1996). With this selected sample it was not the "high BI" group of girls and boys but the "medium BI" group who supported the above findings within a normative sample. "Parallels with normative samples occur if one considers that most of the high scorers in an 'unselected' sample would probably fall into a 'medium shy' group as defined in the present sample" (Stevenson-Hinde & Glover, 1996, p. 186). Here, gender as well as BI will be included in our analyses.

Methods

The original sample (N = 763)

All mothers living within a 10-mile radius of Cambridge (UK) with a focal child aged 50–52 months were posted a letter with a set of questionnaires to complete and return. With approval of the Local District Ethical Committee, their names and addresses had been provided by the Lifespan Healthcare Information Service in Cambridge. Mailings occurred in four waves, spread over 10 months, to 1304 mothers, with 763 returns (59%). Mothers' mean age was 34 years (range 21 to 53), with a mean number of 2.2 children (range 1–8), and 87% living with a spouse or partner. It should be noted that nearly half of the 763 mothers (46%) had anxiety scores above the "normal" range (0–7), compared with only 15% with above "normal" depression scores.

Of the 763 mothers who returned questionnaires, 86% were willing to be contacted further. Their Hospital Anxiety and Depression Scale scores (HADS: Snaith & Zigmond, 1994; see below) for anxiety ($M = 7.5$) and depression ($M = 4.5$, $n = 656$) did not differ from the scores of those unwilling to be contacted further (M anxiety = 7.0; M depression = 4.4, $n = 107$). Further details, including Depression results, may be found in Stevenson-Hinde, Curley, Chicot, and Jóhannsson (2007).

The selected sample (N = 98)

Of mothers willing to be contacted further, selection criteria were: (1) two-parent families (to eliminate any influence of single parenting); (2) 1–3 children (reflecting 92% of the returns); and (3) anxiety scores spread as evenly as possible over three groups based on the Hospital Anxiety and Depression Scale (see below). The selected mothers were visited at home, 1–2 months after the initial mailing. Following an interview, mothers completed a set of questionnaires and a laboratory visit was set up for mother and child.

Anxiety assessment of mothers

The Hospital Anxiety and Depression Scale (HADS: Snaith & Zigmond, 1994) lists seven statements relating to generalized anxiety (e.g., *I feel tense or "wound up"*) and seven to depression (e.g., *I feel cheerful*). Beneath each statement is a choice of qualifiers relating to the past week: *Not at all; Sometimes; Very often; Nearly all the time*, rated from 0 to 3. Thus, the total anxiety (or depression) score may range from 0 to 21, with clinically-related categories: 0–7 = Normal; 8–10 = Medium; 11–14 = Moderate; and 15–21 = Severe.

Within the selected sample described above, consistency in maternal HADS scores administered over about 3 months (initial mailing, home visit, and lab visit) was high, with Pearson correlations of: .70 between the initial mailing and the home visit; .75 between the home and lab visits; and .74 from the first to the third assessment (all with $N = 98$, $p \leq .001$, two-tailed). Therefore to ensure robustness, ratings averaged over all three assessments will be used throughout the Results. The average ratings fell into three groups: Low anxiety (0–<8): $n = 36$ (17 girls + 19 boys); Medium anxiety (8–<11): $n = 34$ (15 girls + 19 boys); and High anxiety (11–21): $n = 28$ (15 girls + 13 boys). The latter group is a combination of clinically-related categories of Moderate (n = 24) and Severe (n = 4). The HADS was chosen because: (1) it was designed for use on non-psychiatric groups, with questions appropriate for a community sample; (2) it takes only minutes to complete, thereby increasing the likelihood of replies in a postal screening; (3) the emphasis on state "within the past week" permits re-administration over time; (4) the content of each question concerns either anxiety or depression but not both, unlike some scales for anxiety (Spinhoven et al., 1997); (5) it provides both *continuous scales* and *categories*; and (6) the HADS has proven reliability and validity worldwide (e.g., Herrmann, 1997). A review of 747 papers confirmed the HADS' 2-factor structure, discriminant validity, and internal consistency (Bjelland, Dahl, Haug, & Neckelmann, 2002, p. 69).

Home visit – ratings of sensitivity

An experienced independent interviewer (C. Jóhannsson) visited each mother and child at home for about an hour. As in previous studies, "during the entire visit, mother/child interactions were observed, with a view to completing rating scales relating to the provision of a secure base" (Stevenson-Hinde & Shouldice, 1995a, p. 586). Immediately after the visit, ratings were made for each of the following dimensions, on a scale from 1 to 7, with 4 as the norm: *Sensitive* (from inappropriate/ignoring to appropriate responses to child's signals); *Meshing* (from intense, unpleasant friction to smooth, coordinated interactions toward mutual goals); *Enjoy* (from negative comments/ attitude toward child to enjoyment of child's company; and *Gentle* (sudden, over-intense voice and/or rough physical contact to soft voice, gentle physical contact). Reliability and validity of the ratings has been demonstrated in two previous samples: a "normal" one (Stevenson-Hinde & Shouldice, 1995a) and one selected for varying levels of behavioral inhibition (Stevenson-Hinde & Glover, 1996). In each sample, the mean of the standardized ratings provided an index of sensitivity, called "maternal style at home".

Laboratory visit – modified strange situation procedure (for assessing child's BI as well as attachment status)

The modified Strange Situation involved a separation of about 20 minutes and one reunion, as found suitable for children older than about 3 years. A behavioral inhibition (BI) test with a stranger was embedded within the Strange Situation, as used successfully in two previous samples (e.g., Stevenson-Hinde & Glover, 1996; Stevenson-Hinde & Marshall, 1999; Stevenson-Hinde & Shouldice, 1995b). The following episodes were video-taped through a one-way mirror:

(1) Mother & child enter room; mother seated & child invited to play with toys: 4 min
(2) Mother negotiates her departure with child
(3) Child alone for 30 sec
(4) Stranger enters & asks a set of questions for the *behavioral inhibition* assessment, then administers picture test: 10–15 min
(5) Child alone: 4 min
(6) Reunion – Mother returns

Attachment coding

Coding focused on the child's behavior to mother during the reunion episode, according a system based on Ainsworth's infancy system but modified, with her guidance and support, for 2.5–4.5-year-olds. The Cassidy and Marvin system (1992) has proven reliability and validity (e.g., Moss, Bureau, Cyr, Mongeau, & St-Laurent, 2004; Solomon & George, 2008; Stevenson-Hinde & Verschueren, 2002).

Ratings

Security was rated on a scale from 1 to 9, with ratings of 5 and above indicating a secure pattern.

Patterns

Secure (B). Full gaze and positive affect. Interactions are calm, while also intimate and indicative of a special relationship.

Insecure-Avoidant (A). Physical and conversational avoidance of calling attention to the relationship; minimal responses to mother's questions; polite maintenance of neutrality.

Insecure-Ambivalent (C). Angry, whiny resistance directed to mother and/or immature, coy behavior, often with ambivalence to physical proximity or contact; emphasis on dependence.

Insecure-Controlling (CN). Child rather than mother structures the reunion, often with inappropriate caregiving or punitive behavior.

Insecure-Disorganized (D) and Insecure-Other (I-O). Disorganization refers to indices of confusion and apprehension immediately upon mother's return. Insecure-Other refers to children judged insecure, but who do not fall into any one of the above patterns or who show a combination of patterns. As in previous studies (Stevenson-Hinde & Marshall, 1999; Stevenson-Hinde & Shouldice, 1995a), our D and I-O children (n = 4) were "forced" into one of the other patterns that had been assigned as an "alternative" classification (one to A, one to C, and two to CN) at the time of coding.

After jointly coding 10 reunions, J.S.H. and A.S. independently coded each remaining child/mother pair. Inter-observer agreement was high, with $r = .91$ ($n = 88$) for the security ratings and 76/88 (86%) matches for all six classifications (Cohen's Kappa = .79). Mismatches were reviewed until a consensus was reached.

Behavioral inhibition (BI) assessment and coding

In Episode 4 of the above Strange Situation, the stranger entered and invited the child to come and sit by her at a small, low table. She then asked the child three sets of questions, of increasing social demand, concerning: favorite toys or things to do; family members; and favorite song, ending with asking the child to stand up and sing the song. BI ratings were made on a scale from 1 to 9, with 4 as "typical for age". (An extension beyond a 7-point scale permits distinguishing the truly high children from those who are only just above the norm.) In a previous sample, BI ratings over a 9-point scale were significantly correlated with temperament questionnaire ratings (Stevenson-Hinde & Glover, 1996) as well as with measures of cardiac functioning (Marshall & Stevenson-Hinde, 1998).

Ratings involved repeatedly viewing Episode 4. Firstly, notes and ratings were made of *Non-verbal anxiety*, from 1: Very relaxed posture & movement. Ease of orientation to stranger. Open facial expression. Eye contact. Clear, unrestricted voice with good range to 9: Extreme physical/visual avoidance & tension. Turns away. Minimal eye contact. Tense/frozen posture & movement. Nervous gestures or coyness. Apprehensive expression (underbrow look, ambivalent smile). Whispering, restrained voice. Secondly, notes and ratings were made of *Verbal responsiveness*, from 1: Extremely responsive, with full extensions and/or initiations or spontaneous comments to 9: Extremely low responsiveness. For each child, the observer synthesized the non-verbal and verbal ratings as well as behavioral notes, to produce one overall rating of BI. Inter-observer reliability over the 9-point scale was r (14) = .89.

Laboratory visit – three tasks: procedures and coding

Following on from the strange situation, R.C. conducted a series of brief interviews interspersed with mother/child tasks, relieved by a 10 min tea break and ending with the child selecting a gift. Of interest here are the two joint tasks and a fear-inducing Black box task, coded from repeatedly viewing video-tapes (for further details of instructions and coding as well as photos of the materials involved, see Chicot, 1999).

Joint tasks

Etch A Sketch®. Mother and child were given an Etch A Sketch® drawing board and shown how it worked. They were then presented with an outline drawing of a simple house consisting of vertical or horizontal lines but with a slanting roof. They were asked to copy it onto the Etch A Sketch®, with the rule that the mother could use only the vertical knob and the child the horizontal knob (after Stevenson-Hinde & Shouldice, 1995a). There was no set time for completion, which ranged from 4 to 8 minutes.

Butterfly wooden puzzle, in four layers (eggs, caterpillar, cocoon, & butterfly). Mother and child were given the wooden base and a photo of each completed layer, along with a box of jigsaw pieces for mother and another box for the child. It was explained that each layer had to be completed before the next, and that the pieces in mother's box were for the right side of the puzzle and child's for the left side.

Ratings reflect three different dimensions of the maternal support needed in order to complete the two tasks (developed and validated by Denham, Renwick, & Holt, 1991; Stevenson-Hinde & Shouldice, 1995a). Ratings of *Sensitive framework* ranged from 1 (either over-controlling or under-controlling; no encouragement) to 7 (providing a sensitive framework in which the child is allowed to take initiative; encouragement), with 4 as the norm. Ratings of *Limit setting* ranged from 1 (no establishment of clear expectations; task never outlined) to 7 (establishment and reinforcement of clear expectations; task outlined beforehand). Ratings of *Allowance of autonomy* ranged from 1 (not taking account of child's individual motives or perspective) to 7 (full recognition of the validity of the child's individual motives and perspectives). Coding was done blind to any other measures, with inter-observer reliabilities of r = .93 for sensitive framework, r = .88 for limit setting, and r = .87 for allowance of autonomy (n = 16, from a previous sample of mothers with a child aged 4.5 years).

Finally, the frequency of occurrence of maternal *Criticizing and cutting in* was coded over the first 3 minutes of each joint task. It was then converted to "relative frequency" by expressing the frequency as a proportion of total maternal turns, defined as a vocal phrase or action preceded and followed by a 2-second pause, or by a clear-cut change in vocal inflection or topic change (following Stevenson-Hinde & Shouldice, 1995a). Inter-observer reliability was $r = .89$ ($n = 16$).

Black box task

It was predicted that anxious mothers should particularly stand out from others on a task with a fear-inducing theme. A 40-cm-cubed wooden box was positioned in front of mother and child. A flowerpot had been set on top of the black box in order to cover a hole and a black cotton sleeve within, which made it impossible to see inside. Mothers were given an instruction card and then left alone in the room. The card stated that there were three "scary" things in the box. Mothers were asked to discuss with their child what might be in there until a knock came (after 30 sec). They should then remove the pot and ask the child to take out the objects if he/she wishes, and to encourage the child if he/she is reluctant (see Chicot, 1999 for further details, including a diagram of the box, along with its small plastic spider and two caterpillars).

Mothers were assessed on three ratings scales ranging from 1 to 5, with 3 as the norm. *Tension* was rated from 1 (relaxed; open posture; calm voice; readily reaches into box) to 5 (tense posture; tense voice; may avoid box). *Regulation of child's emotion* was rated from 1 (encourages child to ignore/minimize fear; does not introduce fear theme) to 5 (winding up child's fear by emphasizing fearful theme; dwelling on child's fear; pestering a fearful child to complete task). *Supportive presence* was rated from 1 (unsupportive; task oriented; unavailable) to 5 (supportive; child-oriented; always available). To ensure independence, the task was coded by two undergraduates who were blind to all other assessments. After training on the system with 12 randomly chosen video-tapes, independent ratings were made before conferencing to agree a final rating. Inter-observer reliabilities (with R.C.) were $r = .96$ for tension making, $r = .92$ for regulation of emotion, and $r = .95$ for supportive presence ($n = 16$).

Ratings on each scale were converted to z-scores, and for Supportive presence the sign of each z-score was reversed. The mean of the three z-scores provided a summary Tension making score for each child.

Results

Descriptive statistics

The sample consisted of intact families with 1–3 children and mothers spread over three anxiety levels: Low (0–7, $n = 36$), Medium (8–10, $n = 34$), and High (11–21, $n = 28$). Mothers' mean age was 34 years (range = 23 to 48), and families covered the spectrum of educational and occupational levels (further information may be found in Stevenson-Hinde et al., 2007).

All the continuous variables to be analyzed are listed in Table 1. *Maternal anxiety* scores ranged from 0.3 to 17.7, with a mean of 8.4. *Behavioral inhibition* (BI) ratings ranged from 1 to 8 with a mean of 4.9, slightly higher than the "norm for age" rating of 4, to be expected in this selected sample. Maternal interactions consist of six sets: four positive and two negative. *Positive maternal style at home* (the mean of four z-scores: ratings of mothers' sensitive responsiveness, meshing, enjoyment of child, and gentleness), with a mean of 0, ranged from –2.33 to 1.65. In the laboratory, the following four

Table 1. Descriptive statistics and intercorrelations (Pearson *rs*) for all the continuous measures.

	Mean (SD)	1.	2.	3.	4.	5.	6.	7.	8.	9.
Characteristics										
1. Maternal anxiety	8.4 (3.9)									
2. Child BI	4.9 (1.9)	.15	–							
Maternal interactions										
3. Maternal style at home[1]	0.0 (.86)	–.34***	–.08	–						
4. Sensitive framework[2]	4.9 (1.5)	–.33***	–.14	.39***	–					
5. Limit setting[2]	5.5 (1.4)	–.31***	–.08	.22*	.74***	–				
6. Allowance of autonomy[2]	4.7 (1.4)	–.29**	.02	.40***	.68***	.38***	–			
7. Criticize and cut in[3]	.05 (.05)	.24**	.08	–.24*	–.68***	–.63***	–.56***	–		
8. Black box tension making[4]	0.0 (.77)	.32***	.17*	–.08	–.35***	–.32***	–.27**	.28**	–	
Attachment										
9. Security ratings	5.0 (2.0)	–.35***	–.22*	.41***	.46***	.46***	.37***	–.47***	–.33***	–

Notes: $N = 98$, except for "Maternal style at home" ($N = 86$).
[1]Mean of four ratings (as *z*-scores): sensitive, meshing, enjoyment, gentle.
[2]Mean rating (1–7) over two laboratory joint tasks (Etch A Sketch® and Butterfly puzzle).
[3]Relative frequency of occurrence over the above two joint tasks.
[4]Mean of three ratings (as *z*-scores) over a fear-inducing task: tension making; regulation of emotion, supportive presence.
$*p < .05$; $**p < .01$; $***p < .001$; 1-tailed.

measures were each averaged over two joint tasks: *sensitive framework* (ratings ranging from 1 to 7), *limit setting* (1 to 7), *allowance of autonomy* (1.5 to 7), and the percentage of *criticizing and cutting in* (0% to 24%). Finally, *tension making* (1.15 to 2.16), involved a mean of three ratings (converted to *z*-scores) during the fear-inducing Black box task. *Security of attachment* ratings covered the whole possible range, from 1 to 9 with a mean of 5.0, the lower limit for a secure pattern. None of the variables showed a significant sex difference.

Table 1 also indicates that maternal anxiety was highly significantly correlated with each of the six maternal interactions (Column 1) and BI with only one – tension making in the Black box task (Column 2). All but one of the 15 intercorrelations between the six maternal interactions were significant (Columns 3–7). Security of attachment ratings (Row 9) were significantly correlated with all other measures: maternal anxiety, BI, and the six maternal interactions.

Is maternal anxiety, as opposed to child's BI or sex, the main predictor of maternal interactions?

Using a GLM Univariate procedure (General Linear Model, IBM SPSS Statistics, Version 21), maternal anxiety and child's behavioral inhibition (as co-variates) and sex (as a fixed factor) were entered as independent (predictor) variables, with each of the six maternal sensitivity measures entered in turn as a dependent variable (Table 2). This procedure permits testing for interactions (i.e., one 3-way and three 2-way) as well as main effects. For each one of the six maternal measures, no significant interaction occurred between maternal anxiety, BI, and/or sex, and sequential deletion revealed that neither BI nor sex was a significant predictor, leaving only maternal anxiety. Table 2 lists Beta and *F*-values for maternal anxiety on its own and then for each non-significant variable – BI and sex – with anxiety controlled for. A partial Eta-squared is the partial variation accounted for, namely the proportion of the effect + error variance that is attributable to the effect ($SS_{effect}/(SS_{effect} + SS_{error})$). Maternal anxiety was a significant predictor of each of the six maternal interactions, with partial eta-squares ranging from .06 for *criticize and cut in* to .12 for *maternal style at home*. BI and sex were not significant, with partial eta-squares ranging from only .00 to .03.

Levels of anxiety and maternal interactions

Table 3 lists means of each standardized maternal interaction across maternal anxiety levels defined by the HADS scale (see Methods). *Low* represents scores within the normal range, whereas *High* indicates clinically-related categories of moderate or severe. The Low and High anxiety mothers' profiles are in sharp contrast: for Low anxiety mothers the four "positive" interactions (positive style at home, sensitive framework, limit setting, allowance of autonomy) were *above* the group mean of zero, and the two "negative" interactions (criticize and cut in, tension making) were *below* the mean.

To test for significance, a GLM multivariate analysis was performed over all six maternal scores in relation to the three levels of maternal anxiety. There were no significant interactions or main effects involving child's sex. The overall MANOVA was significant ($p < .01$; Pillai's trace, $F(12, 158) = 2.54$), thereby permitting univariate analyses and post-hoc tests. As indicated in Table 3, for each type of maternal interaction there was a significant difference between Low and High anxiety groups. Moreover, there

Table 2. GLM univariate analyses of maternal anxiety, child's behavioral inhibition, and sex as predictors of each of the six sets of maternal interactions.

	Maternal anxiety			Behavioral inhibition			Sex		
Maternal interactions	B *SE* (B)	*F*	Partial eta^2	B *SE* (B)	*F*	Partial eta^2	B *SE* (B)	*F*	Partial eta^2
Maternal style at home	–.09 (.03)	11.19***	.12	–.01 (.05)	.04	.00	–.12 (.18)	.47	.01
Sensitive framework	–.13 (.04)	11.75***	.11	–.07 (.08)	.88	.01	+.45 (.29)	.02	.00
Limit setting	–.11 (.03)	10.05**	.10	–.03 (.04)	.13	.00	+.16 (.27)	.33	.00
Allowance of autonomy	–.11 (.04)	9.05**	.09	+.05 (.07)	.40	.00	+.23 (.28)	.69	.01
Criticize and cut in	+.00 (.00)	5.63*	.06	+.00 (.00)	.25	.00	–.01 (.01)	2.78	.03
Black box tension making	+.06 (.02)	10.65**	.10	.05 (.04)	1.71	.02	–.11 (.15)	.01	.00

Notes: Results are given for maternal anxiety on its own as well as for behavioral inhibition and sex alone, in each case controlling for the significant effect of maternal anxiety. $N = 98$, except for "Maternal style at home" ($N = 86$).
A negative Beta for "Sex" indicates that girls had lower values for the dependent variable than did boys.
$^*p < .05$; $^{**}p < .01$; $^{***}p < .001$.

Table 3. Mean *z*-scores (standard deviations) and ANOVA results for the six sets of maternal interactions, according to levels of maternal anxiety.

	Maternal anxiety level			ANOVA	
Maternal interactions	Low (n = 36)	Medium (n = 34)	High (n = 28)	F-value	Between-group diffs.
Maternal style at home	.55	−.01	−.51	8.78***	L>M*>H*
	(.83)	(.91)	(1.01)		L>H***
Sensitive framework	.38	−.14	−.31	4.55**	L>M*
	(.88)	(1.07)	(.95)		L>H**
Limit setting	.43	−.24	−.26	5.67**	L>M**
	(.79)	(.91)	(1.18)		L>H**
Allowance of autonomy	.36	−.19	−.23	4.01*	L>M*
	(.98)	(1.02)	(.89)		L>H*
Criticize and cut in	−.35	.26	.13	3.76*	L<M**
	(.88)	(1.14)	(.86)		L<H*
Black box tension making	−.36	.06	.40	5.08**	L<H**
	(.90)	(1.05)	(.91)		

Notes: df = 2, 95 with the exception of "Maternal style at home" where df = 2, 83. For this variable, the *n*s across anxiety levels were 26, 33, and 27, respectively.
*$p < .05$; **$p < .01$; ***$p < .001$.

were even significant differences between Low and Medium anxiety mothers, with one exception (tension making).

Is maternal sensitivity, as opposed to maternal anxiety or sex of child, the main predictor of security of attachment?

The six sets of maternal interactions were highly significantly intercorrelated (Table 1), and a Principal Component Analysis over the six sets produced a first component with an eigenvalue of 3.16. Therefore a summary score was calculated, in order to obtain one robust measure of overall maternal sensitivity, as follows: Interactions were converted to *z*-scores (with signs changed for the two negative sets), and then means were taken over all six sets (or over five sets for the 12 children with missing home ratings). These were similar to PCA scores (r = .996, N = 86), and were preferred as being more straightforward.

This composite "overall sensitivity" score was significantly correlated with maternal anxiety on the one hand ($r(98) = -.43$, $p = .000$, 1-tailed) and security of attachment ratings on the other ($r(98) = .58$, $p = .000$). To see if it could be considered a mediator between the significantly correlated maternal anxiety and security ratings ($r(98) = -.35$, $p = .000$, Table 1), this overall sensitivity score and maternal anxiety (as co-variates) and sex (as a fixed factor) were entered as independent variables, with security of attachment ratings as the dependent variable. No significant interactions occurred between maternal sensitivity, anxiety, and/or sex, and sequential deletion revealed that overall maternal sensitivity was the only significant predictor of attachment security (Table 4). The F-value for maternal sensitivity was highly significant ($p = .000$) with a partial Eta-squared indicating 33% of the variance accounted for, but only 2% and 1% for maternal anxiety and sex, respectively. Thus, maternal sensitivity may be viewed as a mediator between maternal anxiety and security of attachment (see Zhao, Lynch, & Chen, 2010).

Table 4. GLM univariate analysis of overall maternal sensitivity (the mean of six z-transformed sets of maternal interactions) maternal anxiety, and sex as predictors of security of attachment ratings.

Overall maternal sensitivity			Maternal anxiety			Sex		
B *SE* (B)	*F*	Partial eta^2	B *SE* (B)	*F*	Partial eta^2	B *SE* (B)	*F*	Partial eta^2
1.62 (.23)	48.23***	.33	–.07 (.05)	1.92	.02	–.38 (.34)	1.30	.01

Notes: Results are given for overall sensitivity, as well as for maternal anxiety and sex alone, in each case controlling for the significant effect of overall sensitivity.
$N = 98$; ***$p = .000$.

Maternal interactions and patterns of attachment

We have seen that each of the six sets of maternal interactions was significantly correlated ($p < .001$) with security of attachment ratings (Table 1), and that these interactions mediate the relation between maternal anxiety and security (Table 4). However, one may be insecure in different ways, raising the question of which maternal interactions are associated with each pattern of attachment (Table 5). For the Secure group (B), the four positive maternal interactions were above the sample mean of zero and the two negative interactions fell below it. Profiles of the insecure Ambivalent (C) and Controlling (CN) groups were similar, and in the opposite direction from that of the Secure (B) group. Likewise, for the insecure Avoidant (A) pattern, all four positive maternal interactions fell below the sample mean of zero. However, unlike the Ambivalent and Controlling patterns, but like the Secure pattern, the two negative maternal interactions of the Avoidant group fell below the sample mean.

To test for significant differences, a GLM multivariate analysis was performed over all six maternal interactions in relation to the four main attachment patterns. There were no interaction or main effects due to child's sex. An overall MANOVA was significant ($p < .001$; Pillai's trace, $F(18, 237) = 2.80$). Univariate analyses and post-hoc tests are presented in Table 5. Each of the six sets of maternal interactions showed a significant difference in expected directions between mothers of Secure children and one or more of the insecure groups.

Mothers of the Avoidant group significantly differed from the Secure group for positive style of interactions at home and sensitive framework. They were significantly *lower* than mothers in the insecure Ambivalent or Controlling groups for criticizing and cutting in and *lower* than the Controlling group for tension making.

The Ambivalent and Controlling groups never significantly differed from each other, nor did they significantly differ from Secure on positive maternal style in the more relaxed home setting. In lab tasks, they were each significantly *lower* than Secure for sensitive framework and limit setting and *higher* than Secure for criticizing and cutting in. Finally, unlike all other mothers, those in the Controlling group were significantly *lower* than those in the Secure group for allowing autonomy, and significantly *higher* than Secure (and Avoidant) for maternal tension making in the Black box task. In brief, mothers of Controlling children significantly differed from mothers of Secure children on all five laboratory-based measures.

The last row in Table 5 lists the summary maternal interactions (standardized) or "overall sensitivity score" for each pattern of attachment. Only the Secure group has a mean (.31) above the overall mean of 0. This was significantly different from each of the insecure groups (–.16 for A; –.34 for C; –.44 for CN), which did not differ significantly from each other.

Table 5. Mean z-scores (standard deviations) and ANOVA results for maternal interactions, according to patterns of attachment.

	Pattern of attachment				ANOVA	
Maternal interactions	Avoidant (n = 14)	Secure (n = 52)	Ambivalent (n = 15)	Controlling (n = 17)	F-value	Between-group
Maternal style at home	−.61 (1.21)	.24 (.91)	−.05 (1.02)	−.15 (.87)	2.80*	A<B**
Sensitive framework	−.34 (1.04)	.34 (.76)	−.47 (1.22)	−.35 (1.08)	4.96**	B>A*; C**; CN**
Limit setting	−.02 (.89)	.33 (.63)	−.70 (1.34)	−.38 (1.26)	5.93***	B>C***; CN**
Allowance of autonomy	−.26 (1.15)	.22 (.92)	−.11 (1.07)	−.36 (.95)	1.99	B>CN*
Criticize and cut in	−.12 (.93)	−.35 (.68)	.58 (1.30)	.65 (1.11)	7.50***	A<C*; CN* B<C***; CN***
Black box tension making	−.05 (.92)	−.30 (.85)	.21 (1.06)	.77 (1.08)	5.86***	A<CN* B<CN***
Overall sensitivity	−.16 (.68)	.31 (.54)	−.34 (.80)	−.44 (.79)	8.19***	B>A*; C***; CN***

Notes: *Overall sensitivity* is the mean of the six z-transformed maternal interactions (with the sign of the last two, which are undesirable, reversed); N = 98.
df = 3, 94 with the exception of "Maternal style at home" where df = 3, 82. For this variable the ns across patterns of attachment were 13, 45, 12, and 16, respectively.
$^{*}p < .05$; $^{**}p < .01$; $^{***}p < .001$.

Although the Controlling pattern differed the most from the Secure pattern, it is notable that the *security ratings* (from 1–9, see Methods) of the Controlling group were not the lowest. Their mean rating was M = 3.06 (n = 17), with the Ambivalent group being lowest at M = 2.97 (n = 15). The Avoidant group rating was M = 3.50 (n = 14), and none of the three insecure patterns differed significantly from each other. As may be expected from the attachment coding scheme, the Secure group was above 5, at M = 6.64 (n = 52).

Summary and discussion

Maternal anxiety as a predictor of maternal interactions

We have seen (Table 1) that maternal anxiety was significantly correlated in predictable ways with the six sets of maternal interactions observed in different contexts: at home (*positive maternal style*), in laboratory joint tasks (*providing a sensitive framework, limit setting, allowance of autonomy, criticizing and cutting in*), and in a laboratory fear-inducing task (*tension making*). These sets of interactions overlap with observations of anxious mothers in previous samples, as mentioned in the Introduction. In particular, previous studies showing anxious mothers as less warm and positive overlaps with our current index of positive maternal style at home; less granting of autonomy and more critical and intrusive overlaps with those same interactions in our laboratory joint tasks; and more catastrophizing overlaps with tension making in our fear-inducing task. What seems to be missing in previous studies with anxious mothers are assessments of sensitivity *per se*, as seen in our home observations (*positive maternal style*) and in laboratory joint tasks (*providing a sensitive framework*).

When maternal anxiety, behavioral inhibition (BI), and sex of child were entered as predictors for each of our six sets of maternal interactions, there were no statistically significant interactions between anxiety, BI, or sex. Sequential deletion revealed that neither BI nor sex was a predictor, leaving only maternal anxiety as the significant predictor for each measure (Table 2). In earlier studies, observations of similar maternal interactions did show significant differences according to BI and sex of child (Simpson & Stevenson-Hinde, 1985; Stevenson-Hinde & Glover, 1996). However, the previous two samples were not selected for maternal anxiety, so that most mothers presumably fell within the present "normal anxiety" range of 1–7. The wide spread of anxiety scores (from 0.3 to 17.7) within the present selected sample appeared to overshadow any effects of BI or sex. This is in keeping with results involving 4.9-year-old children of mothers with anxiety disorder (social phobia or generalized anxiety disorder): "There were no significant effects of child BI on any parenting dimension" (Murray et al., 2012, p. 194).

Analyses of variance indicated that the interactions of Medium anxiety as well as High anxiety mothers significantly differed in expected directions from those with Low (i.e., "normal") anxiety (Table 3). This suggests that even moderate levels of anxiety within a community sample may negatively influence aspects of maternal sensitivity.

Maternal sensitivity as a mediator between maternal anxiety and attachment security

Highly significant correlations occurred between maternal anxiety and security, as well as between maternal anxiety and maternal sensitivity, and maternal sensitivity and security. To test for mediation (via a GLM Univariate analysis), overall maternal sensitivity, maternal anxiety, and sex were entered as independent variables, with security of attachment ratings as the dependent variable. The significant effect of anxiety on security disappeared. Instead, the F-value for overall sensitivity was highly significant ($p = .000$) with a partial Eta-squared indicating 33% of the variance in security ratings accounted for, but only 2% and 1% for maternal anxiety and sex, respectively (Table 4). Thus, we have identified maternal interactions which reflect sensitivity and satisfy conditions for being regarded as a mediator between maternal anxiety and security (Zhao et al., 2010). This suggests that maternal anxiety may negatively affect security of attachment primarily through a reduction in maternal sensitivity.

Maternal sensitivity and security

In the original Baltimore study the effect size was $r(21) = .78$ between maternal sensitivity assessed in the home over the first year of life and security ratings in the Strange Situation at one year. This was considerably higher than the combined effect size of $r(1097) = .24$ over the variety of studies in the Leiden meta-analysis (De Wolff & van IJzendoorn, 1997). In our earlier "normative" sample, the correlation between maternal sensitivity at home (assessed at 3.5 years) and security ratings (assessed at 4.5 years) was $r(78) = .32$ (Stevenson-Hinde & Shouldice, 1995a). With our present 4.5-year-olds, the effect size was $r(86) = .41$ between maternal sensitivity at home and security ratings (Table 1). For our overall sensitivity score the effect size was even higher, at $r(98) = .578$. This considerable effect size may be due to the fact that contemporaneous, observational, and robust assessments of maternal sensitivity had been composited into one variable.

From all of the above, we may conclude that Ainsworth's concept of maternal sensitivity is central to the development of a secure attachment bond.

Particular maternal interactions and patterns of attachment

Finally, the six sets of interactions were associated with patterns of attachment in accord with previous findings from infancy and early childhood. Predictably, Secure children had mothers with above average (i.e., > 0) *z*-scores on the four sets of positive interactions, and below average (< 0) *z*-scores on the two sets of negative interactions (see Table 5). Mothers of the Avoidant group significantly differed from the Secure group on only two interactions, both focusing on sensitive responsiveness: positive maternal style at home and sensitive framework in the lab. However, like mothers of Secure children, their negative interactions (criticizing and cutting in on the joint tasks and tension-making on the fear-inducing task) were below the sample mean and significantly lower than mothers in the Ambivalent or Controlling groups, although not as low as mothers in the Secure group. Thus, although insensitive, mothers of Avoidant children expressed slightly below average negative or emotional behavior. This may be seen as a precursor to the child's "maintenance of neutrality" upon reunion with mother, in spite of having being left alone by her.

The Ambivalent and Controlling group of mothers never significantly differed from each other, and they were significantly lower than Secure on two positive measures involving joint tasks, namely sensitive framework and limit setting. While not providing sensitive guidance, mothers of Ambivalent children were nevertheless significantly higher than the secure mothers on criticizing and cutting in. This behavior is compatible with Cassidy and Berlin's (1994) finding that mothers of Ambivalent children were inconsistent and interfering.

What distinguished Controlling from all other mothers was that they significantly differed from Secure on not allowing autonomy in the joint tasks and creating tension in the fear-inducing task. Thus, mothers of Controlling children not only failed to provide a sensitive framework, set limits, or allow autonomy, but also criticized/cut-in and failed to provide a relaxed, supportive presence in a fear-inducing task. With such lack of maternal support, "taking control" is an understandable but burdensome outcome for a 4-year-old. Overall, the above differences reflect what Mary Ainsworth stated some years ago: "mothers who were highly sensitive to infant signals were very similar in their behaviour, whereas insensitive mothers were insensitive in a variety of different ways" (1982, p. 14).

Conclusion and future directions

Within a community sample of mothers selected for a spread of low, medium, or high anxiety levels, we have indicated a main influence of maternal anxiety on maternal insensitivity, leading to insecurity of attachment. Within this same sample, maternal anxiety was related to paternal anxiety, low dyadic adjustment, and poor family functioning (Stevenson-Hinde et al., 2007). Additionally, anxiety was prevalent in the community, with above normal ratings for nearly half (46%) the mothers in our original community sample ($N = 763$) before any selection occurred. All this suggests that more consideration should be given to the physical and social support available to mothers. It also suggests that family intervention may play a key role in decreasing anxiety (see also Bögels & Brechman-Toussaint, 2006).

Thus, family systems theory and attachment theory should be considered jointly, the one complementing the other. "A family systems approach provides a context for the development and maintenance of dyadic attachment relationships. An attachment approach provides a focus on the expression of and response to attachment behavior within a family. Uniting the two approaches has implications for both research and intervention" (Stevenson-Hinde, 1990, p. 218; see also Byng-Hall, 1990). To cite one example, an application of attachment theory to observations of family therapy sessions indicated how insecurity in one relationship may influence expectations and interactions in other relationships, and in turn how sensitivity and security may be promoted within the family (Byng-Hall & Stevenson-Hinde, 1991).

Acknowledgements

This research was supported by the Medical Research Council (UK), including a Research Studentship to R.C. This paper has been greatly improved by the constructive comments of Inge Bretherton.

References

Ainsworth, M. D. S. (1982). Attachment: Retrospect and prospect. In C. M. Parkes & J. Stevenson-Hinde (Eds.), *The place of attachment in human behaviour* (pp. 3–30). London: Tavistock & Basic Books.

Ainsworth, M. D. S., Bell, S. M. V., & Stayton, D. J. (1971). Individual differences in strange-situation behaviour of one-year-olds. In H. R. Schaffer (Ed.), *The origins of human social relations* (pp. 17–57). London: Academic Press.

Ainsworth, M. D. S., Blehar, M. C., Waters, E., & Wall, S. (1978). *Patterns of attachment*. Mahwah, NJ: Erlbaum.

Bakermans-Kranenburg, M. J., van IJzendoorn, M. H., & Juffer, F. (2003). Less is more: Meta-analyses of sensitivity and attachment interventions in early childhood. *Psychological Bulletin*, *129*, 195–215.

Bar-Haim, Y., Dan, O., Eshel, Y., & Sagi-Schwartz, A. (2007). Predicting children's anxiety from early attachment relationships. *Journal of Anxiety Disorders*, *21*, 1061–1068.

Bjelland, I., Dahl, A. S., Haug, T. T., & Neckelmann, D. (2002). The validity of the Hospital Anxiety and Depression Scale. An updated literature review. *Journal of Psychosomatic Research*, *52*, 69–77.

Bögels, S. M., & Brechman-Toussaint, M. L. (2006). Family issues in child anxiety: Attachment, family functioning, parental rearing and beliefs. *Clinical Psychology Review, 26*, 834–856.

Bretherton, I. (2003). Mary Ainsworth: Insightful observer and courageous theoretician. In G. A. Kimble & M. Wertheimer (Eds.), *Portraits of pioneers in psychology* (vol. 5, pp. 317–331). Hillsdale, NJ: Erlbaum.

Byng-Hall, J. (1990). Attachment theory and family therapy: A clinical view. *Infant Mental Health Journal*, *11*, 228–236.

Byng-Hall, J., & Stevenson-Hinde, J. (1991). Attachment relationships within a family system. *Infant Mental Health Journal*, *12*, 187–200.

Cassidy, J., & Berlin, L. J. (1994). The insecure/ambivalent pattern of attachment: Theory and research. *Child Development*, *63*, 1456–1472.

Cassidy, J., & Marvin, R. S. (1992). *Attachment organization in preschool children: Procedures and coding manual* (4th ed.). Unpublished manuscript, MacArthur Working Group on Attachment, Seattle, WA.

Chicot, R. (1999). *Maternal anxiety levels and mother-child interactions* (Unpublished doctoral dissertation). University of Cambridge, Cambridge.

Creswell, C., Apetroaia, A., Murray, L., & Cooper, P. (2013). Cognitive, affective, and behavioral characteristics of mothers with anxiety disorders in the context of child anxiety disorder. *Journal of Abnormal Psychology*, *122*, 26–38.

Degnan, K. A., Almas, A. N., & Fox, N. A. (2010). Temperament and the environment in the etiology of childhood anxiety. *Journal of Child Psychology & Psychiatry, 51*, 497–517.

De Wolff, M. S., & van IJzendoorn, M. H. (1997). Sensitivity and attachment: A meta-analysis on parental antecedents of infant attachment. *Child Development*, *688*, 571–591.

Degnan, K. A., & Fox, N. A. (2007). Behavioral inhibition and anxiety disorders: Multiple levels of a resilience process. *Development and Psychopathology, 19*, 729–746.

Denham, S. A., Renwick, S. J., & Holt, R. W. (1991). Working and playing together: Prediction of pre-school social-emotion competence from mother-child interaction. *Child Development, 62*, 242–249.

George, C., & Solomon, J. (1996). Representational models of relationships: Links between caregiving and attachment. *Infant Mental Health Journal, 17*, 198–216.

Herrmann, C. (1997). International experiences with the Hospital Anxiety and Depression Scale: A review of validation data and the clinical results. *Journal of Pyschosomatic Research, 42*, 17–41.

Hirshfeld-Becker, D. R., Biederman, J., Calltharp, S., Rosenbaum, E. D., Faraone, S. V., & Rosenbaum, J. F. (2003). Behavioral inhibition and disinhibition as hypothesized precursors to psychopathology: Implications for pediatric bipolar disorder. *Biological Psychiatry, 53*, 985–999.

Kertz, S. J., Smith, C. L., Chapman, L. K., & Woodruff-Borden, J. (2008). Maternal sensitivity and anxiety: Impacts on child outcome. *Child & Family Behavior Therapy, 30*, 153–171.

Lyons-Ruth, K., & Jacobvitz, D. (2008). Attachment disorganization: Genetic factors, parenting contexts, and developmental transformation from infancy to adulthood. In J. Cassidy & P. Shaver (Eds.), *Handbook of attachment: Theory, research, and clinical applications* (2nd ed., pp. 666–697). New York, NY: Guilford Press.

Manassis, K., Bradley, B., Goldberg, S., Hood, J., & Swinson, R. P. (1995). Behavioral inhibition, attachment and anxiety in children of mothers with anxiety disorders. *Canadian Journal of Psychiatry, 40*, 87–92.

Marshall, P. J., & Stevenson-Hinde, J. (1998). Behavioral inhibition, heart period, and respiratory sinus arrhythmia in young children. *Developmental Psychobiology, 33*, 283–292.

McClure, E. B., Brennan, P. R., Hammen, C., & LeBrocque, R. M. (2001). Parental anxiety disorders, child anxiety disorders, and the perceived parent-child relationship in an Australian high-risk sample. *Journal of Abnormal Child Psychology, 29*, 1–10.

McLeod, B. D., Wood, J. J., & Weisz, J. R. (2007). Examining the association between parenting and childhood anxiety: A meta-analysis. *Clinical Psychology Review, 27*, 155–172.

Moore, P. S., Whaley, S. E., & Sigman, M. (2004). Interactions between mothers and children: Impacts of maternal and child anxiety. *Journal of Abnormal Psychology, 113*, 471–476.

Moss, E., Bureau, J., Cyr, C., Mongeau, C., & St-Laurent, D. (2004). Correlates of attachment at age 3: Construct validity of the preschool attachment classification system. *Developmental Psychology, 40*, 323–334.

Murray, L., Lau, P. Y., Arteche, A., Creswell, C., Russ, S., Zoppa, L. D., … Cooper, P. (2012). Parenting by anxious mothers: Effects of disorder subtype, context and child characteristics. *Journal of Child Psychology & Psychiatry, 53*, 188–196.

Scher, A., & Mayseless, O. (2000). Mothers of anxious/ambivalent infants: Maternal characteristics and child-care context. *Child Development, 71*, 1629–1639.

Shamir-Essakow, G., Ungerer, J. A., & Rapee, R. M. (2005). Attachment, behavioral inhibition, and anxiety in preschool children. *Journal of Abnormal Child Psychology, 33*, 131–143.

Simpson, A. E., & Stevenson-Hinde, J. (1985). Temperamental characteristics of three-to-four-year-old boys and girls and child-family interactions. *Journal of Child Psychology & Psychiatry, 26*, 43–53.

Snaith, R. P., & Zigmond, A. S. (1994). *The Hospital Anxiety and Depression Scale (HADS)*. Windsor: NFER-Nelson.

Solomon, J., & George, C. (2008). The measurement of attachment security and related constructs in infancy and early childhood. In J. Cassidy & P. R. Shaver (Eds.), *Handbook of attachment: Theory, research, and clinical applications* (2nd ed., pp. 383–416). New York, NY: Guilford Press.

Spinhoven, P., Ormel, J., Sloekers, P. P. A., Kempen, G. I. J., Speckens, A. E. M., & VanHemert, A. M. (1997). A validation study of the Hospital Anxiety and Depression Scale (HADS) in different groups of young Dutch subjects. *Psychological Medicine, 27*, 363–370.

Stevenson-Hinde, J. (1990). Attachment within family systems: An overview. *Infant Mental Health Journal, 11*, 218–227.

Stevenson-Hinde, J., Curley, J., Chicot, R., & Jóhannsson, C. (2007). Anxiety within families: Interrelations, consistency and change. *Family Process, 46*, 543–556.

Stevenson-Hinde, J., & Glover, A. (1996). Shy girls and boys: A new look. *Journal of Child Psychology & Psychiatry, 37*, 181–187.

Stevenson-Hinde, J., & Hinde, R. A. (1986). Changes in associations between characteristics and interactions. In R. Plomin & J. Dunn (Eds.), *The study of temperament: Changes, continuities, and challenges* (pp. 115–129). Hillsdale, NJ: Erlbaum.

Stevenson-Hinde, J., & Marshall, P. J. (1999). Behavioral inhibition, heart period, and respiratory sinus arrhythmia: An attachment perspective. *Child Development, 70*, 805–816.

Stevenson-Hinde, J., & Shouldice, A. (1990). Fear and attachment in 2.5-year-olds. *British Journal of Developmental Psychology, 8*, 319–333.

Stevenson-Hinde, J., & Shouldice, A. (1995a). Maternal interactions and self-reports related to attachment classifications at 4.5 years. *Child Development, 66*, 583–596.

Stevenson-Hinde, J., & Shouldice, A. (1995b). 4.5 to 7 years: Fearful behavour, fears and worries. *Journal of Child Psychology & Psychiatry, 35*, 1027–1038.

Stevenson-Hinde, J., Shouldice, A., & Chicot, R. (2011). Maternal anxiety, behavioral inhibition, and attachment. *Attachment & Human Development, 13*, 199–215.

Stevenson-Hinde, J., & Verschueren, K. (2002). Attachment in childhood. In P. K. Smith & C. H. Hart (Eds.), *Blackwell handbook of social development* (pp. 182–204). Oxford: Blackwell.

van der Bruggen, C. O., Bögels, S. M., & van Zeilst, N. (2010). What influences parental controlling behavior? The role of parent and child trait anxiety. *Cognition & Emotion, 24*, 141–149.

van der Bruggen, C. O., Stams, G. J. J. M., & Bögels, S. M. (2008). Research review: The relation between child and parent anxiety and parental control: A meta-analytic review. *Journal of Child Psychology & Psychiatry, 49*, 1257–1269.

Warren, S., Huston, L., Egeland, B., & Sroufe, A. (1997). Child and adolescent anxiety disorders and early attachment. *Journal of the American Academy of Child and Adolescent Psychiatry, 36*, 637–644.

Weinfield, N. S., Sroufe, L. A., Egeland, B., & Carlson, E. A. (2008). Individual differences in infant-caregiver attachment. In J. Cassidy & P. R. Shaver (Eds.), *Handbook of attachment: Theory, research, and clinical applications* (2nd ed., pp. 78–101). New York, NY: Guilford Press.

Whaley, S. E., Pinto, A., & Sigman, M. (1999). Characterizing interactions between anxious mothers and their children. *Journal of Consulting Clinical Psychology, 67*, 826–836.

Woodruff-Borden, J., Morrow, C., Bourland, S., & Cambron, S. (2002). The behaviour of anxious parents: Examining mechanisms of transmission of anxiety from parent to child. *Journal of Clinical Child and Adolescent Psychiatry, 31*, 364–374.

Zhao, X., Lynch, J. G., & Chen, Q. (2010). Reconsidering Baron and Kenny: Myths and truths about mediation analysis. *Journal of Consumer Research, 37*, 197–206.

Piecing together the sensitivity construct: ethology and cross-cultural research

Germán Posada

Human Development & Family Studies, Purdue University, West Lafayette, IN, USA

Although Ainsworth and Bowlby's perspective on attachment relationships has instinctive underpinnings, they also recognized variability in the ways caregiving is implemented in different ecologies. Ainsworth's naturalistic observations in two different societies provided early evidence about the development of infant–mother attachment, differences in the quality of attachment relationships, and the role of maternal care in attachment development. Further, her research demonstrated the importance of an ethological approach for research within and across cultures. Employing similar concepts and methods, my collaborators and I have tested and expanded Bowlby's and Ainsworth's ideas about the generality of the sensitivity construct and sensitivity-security link. In our research, ethological observations have been key to elaborating the quality of care construct and studying child–mother attachment relationships in different cultures, social contexts, and ages.

Mary Ainsworth's conceptualization of caregiving underlies most contemporary work on links between parental care and infant attachment outcomes (e.g., Atkinson et al., 2000; De Wolff & van IJzendoorn, 1997). Her insights about caregiving, quality of care, and methodology are a reference point for inquiries into caregivers' contributions to their relationships with children.

Ainsworth's cross-cultural research played an important role in the development of her approach to the study of child–mother attachment relationships. Her Uganda and Baltimore studies helped identify characteristics and interactional processes of the caregiving environment that contribute to attachment formation and individual differences in attachment outcomes. In addition, her extended, detailed observations in naturalistic contexts yielded insights that had not been available to less intrepid observers. Bowlby (1969/1982) conceptualized attachment and maternal behavior as species characteristic adaptations, which implies some similarities across cultures. Initial tests of this hypothesis focused on the distribution of Strange Situation (SSP) classifications across cultures (e.g., Sagi et al., 1985; van IJzendoorn & Kroonenberg, 1988). However, unless mothers in all cultures experience similar levels of support and stress, there might well be differences in SSP classifications. Attachment theory requires instead that the meaningful links Ainsworth found between sensitive care and infant security replicate across cultures. Indeed, a careful reading of Bowlby and Ainsworth's logic and emphasis on real life experience suggests that there might well be different distributions of infant security in certain social and cultural contexts. Our work has focused on the cross-cultural and cross-context generality of secure base behavior and the links between maternal sensitivity and infant security in 1 to 5 year olds from different cultures (Posada et al., 1995, 2002, 2013). Further, and central to the aims of this paper, we have studied whether Ainsworth's methodology and her conclusions regarding qualities of maternal care are relevant when investigating child–mother attachment relationships in different social and cultural contexts, and at different ages.

Accordingly, this paper reviews the origins of the sensitivity construct highlighting the cross-cultural lens of Ainsworth's research in Uganda and Baltimore and the role played by the methodology she used. Then, the usefulness of her conceptual model of caregiving and ethological approach for cross-cultural research is illustrated through our research.

The Bowlby-Ainsworth perspective on caregiving

Bowlby deemed that many important insights about infant–mother relationships were at risk of being discarded because psychoanalytic formulations were not empirically accessible. Thus, he proposed a new model of instinctive behavior based on control systems theory, ethology, and his own clinical observations. Specifically, he proposed (1958, 1969/1982) that infant attachment behavior is organized by an underlying control system which emerges through the interaction of biases in infant learning abilities and what he called an "ordinary expectable caregiving environment." This control system maintains a balance between attachment and exploratory behaviors and in emergency situations has the predictable outcome of promoting proximity to the caregiver. He proposed as well that caregiver behavior was organized as a behavioral system (Bowlby, 1969/1982) that meshed with infant behavior to insure protection and safety.

As species characteristic components of our evolutionary heritage, both infant and caregiver control systems are expected to show a predictable pattern and be observable in most members of the species as long as the environment they inhabit is within the range of environmental conditions in which those systems evolved. This is not to say that these behavior patterns, or for that matter any instinctual components of complex human behavior, are stereotyped. On the contrary, Bowlby (1969/1982) was well aware that the details of both infant and caregiver behavior could adapt to both context and culture. His theory required only that the overall organization into complementary patterns of secure base use and support would be characteristic of humans in general, and this only when the context allowed it.

Ainsworth's singular contribution was to identify the aspects of infant care that shaped secure base behavior and the infant's emotional tie to one or a few primary caregivers.

Ainsworth's cross-cultural research: Uganda and Baltimore

The key to many of Ainsworth's insights was her use of naturalistic observations of infant–mother interactions at home in two different cultural contexts, rural Uganda and urban, middle-class Baltimore. Her observations led her to conclude that the organization of maternal behavior is central to an infant's sense of security and his ability to use mother as a secure base.

Much in line with Bowlby's idea about the importance of everyday, real life relational experiences, she deemed observations of child–mother interactions in naturalistic contexts essential to account for the development of attachment (Ainsworth, 1991; Ainsworth & Marvin, 1995). Influenced by ethology, she focused on description and classification of both child and maternal behavior in natural contexts. Her emphasis on longitudinal and extensive observation of behavior at home where the relationship is formed and elaborated served Ainsworth well. In addition to considering individual instances of behavior, typically studied in terms of frequencies and/or duration at the time of her research, she focused on the study of behavioral organization, function, and meaning in consideration of context (Main, 1999). Her work provided the first naturalistic account of the development of attachment in humans and created the field of research examining individual differences in attachment.

An initial safari into infant–mother attachment

Ainsworth's journey in understanding the development of the infant–mother bond and factors that play a main role in that process took a decisive turn in Uganda. After overcoming the many barriers of conducting research in a country/culture different from hers, she recruited a small group of mothers who volunteered for her study. She studied 28 infants in villages about 15 miles from Kampala (Ainsworth, 1964, 1967). Interested in investigating the effects of separation during weaning on infant–mother relationships, Ainsworth organized an observational study. Although she had been told infants were sent away from their mothers to facilitate weaning, soon into her study, Ainsworth realized that this practice was existent no longer. Instead, she found herself observing and describing the normative course of infant–mother interaction and attachment development, as well as some aspects of maternal care (e.g., warmth, amount of care, and feeding) hypothesized at the time to be influential on children' development (Ainsworth, 1967).

Two-hour visits at 2-week intervals were intended, but the schedule could not be followed. The length of visits needed to be changed as mothers forgot appointments, infants were ill, and other demands on mothers' time and availability came up. The median number of visits per family was 23. The youngest infant was two days old and the oldest 80 weeks, with most of the sample between 7–39 weeks of age when first visited. The span of observations ranged from 6 to 38 weeks. Mothers were interviewed about their infant-care practices and mother–infant interaction was observed (Ainsworth, 1967).

Ainsworth was an exceptional observer as her records illustrate. Her field notes, expanded immediately after each visit, reflect that her task was not limited to a register of behavior. Her observations involved an appreciation of the fact that the meaning of behavior depends upon the context in which it occurs, with a particular emphasis on the interactive context, which is in turn impacted by its immediate circumstances, e.g., social and economic conditions (Ainsworth, 1967; Main, 1999).

A new vista on the origins and early growth of first love: key findings

The Uganda study produced a series of discoveries and conjectures that transformed and guided Ainsworth's view (and ours) on a baby's attachment relationship with her/his mother. Amidst those, information on the development of infant attachment, the secure base phenomenon, the development of individual differences in attachment and the likely role played by maternal care, and the context sensitivity of attachment relationships are highlighted.

Her study provided the first evidence of the normative course of attachment development. Ainsworth generated an ethogram of attachment behavioral patterns. She described each of them, 16 in total, as well as a timeline for their appearance in the course of infants' first year. Such a mapping of behavior over time portrayed a dynamic picture of infants becoming attached to mother and actively participating in the process during everyday exchanges. Among those behavioral patterns, she included: differential smiling, differential crying, differential vocalization, crying when the mother leaves, following, burying the face in mother's lap, clapping and lifting arms in greeting, use of the mother as a secure base, flight to the mother as a haven of safety, and clinging (Ainsworth, 1967). Her observations made her realize that Bowlby's perspective on the development of the child-to-mother bond could account for the data she had collected more appropriately than any secondary drive theory proposed either by classical psychoanalysis or learning theory (Ainsworth, 1969). By the same token, the information yielded by her Uganda study played a key role in Bowlby's (1969/1982) further elaboration of his normative developmental model.

A main outcome of her research in Uganda was the secure base concept. There, Ainsworth coined the secure base phenomenon construct, or more accurately rediscovered it (Bretherton, 2003). She noticed that infants "do not always stay close to the mother but rather make little excursions away from her, exploring other objects and interacting with other people, but returning to the mother from time to time" (Ainsworth, 1967, p. 345). Later in Baltimore, Ainsworth linked the use of mother as a secure base with maternal sensitivity. The secure base concept has become a centerpiece for research on attachment relationships (Bowlby, 1988; Waters & Cummings, 2000).

Also, frequent observation of infant–mother interactions gave Ainsworth a first-hand picture of infant attachment variations and the processes by which such differences in attachment behavior organization develop. She described three groups, "the non-attached," "the secure-attached," and "the insecure-attached." This marks the beginning of the study of individual differences in attachment. Importantly, her observations of interactions led her to explore the contributions of maternal childrearing practices in accounting for those differences. Although she did not reach any definitive conclusions, Ainsworth reported on those maternal care variables that she explored and found associated with infant security (attitude to breast feeding, maternal amount of care, and excellence as an informant), and those she did not (e.g., maternal warmth, multiple caregivers, and total amount of care; Ainsworth, 1967). These findings prompted a series of conjectures about maternal behavior and infant–mother interactions that she elaborated in Baltimore. There her explorations on the role of maternal care were formalized and investigated.

Finally, an important and often disregarded point of Ainsworth's research in Uganda was concerned with her placing of maternal and infant behavior in context. Whether maternal care was described as more or less optimal, or whether infants were described as secure, insecure, or non-attached, Ainsworth depicted the dyad's immediate context to provide a better understanding of the reasons that might explain behavior. That is, she portrayed the specific circumstances surrounding each dyad and family (e.g., absent father, or financial difficulties) that favored or impeded the provision of good caregiving practices. Thus, in referring to Nabatanzi, one of the participants, Ainsworth (1967) described her mother as an unmarried cheerful teenager, who lived with her daughter in a tiny two-room hut across from a larger house inhabited by the maternal grandmother, maternal great-aunt, and two children. The older women took care of the children most of the day, although most of the routine care was Nabatanzi's mother's responsibility. Ainsworth further noted that they were very poor as there was no regular cash income; Nabatanzi's father was a driver in a distant town and visited them occasionally. Ainsworth provided such information for each mother–child dyad.

In sum, Uganda was a first step study that illustrates Ainsworth openness to let the information gathered define the phenomenon under study. The ethological approach she used was well suited at a point when she was describing and characterizing the infant–mother attachment relationship. Ainsworth's repeated naturalistic observations convinced her about the importance of studying behavior in context. Later, towards the end of her career, she lamented the fact that attachment researchers have strayed away from this research practice (Ainsworth & Marvin, 1995). The observations in Uganda provided Ainsworth with a wealth of ideas about the development of infant–mother attachment that she used to organize her Baltimore study.

A systematic journey into infant–mother attachment relationships

In Baltimore, Ainsworth studied the development of infant–mother attachment and the influence of maternal care on the quality of the emotional bond during the first year. She was interested in describing the process of becoming attached *and* testing the similarity of her information from Uganda and Baltimore, identifying the origins of differences in the quality of attachment, and teasing out key maternal care factors that account for those individual differences (Ainsworth, 1967, 1977a; Ainsworth, Blehar, Waters, & Wall, 1978). As in Uganda, observations of infant behavior at home constituted the central methodological feature of her approach. In Baltimore, however, Ainsworth's observational technique was more advanced and systematic, both in her confidence and skill; she was able to focus on secure base behavior and gave more detailed attention to maternal behavior. The latter was necessary to find out about a key process of attachment development.

The kind of data she obtained was mainly concerned with behavior during dyadic exchanges such as face-to-face interactions, responsiveness to crying, physical contact, behavior relevant to separations and reunion, and obedience and compliance (Ainsworth et al., 1978). The participants were 26 infant–mother pairs from white, middle-class Baltimore families. As in Uganda, observations were long and frequent. Infant and maternal behaviors were observed in the course of 4-hour visits at 3-week intervals from birth to 54 weeks. The second to last visit, at about 12 months, took place in a laboratory where each infant–mother pair was observed in the SSP (Ainsworth & Wittig, 1969).

In Baltimore, Ainsworth had a clearer sense of the questions she wanted to address. As in Uganda, she was exceptionally sensitive to the interactive context in which infant and maternal behavior occurred. But while the Uganda observations and descriptions were focused on characterizing the issues studied with rich narratives, the Baltimore observations were made with an eye towards quantification. To be sure, Ainsworth did not relinquish the narrative method that had proved so useful in Uganda but, in the processing of information, one of the key differences in Baltimore was the development and utilization of scoring systems and rating scales to better quantify her narrative records (Posada, Waters, Pederson, Moran, & Vaughn, 2014).

Ainsworth scored different aspects of maternal care from the transcripts created. One type of measurement strategy used behavioral coding to obtain percentages, or in some cases frequencies, of maternal behavior during episodes of infant crying, feeding, leaving and entering the room where the baby was, close physical contact (e.g., pick-up and put-down exchanges), face-to-face interaction, and episodes involving mother issuing commands to her infant, among others. Focusing on maternal behavior allowed her to study the links between specific caregiving behaviors early and the organization of secure base behavior at one year. For instance, her findings indicated that during the first quarter of the baby's first year, mothers of securely attached infants at 12 months were more responsive (more minutes per hour) to their infants' crying, were rated lower in aversion to physical contact, and were better at timing initiation, termination, and pacing of the baby during feeding than mothers of insecure babies (Ainsworth et al., 1978). Similarly, during the last quarter of the infant's first year, mothers of secure infants were more responsive to their infants' crying, acknowledged their baby more when entering the room, and less frequently used physical interventions than mothers of insecurely attached infants.

Ainsworth's focus on specific behaviors in such detail gave her a unique view. The data depicted developmental transformations of maternal behavior and allowed her to examine its continuity and change. Above all, the longitudinal data allowed her to perceive the organization of behavior in time and gave her the key insight that it is precisely this organization that matters. It was the patterning of maternal behavior that she found central in accounting for the qualitative differences in infant–mother attachment relationships. Despite discontinuity in specific behaviors, her observational records provided evidence for the continuity in the organization of caregiving behaviors across infants' first year.

Ainsworth's other measurement strategy addressed more directly the organization of maternal behavior. Based on a thorough examination of her narrative records, she developed a set of scales that reflected more general qualities of behavior in caregiving routines. These scales were not drawn up in advance of data collection, but based on the information collected. This proved important for the detail and appropriateness of the behavioral definitions for each scale, and facilitated the task of the raters. She labeled the scales used to conceptualize maternal care during the fourth quarter of a baby's first year as: sensitivity-insensitivity to the baby's signals and communications, cooperation-interference with the baby's ongoing behavior, acceptance-rejection of the baby's needs, and accessibility-ignoring (Ainsworth et al., 1978). The four dimensions turned out to be highly inter-correlated (Ainsworth, Bell, & Stayton, 1971). Certainly, these domains of maternal behavior are more integrative and conceptual than measures based on specific caregiving practices. The emphasis is placed on the organization of certain types of behavior in coordination with that of the child. Importantly, the scales proposed are not measures of "warmth," love, or general "goodness."

Consolidation of a new perspective on infant–mother attachment: key findings

In Baltimore, Ainsworth confirmed and expanded her Uganda findings, and consolidated her theoretical perspective on infant–mother attachment relationships. In addition to revealing the process of attachment formation, this time, her data depicted more clearly infants' different trajectories of becoming attached to their mother during the first year and the role played by maternal behavior in the process. Her in-depth descriptions of infant–mother interactions throughout the first year gave Ainsworth a privileged perspective into the step-by-step organization of attachment and caregiving behavior. From her data, she proposed three distinct patterns of attachment: anxiously avoidant, anxiously resistant, and securely attached. Ainsworth construed differences between these groups in terms of an insecurity-security dimension when using the mother as a secure base (Ainsworth, Bell, & Stayton, 1974). Furthermore, a major outcome of the Baltimore study was the assembly and validation of the SSP. Ainsworth convincingly presented data that demonstrated significant associations between classes of (not specific) infant behavior at home and in the SSP. The availability of a procedure to assess the complexity of infant–mother relationships was a major achievement that changed the research landscape (Grossmann, Grossmann, Spangler, Suess, & Unzner,

1985). Importantly, coding and ratings on the quality of maternal interactive behavior at home during the first year were significantly related to infant classifications in expected ways. Thus, Ainsworth identified features of maternal behavior during interactions with infants most relevant to the development of individual differences in secure base organization.

She found that the patterning of maternal behavior over time, rather than the content or specific individual behaviors, turned out to be key in accounting for the configuration of infants' secure base behavior. The general characteristics of maternal behavior as assessed by her four scales yielded the sharpest differences when comparing secure and insecure groups of infants. Her findings made clear the nowadays relatively well accepted understanding that infants whose mothers are routinely accessible physically and psychologically, accepting of their needs (despite the limitations those impose on her time/plans), sensitive to their signals and communications, and cooperative with their ongoing behavior rather than interfering, learn that their mothers are available and appropriately responsive to their initiatives and behavior in their daily exchanges. In other words, she identified some of the key features of the "ordinary expectable caregiving environment" upon which smoothly functioning attachment relationships depend. Similarly, she identified patterns of inaccessible, rejecting, insensitive, and intrusive care, better described as inattentive and/or inappropriate rather than abusive, which play an important role in the development of attachment insecurity. In so doing, Ainsworth substantiated Bowlby's insight that the cumulative effect of ordinary variations in care could also have an important impact on the development of attachment relationships.

The Baltimore study was a turning point. Subsequently, numerous studies used both Ainsworth's sensitivity construct and her classification system to group infants based on their behavior in the SSP. Simply stated, Ainsworth shaped the study of individual differences in attachment relationships. Her influence has spread to the study of attachment at older ages.

Expanding Ainsworth's journey in different cultures, contexts, and ages

In the Baltimore study, Ainsworth and colleagues (Ainsworth et al., 1978) discovered that the quality of early care, i.e., sensitivity, is a key factor in a child's ability to use her or his mother effectively as a secure base from which to explore the environment and to which to retreat if needed. Ensuing studies have replicated Ainsworth's findings. Thus, research summarized in a meta-analysis of 66 studies (De Wolff & van IJzendoorn, 1997) demonstrated a significant relation between maternal sensitivity and infant security, although the effect sizes reported were, overall, much smaller than those reported by Ainsworth.

Despite the number of reports and consistency of findings, which offer the impression that the sensitivity-security link has been proven to be universal, the majority of the studies has been conducted with middle-class samples from Western industrialized societies. Further, most research that has assessed maternal care using Ainsworth's sensitivity scale provides a summary score after observing mother's behavior generally, but not always, in contrived situations and for shorter time spans than those of the Baltimore study. This is a very different endeavor from that of Ainsworth's (see Ainsworth et al., 1978).

In a more recent review of attachment research conducted in several countries in Africa, China, Japan, and Israel, van IJzendoorn and Sagi (2008) concluded that more cross-cultural studies are required to settle the issue. Importantly, of the 16 reports cited as containing sensitivity related evidence, only four, other than the one by Ainsworth in

Uganda, assessed sensitivity directly, and these four did not exactly follow Ainsworth's conceptualization. One of these studies, conducted in Japan, failed to find a significant link between maternal sensitivity and infant security (Nakagawa, Lamb, & Miyake, 1992), but as van IJzendoorn and Sagi (2008) explain, this study is difficult to evaluate. In the other studies cited, the assessment of maternal sensitivity reported is indirect at best. Thus, in a study conducted on the Gusii society in Kenya (Kermoian & Leiderman, 1986), sensitivity was inferred via mothers' age, household size, and the birth of a new infant, but it was never assessed. Associations between those variables and security were taken as evidence supporting the sensitivity-security relation. Also, in the study by Peterson, Drotar, Olness, Guay, and Kiziri-Mayengo (2001), the association between maternal affect and attachment security was taken as evidence in support of the sensitivity-security link (van IJzendoorn et al., 2008). Thus, research on the ubiquity of the sensitivity-security link, or lack thereof, in diverse cultural and social contexts is needed.

Interested in studying child–mother relationships, and testing whether the Bowlby-Ainsworth perspective and associated methodology are relevant in different cultural and social contexts, our research team (e.g., Posada et al., 1999, 2002) has used Ainsworth's sensitivity construct, methodologies akin to those she used (e.g., long and repeated observations in naturalistic settings, and description of child–mother interactions during everyday activities), and a cross-cultural lens to study this issue.

The sensitivity-security hypothesis in different cultural and socio-economic groups

In a first set of studies, we addressed questions about the cross-cultural generality or cultural specificity of the sensitivity-security link by gathering similar information using samples from diverse social contexts in Colombia and middle-class US families. In these studies we employed the Maternal Behavior Q-Set (MBQS; Pederson & Moran, 1995a) to describe maternal behavior and assess sensitivity, and the Attachment Q-Set (AQS; Waters, 1995) to describe child attachment behavior and assess security. The MBQS was based on Ainsworth's conceptual model of maternal care and inquisitive empirical work (e.g., Pederson et al., 1990). It has 90 items that describe a mother's behavior during interactions with her infant. Most of the items are behaviorally specific. This Q-Set (version 2.1) is used to describe observations in naturalistic settings and allows researchers to make replicable descriptions of the organization of maternal behavior. It yields, among others, a summary quantitative index of the quality of maternal care, i.e., a sensitivity score. Data supporting its validity in North American samples has been reported elsewhere (e.g., Moran, Pederson, Pettit, & Krupka, 1992; Pederson & Moran, 1995b; Pederson et al., 1990). Findings from studies with the MBQS typically indicate higher correlation indices (Atkinson et al., 2000) than those reported in the meta-analytic study aforementioned (De Wolff & van IJzendoorn, 1997).

The AQS was used to assess infant–mother attachment security. Its 90 items allow researchers to describe and assess the organization of secure base behavior in naturalistic settings, such as homes and playgrounds, and can be used with infants and preschool children. It yields a summary quantitative index about the configuration of a child's secure base behavior, i.e., a security score. Its validity has been documented in numerous studies (e.g., van IJzendoorn, Vereijken, Bakermans-Kranenburg, & Riksen-Walraven, 2004).

In our first study, we tested the sensitivity-security link in everyday situations in a middle-class Colombian sample from Bogotá (Posada et al., 1999) in which mother–infant dyads were observed at home during their everyday activities. Two 2-hour visits were conducted to observe maternal behavior and two additional 2-hour visits were made to observe child behavior. Independent observers provided descriptions of maternal behavior with the MBQS and descriptions of infant secure base behavior with the AQS. Results indicated that sensitivity and security were indeed significantly related when assessed during every day ordinary situations ($r = .48$; Table 1).

In a second study (Posada et al., 1999), we asked whether maternal sensitivity during an emergency situation, i.e., children's hospitalization, was related to attachment security. Families in this sample came from a very poor sector of the population. Children were hospitalized due to a moderate-to-serious illness (i.e., bronchitis, pneumonia, vomiting, and/or diarrhea). We observed mothers' behavior during hospital visits early in the morning while they fed, cleaned, administered medications, and played with their children. After two 2-hour observations of maternal behavior at the hospital, two observers used the MBQS to describe maternal behavior immediately after the hospital visits. To collect information about children's secure-base behavior at home, mothers themselves were asked and trained to use the AQS; research assistants could not conduct home visits because the families lived in an unsafe zone of the city. An appointment was set to meet at the hospital on a day after mothers had visited their infant. At this time, a research assistant read and explained the 90 Q-items to each mother and carefully instructed them how to use the Q-set. The researcher accompanied them while doing the Q-sort task and assisted if they requested any help (e.g., answering questions about the items, their child's behavior, or the sorting procedure) to ensure correct completion of the task. Although van IJzendoorn et al. (2004) concluded that AQS descriptions provided by mothers are not valid, we (Posada et al., 1995, 1999) as well as others (e.g., Teti & McGourty, 1996; White & Feldstein, 1994) found that, if given adequate training

Table 1. Correlations of maternal sensitivity and child security.

Study	*N*	Sample	Child age[1]	Measure: Mother	Measure: Child	*r*
Posada et al. (1999)						
Study 1	41	Col.[2] middle class	12.6	MBQ[3]	AQS[4]	.48**
Study 2	43	Col. low SES	26.3	MBQ	AQS	.55**
Posada et al. (2002)						
	60	US middle class	12.7	MBQ	SS[5]	.33*
	61	Col. middle class	12.7	MBQ	AQS	.46**
Posada et al. (2004)						
	30	Col. middle class	6–13	MBQ	AQS	.42**
				Ethnography	AQS	.61**
Posada et al. (2007)						
Study 1	50	US middle class	52	MBPQ[6]	AQS	.31*
Study 2	40	US middle class	36	MBPQ	AQS	.49**
Posada et al. (2009)	44	Latino immigrant Low SES	54	MBPQ	AQS	.42**
Plata et al. (2012)	85	Col. middle/low SES	42	MBPQ	AQS	.49**
Noblega (2012)	30	Peru, middle/low SES	61	MBPQS	AQS	.63**

Notes: * $p < .05$; ** $p < .01$.
[1]Age in months; [2]Colombian; [3]Maternal Behavior Q-Set; [4]Attachment Q-Set; [5]Strange Situation; [6]Maternal Behavior with Preschoolers Q-Set.

and assistance while sorting the AQS, mothers (like any trained observer) are successful in providing descriptions of their child.

As in the first study, findings indicated that maternal sensitivity and security were significantly related (r = .55; Table 1). Thus, results from these two studies supported the notion that the sensitivity-security link holds in a culture different from the one in which the constructs are typically studied, whether observed in everyday or stressful contexts, and in two different socio-economic groups.

Importantly, we also found that mean sensitivity (and security) scores for the low SES sample were significantly lower than those of the middle-class sample. This perhaps reflects the fact that living conditions in low SES groups are not as conducive as those of middle-class groups to the provision of sensitive caregiving and the formation of secure attachment relationships. Furthermore, some aspects of maternal behavior were common and some were specific to the situation (i.e., everyday or emergency), indicating that mothers modified their behavior according to the circumstances of their children so that it likely contributed to their sense of well-being. Far from being a set of fixed attributes that mothers may display in all occasions, specific maternal sensitive behavior seems tailored to the particular situation and condition of the child. Examples of specific maternal behavior associated with infants' security at the hospital, but not at home, included molding their (sick) children to themselves when holding them, being careful to adjust their children's posture either when carrying or repositioning them in the crib or play area, displaying affection by touching, and slowing down the pace in face-to-face interactions in response to their children's signals. These behaviors, among others, show that sensitive mothers responded to their children's compromised health status by being careful in interactions that involved close physical contact and making sure that children were comfortable.

In a third study (Posada et al., 2002) using the MBQS, we posed questions concerning the cross-cultural generality of the sensitivity-security link by comparing middle-class mother–infant dyads from Denver (USA) and Bogotá (Columbia). In both samples, two 2-hour home visits per dyad were conducted to observe maternal behavior and describe it with the MBQS. In Denver infant–mother security was assessed in the lab with the SSP whereas the AQS was used to assess attachment security in Bogotá. For this purpose, two additional 2-hour home visits per family were conducted by independent assistants to observe children's attachment behavior. Findings indicated that maternal sensitivity and infant security were significantly associated in both the Denver and Bogotá samples, r = .33 and r = .46, respectively (Table 1). These two indices were not statistically different (Fisher's z for comparing correlations = .82, ns). The results support the hypothesis that the relation between quality of early care and infant security holds in diverse cultural contexts.

In sum, using repeated and relatively long periods of observation to describe mothers' sensitivity and infants' organization of secure base behavior during interactions in naturalistic contexts, we found the sensitivity-security link to be significant across cultural and socio-economic groups and in different situations.

Sensitivity here and there: an ethnographic study

Comparative research in different cultures provides an opportunity to test the universality and, at the same time, study specific adaptations of the caregiving behavioral system to different ecologies. Indeed, although patterns of behavior that result in the care of children are found in almost all humans and could be considered an element of a common plan (along with mating and attachment behavior) with an obvious survival value, both Ainsworth (1969, 1977b) and Bowlby (1969/1982) acknowledged that the cross-cultural generality of central issues in attachment theory does not exclude culture-specific manifestations.

Thus, rather than taking for granted Ainsworth's conceptualization of care, in the study described below we took a different approach by asking whether the sensitivity construct would arise inductively from ethnographic descriptions of infant–mother interactions at home in a different cultural context. Looking at the quality of maternal care through Colombian lenses (Posada, Carbonell, Alzate, & Plata, 2004), we explored what conceptualizations we could infer to characterize early maternal care in an intensive study of 30 infant–mother dyads from a middle/middle-low class background in Bogotá.

By using an open-ended, ethnographic methodology to gather culturally sensitive information (removed, as much as possible, from theoretical influences), we aimed to arrive at a more indigenous characterization of early maternal care. We then assessed whether these culturally specific characterizations of caregiving (i.e., ethnographic descriptions of maternal care) were associated with maternal sensitivity assessed with the MBQS and infant–mother security assessed with the AQS.

Infants were healthy 6 to 13 month olds from a non-clinical population of intact families. About half were girls. Most infants had one sibling. Mothers were the infant's principal caregiver. Mothers' and fathers' education ranged from incomplete high school to having a university degree. Maternal and child behavior were observed at home in a series of 2-hour home visits at 2-week intervals for a total of 16–18 hours per family for most families (Posada et al., 2004). Unstructured observations of maternal behavior were conducted during the first 4–5 home visits. Mothers were observed during their daily routines that included feeding, cleaning, tending to their babies' signals, and playing with their infants. The same observer conducted all visits for a given family (except for one dyad which had two different observers) and naturally interacted with both mother and infant. Observers were allowed to take succinct notes about behavior observed, but were instructed not to write while they were in the same room with a mother. Thus, observers wrote brief notes when mothers stepped out of the room, as they went about their routines and activities at home; alternatively, observers momentarily left the room where the mother was to write short notes. Similar to Ainsworth's procedures in Baltimore (Ainsworth et al., 1978), immediately after each visit, observers created an initial draft of what occurred in the visit. Then, they developed a detailed narrative of maternal caregiving behavior during mother–infant interactions (see Table 2 for an excerpt from ethnographic transcripts).

Undergraduate students who conducted these visits were trained by participating in a semester-long methodology seminar about ethnographic research. Following Spradley (1980) and Strauss (1987), emphasis was placed on how to conduct participant observations. During the seminar, observers were exposed to ethnographic transcripts (of a study on adolescents) and then conducted five practice visits to observe infant–mother interactions, receiving feedback about the quality of their transcripts after each practice visit.

Two independent psychology professors with no in-depth knowledge of Ainsworth's coding at the time read and analyzed the transcripts, and conducted domain analyses in consultation with an expert ethnographer. Following Strauss (1987) and Spradley's (1980) methodology, they began with "open coding" (Strauss, 1987) to identify broad themes of maternal behavior during infant–mother interactions. A second careful reading was done to refine, specify, and identify new domains and sub-domains (domain analysis, Spradley,

Table 2. Excerpt from ethnographic transcripts.

"The mother started to clean the baby's face; she wiped the baby's forehead, his hair, cleaned his ears, then meticulously cleaned his neck, back, and lastly his legs, buttocks, and genitals. She asked me to accompany the baby for a moment while she brought a cream. Mother took the dirty diaper and went to the kitchen. During the approximately 3 minutes she was in the kitchen, she was always talking to us; she offered me a glass of milk and she told the baby things like: 'and you my love? What do you want? Mommy is coming back now.' The baby remained intently watching the ceiling and occasionally he looked at me, specifically he was watching my mouth; as the mother approached the door, the baby directed his gaze towards it and when he found mommy he smiled, moved his legs and arms vigorously, if uncoordinated. The mother gave me a glass of milk and then approached the baby, bent over and kissed him in the stomach.
... When the mother finished dressing him, she picked up the clothes and other stuff from the bed; she got up and went to the kitchen with the baby's dirty clothes; the baby started to cry (his cry was brief and of low intensity), the mother returned as soon as she heard the baby's cry and approached him, leaned over his face and asked him: 'What happens bebé? Are you tired or are you hungry?' The mother sat again on the bed, picked him up, put the baby in her arms with his head on the right arm inclined in a way that the baby was almost in front of her. The mother uncovered her breast and gave it to the baby. The boy started a strong and constant suction. The mother smiled (as if she was pleased by having guessed correctly the baby's request)."

Note: Example taken from Posada et al. (2004).

1979, 1980; grounded theory, Strauss, 1987). The goal was to evaluate maternal caregiving in the Columbian sample observed by using inductively derived culture-specific categories of maternal behavior based on the information gathered.

The Columbian coders identified the following domains: promptness of response, response effectiveness, behavioral consistency, balance between responding to the baby and other demands, balance between physical caregiving and social-emotional interaction with the baby, enjoyment of interaction, interaction smoothness, frequency and quality of physical contact, and frequency and diversity of functions in maternal verbal communications. Most of these domains bear a remarkable similarity with Ainsworth's conceptualization of quality of infant care (Ainsworth et al., 1978). Thus, issues related to promptness and effectiveness of mothers' responses and participation in harmonious interactions are related to Ainsworth's definitions of sensitivity and cooperation with an infant's ongoing behavior. Further, the balance between responding to the baby and other demands, issues of balancing the physical task of caregiving and interacting socially with the baby, and enjoyment of interaction are associated with Ainsworth's constructs of accessibility and acceptance. Another behavioral domain identified in our descriptions was concerned with issues of frequency and quality of physical contact during interactions. Although not defined in the same manner, they are related to key aspects of caregiving identified by Ainsworth and concerned with close bodily contact such as duration of pick-up episodes, affectionate pick-ups, abrupt interfering pick-ups, tender careful holding, inept holding, routine holding, pick-ups and put-downs, and face-to face interactions. In addition, and unlike Ainsworth, the domains of frequency and diversity of functions in maternal verbalizations when interacting with her baby were identified as salient in our sample. Mothers varied in their use of verbalizations and degree to which they acknowledge their babies as active interlocutors. Specifically, some used language to announce, ask, explain, inform, praise, demand, set limits, reproach, and reprimand among others, while some others restricted their use of language to order, reprimand, and reproach their babies.

Table 3. Ethnographic domains and their associations with sensitivity and security.

	Sensitivity (MBQS) r	Security (AQS) r
Specific domains of early care		
1. Promptness of response	.61**	.51**
2. Response effectiveness .55**	.63**	
3. Behavioral consistency .45**	.51**	
4. Balance between responding to the baby & other demands	.51**	.33*
5. Balance between physical care & social interaction with baby	.36*	.57**
6. Enjoyment of interaction .43**	.76**	
7. Interactive smoothness .49**	.55**	
8. Frequency of physical contact	.40*	.55**
9. Quality of physical contact	.42**	.65**
10. Frequency of verbalizations	.30*	.53**
11. Diversity of functions in maternal verbalizations	.30*	.53**
Overall quality of care .47**	.61**	

Note: ** $p < .01$; * $p \leq .05$.
Content taken from Posada et al. (2004).

From each of these 11 domains, we developed 1–7-point rating scales and independent raters scored each transcript on each domain for each participant. Because the domain scores were highly inter-correlated, a total average score representing the overall quality of maternal care was calculated. Subsequently, we used the domain and total scores to evaluate their associations with the MBSQ and AQS scores. These assessments were independently obtained during four 2-hour additional home visits, two to observe maternal behavior and two to observe child behavior. Mean inter-observer reliability for both Q-sort measures was above .80. A Q-composite description was created for each mother and child by averaging the observers' descriptions.

Analyses indicated that the total (ethnographic) score for the caregiving domains was significantly associated with both the MBQS sensitivity score (r = .42) and AQS security score (r = .61). In addition, the scores for each of the 11 domain were significantly associated with the MBQS sensitivity score (rs ranged from .30–.61; Table 3). Similarly, all 11 domain scales turned out to be significantly associated with AQS security scores (rs ranged from .33–.76; Table 3).

Results show that the conceptualization of early care offered by Ainsworth in the Baltimore project emerged also "from scratch" in this ethnographic study in Columbia. The association between general quality of care (ethnographically derived) and attachment security was robust and relatively close to the one found by Ainsworth (De Wolff & van IJzendoorn, 1997).

The sensitivity-security link in early childhood

Attachment researchers (e.g., Ainsworth et al., 1974; Waters, Kondo-Ikemura, Posada, & Richters, 1991) hypothesize that the quality of caregiving remains a central factor in maintaining and shaping the organization of secure-base behavior throughout childhood. Although relatively unexplored, researchers have begun to provide evidence in support of that notion (e.g., Solomon & George, 2008; Stevenson-Hinde & Shouldice, 1995). To explore the relations between quality of care and security beyond infancy, using key notions such as sensitivity, secure base support, and harmonious interactions (Ainsworth et al., 1971) in naturalistic settings, we constructed the Maternal Behavior with Preschoolers Q-Set (MBPQS; Posada, Kaloustian, Richmond, & Moreno, 2007). The MBPQS has 90 items that describe age-relevant caregiving behavior. In developing this measure, we created a pool of items based on behavior observed or referred to by mothers of preschoolers as well as items adapted from the MBQS and the Parental Secure Base Support and Supervision Q-Set (Waters & Gao, 1998). Items were written and modified so that most of them refer to behavior in context.

The MBPQS provides an overall summary index of the quality of caregiving, i.e., maternal sensitivity and scores on age-salient domains of behavior concerned with maternal contributions to harmonious interactions with her child, provision of secure-base support, supervision, and limit setting (Posada et al., 2007). Based on Ainsworth's notion that sensitive responding to a child's communications and harmonious child–mother exchanges are at the heart of children's use of their mother as a secure base (Ainsworth et al., 1971), a subset of 20 items is specifically concerned with maternal behaviors that contribute (or not) to smooth child–mother exchanges. The items include both behavioral and affective involvement in the transactions of a mother with her child (e.g., "Mother behaves as part of a team, exchanges with child are harmonious," "Is over-controlling, intrusive, in interactions with child, e.g., provides excessive instructions, or physically re-orients child," and "When child expresses positive affect, mother joins in"). Another subset of 22 items taps secure-base phenomena. These items refer to a mother's provision of a haven of safety (i.e., maternal behavior in response to a child's returns to mother, signals of distress, or child accidents) and support of exploration (i.e., behavior regarding a child's exploration away from mother, the balance between interactions at a distance and those in close proximity, and the enhancement of a child's activities and experiences in ways that make the child feel effective and emotionally pleased with her/his transactions with the environment). Examples are "When child goes back to mother, she is unresponsive or business-like in acknowledging child's returns," "Smoothly facilitates explorations away from and returns to her," and "When child shows her something he is playing with, mom asks about it, comments positively on it, encourages child to do something with it." A third subset of eight items is concerned with supervision and/or monitoring. These items refer to a caregiver's ability to keep track of the child, anticipate problematic situations, and balance the tasks of monitoring and participating in the child's activities (e.g., "Follows or moves to a better location to supervise/monitor as child moves from place to place," "Is two steps ahead of child, anticipates conflictive situations and does something to prevent escalation," and "Balanced in her role as supervisor of and participant in child's activities"). Finally, a subset of five items taps limit setting and refers to how a mother sets rules and boundaries for her child's activities, whether she considers the child's wants and desires, and how she handles violations of those rules (e.g., "In limit setting, mother negotiates with child until a mutually satisfying solution is achieved" and "When setting rules and prohibiting an activity to child, explains reasons").

We initially used the MBPQS to describe observations of mothers' behavior during interactions with their children at home and playgrounds in two different middle-class US samples (Posada et al., 2007). In a study of 50 mother–child dyads, independent observers conducted a home (2.5 hours) and a playground (1.5 hours) visit, and described maternal and child behavior with the MBPQS and AQS. A significant but modest association between maternal sensitivity and child security at home was found ($r = .31$; Table 1). In a second study, we recruited 40 mother–child dyads. Here, we increased our observation time, conducting two 2-hour home visits, one to describe maternal behavior with the MBPQS and the other to describe child behavior with the AQS, and one 1.5-hour playground visit, where both maternal and child behavior were described with the MBPQS and AQS, respectively. Observations of both mothers and children's behavior were done by at least two independent observers. Composite scores that integrated the home and park descriptions were calculated for mothers and children. Results indicated that sensitivity and security were significantly related ($r = .49$; Table 1).

In both studies, sensitivity and security at the playground were significantly associated ($r = .39$, Study 1, and $r = .60$, Study 2, both $p < .01$); sensitivity at home was significantly associated with security at home in the first study ($r = .27$, $p < .05$), but not in the second study ($r = .09$). As far as the separate MBPQS domain scores are concerned, the "contribution to harmonious interactions" domain was significantly associated with children's security score in both studies. The more mothers' behavior contributed to smooth child–mother transactions, the more secure their children were. Thus, attachment security was directly linked to what transpired in child–mother interactions. Furthermore, significant associations between sensitive maternal support (safe haven and secure base) and child AQS security were found in the two samples. This backs the idea that concurrent maternal support is as needed at this age as it is during infancy. Appropriate and consistent support of children's explorations away from, as well as retreats to, caregivers is likely to provide children with confidence in the availability and sensitive responsiveness of their caregivers. In those daily exchanges, children construct and maintain their trust on their caregivers as a secure base.

Also, our observations indicated that issues related to supervision and monitoring and how mothers went about them were significantly related to attachment security in both studies. The evidence for how mothers went about setting limits, and whether they took the child's perspective during this type of exchanges, was mixed, however. The association between limit setting and security was significant only in the second study. This discrepancy in results demands more research on the issue.

Using the MBPQS, we have further studied the sensitivity-security link during the preschool years in three additional samples from a cultural background different from that of US middle-class samples, namely, a low SES Mexican sample of immigrants in the US (Posada, Carbonell, Kaloustian, & Lu, 2009), a middle/low class Colombian sample (Plata et al., 2012), and a middle/low class Peruvian sample (Noblega, 2012). We observed both maternal and child behavior during mother–child interactions at home and in playgrounds. The AQS was employed to describe child behavior. Results for the three samples show moderate and significant associations between the constructs studied (Mexican immigrants $r = .42$; Colombian $r = .49$; Peruvian $r = .63$; Table 1). In all three samples, the association between sensitivity and security at the park was significant (Mexican immigrants $r = .38$; Colombian $r = .31$; Peruvian $r = .45$; all $p \leq .01$). Sensitivity and security assessed at home were not significantly related in the sample of Mexican immigrants ($r = .20$), but they were in the Colombian ($r = .47$) and Peruvian ($r = .60$) samples (both $p < .01$).

In summary, use of the MBPQS to describe observations of mothers' behavior with children between 3–5 years of age in five samples from different cultural and socioeconomic backgrounds has consistently found significant associations between overall composite scores for maternal sensitivity and child security. When the security-sensitivity link is analyzed separately by setting, results indicate that the constructs are significantly related at the playground; at home, the evidence is mixed. This latter finding is line with the idea that capturing the relation between the constructs at home becomes more difficult as children mature (Solomon & George, 2008). Thus, assessments in settings other than home where both the caregiving and attachment behavioral systems are taxed may be necessary. Overall, these studies confirm that the quality of concurrent maternal care continues to play an important role in the organization of secure base behavior during early childhood. Further, they are consistent with Ainsworth's assertion that the key feature of maternal behavior associated with infant security is sensitive responding to her/his signals and communications, and the ability to establish an atmosphere of harmony and cooperation in interactions with her infant (Ainsworth et al., 1971). Our findings extend that notion to the preschool years.

Conclusion

Ainsworth delineated the caregiving construct in attachment theory through careful empirical research on infant–mother interactions during the first year of life in two different cultures. She conceptualized a model of care that focuses on the organization of caregiving behavior and coined the construct of sensitivity. These notions have been useful in our exploration of the contributions of maternal care to child–mother interactions and relationships in different ecologies.

Although much remains to be investigated about caregiving and the development of child–mother attachment relationships, we have taken some steps to answer questions concerned with key hypotheses in attachment theory. Thus, we have found support for the sensitivity-security link in diverse cultural and social contexts, and at different ages. Although encouraging, an important limitation of the studies presented is their cross-sectional assessment of sensitivity and security, even if done during several different observation periods and with different observers. As crucial as studying the phenomenon longitudinally was for Ainsworth, for it provided her with a developmental perspective on attachment relationships during infancy, we expect a longitudinal approach to be essential in research about the elaboration of those relationships beyond the first year. In doing this, we deem critical the use of a dyadic perspective and the investigation of mother–preschooler behavioral exchanges at a time where attachment relationships are consolidating.

The use of Q-methodology to describe both maternal and child behavior has provided us with a useful assessment tool. The MBQS and MBPQS allowed us to study sensitivity at the level of organization of behavior while remaining grounded on maternal specific behavior during interactions with her child. That is, the use of these Q-sets has let us go beyond global assessments of sensitivity, specify what mothers do during exchanges with their children, and conduct more nuanced analyses. Accordingly, we have been able to operationalize, reliably describe, and evaluate different aspects of care that are subsumed under summary labels such as quality of care, sensitivity, or maternal secure base support.

Relatedly, it is important to highlight our recent explorations of maternal care during early childhood. First, results support the validity of the MBPQS as it was found to be associated with security as predicted by the theory. Of course, more research is needed to revise and refine this tool, e.g., the domain concerned with setting limits may need to be modified to determine if and under what circumstances it taps on sensitive responding. Further, the MBPQS provides an age-relevant assessment of maternal behavior and it elaborates the construct of sensitivity by operationalizing some of its different manifestations during early childhood, e.g., secure base support and supervision. Here, it is important to note that although the domains we have studied are likely to be relevant in understanding the sensitivity-security link, they are by no means exhaustive of all aspects of caregiving. Lastly, initial evidence indicates that findings with US samples can be replicated with samples from different cultural contexts.

Based on the evidence presented, we consider that an ethological perspective and cross-context research on sensitivity (and secure base behavior) are important when studying caregiving and attachment relationships. Observation and description of maternal behavior in naturalistic settings are necessary, to identify common and specific characteristics of maternal care in different environments, and to test central propositions such as the sensitivity-security link in infancy and during childhood. Our ethnographic characterization of maternal caregiving behavior in a Columbian sample allowed us to examine Ainsworth' construct of sensitivity as appropriate to use in samples from different cultures. In addition to providing confirmatory evidence, it highlighted domains concerned with maternal verbalizations not typically emphasized when studying attachment relationships during infancy, but until later.

Findings reported underline the relevance of considering the immediate context and situation of the mother–child dyad. Thus, SES seems to impact mothers' ability to provide sensitive care and children's use of mother as a secure base, and maternal specific behavior during interactions varied depending on her child's condition (e.g., health). This showed that sensitivity, far from being a fixed trait-like characteristic, should be studied in consideration of a child's behavior, and the dyad's situation and ecology.

In undertaking the work presented, we have built upon invaluable insights offered by Ainsworth's conceptualizations and methods. Her exploratory excursion in Uganda and her systematic journey in Baltimore provide us with enduring lessons. Ainsworth's conceptualization of quality of care, emphasis on a broad sampling of child–caregiver interactions, use of a dyadic lens, and utilization of methodologies that tap the phenomenon under investigation in naturalistic contexts using a longitudinal perspective are important lessons to keep in mind.

Acknowledgements

Some of the ideas and data presented were supported by grants from the National Science Foundation (BCS-0645530), the Kinley Trust, and the Purdue Research Foundation. Special thanks to the families who generously offered their time, and the graduate and undergraduate students whose help has been crucial. Special thanks to Gloria Alzate, Olga Carbonell, Garene Kaloustian, Ting Lu, Amanda Moreno, Magaly Noblega, Sandra Plata, Melissa Richmond, and Jill Trumbell for their invaluable collaboration.

References

Ainsworth, M. D. S. (1964). Patterns of attachment behavior shown by the infant in interaction with his mother. *Merrill Palmer Quarterly, 10*, 51–58.

Ainsworth, M. D. S. (1967). *Infancy in Uganda: Infant care and the growth of love*. Baltimore, MD: John Hopkins University Press.

Ainsworth, M. D. S. (1969). Object relations, dependency, and attachment: A theoretical review of the infant-mother relationship. *Child Development, 40*, 969–1025.

Ainsworth, M. D. S. (1977a). Infant development and infant-mother interaction among Ganda and American families. In P. H. Leiderman, S. R. Tulkin, & A. Rosenfeld (Eds.), *Culture and infancy* (pp. 119–149). New York, NY: Academic Press.

Ainsworth, M. D. S. (1977b). Attachment theory and its utility in cross-cultural research. In P. H. Leiderman, S. R. Tulkin, & A. Rosenfeld (Eds.), *Culture and infancy* (pp. 49–67). New York, NY: Academic Press.

Ainsworth, M. D. S. (1991). Attachment and other affectional bonds across the life cycle. In C. M. Parkes, J. Stevenson-Hinde, & P. Morris (Eds.), *Attachment across the life cycle* (pp. 33–51). London: Routledge.

Ainsworth, M. D. S., Bell, S. M., & Stayton, D. F. (1971). Individual differences in strange situation behavior of one-year-olds. In H. R. Shaffer (Ed.), *The origins of human social relations* (pp. 17–57). London: Academic Press.

Ainsworth, M. D. S., Bell, S. M., & Stayton, D. F. (1974). Infant-mother attachment and social development: Socialization as a product of reciprocal responsiveness to signals. In M. P. M. Richards (Ed.), *The integration of a child into a social world* (pp. 99–135). New York, NY: Cambridge University Press.

Ainsworth, M. D. S., Blehar, M. C., Waters, E., & Wall, S. (1978). *Patterns of attachment*. Hillsdale, NJ: Erlbaum.

Ainsworth, M. D. S., & Marvin, R. S. (1995). On the shaping of attachment theory and research: An interview with Mary D. S. Ainsworth. *Caregiving, Cultural, and Cognitive Perspectives on Secure-Base Behavior and Working Models: New Growing Points of Attachment Theory and Research. Monographs of the Society for Research in Child Development, 60* (2–3), 3–21.

Ainsworth, M. D. S., & Wittig, B. A. (1969). Attachment and exploratory behavior of one- year-olds in a strange situation. In B. M. Foss (Ed.), *Determinants of infant behaviour IV* (pp. 111–136). London: Methuen.

Atkinson, L., Paglia, A., Coolbear, J., Niccols, A., Leung, E., Poulton, L., ... Chisholm, V. C. (2000). Assessing maternal sensitivity in the context of attachment security: A meta-analysis. In G. M. Tarabulsy, S. Larose, D. R. Pederson, & G. Moran (Eds.), *Attachement et développement: Le rôle des premieres relations dans le développement humain* [Attachment and development: The role of first relationships in human development] (pp. 27–56). Québec: Presses de l'Université du Québec.

Bowlby, J. (1958). The nature of the child's tie to his mother. *International Journal of Psycho-Analysis, 39*, 350–373.

Bowlby, J. (1969/1982). *Attachment and loss (Vol. I): Attachment.* New York, NY: Basic Books.

Bowlby, J. (1988). *A secure-base*. New York, NY: Basic Books Inc.

Bretherton, I. (2003). Mary Ainsworth: Insightful observer and courageous theoretician. In G. A. Kimble & M. Wertheimer (Eds.), *Portraits of pioneers in psychology* (pp. 317–331). Hillsdale, NJ: Erlbaum.

De Wolff, M. S., & van IJzendoorn, M. H. (1997). Sensitivity and attachment: A meta-analysis on parental antecedents of infant attachment. *Child Development, 68*, 571–591.

Grossmann, K., Grossmann, K. E., Spangler, G., Suess, G., & Unzner, L. (1985). Maternal sensitivity and newborns' orientation responses as related to quality of attachment in Northern Germany. *Growing Points of Attachment Theory and Research. Monographs of the Society for Research in Child Development, 50* (1–2), 233–256.

Kermoian, R., & Leiderman, P. H. (1986). Infant attachment to mother and child caretaker in an East African community. *International Journal of Behavioral Development, 9*, 455–469.

Main, M. (1999). Mary D. Salter Ainsworth: Tribute and portrait. *Psychoanalytic Inquiry, 19*, 682–730.

Moran, G., Pederson, D. R., Pettit, P., & Krupka, A. (1992). Maternal sensitivity and infant-mother attachment in a developmentally delayed sample. *Infant Behavior and Development, 15*, 427–442.

Nakagawa, M., Lamb, M. E., & Miyake, K. (1992). Antecedents and correlates of the strange situation behavior of Japanese infants. *Journal of Cross-Cultural Psychology, 23*, 300–310.

Noblega, M. (2012). *Conducta de base segura y sensibilidad en niños y madres del distrito de los Olivos* (Unpublished Dissertation, Pontificia), Universidad Católica del Peru.

Pederson, D. R., & Moran, G. (1995a). Maternal behavior Q-set. *Caregiving, Cultural, and Cognitive Perspectives on Secure-Base Behavior and Working Models: New Growing Points of Attachment Theory and Research. Monographs of the Society for Research in Child Development, 60* (2–3), 247–254.

Pederson, D. R., & Moran, G. (1995b). A categorical description of infant-mother relationships in the home and its relation to Q-sort measures of infant-mother interaction. *Caregiving, Cultural, and Cognitive Perspectives on Secure-Base Behavior and Working Models: New Growing Points of Attachment Theory and Research. Monographs of the Society for Research in Child Development, 60* (2–3), 111–132.

Pederson, D. R., Moran, G., Sitko, C., Campbell, K., Ghesquire, K., & Acton, H. (1990). Maternal sensitivity and the security of infant-mother attachment: A Q-sort study. *Child Development, 61*, 1974–1983.

Peterson, N. J., Drotar, D., Olness, K., Guay, L., & Kiziri-Mayengo, R. (2001). The relationship of maternal and child HIV infection to security of attachment among Ugandan infants. *Child Psychiatry and Human Development, 32*, 3–17.

Plata, S. J., Posada, G., Carbonell, O. A., Perez, J., Peña, P. A., Suarez, L. C., ... Villanueva, C. (2012, January). *Maternal secure base support and children's secure base behavior in Colombian preschoolers*. Paper presented at the 2nd meeting of the Iberian-American Attachment Network. Santiago, Chile.

Posada, G., Carbonell, O. A., Alzate, G., & Plata, S. J. (2004). Through Colombian lenses: Ethnographic and conventional analyses of maternal care and their associations with secure base behavior. *Developmental Psychology, 40*(*4*), 508–518.

Posada, G., Carbonell, O. A., Kaloustian, G., & Lu, T. (2009, April). *The maternal secure base support–child secure base use link in preschoolers: Findings in two different cultural groups*. Poster presented at the meeting of the Society for Research in Child Development, Denver, Colorado.

Posada, G., Gao, Y., Wu, F., Posada, R., Tascon, M., Schoelmerich, A., ... Synnevaag, B. (1995). The secure-base phenomenon across cultures: Children's behavior, mothers' preferences, and experts' concepts. In E. Waters, B. E. Vaughn, G. Posada, & K. Kondo-Ikemura (Eds.), *Caregiving, Cultural, and Cognitive Perspectives on Secure-Base Behavior and Working Models: New Growing Points of Attachment Theory and Research. Monographs of the Society for Research in Child Development, 60*(2–3), 27–48.

Posada, G., Jacobs, A., Carbonell, O. A., Alzate, G., Bustamante, M. R., & Arenas, A. (1999). Maternal care and attachment security in ordinary and emergency contexts. *Developmental Psychology, 35*, 1379–1388.

Posada, G., Jacobs, A., Richmond, M., Carbonell, O. A., Alzate, G., Bustamante, M. R., ... Quiceno, J. (2002). Maternal caregiving and infant security in two cultures. *Developmental Psychology, 38* (1), 67–78.

Posada, G., Kaloustian, G., Richmond, M. K., & Moreno, A. (2007). Maternal secure base support and preschoolers' secure base behavior in natural environments. *Attachment & Human Development, 9*, 391–411.

Posada, G., Lu, T., Trumbell, J., Kaloustian, G., Trudel, M., Plata, ... Lay, K. L. (2013). Is the secure base phenomenon evident here, there, and anywhere? A cross-cultural study of child behavior and experts' definitions. *Child Development*. doi:10.1111/cdev.12084

Posada, G., Waters, E., Pederson, D. R., Moran, G., & Vaughn, B. (2014). Mary Ainsworth, ethology, and maternal sensitivity. In E. Waters, B. E. Vaughn, & H. S. Waters (Eds.), *Measuring attachment*. New York, NY: Guilford.

Sagi, A., Lamb, M. E., Lewkowicz, K. S., Shoham, R., Dvir, R., & Estes, D. (1985). Security of infant–mother, –father, and –metapelet attachments among kibbutz-reared Israeli children. *Growing Points of Attachment Theory and Research. Monographs of the Society for Research in Child Development, 50* (1–2), 257–275.

Solomon, J., & George, C. (2008). The measurement of attachment security and related constructs in infancy and early childhood. In J. Cassidy & P. R. Shaver (Eds.), *Handbook of attachment: Theory, research, and clinical applications* (2nd ed., pp. 383–416). New York, NY: The Guilford Press.

Spradley, J. P. (1979). *The ethnographic interview*. New York, NY: Holt, Rinehart & Winston.

Spradley, J. P. (1980). *Participant observation*. New York, NY: Holt, Rinehart & Winston.

Stevenson-Hinde, J., & Shouldice, A. (1995). Maternal interactions and self-reports related to attachment classification at 4.5 years. *Child Development, 66*, 583–596.

Strauss, A. L. (1987). *Qualitative analysis for social scientists*. New York, NY: Cambridge University Press.

Teti, D. M., & McGourty, S. (1996). Using mothers versus trained observers in assessing children's secure base behavior: Theoretical and methodological considerations. *Child Development, 67*, 597–605.

van IJzendoorn, M. H., & Kroonenberg, P. M. (1988). Cross-cultural patterns of attachment: A meta-analysis of the strange situation. *Child Development, 59*, 147–156.

van IJzendoorn, M. H., & Sagi, A (2008). Cross-cultural patterns of attachment. In J. Cassidy, & P. R. Shaver (Eds.), *Handbook of attachment* (2nd ed., pp. 880–905). New York, NY: The Guilford Press.

van IJzendoorn, M. H., Vereijken, C. M., Bakermans-Kranenburg, M. J., & Riksen-Walraven, J. M. (2004). Assessing attachment security with the attachment q-sort: Meta-analytic evidence for the validity of the observer AQS. *Child Development, 75*, 1188–1213.

Waters, E. (1995). The Attachment Q-set (version 3). *Caregiving, Cultural, and Cognitive Perspectives on Secure-Base Behavior and Working Models: New Growing Points of Attachment Theory and Research. Monographs of the Society for Research in Child Development, 60* (2–3), 234–246.

Waters, E., & Cummings, E. M. (2000). A secure base from which to explore close relationships. *Child Development, 71*, 164–172.

Waters, E., & Gao, Y. (1998). *Parental secure base support and supervision Q-set.* Unpublished manuscript. Department of Psychology, State University of New York, Sony Brook.

Waters, E., Kondo-Ikemura, K., Posada, G., & Richters, J. E. (1991). Learning to love: Mechanisms and milestones. In M. R. Gunnar & L. A. Sroufe (Eds.), *Self processes and development. Minnesota symposia on child psychology* (Vol. 23, pp. 217–255). Hillsdale, NJ: Erlbaum.

White, K. A., & Feldstein, S. (1994, June). *Infants' secure base behavior as assessed by the strange situation and the Q-sorts of mothers and observers: Comparisons within and across methods.* Paper presented at the ninth International Conference on Infant Studies, Paris, France.

Individual dispositions as precursors of differences in attachment quality: why maternal sensitivity is nevertheless important

Gottfried Spangler

Friedrich-Alexander-University Erlangen-Nuremberg, Erlangen, Germany

This paper explores the interplay of maternal sensitivity (or, more generally, the quality of the caregiving social environment) and infant individual dispositions in predicting infant–mother attachment. After a brief theoretical introduction, the focus turns to studies conducted during the 1980s that predicted attachment security vs. insecurity at 12 months from newborns' ability to regulate orientation and arousal. A re-analysis of two longitudinal studies, formerly coded only with the ABC system, subsequently revealed that disorganized (vs. organized) attachment was predictable from newborns' regulatory abilities, whereas secure (vs. insecure) attachment was predictable from the quality of maternal care. This suggested that the two dichotomies represented distinct dimensions and that – in low risk samples – disorganized SSP behavior may be associated with infant behavioral dispositions. More recent attempts to predict disorganized attachment from infant genetic (as opposed to newborn behavioral) dispositions yielded inconsistent results when only main effects models were examined. A set of subsequent studies examining the interplay of genetic and caregiving influences in the prediction of disorganized attachment suggested that maternal sensitivity is of particular importance in cases of genetic risk.

> Whatever role may be played by the baby's constitutional characteristics, it seems quite clear that the mother's contribution to the interaction and the baby's contributions are caught up in an interacting spiral. It is because of these spiral effects – some vicious and some virtuous – that the variables are so confounded that it is not possible to distinguish independent from dependent variables. (Ainsworth & Bell, 1969, p. 160)

This quote very aptly addresses the central theme of this paper: the interplay between the quality of maternal care and infants' individual dispositions in predicting developing infant–mother attachment patterns. After a brief introductory discussion of attachment and maternal sensitivity as relational constructs, findings documenting associations between newborns' regulatory abilities and secure attachment at 12 months are reviewed and reasons suggested why infant dispositional characteristics should be more systematically studied. A re-analysis of two longitudinal studies is then presented that became possible after the early 1990s when the D-classification for SSP behavior had been identified and video-records, previously coded only for the traditional ABC groups, could be examined for D-criteria. Two dichotomous variables based on SSP classifications (security vs. insecurity and disorganization vs. organization) were related to different antecedents. Subsequent efforts to predict disorganized attachment from gene variants or polymorphisms (rather than from newborn behavioral characteristics) yielded inconsistent findings as long as only main effects were analyzed. However, several subsequent investigations – including one by the author – revealed various ways in which genes and caregiving can interact or co-act in predicting the disorganized attachment. The final section focuses on a discussion of hypothesized relational and individual pathways in the development of disorganized attachment and considers the findings in light of Belsky and Pluess' (2009) model of differential (infant) susceptibility to environmental influences.

Caregiver sensitivity and quality of attachment: theoretical background

Attachment, conceived as an emotional tie between infant and caregiver (Ainsworth, Blehar, Waters, & Wall, 1978; Bowlby, 1969), is, by definition, a relational construct. Bowlby (1988) described the parental caregiving system and the child's attachment behavioral system as two biologically rooted, complementary systems. According to this view, both caregiver and child characteristics play a role in shaping the developing attachment relationship.

Ainsworth (1979, p. 42) similarly maintained that infants are pre-adapted to their social environment and that one important feature of this environment is a mother-figure who is responsive to the infant's behavioral cues. Although infants will become attached to an insensitive, even maltreating, mother-figure or primary caregiver, the developing attachment under these circumstances will be insecure. Ainsworth particularly stressed the importance of caregivers' psychological availability and sensitive responsiveness in the development of a secure versus insecure attachment. Sensitive parents are able to perceive and interpret their infants' idiosyncratic signals and to respond to them promptly and appropriately (Ainsworth et al., 1978). Because sensitive parents gear their behavior to differences in the frequency and intensity with which individual infants express their needs, caregiver sensitivity, as conceptualized by Ainsworth, should be regarded as a relational construct.

In addition to physical protection, a related caregiving function is physiological and emotion regulation of the infant (Cassidy, 1994). To the extent that the caregiver is able to support the infant's state-, arousal- and affect-regulation (e.g., by alleviating distress through comforting), the infant will build up positive expectations about the caregiver's emotional availability and eventually develop more or less adaptive autonomous regulatory strategies. Sroufe (1979) addressed this point in his theoretical model of development wherein he proposed age-appropriate developmental tasks for both the child and the caregiver. Relevant here, during the first year Sroufe saw it as the parent's main task to provide external regulation and support for infant physiological and emotional functioning, and to serve as a secure base for the child's exploration and autonomy.

Caregiver sensitivity and attachment quality: empirical evidence

Mary Ainsworth and her colleagues (Ainsworth, Bell, & Stayton, 1971; Ainsworth et al., 1978) were the first to report that maternal sensitivity was a predictor of infant–mother attachment security. They showed that infants, classified as secure in the Strange Situation Procedure (SSP) at 12 months, had mothers who were rated as highly sensitive on the basis of lengthy home observations in the last quarter of the first year. In contrast, mothers whose caregiving behavior was judged to be insensitive had infants classified as avoidant or resistant in the SSP.

These findings from Ainsworth's Baltimore study were partially replicated in Germany by Klaus Grossmann's group in their Bielefeld Longitudinal Study, whose first year phase was modeled closely on methods employed in Baltimore (Grossmann, Grossmann, Spangler, Suess, & Unzner, 1985). In the Bielefeld study, secure attachment at 12 months was significantly correlated with maternal sensitivity ratings of 2-hour home visits at 3 and 6 months, although, unexpectedly, not at 9 months.

Results from the Bielefeld study, along with findings from 65 other studies, were later included in a meta-analysis by De Wolff and van IJzendoorn (1997). Their overall analysis confirmed the expected associations between various global measures of maternal sensitivity and infant attachment security, but the obtained effect sizes, although significant, were more modest than those reported by Ainsworth. Furthermore, effect sizes were not significantly larger when only studies using the original Ainsworth Sensitivity Scale (Ainsworth & Bell, 1974) were taken into account.

Commenting on these findings, Belsky and Fearon (2008, p. 304) suggested that other characteristics of parental behavior, as well as infant emotional dispositions, may moderate the influence of sensitivity on attachment security and thus explain what they called the "moderator gap."

Early research on infant individual dispositions, maternal sensitivity and attachment quality

Although attachment researchers initially focused almost exclusively on the role of maternal sensitivity in the development of attachment security, a small number of studies conducted during the 1980s (e.g., Grossmann et al., 1985; Waters, Vaughn, & Egeland, 1980) showed that measures of newborn behavioral organization (i.e., orientating ability and irritability) predicted infant–mother attachment security at the end of the first year. Reviewing this and other empirical evidence, Sroufe (1985) persuasively argued for a distinction between attachment and temperament as orthogonal constructs. He assumed that temperament may (at most) explain differences between insecure avoidant and resistant categories or differences within the attachment subgroups (B1 versus B4). In their review, Vaughn, Bost, and van IJzendoorn (2008) likewise considered temperament and attachment to be separate domains that contribute to infants' interpersonal and intrapersonal developmental adaptation, either as direct effects or as products of their (statistical) interaction with caregiver sensitivity.

A possible reason why attachment researchers became less keen to include the assessment of individual dispositions in their studies was that some developmental psychologists attempted to explain infant attachment patterns as due to infant temperament (e.g., Kagan, 1982). There may, however, be a number of different ways in which temperament and attachment quality can interact. For example, an irritable infant may learn effective regulation strategies within a sensitive caregiving environment and, as a result, *not* develop an insecure attachment (e.g., Washington, Minde, & Goldberg, 1986). Alternatively, individual differences in early regulatory capacities may not have the same effect on the developmental process of attachment formation in all children (see Belsky, 1997). For some children, a midrange of maternal sensitivity may be "good enough," while others may need a highly sensitive parent to develop a secure attachment. In addition, temperament dispositions may influence the quality of attachment by affecting maternal sensitivity. For example, the intensity of a difficult infant's demands may overtax a mother's ability to provide sensitive care, ultimately fostering an insecure attachment relationship (Ainsworth, 1979).

Attachment security and disorganization as distinct dimensions

The categorical SSP designation "organized" was first applied to the traditional ABC classifications by Main (1990) to distinguish them as a group from the *disorganized* (D) form of infant–mother attachment that she and Solomon (1990) had identified and defined. As a potential explanation of caregiving qualities associated with the disorganized/disoriented behavior shown by infants in the SSP, Main and Hesse (1990) posited frightening or frightened (FR) maternal behaviors that could be traced to the mothers' unresolved traumatic experiences. FR behaviors were, indeed, subsequently observed in mothers of disorganized infants, either during home observations (Schuengel, Bakermans-Kranenburg, & van IJzendoorn, 1999) or in the SSP itself (e.g., Goldberg, Benoit, Blokland, & Madigan, 2003). The latter study used a broader combined assessment of disturbed and FR behaviors Lyons-Ruth, Bronfman, and Parsons (1999) had developed for a study of high-risk families (the Atypical Maternal Behavior Instrument for Assessment and Classification or AMBIANCE). Lyons-Ruth and others had found infant disorganization to be disproportionately frequent in high-risk samples and to be predictable from hostile-intrusive maternal behavior and communication errors assessed with AMBIANCE (e.g., Barnett et al., 1999; Lyons-Ruth et al., 1999; Lyons-Ruth & Jacobvitz, 1999; Madigan, Moran, & Pederson, 2006; for a review from the FR perspective, see Hesse & Main, 2006).

Yet, surprisingly few studies with non-risk samples have reported associations between infant attachment disorganization and low maternal sensitivity ratings (Moran, Forbes, Evans, Tarabulsy, & Madigan, 2008; van IJzendoorn, Schuengel, & Bakermans-Kranenburg, 1999). This suggests either that maternal behaviors contributing to attachment disorganization may have aversive characteristics not included in traditional definitions of insensitivity or, as considered below, that there may be a dispositional – in addition to or instead of – a relational explanation for attachment disorganization.

A complication that will become relevant in the presentation of the re-analysis of the Bielefeld and Regensburg Studies (presented below) is that infants' classified as disorganized in the SSP are given a secondary "organized" designation, if an underlying secure, avoidant or resistant strategy can be discerned. Disorganized infants assigned these secondary avoidant or resistant classifications are referred to as "force-classified."

Re-analysis of the Bielefeld and Regensburg studies

At the beginning of the 1990s, studies evaluating the quality of maternal care given to infants with the newly identified "D" classification had not yet been conducted. However, it was possible to reanalyze the still existing SSP videotapes from the Bielefeld Longitudinal study (Grossmann et al., 1985) and the Regensburg Longitudinal Study III and code them for D-characteristics (e.g., Spangler & Grossmann, 1993). Also important, both longitudinal studies included newborn assessments of arousal regulation and ratings of observed maternal sensitivity during the first year.

To increase the number of subjects and the statistical power, the two samples were combined. The aim was to examine newborn behavioral organization and maternal sensitivity as predictors of two dichotomous SSP variables at 12 months: (1) attachment security versus insecurity and (2) organized versus disorganized attachment. With respect to (1), all infants classified as secure or force-classified as D-secure were compared with all infants traditionally or force-classified as avoidant or resistant. With respect to (2), all infants with any D-classification were compared to all infants assigned to the traditional secure, avoidant or resistant groups (the "organized" group).

Separate analyses with the two dichotomies yielded quite different results (Spangler, Fremmer-Bombik, & Grossmann, 1996), suggesting that security and disorganization may represent two distinct dimensions. Confirming the importance of maternal sensitivity for attachment security, mothers of secure infants had significantly higher sensitivity ratings than mothers of insecure infants, but mothers of disorganized and organized infants did not differ in sensitivity. In contrast, the newborns' reduced ability to regulate arousal or behavior predicted disorganized attachment at 12 months, but secure and insecure infants did not differ in newborn regulation ability. These findings agree with other empirical research, and are further corroborated by the Grossmanns' Regensburg Longitudinal Study I in which significant associations between infant attachment disorganization were reported in relation to mother and father (Spangler & Grossmann, 1999).

Given the association of infant security with maternal sensitivity, we interpreted the security variable as a relational component of the SSP classifications. In contrast, because disorganized SSP classifications in our low-risk sample were associated with poorer newborn behavioral regulation, we interpreted the disorganization variable as a dispositional or individual variable. This conclusion agrees with findings by Goldberg and colleagues (2003) that mothers of disorganized and organized infants did not differ in terms of fearful or intrusive behaviors. Goldberg et al. (2003) surmised that, under some conditions, infant and contextual factors might contribute to the development of attachment disorganization. Additional studies indicated that neurological impairment can produce behavioral characteristics that resembled attachment disorganization (Pipp-Siegel, Siegel, & Dean, 1999), supporting our hypothesis.

We are not making the claim that attachment disorganization is *always* related to individual child factors, only that there may be different pathways to the development of a disorganized attachment pattern. Particularly in high risk families, in which disturbed parental behavior is likely to occur more frequently, infants may become disorganized as a result of experiences with an attachment figure who exhibits FR, atypical, hostile or maltreating behaviors. In low-risk families, in which these disturbed behaviors are likely to be less frequent, infants may exhibit disorganized behaviors during the SSP because of difficulties in behavioral organization from birth onward.

Prediction of quality of attachment by genetic dispositions

We turn, now, to studies in which infant individual dispositions were assessed by the presence/absence of gene variants or polymorphisms with known involvement in various aspects of social-emotional regulation (e.g., Ebstein, 2006) and that have, therefore, been considered relevant in the study of attachment processes.

The most important gene candidates used in these studies were:

- DRD4 (*the dopamine receptor D4 gene*) and –521 C/T SNP (*a single nucleotide polymorphism in the regulatory region of the DRD4 gene*), genetic markers of the dopaminergic system, and COMT (the *catechol-O-methyltransferase gene*) involved in the inactivation of dopamine (and other catecholamines). These genetic markers and regulators of the dopaminergic system are involved in attentional, motivational and reward mechanisms and associated with negative emotionality and stress reactivity (Diamond, 2001);

- 5-HTTLPR (*a linked polymorphic region of the 5-hydroxytriptamine or serotonin transporter gene*). This genetic marker of the serotoninergic system is linked to emotional reactivity and regulation, specifically with respect to fear, anxiety, impulsiveness and aggressivity (e.g., Carver & Miller, 2006; Caspi et al., 2003; Lesch et al., 1996);
- OXTR (*Oxytocin receptor gene*). This genetic marker of the oxytonergic system is involved in social and parenting behavior (Bakermans-Kranenburg & van IJzendoorn, 2008);
- GR (*glucocorticoid receptor gene*) and MR (*mineralocorticoid receptor gene*). These two genes are involved in regulating stress, specifically in the hypothalamic-pituitary-adrenal or HPA axis (e.g., DeRijk & De Kloet, 2008).

In their pioneering study of a Hungarian low-risk sample, Lakatos and colleagues (2000) reported a significant association between attachment disorganization and gene markers of the dopaminergic system. Specifically, the 7-repeat allele of the dopamine receptor D4 gene (DRD4) was significantly more frequent in disorganized than organized infants. Later findings indicated involvement in D-attachment of a polymorphism of the –521 C/T single nucleotide in the regulatory region of the DRD4 gene (Lakatos et al., 2002). These positive findings were, however, soon followed by studies with negative or mixed results.

The first replication attempt in a Dutch Twin study failed (Bakermans-Kranenburg & van IJzendoorn, 2004), nor were these results replicated in our German sample (Spangler, Johann, Ronai, & Zimmermann, 2009). Instead, we found that infants carrying one or two short alleles of the serotonin transporter polymorphism 5-HTTLPR were significantly more likely to be classified as disorganized than those with two long alleles. Importantly, these polymorphisms were not associated with the secure-insecure attachment dichotomy.

Frigerio and colleagues (2009) studied a number of different genetic markers and infant attachment as predictors of infant biochemical stress responses (also assessed during the SSP). In that context, they also checked on the association of attachment with several genetic markers, finding none for the 5-HTTLPR, DRD4, COMT or GABRA6 (*Gamma-Aminobutyric Acid Receptor Subunit Alpha-6 gene,* involved in inhibitory processes).The only significant association involved the –521 C/T single nucleotide polymorphism of the serotonin transporter gene (5-HHT). Infants classified as avoidant had a higher proportion of T-alleles whereas infants classified as ambivalent had a higher proportion of C-alleles.

Finally, Luijk, Roisman, et al. (2011) combined two very large samples (the Dutch Generation-R sample and the sample of the NICHD Study of Early Child Care and Youth Development) to analyze effects of DRD4, DRD2, COMT, 5-HTT and OXTR on attachment disorganization and security. None of the genes tested predicted SSP security ratings, but there was one significant effect for disorganization with respect to the COMT gene. Infants with the Val/Met alleles (i.e., heterozygous) received significantly higher disorganization ratings, and the effect was independently found in both samples.

Taken together, the findings reported in this section suggest two theoretically important points. First, that there is no systematic indication of genetic effects when a security-insecurity dichotomy or a security scale is used. This fits well with the theoretically and empirically founded notion of attachment as a relational construct. Second, indications of a genetic basis for the disorganization (classifications or ratings) are inconsistent. Although genetic associations were identified in some studies, the findings often included different gene candidates and could not be systematically replicated.

The possibility that inconsistent findings may be due to methodological problems can, of course, not be ruled out, because the studies used different designs and assessment methods and are, thus, only partially comparable. On the attachment side, while some studies employed the SSP attachment categories (e.g., Lakatos et al., 2000) others used SSP rating scales (e.g., Luijk, Roisman, et al., 2011). Moreover, although the latter study was composed of two large samples, giving it more statistical power, the pre-separation and the separation episodes of the SSP for the Generation- R sample were each shortened by 1 minute. On the genetic side, the inconsistent findings may be due to the fact that only main-effects models were analyzed. Testing for interactions of genetic dispositions and caregiving quality in the prediction of attachment may provide better explanations. This topic is discussed in the next section.

The interplay of genetic dispositions and caregiving quality in the prediction of quality of attachment

Based on the concept of multi-causality (Cicchetti & Rogosch, 1996), different developmental pathways to the same phenotypic attachment outcomes may be assumed. In this section, studies examining possible gene × caregiving interactions in the prediction of attachment qualities are reviewed, beginning with a study by the author. All studies in the first set included the serotonin transporter polymorphism 5-HTTLPR, whereas findings in the second set were based on a variety of other gene-markers.

Studies using the serotonin transporter gene polymorphism 5-HTTLPR

Findings from the Regensburg Longitudinal sample IV

Spangler and colleagues (1996) hypothesized that, in low-risk samples, a genetic (dispositional) pathway may influence the development of regulatory capacities, present from birth, and explain subsequent disorganized behavior in the SSP. In high-risk samples, by contrast, in which atypical maternal behaviors may be more common and more severe, maternal caregiving qualities (insensitivity) may explain the high proportion of disorganized infants. In accord with this assumption, Cicchetti, Rogosch and Toth (2011) found high rates of disorganized attachment but no genetic contributions by 5-HTTPLR and DRD4 polymorphism to attachment disorganization in a sample of maltreated infants from low-income families, neither was the effectiveness of their intervention programs correlated with infant genetic risk. In contrast, among the comparison group of nonmaltreated infants, *5-HTTLPR* and *DRD4* polymorphisms predicted attachment security and disorganization at age 2. At that age 75% of securely attached infants in the nonmaltreated comparison group carried two long 5-HTTLPR alleles, suggesting that this genotype may have conferred protection against developing insecure or disorganized attachment.

Rather than positing separate dispositional and experiential pathways that may operate in parallel, Spangler et al. (2009) hypothesized that genetic dispositions and experience may interact through the interplay of underlying behavioral and biological systems or by one system moderating the effect of the other. The interplay between attachment security, disorganization and biological regulatory systems has been repeatedly demonstrated (e.g., Nachmias, Gunnar, Mangelsdorf, & Parritz, 1996; Spangler & Grossmann, 1993; Spangler & Schieche, 1998). More studies including both genetic and environmental measures may thus help to show whether dispositional risk factors are moderated by caregiver behavior (Moffitt, Caspi, & Rutter, 2006).

Toward this aim, Spangler and colleagues investigated gene × environment interactions in the prediction of security and disorganization in the Regensburg Longitudinal Study IV. The sample consisted of 106 low-risk infants (53 girls) from a fairly wide range of lower to upper middle class families. Attachment security and disorganization were assessed with the SSP at 12 months. After the SSP, infants and mothers were observed in a free play session during which mothers were asked to fill out a questionnaire but were free to respond to the infant as they normally would. The quality of observed maternal behavior during the play session was assessed with the Ainsworth Sensitivity-Insensitivity scale, supplemented by two subscales that focused on specific components of maternal sensitivity as laid out in the Ainsworth scale (Ainsworth & Bell, 1974). The two subscales assessed Maternal Responsiveness (describing maternal perception of and prompt response to infant signals) and Maternal Regulatory Quality (appropriateness and sustained maternal regulation of infant behavior). In a follow-up assessment at 12 years of age, cheek cells were collected for genetic analyses from 96 of the original 106 participant children, and tested for two candidates from the dopaminergic system (DRD4, –521 C/T) and from the serotonergic system (the long and short 5-HTTLPR alleles).

Disorganized vs. organized attachment was unrelated to the DRD4 and the –521 C/T single nucleotide polymorphisms, but it was significantly predicted by the 5-HTTLPR genotype, linear χ^2 (2, N = 96) = 6.57, p = .02. Among infants with two long alleles (11.4%), the proportion of disorganized infants was very low, but it doubled in infants with one short allele and increased almost fourfold among those with two short alleles (see Table 1).

After ruling out passive gene-environment associations (there were no correlations between maternal sensitivity ratings and infant genotypes), Spangler and colleagues investigated whether the genetic effects on disorganization were moderated by the quality of maternal caregiving, thus qualifying the genetic main effect. An ANOVA revealed a significant interaction of maternal responsiveness (low vs. high) with variations in the 5-HTTLPR allele (long-long, short-long, short-short) in the prediction attachment disorganization status, F(2,89) = 3.58, p = .03. Post hoc inspection of the distributions of attachment disorganization showed that the proportion of D-infants was low and independent of the 5-HTTLPR genotype when the infant had a highly responsive mother (see Table 1). However, the proportion of D-classifications increased markedly with the number of short alleles if infants had experienced low maternal sensitivity. No gene × caregiving interaction effects were found for the two additional maternal scales (Regulation Quality and the global scale).

Table 1. Proportion of infants classified as disorganized by 5-HTTLPR alleles and maternal responsiveness.

	Serotonin transporter polymorphisms (5-HTTLPR)*		
Sample (N = 95)	ll	Ls	Ss
Total	.09	.26	.42
Low maternal responsiveness	.00	.29	.67
High maternal responsiveness	.15	.22	.20

Notes: ll = two long alleles; ls = one long and one short allele;
ss = two short alleles.
*Hydroxy Tryptamine Transporter Linked Polymorphic Region.

In sum, in the Regensburg sample IV, the presence of short variants of the 5-HTTLPR allele predicted attachment disorganization, but only in children whose mothers received low ratings for sensitive responsiveness. In contrast, and in accord with theoretical expectations, none of the gene-candidates included in the study predicted secure versus insecure attachment, nor were there gene × caregiving interactions in the prediction of attachment security vs. insecurity.

These findings confirm that infant's individual dispositions, assessed by a gene-marker, can affect the development of attachment disorganization (Spangler et al., 1996). One possible developmental pathway would lead from difficulties in arousal and attention regulation, already found in the newborn, to disorganized behavior at 12 months in a stressful situation such as the SSP. The poorer orientation ability and high negative emotionality found in newborns carrying two short 5-HTTLPR alleles (e.g., Ebstein et al., 1998) supports this perspective.

Additional findings

The 5-HTTLPR genotype has been included in several other studies examining the interplay of genes, caregiving, behavior regulation and attachment. Barry, Kochanska, and Philibert (2008) found that insecure infant–mother attachment was predicted by low maternal responsiveness, but only in infants carrying a short 5-HTTPLR allele. The authors interpreted this finding as an indicator that infants with a short allele (hetero- or homozygous) were more vulnerable to disorganization. At first sight, their result suggests a gene × caregiving interaction in predicting attachment security, but unfortunately they had combined insecurely attached and disorganized infants into one group. However, a closer look at their data revealed that all disorganized infants were carriers of one or two short 5-HTTLPR alleles.

In a related follow-up study of the same sample, Kochanska, Philibert, and Barry (2009) found an interaction of genetic risk with attachment quality in the prediction of self-regulation. Children who were insecurely attached at 15 months and were carriers of a short 5-HTTPLR allele had poor deliberate self-regulation as preschoolers. In contrast, children with a short allele and secure attachment were indistinguishable from secure children with two long alleles. The authors interpreted their findings as a demonstration that secure attachment may serve as a protective factor in the presence of risk conferred by a genotype.

The protective role of two long 5-HTTLPR alleles in the context of insensitive care has also been shown in a recent, albeit quite small, study by Bakermans-Kranenburg, Dobrova-Krol, and van IJzendoorn (2012). Ukrainian preschool children raised in institutions and seen in a modified SSP with their favorite caregiver were more often disorganized than family-raised children seen with a parent, but only when they had at least one short 5-HTTLPR allele. Children with two long alleles seemed to be somewhat protected against disorganization, even in an adverse caregiving environment. Gene × environment effects in this study were also tested with respect to symptoms of attachment disorder and indiscriminate friendliness, with no significant results. This contrasts with the Budapest Early Intervention project where an effect of early institutional care on indiscriminant friendliness was detected, but only in children with at least one short 5-HTTLPR allele (Drury et al., 2012). The latter two studies did not investigate differences in maternal sensitivity within the normal range of low-risk samples. Instead, they focused on gene × caregiving interactions by comparing low and high risk environments.

In another recent study based on data from the Minnesota Longitudinal study, Raby et al. (2012) investigated the 5-HTTLPR polymorphism and maternal responsivity as predictors of emotional reactivity and security in the SSP at 12 months and 18 months (only the 12 months findings are reviewed here). A distress reactivity variable was created by grouping children by their tendency to become distressed during the SSP. Insecure-avoidant A1 and A2 infants and secure B1 and B2 infants were placed in a low reactivity group while secure B3 and B4 infants and ambivalent C1 and C2 infants were assigned to a high reactivity group (known as the "Belsky-split," see Belsky & Rovine, 1987). The authors found that one or two short alleles of the 5-HTTLPR genotype predicted high emotional reactivity in the SSP, whereas two long alleles predicted low reactivity. No genetic effect was found for the secure-insecure dichotomy which was, instead, correlated with sensitive maternal responsiveness. Rather than a gene × caregiving interaction, these findings indicated the co-action of a genetic disposition and caregiving quality in the prediction of attachment security. Raby and colleagues (2012) concluded that sensitive-responsive maternal care affects the infant's ability to rely on the mother for emotion regulation. However, the correlation of SSP reactivity and the short 5-HTLLR was not replicated in a recent analysis of the NICHD SECCYD sample (Roisman, Booth-Laforce, Belsky, Burt, & Groh, 2013).

The protective function of two long 5-HTTLPR alleles regarding emotional regulation has, incidentally, also been noted in developmental studies unrelated to attachment. It was shown, for example, by Caspi and colleagues (2003) who assessed the influence of stressful life events on the development of depression. Additionally, in a nonhuman primate study, Barr et al. (2003) reported that peer-reared rhesus macaques carrying the short serotonin transporter allele had difficulties with emotional regulation compared to mother-reared primates.

Gene × caregiving interactions in studies using other gene candidates

Gene × caregiving interactions with respect to attachment disorganization have also been reported for a dopaminergic gene candidate. van IJzendoorn and Bakermans-Kranenburg (2006) examined infant genetic characteristics, unresolved maternal trauma assessed with the AAI (distal predictor) and maternal FR behavior (proximal predictor) as predictors of attachment disorganization. They found that infants of unresolved mothers were more likely to be classified as disorganized, but only if they carried the DRD4 7-repeat allele. A similar moderating effect was, however, not seen for FR behavior.

These findings contrast with a report by Gervai and colleagues (2007) who combined a Hungarian low-risk and a US high-risk sample to examine the interplay of DRD4 polymorphisms and disrupted forms of maternal affective communication in the prediction of disorganized attachment. A main effect of maternal disrupted communication on infant disorganization emerged independently in both of these samples, but further examination showed that the association held only for the majority of infants who carried the short DRD4 allele. Among carriers of the (long) 7-repeat DRD4 allele, there was no relation between atypical maternal behavior and infant disorganization, and this effect was independent of degree of social risk and maternal DRD4 genotype. The authors speculated that functional variations in the DRD4 gene, expressed preferentially in brain regions of the reward circuit, might modulate *infant* sensitivity to variations in maternal caregiving behavior.

The two studies with the DRD4 polymorphism produced somewhat inconsistent results although both pointed to a moderating role of the DRD4 polymorphism. In the van IJzendoorn and Bakermans-Kranenburg (2006) study, the 7-repeat allele was associated with a higher susceptibility to (distal) maternal influences represented by unresolved maternal AAI status, but not with the (proximal) influences represented by maternal FR behavior. In the Gervai et al. (2007) study, maternal disruptive communication (severe insensitivity assessed with AMBIANCE) was predictive of disorganization in infants who were carriers of the short DRD4 allele.

Only one study (Luijk, Tharner, et al., 2011) has reported an interaction between maternal sensitivity and the MR gene-marker which is involved in stress reactivity. Using data from the Dutch Generation-R study, the authors found no genetic main effect, but infants carrying the minor MR allele (G) were rated as *more* secure during the SSP if their mothers' caregiving was sensitive-responsive (assessed with the Ainsworth sensitivity and cooperation scales in one context). Infants with this allele were rated *less* secure if their mothers showed extremely *insensitive* behaviors (assessed in a second context with a measure of Disconnected and Extremely Insensitive Parenting or DIP, developed by Out, Bakermans-Kranenburg, & van IJzendoorn, 2009). Luijk and colleagues speculate that infants with the G allele of the MR gene are faster and better processors of information related to maternal responsiveness in stressful circumstances and might therefore be more susceptible to the effects of both positive care (sensitive responsiveness) and negative care (extreme insensitivity). They suggest that this issue should be examined in future biochemical and behavioral studies.

Concluding remarks

As shown earlier in the history of intelligence research (Anastasi, 1958), in the study of parental care and individual dispositions it is more productive to ask questions regarding the *interplay* of caregiving and dispositional influences on the development of attachment than to search for their separate main effects (Rutter, 2003). The G × E studies that relate gene-markers involved in the regulation of emotion, arousal and motivation to different attachment patterns are important first steps toward describing and understanding this interplay. Although the effect sizes associated with these studies tend to be modest and are not always consistent, they nevertheless suggest some systematic trends.

Pathways to disorganization

The overall pattern of findings reviewed here supports the notion of (at least) two possible pathways in the development of attachment disorganization. One pathway, more often seen in studies of high-risk families, is related to mothers' or other primary caregivers' atypical or disturbed behaviors and communication (e.g., Beebe et al., 2010; Lyons-Ruth et al., 1999; Main & Hesse, 1990). The caregiver behavior captured by these measures goes far beyond simple insensitivity and seems to strongly compromise infants' ability to develop organized strategies of attachment behavior.

A second developmental pathway to disorganized attachment that seems to be more typical for low-risk infants starts with an individual (behavioral or genetic) disposition. Strong empirical arguments for this position can be found in genetic studies reported above, but have also been provided on the behavioral level by Spangler et al. (1996). They showed that low newborn orientation and state regulation, but not low maternal sensitivity, predicted infant–mother attachment disorganization. Such regulatory problems at birth are, of course, not necessarily due to genetic dispositions, but could be caused by maternal stress during pregnancy, as shown in a nonhuman primate study by Schneider and Coe

(1993). However, whether related to genetic or environmental causes, general difficulties in orienting, state and emotion regulation are likely to interfere with infant–caregiver interactions and – by affecting the caregiver – could constitute a risk factor for the development of attachment disorganization.

Disposition × caregiving interactions

The findings reviewed here suggest that: (1) a dispositional or genetic risk for the development of attachment disorganization may be realized or exacerbated in an environment of insensitive or adverse care, (2) sensitive caregiving can serve as a protective factor against this risk, and (3) some genetic dispositions act as protective factors in adverse caregiving environments. Several studies reviewed here showed that homozygosity for the long 5-HTTLPR alleles seemed to shield infants against developing a disorganized attachment, even under adverse circumstances. In contrast, hetero- or homozygosity for the short allele conferred a risk for disorganized attachment, but this risk was unrealized in the context of experiencing sensitive care, a finding that several authors interpreted as evidence for infants' sensitivity to maternal sensitivity.

Based on a thorough review of research on attachment disorganization, Bernier and Meins' (2008) proposed an explanatory model wherein the threshold at which caregiving behavior has an impact on the development of attachment disorganization varies for different infants. The putative threshold is heightened or lowered, depending on each infant's characteristics (genes, behavior regulation) and social context. In Bernier and Meins' view, this individualized threshold determines an infants' vulnerability or resilience in the face of atypical or highly insensitive care by an attachment figure.

Going further, and illustrating their arguments with re-analyses of extant findings, Belsky and Pluess (2009) proposed that specific genes may not so much function as "vulnerability factors" but as "plasticity factors." That is, not only may some individuals be genetically more susceptible to the negative effects of adversity, but the very same individuals may, in the context of experiencing sensitive and appropriate care by their attachment figure, manifest particularly beneficial effects. This provocative notion deserves study in an attachment context.

There is, as yet, no evidence that infants carrying genes that confer a risk for disorganized attachment in the context of caregiver insensitivity also reap disproportionately greater benefits when experiencing sensitive care. Nevertheless, the findings *are* suggestive of differential susceptibility to variations in care. The gene × caregiving effects reviewed above support the view that sensitive and responsive caregiving may help genetically at-risk infants to improve their ability to regulate and organize their behavior within the attachment relationship. Maternal sensitivity is particularly important for such infants because it can counteract and even eliminate the effect of potentially deleterious individual dispositions, which has been convincingly shown with respect to attachment security by van den Boom (1994) in her intervention study with irritable infants. In a sense this was anticipated by Mary Ainsworth more than 30 years ago in her 1979 article (1979, p. 42) in which she addressed the geneticists' notion of "phenotypical buffering" of genetic variation and emphasized the role of maternal behavior to accomplish such buffering.

Acknowledgements

This research was supported by the Köhler-Stiftung (Munich, Germany), the German Research Foundation (SP 312/16-1 and ZI 511/13-1) and the Department of Developmental Psychology at the

University of Regensburg (Prof. Dr. Klaus Grossmann). I want to thank Klaus and Karin Grossmann for their valuable advice and enduring extraordinary support for my research, Fabienne Becker-Stoll, Elisabeth, Fremmer-Bombik, Ursula Ilg, Klaudia Kramer, Iris Rainer, Michael Schieche and Peter Zimmermann for their support in data assessment and psychological data analyses, and Monika Johann and Zolt Ronai for conducting genetic analyses. Also I need to acknowledge a special tribute to the families who made these studies possible. Finally, I want to underline my special gratitude to Inge Bretherton for her challenging and valuable comments to former versions of the paper.

Funding

This research was supported by the Köhler-Stiftung (Munich, Germany), the German Research Foundation [SP 312/16-1 and ZI 511/13-1].

References

Ainsworth, M. D. S. (1979). Attachment as related to mother-infant interaction. *Advances in the Study of Behaviour, 9*, 2–52.

Ainsworth, M. D. S., & Bell, S. M. (1969). Some contemporary patterns of mother-infant interaction in the feeding situation. In A. Ambrose (Ed.), *Stimulation in early infancy* (pp. 133–170). London: Academic Press.

Ainsworth, M. D. S., & Bell, S. M. (1974). Mother–infant interaction and the development of competence. In K. J. Connolly & J. Bruner (Eds.), *The growth of competence* (pp. 97–118). New York, NY: Academic Press.

Ainsworth, M. D. S., Bell, S. M., & Stayton, D. J. (1971). Individual differences in strange situation behaviour of one-year-olds. In H. R. Schaffer (Ed.), *The origins of human social relations* (pp. 17–57). London: Academic Press.

Ainsworth, M. D. S., Blehar, M. C., Waters, E., & Wall, S. (1978). *Patterns of attachment: A psychological study of the strange situation*. Hillsdale, NJ: Lawrence Erlbaum.

Anastasi, A. (1958). Heredity, environment and the question "how". *Psychological Review, 65*, 197–208.

Bakermans-Kranenburg, M. J., Dobrova-Krol, N., & van IJzendoorn, M. (2012). Impact of institutional care on attachment disorganization and insecurity of Ukrainian preschoolers: Protective effect of the long variant of the serotonin transporter gene (5HTT). *International Journal of Behavioral Development, 36*(1), 11–18.

Bakermans-Kranenburg, M. J., & van IJzendoorn, M. H. (2004). No association of the dopamine D4 receptor (DRD4) and –521 C/T promoter polymorphisms with infant attachment disorganization. *Attachment & Human Development, 6*, 211–218.

Bakermans-Kranenburg, M. J., & van IJzendoorn, M. H. (2008). Oxytocin receptor (OXTR) and serotonin transporter (5-HTT) genes associated with observed parenting. *Social Cognitive & Affective Neuroscience, 3*, 128–134.

Barnett, D., Hunt, K. H., Butler, C. M., McCaskill, J. W., Kaplan-Estrin, M., & Pipp-Siegel, S. (1999). Indices of attachment disorganization among toddlers with neurological and non-neurological problems. In J. Solomon & C. George (Eds.), *Attachment disorganization* (pp. 189–212). New York, NY: Guilford Press.

Barr, C. S., Newman, T. K., Becker, M. L., Parker, C. C., Champoux, M., & Lesch, K. P., … Higley, J. D. (2003). The utility of the non-human primate model for studying gene by environment interactions in behavioral research. *Genes, Brain & Behavior, 2*, 336–340.

Barry, R. A., Kochanska, G., & Philibert, R. A. (2008). G × E interaction in the organization of attachment: Mothers' responsiveness as a moderator of children's genotypes. *Journal of Child Psychology and Psychiatry, 49*, 1313–1320.

Beebe, B., Jaffe, J., Markese, S., Buck, K., Chen, H., Cohen, P., … Feldstein, S. (2010). The origins of 12-month attachment: A microanalysis of 4-month mother-infant interaction. *Attachment & Human Development, 12*, 3–141.

Belsky, J. (1997). Variation in susceptibility to rearing influence: An evolutionary argument. *Psychological Inquiry, 8*, 182–186.

Belsky, J., & Fearon, R. M. P. (2008). Precursors of attachment security. In J. Cassidy & P. R. Shaver (Eds.), *Handbook of attachment: Theory, research, and clinical applications* (2nd ed.) (pp. 295–316). New York, NY: Guilford Press.

Belsky, J., & Pluess, M. (2009). Beyond diathesis stress: Differential susceptibility to environmental influences. *Psychological Bulletin, 135*, 885–908.

Belsky, J., & Rovine, M. (1987). Temperament and attachment security in the strange situation: An empirical rapprochement. *Child Development, 58*, 787–795.

Bernier, A., & Meins, E. (2008). A threshold approach to understanding the origins of attachment disorganization. *Developmental Psychology, 44*, 969–982.

Bowlby, J. (1969). *Attachment and loss* (Vol. 1: Attachment). New York, NY: Basic Books.

Bowlby, J. (1988). *A secure base*. New York, NY: Basic Books.

Carver, C. S., & Miller, C. J. (2006). Relations of serotonin function to personality: Current views and a key methodological issue. *Psychiatry Research, 144*, 1–15.

Caspi, A., Sugden, K., Moffitt, T. E., Taylor, A., Craig, I. W., Harrington, H., … Poulton, R. (2003). Influence of life stress on depression: Moderation by a polymorphism in the 5-HTT gene. *Science, 301*(5631), 386–389.

Cassidy, J. (1994). Emotion regulation: Influences of attachment relationships. *Monographs of the Society for Research in Child Development, 59*(2–3, Serial No. 240), 2228–2249.

Cicchetti, D., & Rogosch, F. A. (1996). Equifinality and multifinality in developmental psychopathology. *Development and Psychopathology, 8*, 597–600.

Cicchetti, D., Rogosch, F. A., & Toth, S. L. (2011). The effects of child maltreatment and polymorphisms of the serotonin transporter and dopamine D4 receptor genes on infant attachment and intervention efficacy. *Development and Psychopathology, 23*, 357–372.

De Wolff, M., & van IJzendoorn, M. (1997). Sensitivity and attachment: A meta-analysis on parental antecedents of infant attachment. *Child Development, 68*, 571–591.

DeRijk, R. H., & De Kloet, E. R. (2008). Corticosteroid receptor polymorphisms: Determinants of vulnerability and resilience. *European Journal of Pharmacology, 583*, 303–311.

Diamond, A. (2001). A model system for studying the role of dopamine in the prefrontal cortex during early development in humans: Early and continuously treated phenylketonuria. In C. A. Nelson & M. Luciana (Eds.), *Handbook of developmental cognitive neuroscience* (pp. 433–472). Cambridge, MA: MIT Press.

Drury, S. S., Gleason, M. M., Theall, K. P., Smyke, A. T., Nelson, C. A., Fox, N. A., & Zeanah, C. H. (2012). Genetic sensitivity to the caregiving context: The influence of 5httlpr and BDNF val66met on indiscriminate social behavior. *Physiology & Behavior, 106*, 728–735.

Ebstein, R., Levine, J., Geller, V., Auerbach, J., Gritsenko, I., & Belmaker, R. H. (1998). Dopamine D4 receptor and serotonin transporter promoter in the determination of neonatal temperament. *Molecular Psychiatry, 3*, 238–246.

Ebstein, R. E. (2006). The molecular genetic architecture of human personality: Beyond self-report questionnaires. *Molecular Psychiatry, 11*, 427–445.

Frigerio, A., Ceppi, E., Rusconi, M., Giorda, R., Raggi, M. E., & Fearon, P. (2009). The role played by the interaction between genetic factors and attachment in the stress response in infancy. *Journal of Child Psychology and Psychiatry, 50*, 1513–1522.

Gervai, J., Novak, A., Lakatos, K., Toth, I., Danis, I., Ronai, Z., … Lyons-Ruth, K. (2007). Infant genotype may moderate sensitivity to maternal affective communications: Attachment disorganization, quality of care, and the DRD4 polymorphism. *Social Neuroscience, 2*(3–4), 307–319.

Goldberg, S., Benoit, D., Blokland, K., & Madigan, S. (2003). Atypical maternal behavior, maternal representations, and infant disorganized attachment. *Development and Psychopathology, 15*, 239–257.

Grossmann, K., Grossmann, K. E., Spangler, G., Suess, G., & Unzner, L. (1985). Maternal sensitivity and newborns'orientation responses as related to quality of attachment in Northern Germany. *Monographs of the Society for Research in Child Development, 50*, 233–256.

Hesse, E., & Main, M. (2006). Frightened, threatening, and dissociative parental behavior in low-risk samples: Description, discussion, and interpretations. *Development and Psychopathology, 18*, 309–343.

Kagan, J. (1982). *Psychological research on the human infant: An evaluative summary*. New York, NY: W. T. Grant Foundation.

Kochanska, G., Philibert, R. A., & Barry, R. A. (2009). Interplay of genes and early mother-child relationship in the development of self-regulation from toddler to preschool age. *Journal of Child Psychology and Psychiatry, 50*, 1331–1338.

Lakatos, K., Nemoda, Z., Toth, I., Ronai, Z., Ney, K., Sasvari-Szekely, M., & Gervai, J. (2002). Further evidence for the role of the dopamine D4 receptor (DRD4) gene in attachment disorganization: Interaction of the exon III 48bp repeat and the –521 C/T promoter polymorphisms. *Molecular Psychiatry, 7*, 27–31.

Lakatos, K., Toth, I., Nemoda, Z., Ney, K., Sasvari-Szekely, M., & Gervai, J. (2000). Dopamine D4 receptor (DRD4) gene polymorphism is associated with attachment disorganization in infants. *Molecular Psychiatry, 5*, 633–637.

Lesch, K.-P., Bengel, D., Heils, A., Sabol, S. Z., Greenberg, B. D., Petri, S., … Murphy, D. L. (1996). Association of anxiety-related traits with a polymorphism in the serotonin transporter gene regulatory region. *Science, 274*(5292), 1527–1531.

Luijk, M. P. C. M., Roisman, G. I., Haltigan, J. D., Tiemeier, H., Booth-LaForce, C., & van IJzendoorn, M. H., … Bakermans-Kranenburg, M. J. (2011). Dopaminergic, serotonergic, and oxytonergic candidate genes associated with infant attachment security and disorganization? In search of main and interaction effects. *Journal of Child Psychology and Psychiatry, 52*, 1295–1307.

Luijk, M. P. C. M., Tharner, A., Bakermans-Kranenburg, M. J., van IJzendoorn, M. H., Jaddoe, V. W. V., Hofman, A., … Tiemeier, H. (2011). The association between parenting and attachment security is moderated by a polymorphism in the mineralocorticoid receptor gene: Evidence for differential susceptibility. *Biological Psychology, 88*, 37–40.

Lyons-Ruth, K., Bronfman, E., & Parsons, E. (1999). Maternal frightened, frightening, or atypical behavior and disorganized infant attachment patterns. *Monographs of the Society for Research in Child Development, 64*, 67–96.

Lyons-Ruth, K., & Jacobvitz, D. (1999). Attachment disorganization: Unresolved loss, relational violence, and lapses in behavioral and attentional strategies. In J. Cassidy & P. R. Shaver (Eds.), *Handbook of attachment: Theory, research, and clinical applications* (pp. 520–554). New York, NY: Guilford Press.

Madigan, S., Moran, G., & Pederson, D. R. (2006). Unresolved states of mind, disorganized attachment relationships, and disrupted interactions of adolescent mothers and their infants. *Developmental Psychology, 42*, 293–304.

Main, M. (1990). Cross-cultural studies of attachment organization: Recent studies, changing methodologies, and the concept of conditional strategies. *Human Development, 33*, 48–61.

Main, M., & Hesse, E. (1990). Parents' unresolved traumatic experiences are related to infant disorganized attachment status: Is frightened and/or frightening parental behavior the linking mechanism? In M. T. Greenberg, D. Cicchetti, & E. M. Cummings (Eds.), *Attachment in the preschool years: Theory, research, and intervention* (pp. 161–182). Chicago, IL: University of Chicago Press.

Main, M., & Solomon, J. (1990). Procedures for identifying infants as disorganized/disoriented during the Ainsworth strange situation. In M. Greenberg, D. Cicchetti, & M. Cummings (Eds.), *Attachment in the preschool years* (pp. 121–160). Chicago, IL: University of Chicago Press.

Moffitt, T. E., Caspi, A., & Rutter, M. (2006). Measured gene-environment interactions in psychopathology: Concepts, research strategies, and implications for research, intervention, and public understanding of genetics. *Perspectives on Psychological Science, 1*, 5–27.

Moran, G., Forbes, L., Evans, E., Tarabulsy, G. M., & Madigan, S. (2008). Both maternal sensitivity and atypical maternal behavior independently predict attachment security and disorganization in adolescent mother-infant relationships. *Infant Behavior & Development, 31*, 321–325.

Nachmias, M., Gunnar, M., Mangelsdorf, S., & Parritz, R. H. (1996). Behavioral inhibition and stress reactivity: The moderating role of attachment security. *Child Development, 67*(2), 508–522.

Out, D., Bakermans-Kranenburg, M. J., & van IJzendoorn, M. H. (2009). The role of disconnected and extremely insensitive parenting in the development of disorganized attachment: Validation of a new measure. *Attachment & Human Development, 11*, 419–443.

Pipp-Siegel, S., Siegel, C. H., & Dean, J. (1999). Neurological aspects of the disorganized/disoriented attachment classification system: Differentiating quality of the attachment relationship from neurological impairment. *Monographs of the Society for Research in Child Development, 64*, 25–44.

Raby, K. L., Cicchetti, D., Carlson, E. A., Cutuli, J. J., Englund, M. M., & Egeland, B. (2012). Genetic and caregiving-based contributions to infant attachment: Unique associations with distress reactivity and attachment security. *Psychological Science, 23*, 1016–1023.

Roisman, G. I., Booth-Laforce, C., Belsky, J., Burt, K. B., & Groh, A. M. (2013). Molecular-genetic correlates of infant attachment: A cautionary tale. *Attachment & Human Development, 15*, 384–406.

Rutter, M. (2003). Commentary: Nature-nurture interplay in emotional disorders. *Journal of Child Psychology and Psychiatry, 44*, 934–944.

Schneider, M. L., & Coe, C. L. (1993). Repeated social stress during pregnancy impairs neuromotor development of the primate infant. *Journal of Developmental and Behavioral Pediatrics, 14*(2), 81–87.

Schuengel, C., Bakermans-Kranenburg, M. J., & van IJzendoorn, M. H. (1999). Frightening maternal behavior linking unresolved loss and disorganized infant attachment. *Journal of Consulting and Clinical Psychology, 67*, 54–63.

Spangler, G., Fremmer-Bombik, E., & Grossmann, K. (1996). Social and individual determinants of infant attachment security and disorganization. *Infant Mental Health Journal, 17*, 127–139.

Spangler, G., & Grossmann, K. (1999). Individual and physiological correlates of attachment disorganization in infancy. In J. Solomon & C. George (Eds.), *Attachment disorganization* (pp. 95–124). New York, NY: Guilford Press.

Spangler, G., & Grossmann, K. E. (1993). Biobehavioral organization in securely and insecurely attached infants. *Child Development, 64*, 1439–1450.

Spangler, G., Johann, M., Ronai, Z., & Zimmermann, P. (2009). Genetic and environmental influence on attachment disorganization. *Journal of Child Psychology and Psychiatry, 50*, 952–961.

Spangler, G., & Schieche, M. (1998). Emotional and adrenocortical responses of infants to the strange situation: The differential function of emotional expression. *International Journal of Behavioral Development, 22*, 681–706.

Sroufe, L. A. (1979). The coherence of individual development: Early care, attachment, and subsequent developmental issues. *American Psychologist, 34*, 834–841.

Sroufe, L. A. (1985). Attachment classification from the perspective of infant-caregiver relationships and infant temperament. *Child Development, 56*, 1–14.

van den Boom, D. C. (1994). The influence of temperament and mothering on attachment and exploration: An experimental manipulation of sensitive responsiveness among lower-class mothers with irritable infants. *Child Development, 65*, 1457–1477.

van IJzendoorn, M. H., & Bakermans-Kranenburg, M. J. (2006). DRD4 7-repeat polymorphism moderates the association between maternal unresolved loss or trauma and infant disorganization. *Attachment & Human Development, 8*, 291–307.

van IJzendoorn, M. H., Schuengel, C., & Bakermans-Kranenburg, M. J. (1999). Disorganized attachment in early childhood: Meta-analysis of precursors, concomitants, and sequelae. *Development and Psychopathology, 11*, 225–249.

Vaughn, B. E., Bost, K. K., & van IJzendoorn, M. H. (2008). Attachment and temperament: Additive and interactive influences on behavior, affect, and cognition during infancy and childhood. In J. Cassidy & P. R. Shaver (Eds.), *Handbook of attachment: Theory, research, and clinical applications* (2nd ed.) (pp. 192–216). New York, NY: Guilford Press.

Washington, J., Minde, K., & Goldberg, S. (1986). Temperament in preterm infants: Style and stability. *Journal of the American Academy of Child Psychiatry, 25*, 493–502.

Waters, E., Vaughn, B. E., & Egeland, B. R. (1980). Individual differences in infant–mother attachment relationships at age one: Antecedents in neonatal behavior in an urban, economically disadvantaged sample. *Child Development, 51*(1), 208–216.

Epilogue: reflections on a Special Issue of *Attachment & Human Development* in Mary Ainsworth's 100th year

Everett Waters[a], Dean Petters[b] and Christopher Facompre[a]

[a]*Department of Psychology, SUNY Stony Brook, Stony Brook, NY, USA;* [b]*Department of Computer Science, University of Birmingham, Birmingham, UK*

A Special Issue such as this, celebrating the 100th year since Mary Ainsworth's birth, reflects unusual fondness and appreciation. For the editors and contributors, and for Mary Ainsworth's students as well, it is a special treat to revisit her accomplishments and, by clarifying and elaborating, see her remarkable contributions shared and sustained through new generations.

Mary Ainsworth's first study of infant–mother interaction and attachment appeared in the *Determinants of Infant Development* series edited by Brian Foss (Ainsworth, 1963). She was 50 years old. Over the years she published two good books, two dozen empirical articles, and as many theoretical articles and reviews. Emphasizing quality over quantity, she may have done more than John Bowlby himself to explain the new attachment paradigm to psychologists and open conceptual doors for new generations that would give attachment study the depth and scope reflected in journals, handbooks, and this Special Issue. Indeed, it doesn't diminish John Bowlby's contributions to suggest that, absent Mary Ainsworth's contributions, his great trilogy might not have carried the day.

This Special Issue could well have focused on the Strange Situation for it was certainly the individual differences perspective and its promise of clinical implications that attracted much of the early interest in attachment study. However, as Mary Ainsworth explained when she received the APA's 1989 Distinguished Scientific Contribution Award, the Strange Situation is a tool to be used while it is needed; the better use we make of it, the sooner we will put it aside. In fact, her lasting impact rests as much on her insights into the meanings infants find in countless real-world interactions with a primary caregiver as on the Strange Situation. By focusing on maternal sensitivity and attachment security rather than the Strange Situation, this Special Issue will draw much new attention to Mary Ainsworth's Uganda research. This is long overdue. In addition, the contributors to this Special Issue focus on two areas in which Mary Ainsworth had singular insights: (1) the nature of the infant's interactions with its mother and (2) the evolution of security in their relationship.

The biographies and histories are important vehicles for maintaining theoretical and programmatic coherence across disciplines and generations. Thus, we are fortunate to have good biographies and broadly drawn histories of attachment theory and research (e.g., Ainsworth & Bowlby, 1991; Ainsworth & Marvin, 1995; Ainsworth, 1982;

Bretherton, 1985; 2003; Main, 1999). These have helped explain and consolidate the attachment paradigm in the mainstream of scientific psychology. However, we have less in the way of working histories, detailed recollections of how specific problems were formulated, how constructs were defined and revised, and what we learned from experience developing and teaching measures like the Strange Situation and the Maternal Behavior Scales. Fortunately, Inge Bretherton (pp. 475–499; this issue) has provided valuable clarifications and new information about the logic and evolution of Mary Ainsworth's maternal sensitivity construct. In addition, many contributors to this Special Issue have enriched their articles with first-hand accounts of Mary Ainsworth's advice, feedback, and encouragement as they charted new directions for theory and research on infant–mother interaction and attachment security.

Reflections on Mary Ainsworth and attachment study

An epilogue allows an author or main character to address readers directly or, from a privileged perspective, to reveal the fates of the characters or hint at a sequel. Of course, there is no privileged perspective in science, no way to foresee the directions a field will take. That said, it can still be useful and, we hope, encouraging about the prospects for attachment study to highlight some ideas brought to mind in reading this Special Issue. Topics include: (1) reviewing and refreshing the goals of attachment study; (2) language and attachment study; (3) what is learned in infant–mother interactions; (4) sensitivity, security, and representations; and (5) new methods for exploring attachment and learning in infant–mother dyads.

Reviewing and refreshing the goals of attachment study

Psychologist Paul Meehl once suggested that, in the course of any scientific undertaking, it helps now and then to go back to the beginning and reflect on just what we are trying to do (Meehl, 1959, p. 102). Absent this, any field risks becoming an instrument-driven search for nothing more than significant correlations.

When Mary Ainsworth was relocating to Uganda she anticipated obtaining unique data on separation and early experience. Experts familiar with Ugandan culture confidently told her that as many as half of Ganda infants were separated from their mothers at weaning and sent to be raised by relatives. This would afford her a rare opportunity to study the effects of early separation on attachment development, without the confounds of community, family, and individual disturbances that so often accompany such separations in Europe or North America. As sometimes happens, her informants were misinformed. Fortunately, she recognized that her stay in Uganda also afforded an opportunity evaluate some key postulates of Bowlby's evolving attachment theory. Indeed, in later years, she often said she had not set out to *confirm* Bowlby's view. She would look for herself and see if the theory fit the facts. If so, fine; otherwise, the sooner to find out the better.

Departing significantly from his psychoanalytic roots, John Bowlby had long emphasized the importance of actual experiences (as opposed to *phantasies*) for attachment development. He also hypothesized that clinical problems don't depend exclusively on trauma. Garden-variety separations and lapses in maternal care, which are much more frequent than trauma, could also be important. Of course, validating this hypothesis required sorting out *which* early behaviors mattered. Psychoanalysts, learning theorists, ethologists, and even baby care specialists had their favorites. Mary Ainsworth would give them all a fair test.

Then there was the matter of what to use to evaluate relevance to attachment onset. At the time, many developmental psychologists accepted Schaffer and Emerson's (1964) work on crying in response to separation as a criterion for attachment onset. However, Mary Ainsworth's good eye for behavior, experience as an observer, and common sense raised doubts about separation protest as the sole criterion. Accordingly, she formulated a list of 16 behavior patterns (e.g., differential crying, following, clapping hands in greeting, approach, exploration away from mother as a secure base) that were characteristic of babies who clearly seemed attached to their mothers (Ainsworth, 1967, p. 332). In addition, she recognized that the kind of programmatic theory and research she and John Bowlby were initiating would require a good normative description of behavior up to and beyond attachment onset. Moreover, there were important differences among babies who were judged attached to their mothers. That is, being *attached* was quite a different matter than being *secure* in the relationship. So, it would be important to avoid treating individual differences as mere noise. Key here is that Mary Ainsworth's plans were always built on her clear understanding of what kind of data would do the most to advance attachment theory. Sometimes, this meant descriptive data. Sometimes, it meant checking hypotheses against naturalistic observations. It was never a matter of simply chasing significant correlations and then cynically spinning journal articles to suggest that whatever was found was what they had been looking for in the first place (*cf.* Bem, 1987). Mary Ainsworth was a terrific model in this respect. Nonetheless, it is important to ask, what will drive the next decade of attachment study? Can we stay focused on testing theory driven hypotheses or will we fall prey to pressure to publish (or obtain external funding) or perish? Ultimately, the best way to keep theoretical issues in the driver's seat, the best defense against becoming an instrument driven science, is to keep the theoretical underpinnings of attachment theory and measures as explicit as possible so they can continue to inform both construct validation and applied research. The contributors to this Special Issue have clearly cast their votes for the kinds of theory driven, labor intensive, construct validation studies Mary Ainsworth favored, and in doing so they too are serving as good models for next generations.

Language and attachment study

Attachment theory has always had more than its share of difficulties finding adequate language to express genuine insights. This problem arises because some of the key insights are subtle and their manifestations in behavior and emotion expression often reside in fine details and change dramatically with age. In addition, where ethologists' knowledge of an animal's behavior is based on naturalistic observations, psychologists too often base their knowledge of human behavior on being humans and having raised children.

Mary Ainsworth's observations of infant–mother interaction and the way she mapped keen observations into clear language represent a high water mark for behavioral sciences research. Unfortunately, her methods required a virtual apprenticeship to master even "standard" measures. Consider, for example the four "maternal sensitivity" scales she developed for assessing qualities of infant–mother interactions. Each scale has a title, an accompanying essay (approximately 200 words) explaining the construct to be measured, describing the relevant behavior and behavioral dynamics, and elaborating on how the behaviors play out in different contexts. These essays also highlight difficulties that might be encountered when observing or scoring the relevant behaviors, and the kinds of misinterpretations that can compromise scoring. Finally, the odd points of the 9-point scale are anchored to prototypical behavior descriptions that run from 100–300 words. More than mere scales, each of these is a virtual seminar on infant and maternal behavior.

Importantly, these scales are not broad-band Mary Ainsworth formulations of "good mothering". Commonly known as "maternal sensitivity", "cooperation", "accessibility", and "acceptance-rejection", each scale focuses on a specific facet of maternal behavior to be evaluated as potentially significant for attachment development and outcomes. Even the scale names convey important meaning.

Imagine a novice researcher coming across these scale labels in a journal article. There would be brief definitions but not much about how they are used. Certainly nothing compared to Mary Ainsworth's introductory essays and detailed behavioral anchors. Yet, being human and having raised (or cared for) children, they might very well feel that they had a fair sense of the constructs and how to score them. They just work with the meaning conveyed by the labels ordinary connotations and semantic associations, or develop their own scales to measure these constructs. *Sensitivity* suggests warmth, tenderness, and attention to detail. *Cooperation,* connotes patience and flexibility. *Accessibility* suggests patience and attentiveness. *Acceptance* suggests perhaps some sort of non-specific positive regard. This is the level at which infant–mother interaction is assessed in many published studies. However, these are not even the full names and the scales are based on actual behavior from extended home observations, not linguistic connotations or associations.

Imagine then learning for the first time that the *Sensitivity* scale was designed to assess S*ensitivity to infant signals,* where *sensitivity* refers to a radio receiver's ability to detect a weak broadcast signal. Suddenly, notions of warmth and tenderness (perhaps with a glowing fire and violins in the background) seem quite irrelevant. The key is for the mother to (1) detect behaviors that might potentially convey information, (2) interpret the behavior as meaningful, (3) interpret it correctly, (4) settle on an appropriate response, and (5) deliver it in a timely manner. The key phenomenon is the mother's behavior, not semantic connotations of the label *sensitivity.* At best, abbreviated scale names are mnemonic devices that help observers access their knowledge of the relevant behaviors, scoring criteria, and patterns.

Continuing on to the other constructs, the complexities and potential difficulties remain the same. *Cooperation* connotes patience and attention. However, the full scale title, *Cooperation with the infant's ongoing behavior*, suggests that the scale focuses primarily on scaffolding and facilitating infant behavior during manual and locomotor exploration. This certainly requires attention and patience, but the key is how the caregiver affects the way the baby experiences exploration and helps the baby become familiar with working in dance-like coordination with its primary caregiver.

Similarly, *Acceptance* is properly *Acceptance vs. Rejection of the Baby's Needs* and is primarily about accepting that "baby" is shorthand for "a little package of this and that, that requires this, that, and the other, which it can't help requiring, and who's requirements are inherent to it, not efforts to compete or coerce the caregiver". In effect, if you wanted a baby, this is what you signed up for. Accordingly, the scale is about accepting that the baby is defined by a set of behaviors and requirements, which it can't intentionally coordinate this with your needs.

Clearly, Mary Ainsworth's goal here was not on making a sweeping evaluation. She was focused on behavioral manifestations of a very specific aspect of a caregiver's perspective and motivation in parenting. In the end, only one scale, *Accessibility* (vs. *Ignoring*), seems to be passingly well represented by its shorthand label. Yet, even here, the full scale title, *Physical and psychological availability vs. ignoring and neglecting*, helps clarify Mary Ainsworth's intentions.

What does our hypothetical novice do in the face of all this complexity? How to avoid drowning in the subtleties? Or is this scenario too improbable? How confident can we be that we are all shooting at the same target, and at the right target?

Mary Ainsworth was a careful and explicit model in such matters. However, it is important to have contemporary models as well. The contributors to this Special Issue also seem quite sensitive to issues of meaning. Where they want intentionally to diverge somewhat from Mary Ainsworth's constructs (perhaps in order to better understand them), they remain, for the most part, solidly grounded and explicit about what they are doing. Our hypothetical novice, indeed anyone interested in research on maternal sensitivity (not to mention sensitivity), would do well to look closely at the Special Issue and at early work like *Infancy in Uganda* and papers from the Baltimore study before stepping into the deep end of the pool.

Don't let the language fool you

Technical language, terms of art (ordinary terms that have special meaning in a given context), and short-hand labels are necessary for efficient scientific communication. However, they can be obstacles as well. So much so that Waters and McIntosh (2011) have suggested that attachment theory, research, and applications would benefit if, now and then, we would dispense with the technical terms and say what we mean. That is, when using attachment terms and labels, we should make sure that we could just as easily have spelled out what the shorthand is shorthand for. The authors and editors of this Special Issue have done a great service by trying to be as careful about this as Mary Ainsworth was.

It is worth keeping in mind that, for John Bowlby and Mary Ainsworth, the behavior was primary. If anything, the challenge was to find language adequate to their observational, behavioral insights. In more recent work, the challenge is often more a matter of construct definition and validation. That is, we start out with a verbal/theoretical concept and try to see how it plays out in observable behavior. Both are reasonable approaches and have proven useful. However, it is important to keep in mind that they are different kinds of problems.

We should also keep in mind the difference between developing terminology and validating constructs for typical and atypical behaviors. Behavior patterns that are typical of most infants and mothers are often easier to observe and more familiar to observers; and it is easier to compile large numbers of exemplars from different contexts. This makes it relatively easy to standardize and qualify descriptions and develop useful measures and labels. However, definitions, measures, and labels that seemed relatively easy to describe in early work for ordinary attachment behavior proved somewhat difficult to extend to the full range of normal individual differences. Even terms like avoidance and resistance have been problematic at times. As we move increasingly into very low frequency behaviors and attachment in clinical contexts, coordinating concepts, observations, and language is likely to become increasingly more difficult.

Finally, it is important to distinguish between contexts in which the construct is pretty close to behavior (e.g., proximity seeking) and contexts in which the construct is more difficult to operationalize in behavioral terms (e.g., disorganization and mindedness). From the start, Bowlby was committed to building an empirically accessible attachment theory. Thus both he and Mary Ainsworth often worked with research definitions of key phenomena, knowing full well that such definitions did not exhaust the full conceptual or clinical meaning of the constructs. For example, they understood that attachment is not merely a matter of using one or a few caregivers as a secure base and a haven of retreat, and that there is more to security than behavioral indicators of confidence in caregiver's availability and responsiveness. It just seemed better to work first with empirically accessible formulations, then sketch out key relationships and answers, and afterward see what else had to be gathered in for theory and research to translate into useful clinical tools. Better, at least, than starting with muddled constructs and measures that were subject to methodological criticisms before the work could get off the ground. If we are not explicit about such strategies, and Bowlby was not always explicit enough about it, we risk reifying and settling for operational definitions and measures that aren't adequate to the underlying descriptive insights.

There is so much interesting work to do, so many facets of behavior to be described, and so many interesting questions about how it is all coordinated within and across contexts and ages. Moreover, answers can open the door to important new directions in attachment theory and clinical applications. From the inside looking out, the prospects for attachment seem as exciting as ever. It seems more like we have finally done the easy studies that make it possible (and not too risky) to do the really ambitious ones. Many of the papers in this Special Issue are convincing on this point.

An aside: One of the enduring difficulties in this area has been that, for some time, the full set of Ainsworth's Maternal Behavior Scales has only been available in mimeograph and more recently online. Fortunately, Taylor & Francis have undertaken to reissue in 2014 *Patterns of Attachment* in both hardback and paperback bindings for their *Classic Editions* series. The original text will be preserved but there will be a new introductory essay reflecting on work with the Strange Situation procedure since the book first appeared. In addition, Mary Main is contributing an essay reflecting work on the Disorganized classification, which was discovered and became the focus of much interesting work after 1978. Importantly for present purposes, there will also be a new Appendix that includes the full set of four Maternal Behavior Scales.

What is learned in infant–mother interactions?

Over the years, attachment theory and research have been fairly criticized for inattention to the mechanisms underlying key phenomena and findings. Collecting data for their influential meta-analysis of links between maternal sensitivity and infant security, De Wolf and Van IJzendoorn (1997) identified 30 studies reporting such correlations. Yet, there are at most a handful of studies (correlational or experimental) examining links between specific aspects of maternal sensitivity and acquisition of specific components of infant security. Moreover, there are only a handful of studies that try to explain such correlations in terms of ordinary learning mechanisms. Aggregate measures of complex constructs like sensitivity and security can highlight where causal relations are in play. However, when it comes to specifying how maternal sensitivity, broadly construed, affects infant security, such studies leave a great deal to the imagination.

One of the key postulates of Bowlby's attachment theory is that an infant's attachment control system arises from biases in infant learning abilities playing out in "an ordinary expectable caregiving environment". As mentioned above, one of Mary Ainsworth's goals in her Uganda study was to identify the aspects of maternal care that are most relevant to attachment development. Logically, the next step would be to formulate hypotheses about how these lead to the infant becoming sensitive to attachment-related cues and contexts, and acquiring and organizing behavior patterns associated with the attachment-exploration balance. Parsimony dictates examining ordinary learning mechanisms before hypothesizing attachment specific learning mechanisms (e.g., unlearned sensitivity to certain types of attachment-relevant stimuli). It would also make sense to leave for later more exotic mechanisms, such as aspects of maternal care instinctually activating species specific "blueprints" that define the attachment control system. Although Bowlby (1969) alludes to such mechanisms and writes at length about the notion of instinct, such innate triggering would immediately raise questions regarding the mechanisms through which it was accomplished. That is, the explanation would demand an explanation; all the more reason to look first at ordinary learning.

What then can an infant learn from a primary caregiver's sensitivity to its signals and cooperation with its ongoing behavior? Most obviously, it can acquire alertness to certain cues and contexts, and learn to identify and perhaps prefer the primary caregiver. It can also build up expectations regarding the caregiver's availability and responsiveness in a fairly narrow range of behavioral contexts (e.g., face-to-face games, during negative reactions to novelty, etc.), and learn to elicit or modify certain caregiver behaviors (as a function of caregiver characteristics such as experience, motivation, competing demands on caregiver time, etc.) These are the kinds of phenomena Bowlby (1969) described as undiscriminating and discriminating social responsiveness.

Much of this interaction is accompanied by maternal and infant affect expression. Yet, there is little research on the role these play in attachment learning. Indeed, almost all recent work on attachment and emotion falls under the rubric of attachment and emotion regulation. What roles does accompanying affect play in attachment development? Does it potentiate the bonding mechanism that ties the infant to one or a few primary caregivers? Ethologists and neurobiologists have developed very detailed models of learning processes in imprinting, several of which explicitly address emotion (e.g., Bolhuis & Honey, 1998). In light of new methods for imaging brain activity and assaying gene activity, the possibilities here are quite exciting. Moreover, pursuing them will help clarify the distinction between bond formation and attachment security. Emotion expression also has also been shown to influence gene expression and whether memories are consolidated or opened for revision (e.g., Krugers, Hoogenraad, & Groc, 2010). The emotional correlates of infant–mother interaction could also play a role in learning expectations. Most interestingly, emotion could also play a role in adding meaning to attachment-related interactions and tagging prototypical or singular events.

As we begin to investigate such mechanisms, we should try to explain as much as possible with ordinary, non-specific mechanisms and be cautious about proposing attachment-specific learning, genetic, and physiological processes and neural structures. At a certain point, evolution demands certain economies. Thus it makes sense to investigate what can be done with non-specific, "off the shelf" processes and mechanisms before hypothesizing dedicated mechanisms for every phenomenon in behavior, cognition, and emotion. There is nothing magical about contingent responsiveness leading to familiarity, preference, and simple expectations. It is less clear, however, that sensitive, cooperative care can explain distinct attachment-related behaviors becoming coordinated and beginning to act as a coherent, context sensitive behavioral system. Waters, Kondo-Ikemura, Posada, and Richters (1991) proposed that explicit teaching plays a key role in the infant learning to use its mother as a secure base from which to explore. Indeed, mothers are frequently observed playing chase and follow games and "come to Mommy", with generous emotional accompaniment and reinforcement of key junctures in the interactions. Although sensitivity to infant signals and cooperation with ongoing behavior may predict maternal engagement in such games, it is the secure base game, not sensitivity *per se*, that knits such attachment behavior patterns together. If the learning here is facilitated by some sort of species specific or primate specific biases in the infants' learning abilities, it would be very interesting to characterize them in some detail and study them in depth. However, this isn't likely to happen as long as attachment theory implicitly suggests that maternal sensitivity causes attachment or attachment security. That is simply painting with too broad a brush.

One of the most interesting aspects of the attachment security construct is its relevance across the life-span. Indeed, the attachment patterns described by Ainsworth, Blehar, Waters, and Wall (1978) have analogues in Adult Attachment Interview classifications (Main, Goldwyn, & Hesse, 2003) in adolescence and adulthood. Similarly, the insights underlying Mary Ainsworth's four maternal sensitivity constructs have analogues in adult–adult marital interactions (Crowell et al., 2002).

John Bowlby was well aware that attachment-related behavior, expectations, and representations continue to develop, and to be revised in light of experience, throughout childhood and adolescence. Unfortunately, his well-known four-stage model of attachment development concludes at age three with the child acquiring the ability to maintain a goal-corrected partnership with one or a few primary caregivers. This implicitly closes the door on further caregiver input into attachment development. As a result, there has been very little research on the roles sensitivity to signals, cooperation with ongoing behavior, acceptance *vs.* rejection of the child's needs, and physical-psychological accessibility influence play in the child's acquiring the secure-base experiences and world knowledge necessary to expand secure base use over greater distances, longer time spans, and more diverse contexts, not to mention their roles in building independence.

As cognitive psychologists well know, formulating, integrating, and updating representations of daily life experiences and critical life events entails considerable effort. Such representations do not arise passively. They are actively constructed, often in a social context. Thus it is important to follow analogues of sensitivity and cooperation as we see them in infant mother interactions into childhood and adolescence in order to understand their roles in emerging attachment representations. Waters and Waters (2006) have described several studies in which mothers can be observed helping toddlers integrate daily experiences and story-telling tasks into script-like attachment representations. No doubt the same can be observed in adolescence and even in marital relationships. In brief, Mary Ainsworth's work on maternal sensitivity (broadly construed) and the work represented in this Special Issue are just the starting points for extending attachment theory and research into childhood, adolescence, and adulthood, and beyond parent–child interactions into marriage and care for elderly parents (e.g., Chen et al., 2013).

The nice thing about attachment study

Not long ago, after an exciting lecture on attachment study, undergraduate Introductory Psychology students at a renowned West Coast university asked their distinguished professor whether attachment study would be a good choice for a career in psychology. The professor replied: "There is some great work there. But it is a mature field now and I think all the big studies have been done". To be sure, there is some great work there. However, if there is a message in this Special Issue for next generations, it is that attachment study is alive and well, with a great deal of exciting work ahead. Although there is no privileged perspective from which to predict the future in science, for students interested in attachment study, this feels like the moment to step aboard. The nice thing about attachment study is that you don't have to start until you are 50 years old. And if you take it up, Mary Ainsworth will always be there for you.

References

Ainsworth, M. D. (1963). Development of infant–mother interaction among the Ganda. In: B. M. Foss (Ed.), *Determinants of infant behaviour, II* (pp. 67–104). London: Methuen.

Ainsworth, M. D. S. (1967). Infancy in Uganda: Infant care and the growth of love. Baltimore, MD: Johns Hopkins University Press.

Ainsworth, M. D. S. (1982). Attachment: Retrospect and prospect. In C. M. Parkes & J. Stevenson-Hinde (Eds.), *The place of attachment in human behavior* (pp. 3–30). New York: Basic Books.

Ainsworth, M. D. S., Blehar, M. C., Waters, E., & Wall, S. (1978). *Patterns of attachment: A psychological study of the strange situation*. Hillsdale, NJ: Lawrence Erlbaum Associates.

Ainsworth, M. D. S., & Bowlby, J. (1991). An ethological approach to personality development. *American Psychologist, 46*, 333–341.

Ainsworth, M. D. S., & Marvin, R. S. (1995). On the shaping of attachment theory and research: An interview with Mary D. S. Ainsworth (Fall 1994). *Monographs of the Society for Research in Child Development, 60*(2/3), 2–21.

Bem, D. J. (1987). Writing the empirical journal article. In M. P. Zanna & J. M. Darley (Eds.), *The compleat academic: A practical guide for the beginning social scientist* (pp. 171–201). New York: Random. House.

Bolhuis, J. J., & Honey, R. C. (1998). Imprinting, learning and development: From behaviour to brain and back. *Trends in Neuroscience, 21*(7), 306–311.

Bowlby, J. (1969). *Attachment and loss (vol. 1), attachment*. New York: Basic Books.

Bretherton, I. (1985). Attachment theory: Retrospect and prospect. In I. Bretherton & E. Waters (Eds.), *Growing points of attachment theory and research. Monographs of the Society for Research in Child Development 50*(1–2), 3–35.

Bretherton, I. (2003). Mary Ainsworth: Insightful observer and courageous theoretician. In G. A. Kimble & M. Wertheimer (Eds.), *Portraits of pioneers in psychology* (Vol. 5). Washington, DC: American Psychological Association.

Chen, C. K., Waters, H. S., Hartman, M., Zimmerman, S., Miklowitz, D., & Waters, E. (2013). The secure base script and the task of caring for elderly parents: Implications for attachment theory and clinical practice. *Attachment & Human Development, 15*(3), 332–348.

Crowell, J. A., Treboux, D., Gao, Y., Fyffe, C., Pan, H., & Waters, E. (2002). Assessing secure base behavior in adulthood: Development of a measure, links to adult attachment representations, and relations to couples' communication and reports of relationships. *Developmental Psychology, 38*, 679–693.

De Wolff, M. S., & Van IJzendoorn, M. H. (1997). Sensitivity and attachment: A meta-analysis on parental antecedents of infant attachment. *Child Development, 68*, 571–591.

Krugers, H. J., Hoogenraad, C. C., & Groc, L. (2010). Stress hormones and AMPA receptor trafficking in synaptic plasticity and memory. *Nature Reviews. Neuroscience, 11(10)*, 675–681.

Main, M. (1999). Mary D. Salter Ainsworth: Tribute and Portrait. *Psychoanalytic Inquiry, 19*, 682–736.

Main, M., Goldwyn, R., & Hesse, E. (2003). *Adult attachment scoring and classification systems. Ver. 7.2*. Berkeley: Department of Psychology, University of California.

Meehl. (1959). Some ruminations on the validation of clinical procedures. *Canadian Journal of Psychology, 13*, 102–128.

Schaffer, H. R., & Emerson, P. E. (1964). The development of social attachment in infancy. *Monographs of the Society for Research in Child Development, 29*(3), 1–77.

Waters, E., Kondo-Ikemura, K., Posada, G., & Richters, J. (1991). Learning to love: Mechanisms and milestones. In M. Gunner & A. Sroufe (Eds.), *Minnesota Symposium on Child Psychology* (*Vol. 23: Self Processes and Development*, pp. 217–255). Minneapolis: University of Minnesota Press.

Waters, E., & McIntosh, J. (2011). Are we asking the right questions about attachment? *Family Court Review, 49*, 474–482.

Waters, H., & Waters, E. (2006). The attachment working models concept: Among other things, we build script-like representations of secure base experiences. *Attachment & Human Development, 8*, 185–197.

Index

Note: Page numbers in **bold** type refer to figures
Page numbers in *italic* type refer to tables

For Product Safety Concerns and Information please contact our EU representative GPSR@taylorandfrancis.com
Taylor & Francis Verlag GmbH, Kaufingerstraße 24, 80331 München, Germany

www.ingramcontent.com/pod-product-compliance
Ingram Content Group UK Ltd.
Pitfield, Milton Keynes, MK11 3LW, UK
UKHW050754180926
475701UK00007B/1048
9780367739263